BIRD ON AN ETHICS WIRE

BIRD *on an* ETHICS WIRE

Battles about Values in the Culture Wars

Margaret Somerville

McGill-Queen's University Press
Montreal & Kingston • London • Chicago

ISBN 978-0-7735-4640-0 (cloth)
ISBN 978-0-7735-9814-0 (ePDF)
ISBN 978-0-7735-9815-7 (ePUB)

Legal deposit fourth quarter 2015
Bibliothèque nationale du Québec

Printed in Canada on acid-free paper that is 100% ancient forest free (100% post-consumer recycled), processed chlorine free

McGill-Queen's University Press acknowledges the support of the Canada Council for the Arts for our publishing program. We also acknowledge the financial support of the Government of Canada through the Canada Book Fund for our publishing activities.

Library and Archives Canada Cataloguing in Publication

Somerville, Margaret A., 1942–, author
Bird on an ethics wire : battles about values in the culture wars / Margaret Somerville.

Includes bibliographical references and index.
Issued in print and electronic formats.
ISBN 978-0-7735-4640-0 (cloth).–ISBN 978-0-7735-9814-0 (ePDF).
–ISBN 978-0-7735-9815-7 (ePUB)

1. Social values. 2. Ethics. 3. Culture conflict. I. Title.

HM681.S64 2015 303.3'72 C2015-905189-4
C2015-905190-8

For all the people, especially those I know, who work tirelessly to hold values in trust for the world of the future and have the courage to fight for what they believe to be ethical, even when it means facing adversity personally

Contents

Preface ix

Acknowledgments xv

Introduction 3

1 Should Religion Be Evicted from the Public Square? 13

2 Are Our "Values Conversations" Sufficiently Open and Free? The University as a Test Case 46

3 Is the Concept of Human Dignity Useful, Useless, or Dangerous? 87

4 Legalizing Euthanasia: Evolution or Revolution in Societal Values? 117

5 Is Every Life Beautiful? 167

6 How Might a Problem – a Crisis Pregnancy – Be Converted to a Mystery, the Gift of Life? 200

7 How Might the Involvement of "Applied Ethics" in Law Affect Our Societal Values? Ethics as "First Aid" for Law 229

8 What Questions Are We Asking in Contemporary Cultural Values Conversations, and What Messages Are They Communicating? 261

APPENDICES

A The Best Teacher I Ever Had Was My Father, George Patrick Ganley 295

B Three Statements on Academic Freedom 303

C Use of the Concept of Human Dignity in Four International Instruments 308

D The Declaration of Montreal 315

Notes 321

Index 347

Preface

This is a book about values and how we understand them as individuals and as a society. Values constitute a seamless web, which means, as I endeavour to show in the following pages, that when we unravel one thread – for instance, the values governing birth and abortion – we can also unravel the values in another thread – for example, those consisting of our beliefs that govern death and euthanasia. This correlation should not be surprising, because there is a connection between the values brought into play in birth and death and those in abortion and euthanasia. What we decide in relation to the values in one context is thus likely to reflect and also predict what we will decide about them in others. In exploring the battles about the values that should govern birth and death and other struggles about values, my goal is to articulate a "values map" that represents an overview of our contemporary "values universe" in which some values are highlighted. As readers will see, this universe is a contested landscape where contemporary battles about values within our western democracies collectively make up what many call our current "culture wars." These wars, which are the ones I explore in this book, can be distinguished from the larger-scale "clashes of civilizations"[1] in that they occur within a given society, whereas the latter are between societies or the nations that represent those societies, although the two types of conflict can often be related.

The essential question we all must ponder is: How can we first identify and then both protect and promote in each society the values that will maintain a world in which reasonable people would want to live? Or, asked another way: What are the values we must embrace if we, as individuals and as societies, are to maintain respect for human life, human dignity, and the essence of our humanness? Asking these questions demands that we ask further ones: What does it mean to be human, and why is being human important? A lot of heady philosophy has long been elicited by such questions. However, as I write in chapter 5, one way to explore possible responses is to talk about experiences of "amazement, wonder, and awe."

This approach might seem too ephemeral, too "modern-age" – even "flakey" – but we need to prepare the metaphorical soil in which the values we want to flourish can take root and grow. We cannot do so through a coercive or, often, a direct approach but only by persuasion and by creating metaphorical and perhaps even emotional spaces, which people will choose to enter and where they can encounter and find appealing the values we hope will prevail. Consequently, as I explain in this book, we should be open to experiencing amazement, wonder, and awe in many situations, as often as possible, hoping that such experiences will open us and, through diffusion or even contagion, open others to encountering re-enchantment of the world. Any risks that such an approach engenders can and should be avoided by a stringent use of reason as a "secondary verification process" to ensure that our decisions about values are wise and ethical. (I use "secondary" here in a chronological sense, not as indicating that reason is of secondary importance.)

I suggest that experiencing "amazement, wonder, and awe" enriches our lives and can help us to find meaning, which is of the essence of being human, in a way that traditional philosophy alone cannot. It can change how we see the world, the decisions we make, especially regarding values and ethics, and how we live our lives. And it can put us in touch with the sacred (for some, that's a "religious sacred," for others a "secular sacred"), that to which we must not lay waste but must hold in trust for future generations. Experiencing amazement, wonder, and awe opens up the possibility of experiencing transcendence, the feeling that we belong to something larger than ourselves and that our actions matter, for good or harm, beyond just us. That experience can generate hope, the oxygen of the human spirit. Without hope, our human spirit dies; with it, we can overcome even seemingly insurmountable obstacles. And might not experiencing amazement, wonder, and awe about the new knowledge gained through science be a condition precedent to its conversion to wisdom and its wise govermance?

Each of us individually and as members of a society needs to understand where our own values came from and how they were formed, if we are to have the insights necessary to make wise decisions about whether we want to keep or change them. With that in mind, I have included as Appendix A an autobiographical essay I wrote, which caused me to realize that my own values were powerfully influenced by what I learned from my father.

I have long argued that an important aspect of an academic's "repayment" for the privilege of being one is to inform members of the public in such a way that they can participate effectively in the public and social policy debates relating to values that affect all of us in the present and will affect the world we leave to future generations. I believe members of the public have a "right to know" and academics have a responsibility to inform them, that is, to engage in what can be called "effective informing." That is what I try to do in this book.

Effective informing requires abandoning "mystery and mastery" – the use of concepts and language that average people cannot understand – which is an exercise of control and exclusion of those not among the "chosen few" initiated into the "mystery." Contemporary moral philosophy and applied ethics, including sometimes bioethics, are largely inaccessible to all but the "chosen few." Many philosophers – although certainly not all, as my eminent philosopher colleague Professor Charles Taylor shows us – typically employ a form of communication that is rarely readily understandable to the average citizen. As well, they can object strongly to people such as myself who act as "translators." In the early days of my participation in "public square" debates about values, I was frequently accused by some philosophers of vulgarizing the knowledge I was communicating; in doing so, I was vulgar in the derogatory sense of that word. They also accused me of oversimplifying complicated ethical issues. My defence was that engaging in such translation is neither to deny the complexity of the issues and concepts that are translated, nor to condone the introduction of errors, nor to be simplistic – although that translation can have the immensely valuable attribute of being simple. I have long adopted this general approach when interacting with the public, and the most frequent response I have received is people saying, "Thank you for what you said. I knew what I believed, but I didn't know how to say it, I didn't have the words. Now I do."

In contrast to such gratitude, others, including some members of the academy, have severely critiqued my participation in the public square. They have sought to dismiss my arguments on the grounds that they are based on what they perceive to be my political, ideological, or (especially) religious beliefs; and they claim that, as a result, the positions I advance oversimplify complicated ethical, medical, social, or technical issues. My response has been to ask them to judge me on the basis of the arguments I present and the ethical values I advance, rather than on the basis of what they think I may believe. The debate about what our values should be is too important to be obscured by assumptions that limit debate before it begins.

In undertaking the "translation" I've described, I am also sometimes criticized by those who oppose my views, on the grounds that I do not understand philosophy. This book reflects, however, a deep respect for philosophy and classical ethics as a subdiscipline of moral philosophy. But it has a much broader basis than philosophy: it draws on research and study that is the work of the academy, on what the public-health experts, scientists, sociologists, research psychologists, anthropologists, jurists, humanities scholars, policy experts, and statisticians as well as bioethicists, ethicists, and philosophers have argued, said, and published. Moreover, this book is not written for philosophers but is intended for a broad audience and venues distinctly in the public square, as a contribution in the search for values we can all embrace.

In this last regard, this book is a sequel to another of my books, *The Ethical Imagination: Journeys of the Human Spirit*, which was based on my 2006 CBC Massey Lectures. The theme running through those lectures was how we might be able to find some shared values. Moreover, as that lecture series powerfully demonstrates, public intellectuals and scholars can successfully bring the best of a world of learning and expertise to a general audience when they don't talk down or simplify issues unnecessarily but use their skills as writers and thinkers to explain complex issues in all their complexity in a way that is understandable and valuable to non-scholars. Indeed, as I have argued, this task is their obligation. As scientists from Albert Einstein to Karl Steinmeitz have said, if you can't make it clear to others, you are not clear yourself.

This clarity is what I am attempting to realize in this book. Its goal is not to advocate or argue by assertion but to show how to "do ethics" in a way that does not underestimate the complexity of the ethical issues at play, yet can be readily understood. Its subject is values, because they are the heart of the ethics we propose, the groundwork on which our beliefs are built and from which our policies and decisions flow. And because we live in democracies where the perspective of average people matters, the whole is, I hope, accessible to non-academic as well as professional audiences.

I was asked, "What is new in this contribution to public debate?" My answer is that we can no longer assume, as we once could, that we all share more or less the same fundamental values. If society was ever that homogenous, those days are long gone. What is perhaps new in this book is that it insists on the perspective that all can and should be involved in the debates about values in our societies.

The need for a broad spectrum of involved citizens is especially critical with respect to governing the extraordinary powers opened up by astonishing "technoscience advances." On 18 April 2015, Chinese scientists announced that they had "edited" the genes of human embryos,[2] that is, intentionally changed the human germline (the genes we pass on from generation to generation) which is the outcome of the billions of years of evolution of life on Earth. We thought that there was an international consensus that such alteration would be inherently wrong and must never be undertaken. We were wrong. Now we are faced with possibilities such as "genetically enhancing" our children – for instance, increasing their intelligence, or "designing" their physical characteristics. What values and ethics must govern such procedures? As this example (one of many) demonstrates, what we decide about values, and what that means we may or must not do, will be among our most important collective decisions in coming decades.

I was also asked, "What do you want readers to know that they did not perceive before?" My answer is, first, I want them to to realize that their opinion matters and, if they wish, it can be one informed by academic and popular arguments that do not require a PhD to be understood. Second, I want to convey that there are strong links among all the current debates about values, and that in thinking about values – what we believe, and why – we all may develop an informed and consistent perspective as citizens. It does not matter if one's values are founded in human rights or a religious perspective or humanism or atheism (which is, of course, just as much an informing principle of one's worldview as religion). All must be respected; all must be considered respectfully as we seek possible accommodations among them.

If I were asked to articulate a single point that I would hope readers might take from this book, it is that we are in a crisis of conflict between respect for individual autonomy and protection of the common good. I believe the balance has swung dangerously towards the former and that this situation urgently needs to be corrected.

A second and related point (a corollary) might be simply this: in the past few decades, we have recognized that our physical ecosystem is not indestructible – indeed, it is vulnerable, and can be irreparably damaged – and that we have obligations to future generations to care for it. The same is true of our metaphysical ecosystem, the values, principles, attitudes, beliefs, shared stories, and so on, on the basis of which we form our society. Holding our metaphysical ecosystem in trust will require of all of us – young and old – wisdom, ethical restraint (the old virtue of prudence), hope, and courage, as we participate in the battles about values that constitute the current culture wars.

Margaret Somerville
Montreal
April 2015

Acknowledgments

Many people around the world, through the miracles of travel and twenty-first century communications technology, have contributed to this book. Some have done so by agreeing with me and expanding my knowledge, others – especially my students – by disagreeing with me and challenging me to explain why I hold the views I do. I thank all of you.

As I explain in the introduction, a substantial amount of the text in this book began as speeches I was invited to deliver. I am deeply grateful to the people who invited me and who often needed to persuade or push me to accept. In exploring and developing the wide variety of topics and issues they asked me to address, I came to see the common threads linking those topics and issues and how the different prioritizations of the underlying values informing people's approaches to them gave rise to the resulting conflicts of values.

My thanks also to the three anonymous reviewers whose comments challenged, helped, and even forewarned me. As one of them pointed out, my arguing for "the enduring significance of historic, traditional values, [i]n an age of progressive novelty … [in which] others have jumped on bandwagons of progressivism and flippantly, sometimes even cheerfully, tossed overboard values widely held to be sacrosanct only a generation ago … [means] people will not necessarily *like* the book."

As always, I'm indebted to the wonderful team at McGill-Queen's University Press, so ably led by my colleague and friend Philip Cercone. Special thanks are owed to Philip for critiquing the manuscript and suggesting improvements. I thank also Ryan Van Huijstee for his ready assistance, my excellent copy editor, Maureen Garvie, and David Drummond for designing the front cover.

Thanks to esteemed sculptor Marcel Braitstein both for his gift of the sculpture *Bird on an Ethics Wire* and his permission to use a detail of the image on the cover of this book. I am also very grateful to his wife, my friend Elaine Steinberg, for instigating this gift as a "thank you" for a speech by the same name, which I gave at a charity event.

I am grateful to bioethicist Dr Tom Koch for some valuable editing of the preface, and to Sean Murphy of the Protection of Conscience Project and Barbara Maloney for helpful information and exchange of ideas.

My assistant Libby Parker invariably makes my work easier and my life more tranquil with her calm and patient help, and I am very grateful to her. I thank as well Solange Roch for secretarial assistance with this book in the early days of its preparation.

As always, I'm deeply grateful to my stalwart friends for their kindness, encouragement, and unfailing and unflinching support in good times and bad, whether they agree or disagree with me. The latter is the litmus test of real friendship.

I acknowledge the important role model that my dear aunt, Veronica Rowe, has been for me for my entire life and I thank her for her love and care.

And, as is my custom, I note that I am grateful to have the companionship of my interspecies friends, Didji and Tazzie, and for their reassuring purrs at critical moments.

◆◆◆

I thank Emeritus Professor John Furedy and Emerita Professor Christine Furedy for permission to quote from their texts, as I do in chapter 2.

I am grateful to Father J. Leon Hooper, SJ, Woodstock Jesuit Theological Library, Georgetown University, Washington, DC, for permission to quote from the writings of the late Father Thomas Courtney Murray, SJ, again in chapter 2.

I thank Dr Harvey Max Chochinov and his colleagues for permission to reproduce the table from the article "Dignity Therapy: A Novel Psychotherapeutic Intervention for Patients near the End of Life," *Journal of Clinical Oncology* 23 (2005): 5520–5.

The analysis of the trial-level judgment of the *Carter* case used as a basis for the discussion in chapter 4 was first published in *Suffering and Bioethics*, edited by Ronald M. Green and Nathan J. Palpant (New York: Oxford University Press 2014), as "Exploring Interactions between Pain, Suffering, and the Law," 201–27. I am grateful for the kind permission of the editors and publisher to use the content of that chapter.

Chapter 7 was first published as "Law Marching with Medicine but in the Rear and Limping a Little: Ethics as 'First Aid' for Law," in *Ethik und Recht – Die Ethisierung des Rechts* (Ethics and law – the ethicalization of law), edited by Silja Voneky and colleagues (Heidelberg, New York, Dordrecht, London: Springer 2013). I thank Professor Voneky for her permission to include it here.

◆◆◆

Never give up, no matter the odds
– motto of my mother's Fitzgerald family

Old warrior
– meaning of Ganley, my father's family name and my maiden name

Noli timere. (Be not afraid.)
– from the Bible, a part of my cultural-religious heritage

Introduction

A cartoon shows a long row of birds perched on a telephone wire between two poles. All the birds are facing forward, except for one. The bird next to him asks, "Can't we talk about it?"

I know how that bird facing the opposite way from the rest of the flock feels. I have often found myself in an analogous position when debating ethics issues or expressing an opinion on values. I also know that if I were asked that question, my answer would always be: "Yes, we *must* talk about it." This book is a collection of essays that talk about some of our most important contemporary values issues and the heated debates and conflicts they engender.

Because they can fly, birds are often a metaphor for freedom or, for those who feel imprisoned in some way, a metaphor for the longing to be free. Others of us recognize that to maintain freedom we must have the restrictions necessary to ensure the conditions that make freedom possible. That balance struck between liberty and its restriction can be referred to as "freedom in fetters." Those fetters often consist of long-standing, fundamental, previously shared values. Disagreements about where we should draw the lines between the values we will continue to accept and implement and those we will reject is yet another way to describe the genesis of our current values conflicts.

A friend emailed me recently saying, "I sent my article 'On Old Age' to the magazine *Eureka Street* … The Editor wrote back and said it was written very well, and he had circulated it around his staff, but the decision was to decline it *because there was too much Cicero in proportion to my opinion.* I was surprised – how could anyone prefer my silly opinion to that of the old master? But I shouldn't have been. I've had something else rejected on the same grounds by the *Scholars* journal – that time I quoted Ovid and Edward Gibbon and someone else. I just thought that editor didn't know what she was talking about."

I see a larger message in the two incidents my friend describes. The self-styled, so-called progressives, regarding the values they espouse, tend to treat history (human memory[1]) as old-fashioned and irrelevant and see the lessons it can provide as restrictive. They've started calling people who have conservative values "restrictives" – although the antonym of that word is "permissives," not progressives, and I doubt that they would welcome that characterization. Their informing principle is "choice and change." The underlying, linking theme among the chapters in this book is the battles between these radically different values stances, explored through an examination of the arguments, strategies, tactics, rhetoric, and claims of each.

Labels and definitions matter. They are not neutral. We have moved from labelling the competing values stances as liberal or conservative and left-wing or right-wing to neo-liberal or neo-conservative, and now progressives/permissives or restrictives. Moreover, increasingly, a division through characterization is being made between the secular and the religious, usually to dismiss the values of religious people, even if they are not based on their religious beliefs.

We create our multiple, complex identities, whether as individuals, families, communities, or a society, through the stories that we tell and mutually buy into. We are or become those stories, and so in telling them our choice of words and their persuasiveness is a critical issue. From this perspective, the present battles about values and culture wars can be seen as being between competing narratives, each struggling to predominate in establishing societal values. In contemporary secular societies, the most important of the values we distil from our collective stories are institutionalized in law, which can be seen as the most important meta-narrative in those societies. So it is to be expected, as is the case, that there will be heated battles over the law that should govern, for example, abortion or euthanasia.

Sometimes, especially in relation to novel situations that raise ethical issues, such as assisted reproductive technologies, our collective values are instantiated, at least temporarily when we are uncertain of what the law should be, in ethical precepts. One way to envisage the relation of law and ethics in contemporary western democratic societies is to see the law as their mind and ethics their soul. It merits noting that we may intuit what is ethical or unethical before we can clarify the reasons for our conclusions, which can help to explain why ethical governance of new technologies, for instance, can precede their legal regulation. For people who are religious, faith beliefs can also play a role in what they perceive as ethical or unethical and, consequently, what they would choose as their society's collective values. As I discuss in the chapters that follow, legal, ethical, and religious approaches to establishing collective societal values do not necessarily give consistent answers and can result in conflict as to what those values should be.

One of my goals in writing this book is to show how important our perceptions are in what we decide about ethics and values. I emphasize how radically one person's perception of a situation, belief, or argument can differ from another's, and the major impact those different perceptions can have with regard to what each sees as ethical or unethical. I also try to show how our perceptions can play a role in whether or not we can find meaning in the life events we encounter, especially when those events involve suffering, and how applied ethics and law function to put into practice the values that flow from our perceptions.

A theme running through all the chapters is the powerful influence of the language we choose to describe our perceptions of a situation, principle, or belief. Words affect our intuitions, including our moral intuitions, and our emotions, which both play a role in our decisions about ethics. Words also often determine who prevails in a conflictual social policy debate in the public square. They are weapons in our battles about values and culture wars.

Words occurring frequently throughout this book are "abortion," "reproductive technologies," "transhumanism," and "euthanasia." They represent the postmodern contexts of birth and death, which now can involve technological intervention in our coming-into-being, in the essence of our innate being, that which makes us human, and in how we leave life. As has always been true for birth and death, and is now true for technoscience interventions on the natural human being that affect birth and death, these are the contexts in which we form and uphold or destroy our most important shared values.

Many of the situations discussed in this book reflect the danger that our perceptions, and as a result our ethics and values, can be intentionally manipulated or radically changed through the choice and use of words. One such strategy is to label individuals as religious and dismiss them and their arguments from consideration without addressing the substance of those persons' arguments. Other approaches include automatically labelling opposition to a politically correct or "progressive values" stance as wrongful discrimination, or claiming that unborn children are "just bunches of cells" and not living human beings deserving of protection of their lives. Our perception of an unborn child as either a "problem" or a "miracle" will radically alter our decisions about the ethics of our behaviour in regard to that child. Likewise, people who want to destroy traditional values and label themselves as "progressives" and their opponents as "restrictives" are using a word strategy to further their cause.

We've learned to discount the old chant often sung by children, "Sticks and stones can break my bones but words can never hurt me." Through their power to harm values and ethics and, as a result, individuals, communities, and societies, our words, unless we choose them with wise ethical restraint (the old virtue of prudence), can perpetrate serious and far-reaching harm at all levels of our existence in the present and for the future. Thus we must always choose and use words wisely in engaging in the battles about values and the culture wars that confront us.

There are valuable lessons to be learnt from some of the arguments and positions espoused by the "progressives/permissives" values advocates, but if their claims are not balanced by those of people with countervailing values, the result will eventually prove to be an ethical disaster for our societies. The progressives/permissives advocates are values deconstructionists, often without viable replacements to offer. Their stance is accurately described, as it was recently by Pope Francis, as "adolescent progressivism." It is often also "utopian totalitarianism." They see themselves as creating a better world and as entitled to impose their values, even at great cost to those who disagree with them, in order to achieve that goal. This attitude brings to mind an old saying in human rights: "Nowhere are human rights more threatened than when we act purporting to do only good." Sole focus on the good we hope to achieve can blind us to the risks and harms unavoidably also present. As I argue in several chapters, it would be a serious error to believe we should have no restrictions on our freedoms. Rather, we must strike a balance between unlimited liberty and the safeguards or "fetters" needed to protect our most important values, including freedom itself.

We need to understand better the bases on which we make moral and ethical decisions and the values that come into play when we do so, and these essays should be read with that caveat in mind. For instance, we have unconscious biases that influence our decisions about ethics.[2] Research psychologists, and in particular New York University social psychologist Jonathan Haidt,[3] have articulated six moral foundations that underlie our values-based decisions. Their findings show that the interpretation and adoption of these moral foundations can differ between liberals and conservatives.[4] The moral foundation "Care/Harm" – protect others and do not harm them – was important to everyone, as was "Liberty/Oppression," although liberals interpreted this latter foundation as requiring egalitarianism and protecting the rights of vulnerable groups, while conservatives saw it as the right to be left alone. Both groups supported the value of fairness and rejected cheating. But conservatives had much a stronger attachment to loyalty than did liberals, and more adamantly rejected betrayal, a value foundation that makes people willing to sacrifice for the group or community. Likewise, conservatives had a much stronger attachment to respect for authority and scorn for subversion, positions that help to maintain social order through hierarchies. Conservatives, unlike liberals, also sought and used a sense of sanctity and eschewed degradation, stances that allow humans to bond to form mutually beneficial, large, cooperative societies.

◆◆◆

The essays making up the chapters in this book originated in requests to speak at conferences or to write articles for the comments sections of newspapers. They show how our perceptions of a situation can vary widely with respect to the ethics involved, how the words we choose matter in what we see as ethical or unethical and which values we choose to adopt, and how the vast majority of us are searching for meaning in life, whether through our agreements or our disagreements about these values issues. The essays also show the wide diversity of situations and places in which values conflicts can arise – from a court or a legislature to the public square, in academia, cinematographic art, a hospital, a science laboratory, an abortion clinic, or a crisis pregnancy counselling centre.

Chapter 1, "Should Religion Be Evicted from the Public Square?," was delivered as the 2011 Warrane Lecture at Warrane College at the University of New South Wales. In it I argue that we all have a belief system on which we found our most important values and that it is anti-democratic to eliminate those whose belief system is informed by their religion. Moreover, doing so not only harms excluded individuals but also seriously harms society. The chapter also explores the major difference between a society being based on religious or theological tenets and a society respecting the rights of religious citizens in a secular democratic society to have their voices heard in the public square.

Chapter 2, "Are Our "Values Conversations" Sufficiently Open and Free? The University as a Test Case," originated in a plenary address, "What Are and Are Not Legitimate Restrictions on Academic Freedom? 'Freedom in Fetters' in the University," I gave at the conference Christian Faith and the University: From the Reformation to W. Stanford Reid held in Montreal in September 2013. It examines the use of "political correctness" in our universities, with its goal of promoting and inculcating "progressive values" in students. The case I present is that "political correctness" can function to eliminate certain values, views, discussions, and topics of conversation by suppressing certain freedoms. These freedoms include freedom of conscience and religion; freedom of thought, belief, opinion and expression, including freedom of the press and other media of communication; freedom of peaceful assembly; and freedom of association. Because upholding these freedoms is central to maintaining and defending some of society's most important values, the challenge is how to protect them. I propose that we can do so in the university context through correctly understanding and applying the concept of "academic freedom" in particular, and that respect for this freedom benefits not only academics but society.

Chapter 3, "Is the Concept of Human Dignity Useful, Useless or Dangerous?," was a speech presented at the World Youth Alliance's Decade of Dignity and Development Conference at Yale University in September 2009. Pointing to the ubiquitous use of the concept of human dignity and its history, I summarize the views of leading scholars from a wide variety of disciplines to show that there is no agreement on how to define dignity or what is required to respect it. I focus particularly on the rallying cry of euthanasia advocates, "death with dignity," and describe the work of Canadian psychiatrist Dr Harvey Max Chochinov and his colleagues in developing a new treatment approach for helping terminally ill people, which they call "dignity therapy."

Chapter 4, "Legalizing Euthanasia: Evolution or Revolution in Societal Values?" builds on an analysis of the trial-level judgment in the *Carter* case first published in a chapter in *Suffering and Bioethics* (2014) edited by Ronald Green and Nathan Palpant.[5] This case was appealed to the Supreme Court of Canada, which upheld the trial judge's findings of fact and legal reasoning to strike down the absolute prohibition of assisted suicide in the Canadian Criminal Code to allow "physician-assisted death" – physician-assisted suicide and, arguably, euthanasia. Because the Supreme Court of Canada so strongly endorsed the trial judgment, analysis of it is much more important than it usually is for a case that has been appealed. I believe that history will view what we decide about legalizing "physician-assisted death" as one of the most momentous societal decisions of the twenty-first century, because of the unavoidable serious harm that allowing it will cause to the value of respect for life at both individual and societal levels, and to vulnerable people. (The other momentous decision is whether we will allow alteration/editing of the human germline, the genes passed on from generation to generation, which has just become possible for the first time in human history.)

Chapter 5, "Is Every Life Beautiful?," was an address given as part of the 2011–12 lecture series "The Power of Beauty," co-sponsored by the Current Affairs Exchange Forum, the BEST Club, and Inquire@UofT, at the University of Toronto. It explores what I judge to be the world's most dangerous idea, namely, that there is nothing special about being human – we are just another animal in the forest, and all animals should be treated equally. This concept leads to the conclusion that not all human life deserves respect and protection. I propose that whether or not we see all human life as beautiful could affect our views of suffering and, as a result, the ethics that should govern, for example, euthanasia. Likewise, whether we see all life as beautiful is ethically relevant at the other end of the human lifespan, as it can affect ethical decisions about the use of reproductive technologies and about abortion (including sex-selection abortion), and the ethical acceptability of the consequences of a search for perfection in our children through the use of technology. Being open to experiences of amazement, wonder, and awe, I suggest, can help us to see all life as beautiful, and doing so could assist us in protecting the essential essence of our humanness to the benefit of both ourselves and future generations.

Chapter 6, "How Might a Problem – a Crisis Pregnancy – Be Converted to a Mystery, the Gift of Life?," is the text of a speech given at the Canadian Association of Pregnancy Support Services (CAPSS) National Conference in June 2014. It starts with the story of Anna, a young woman who experienced a crisis pregnancy, and her hopes for what others could learn from her trauma and suffering. It emphasizes the need for those making decisions about the ethics and law that should govern abortion, and for those engaging in the abortion debate, to know and keep up to date with the relevant science if they are to make wise ethical and legal decisions. The impact on the wider community of societal-level decisions about issues such as abortion must also be considered. The concluding section questions how we should handle the situation in which we find ourselves in Canada, that of the absence of any law restricting abortion, and where we should go from here.

Chapter 7, "How Might the Involvement of Applied Ethics in Law Affect Our Societal Values? Ethics as 'First Aid' for Law," was an invited speech delivered at the Ethicalization of Law Symposium, held at the Max Planck Institute for Comparative Public Law and International Law in Neuenheimer, University of Freiburg, Germany, in September 2011.[6] This chapter examines the emergence since the 1970s of applied ethics and its practitioners and the contemporary explicit interaction of ethics with the law, especially in courts and legislatures in the area of bioethics. We see how, as the law has faced unprecedented issues arising from scientific advances, in particular in the area of assisted human reproduction, the order of analysis has changed from assuming that the law reflected ethics and therefore using the law to inform ethics, to turning first to ethics and using ethics to inform law. When values conflict, this change in the order of analysis can result in different values taking priority than would otherwise be the case. Also discussed is the use of human-rights language to implement ethics through law, as well as the current importance of medicine and medical science as a context for the formation of societal values more generally, because this is a context to which we all personally relate.

We sometimes say in ethics that the questions we ask can be more important than the answers we give in helping us to identify ethical issues and gain insight into how we should deal with them. Indeed, it's no accident that the titles of all the chapters in this book are questions. In the final chapter, chapter 8, "What Questions Are We Asking in Contemporary Cultural Values Conversations, and What Messages Are They Communicating?," I address some recent questions I've been asked to ponder and respond to by newspaper editors. These questions include: "What lessons could we learn from two films, *Amour* and *Never Let Me Go*, and from the documentary *End Credits*?" "How do you think the human race will end?" "What will future generations see as the defining event of the first decades of the twenty-first century?" To say the least, these questions lead to thought-provoking and insight-producing enquiries.

To describe the contents of the book in a slightly different way, the first two chapters deal with liberty rights and the values that protect them: in chapter 1, in the general context of the public square, and in chapter 2, in the special context of the university. Chapters 3 to 6 explore the value of respect for life and its protection or the contrary, and examine situations in which there is conflict between upholding the value of respect for life and the value of respect for individual autonomy. Chapters 7 and 8 look at how we establish, uphold, or eliminate our societal values and communicate them, in the formal institutional settings of courts and legislatures (chapter 7) and in informal cultural contexts (chapter 8).

Our battles about values are often not easy and sometimes not pleasant, but we should be grateful that we live in a democratic society where we can engage in them with openness and largely without fear of reprisals – or so it seemed until the recent horrific terrorist attacks in several western democracies, including Canada. It is of the utmost importance that such "safe engagement" should continue to be true, which will require a *sine qua non* of mutual respect on all our parts, because respect is always a two-way street.

1

Should Religion Be Evicted from the Public Square?

In North America a pink slip in your pay-packet means you've been fired. My original title for this chapter was "Is Religion a 'Pink Slip' in the Public Square?" – that is, are some voices and views being dismissed simply on the basis that they are religious? When I suggested this title to Arthur Escamilla, the dean of Warrane College at the University of New South Wales where I'd been invited to give the 2011 Warrane Lecture, he informed me that in Australia a "pink slip" means that your car has been certified as roadworthy. So, it didn't quite fit, even for me who loves finding imaginative connections among apparently unconnected entities, which can provide otherwise unavailable insights. Consequently, I changed the title to "Should Religion Be Evicted from the Public Square?"

But no matter how we ask it, the response to this question in secular western democracies over the past twenty or so years has been that religion is indeed being banished from the public square and an ever-larger number of people are resoundingly affirming that it should be so banished. In other words, some voices and views are being dismissed from the public square simply because they are religious.[1] Many of the people seeking to evict religion are not only openly hostile to any such participation but also openly hostile to religion itself.

Observing this hostility leads to other questions, the primary one being, "Are these people evicting religion doing the right thing?" My response is an absolute "No," and my hope is to convince others to adopt that stance.

What are the arguments *against* religious voices having a valid claim to be heard in the public square? Where do they originate? Why are they being presented? And what are the arguments *for* religious voices having a valid claim, even a right, to be heard in the public square?

What Issues Are Being Debated in the Contemporary Public Square?

In ethics it's a truism, but no less important for being so, that "good facts are essential to good ethics." So let's start with some facts. What are some of the issues currently being debated in the public square?

Whether you live in Canada, Australia, or another western democracy, if you read the newspapers, listen to documentaries on radio, or watch the news on TV, you'll see numerous reports on topics such as euthanasia and physician-assisted suicide; withdrawal of life-support treatment; treatment of seriously disabled newborn babies; access to health care, especially expensive new treatments; abortion; prenatal genetic screening; assisted human reproduction technologies; reproductive tourism; sperm and ova donation; surrogate motherhood; "designer babies"; "saviour siblings"; cloning; human embryo stem cell research; same-sex marriage; artificial sperm and ova, including making embryos from two same-sex adults; creating babies with three genetic parents; altering the human germline, the genes inherited from generation to generation; polygamy; sex education of children; the use of animals in research; "manimals" (embryos with both human and animal genes); synthetic biology; xenotransplantation (the use of animal organs in humans); transplant tourism; being soft/hard on crime and drugs; needle exchange clinics; safe injecting sites; capital punishment; law and ethics governing armed conflict; the ethics of robotic warfare; business ethics; corruption; environmental ethics; aid to developing countries; and so on.

These issues involve some of our most important individual and collective social-ethical-legal values. In part that is true because many of them are connected with respect for life, and with birth or death, the two events around which we have always formed our most important individual and collective values. Those values, together with our principles, attitudes, beliefs, myths, and so on make up the societal-cultural paradigm on which our society is based. That "shared story" that we tell each other and buy into forms the glue that binds us as a society.

So, in "secular societies" such as Australia and Canada, does religion have any valid role to play in determining what these values should be?

Let's look, first, at the nature of the conflicts we are experiencing with respect to the values we should adopt.

Values Conflicts

What our collective values should be in contemporary western democracies is currently a source of conflict some call "culture wars." These conflicts are often described as having two sides: a traditional, conservative, often religious side doing battle against a postmodern, liberal, moral relativist, often secularist side. Lately, as I mentioned in the preface, the sides are sometimes being called "the restrictives" and "the progressives." This division into two well-defined camps can be useful as shorthand to discuss these values issues, but it is an oversimplification, especially in relation to many of our current values issues, such as those I just listed, when they are viewed as packages.

Many variations are possible between one person's "values package" and another's. And it merits noting here that there is no one monolithic religious voice or, indeed, secular voice; rather, each of these two broad groupings is a collection of many different voices. In other words, the reality is far more mixed and complex than two "camps," an important reality to recognize as it tells us that, although we might disagree with "the other side" on some issues, we can agree on others.

That recognition is also important because, as I will propose, searching for agreements – for what I call a "shared ethics" – in pluralistic, multicultural, multi-religious, secular, postmodern, democratic societies like Australia and Canada, is crucial to finding a values structure that will allow us as individuals and as a society to flourish in the sense of realizing the fullness of our human spirit.[2]

The idea is to find what we have in common ethically so that we can experience ourselves as belonging to the same moral community. As those experiences accumulate, we will be more able to find common ground than we can in any other way. But to do so will require the presence of goodwill and the absence of hostility towards religion and religious people and their views in the public square.

Some people question whether there is such hostility. A telling expression of concern about its presence and the absence of goodwill comes from American theologian George Weigel, writing about a seminar for young Catholic Europeans held in Poland in 2009:

> What these young people … know … is that they are coming to Catholic maturity in a Europe increasingly hostile to public manifestations of Catholic faith. When the Tertio Millennio Seminar started in 1992, our debates were about church-state law, democratic theory, and the structure of the free economy; now, they're about the nature of marriage, the challenge of biotechnology, the life issues, Islam [Islamism], and an aggressive secularism that tries to keep religiously informed moral argument out of the European public square … [We need] to help shape a lay leadership in these new democracies that can develop the voice of religiously informed public moral argument. The task is a huge one.[3]

Note that the hostility that Weigel describes arises around precisely many of the same issues I listed earlier in this chapter. To understand and deal with this hostility, we must first have some understanding of how those opposed to religious values in the public square view religion.

Addressing the theme "Free to Believe? A Religious Conscience in a Secular Society," Professor Roger Trigg, the academic director of the Centre for the Study of Religion in Public Life at Kellogg College, Oxford, has noted that "religious viewpoints are frequently not respected or even accommodated. European authorities are inclined to see religion as a threat that must be controlled." He continues, "What is developing is not neutrality but often hostility to religion, with an ideology of human rights taking its place. I am an advocate of respect for human rights, but, as I will explain shortly, I believe it is a mistake to promote those rights to the exclusion of the religiously informed conscience of those who have such."[4] Similarly, Bishop Michael Nazir-Ali, the former Anglican bishop of Rochester, England, has warned that "aggressive secularism is leading to an 'encroaching totalitarianism' that has become a threat to freedom of conscience."[5]

These were prescient and valid warnings. Adherents of "progressive values" are using human-rights rhetoric, mechanisms, and institutions to promote their values and to deny freedom of conscience to those with conflicting values. A clear example is the efforts of some feminists to try to force physicians with conscientious objections to abortion to provide this procedure and to refer women to physicians willing to do so.

The Need to Cross Divides: Abandoning Either/Or

We need to be able to cross our traditional divides if we are to find some shared ethics in relation to issues such as I identified above. And when those divides are places of serious conflict, we must try even harder to find what we share and where we can agree. That is, not only *can* we cross the secular/religious divide, the science/religion divide and the divide between religions, but we *must* if we are to find a "shared ethics" in our world.[6]

The starkest examples of refusals to cross these divides are the fundamentalist religious people and the fundamentalist neo-atheists such as Richard Dawkins, the late Christopher Hitchens, Daniel Dennett, Michel Onfray, and Sam Harris. In my opinion, both groups are seriously misguided, but let's look at the latter.[7]

Like all fundamentalists, the neo-atheists want first to impose their views on everyone else. One of the most egregious current examples, an extension and putting into practice of their "religion has no place in the public square" approach, is the one just mentioned, that physicians acting in their professional capacity have no right to respect for their freedom of conscience and their ethical and moral values. (I discuss this position further in the next chapter, including in relation to the Ontario Human Rights Commission's startling view that physicians' own values have no place in the physician-patient encounter.[8])

Second, like all fundamentalists, neo-atheists take an either/or approach – either my beliefs or yours, either science or religion, either reason or faith – when we need to accommodate both sides of each of these divides. Fundamentalists, whether secular or religious, then seek to reconcile what they see as the conflicts between the two elements that make up each of these pairings, by dropping one or the other. Richard Dawkins's call for the elimination of religion, except as a purely private pursuit, demonstrates such a choice on his part.

And, third, they engage in proselytizing. An example that attracted a great deal of media and public attention was an advertising slogan on buses in Britain and Canada: "There's probably is no God. Now stop worrying and enjoy your life." New York City atheists had some two dozen buses rolling through Manhattan, with a twelve-foot long, three-foot high message, "You don't have to believe in god to be a moral or ethical person."

One problem with this either/or approach is that proposing that science and religion or reason and faith are in conflict is *not neutral* in terms of its impact on finding a "shared ethics." It is very harmful to attaining that goal.

The neo-atheists would like to reduce religion to nothing more than a personal fantasy or superstition. But that is not realistic; it's an impossible dream on their part. At best it will fail, at worst do serious harm – it will exacerbate the acrimony of the values conflicts and make it more likely, not less so, that religion will become a focus of serious conflict. Also, because culture and religion are linked, even within democratic, multicultural, pluralistic western societies it will increase the number and intensity of the current values clashes and may contribute to culture wars.

And it is essential to recognize that, like the fundamentalist neo-atheists, fundamentalist religious people, especially those who act militantly in what they see as "the cause of their faith," also make finding a shared ethics much more difficult, even impossible.

One way of trying to cross some of our current divides would be to see whether we might be able to find ethical universals common to all people, whether religious or not, and if so, no matter which religion they espouse. Might we able to say that these ethical universals are so widely shared over such a long period of time across so many different cultures that they can be taken as characteristics of being human – that is, they are innate to being human?

Might the various religions be one source of the shared ethics wisdom that we seek? For instance, some version of the Golden Rule is to be found in all major world religions. Some scholars – theologians, philosophers, and religious-studies academics – are looking at a range of world religions and analyzing their relation to human rights declarations. And some secular philosophers, for instance, the German philosopher Jürgen Habermas, are suggesting as a possibility for finding some common ethics ground a concept of an "ethics of the [human] species,"[9] which, it can be argued, might have an epigenetic base.[10] I'd call this concept "human ethics."

And it is not only our traditional divides that we need to be concerned about. The American author and journalist Colleen Carroll Campbell describes "the quintessential modern impulse [as being] … to separate – to sever faith from reason, morality from politics, and spirituality from community and history."[11] The elements she names are all "human ways of knowing" and being. She insists, "We urgently need to stop separating them and, rather, to accommodate, reintegrate, and use all them, if we are to make wise and ethical decisions about the values we espouse."[12]

Now, let's look at what we mean by a secular society.

Secular Societies

By a secular society I specifically do not mean a society in which religious and spiritual voices are excluded from the public sphere. As I've explained, I do not agree with the secularist argument that religion has no valid role in our shared values formation and no place in the public square, or at least nothing valuable to contribute, or certainly nothing valuable beyond the purely private sphere. At the same time, I recognize that religion cannot function in the public square as it did in the past.

We form society through a journey of the collective human imagination. In an article in the *Globe and Mail*,[13] journalist Michael Valpy quotes American political scientist Benedict Anderson to the effect that "a nation is an imagined community." Valpy points out that we have to understand our fellow citizens with whom we interact and "share values, community knowledge and mythology," if we are to hear and understand each other. Doing that is "what enables Canadians to live together with sufficient levels of trust and security and to conduct their democracy under the rubric of having a common purpose and serving the common good." Unfortunately, we can no longer assume a shared knowledge – "the cohesive core of common information is shrinking" – and we are becoming more polarized in our attitudes, and that is undermining social cohesion.

In the past, a given group or society found their collective human imagination and undertook the journey of their collective human imagination through religion. In other words, among other functions, a shared religion was used to create and carry the community's collective imagination. To state the obvious, this situation has changed in two ways: first, in our postmodern interconnected world, the collectivity involved in searching for a shared ethics goes far beyond one more or less homogenous, isolated community. Now the entire world – literally – is, in some senses although certainly not all, our local community. And, of course, we do not have a universally shared religion in either our national or global communities. Moreover, in addition to our myriad of religious traditions, some people are not religious, and some of these are militantly anti-religious, just as some religious people are militantly religious.

So, if we cannot use religion to find our collective imagination and bind ourselves together, how do we do that? Can, as fundamentalist neo-atheists propose, a purely secular approach replace religion in fulfilling this need? Can an approach that expressly excludes religious voices do so?

I have long pondered why fundamentalist neo-atheists are so passionate about their disbelief.[14] Why aren't they just indifferent to religion and to people who are religious? Hate is not the opposite of love – both are similar passions, but of opposite emotional content. *Indifference* is the opposite of both.

I've spoken elsewhere[15] about epigenetics, the breakthrough science that shows that genes can be physically changed by environmental triggers (imprinted) and that those changes can have an impact on behaviour. More recently, I've been hypothesizing that humans' search for spirituality might have a genetic base and be an epigenetic phenomenon – that is, the genetic base must be imprinted (activated) by an environmental trigger.[16] If so, it would not be surprising that humans experience an inner space that needs to be filled, and if it is not filled by religion in its traditional mode, then it will need to be filled by something else that can function in a similar manner. Atheism can be seen as one example of what religious studies scholars Katherine Young and Paul Nathanson have called "secular religions,"[17] and atheists' passion for their position could show that we have a need for some form of powerful belief (or disbelief) in order to find meaning in life.

The word religion comes from *religare*, to bind together. We may need to bind together to experience transcendence – the feeling that we belong to something larger than ourselves – an experience that we could require if we are to find meaning in life. Values surveys have found that a longing for transcendence is a rapidly escalating phenomenon in our intensely individualistic western societies. And today much more than in the past, we humans need to bind together across our differences to form a society. Doing so is a major challenge even within our local or national societies in the West, as they become more and more internally diverse. One response could be the emergence of secular religions.

Secular Religions

Secular religions are shared beliefs that have the characteristics of a religion in the ways that they function, but are not based on a belief in a supernatural being.[18] They are forums for values formation and affirmation. It is indisputably true that humanism and atheism function as secular religions binding their adherents through common belief and ideology. They are expressed as secularism, which has more and more become "aggressive or radical secularism."

Science can also function as a secular religion and does so when it becomes scientism. The same is true of ethics when it becomes moralism and sport, when it becomes sportism, especially when that is combined with another powerful "ism," nationalism. And environmentalism is at least a secondary religion for more and more people – but even that has its disbelievers and critics. And I've been told that in the last census some Australians listed "Jedi" as their religion; I will leave how that should be classified as an open question. Surveys that ask for religious affiliation and list "none" as a possible response have resulted in "none" being described as America's new religion. In short, we are witnessing the emergence of a very large number and range of secular religions.

None of these "isms" is harmful in itself, but they are harmful to finding a shared ethics when they are promoted – as, for instance, Dawkins does with scientism – to deny any space for spirituality and traditional religion in the public square and to replace those with *secularism*, the most encompassing secular religion, which functions as a basket holding all the others.

In other words, I am arguing that it is a mistake to accept that secularism is neutral, as its advocates claim. It too is a belief system used to bind people together. And if, despite being a belief system, secularism is not excluded from the public square, then religious voices should not be excluded on that basis. The mistake is in taking a disjunctive (either secularism or religion) approach to a situation that requires a conjunctive (both this and that, secularism and religion) approach. We need all voices to be heard in the democratic public square.

Secular Societies and Democracy

Liberty and equality are the basic principles on which democracy is founded. The genius of democracy at its best is that it functions by allowing us to live peacefully together, despite our differences, by enabling us to find where we can agree and to hold in creative tension the issues we disagree about, rather than engaging in destructive conflict. To privilege secularism, as its advocates urge, is to contravene the liberty and equality principles of democracy and to prevent democracy from functioning as it should. In short, privileging secularism is profoundly anti-democratic.

As an aside, I'd like to focus briefly on the possible benefits of living with such tension by quoting French philosopher Rémi Brague. Western civilization, Brague says,

> is something very strange and unusual. Most civilizations have only one centre. Islam has Mecca. Ancient Egypt had Memphis. Babylon had Babylon. But Western civilization had two sources, Athens and Jerusalem – the Jewish and later Christian tradition and that of pagan antiquity – often described as being in dynamic conflict. This opposition is founded on the opposition of Jew and Greek, borrowed from Saint Paul, which was then systemized in different ways: Hellenism versus Hebraism, the religion of beauty versus the religion of obedience, reason versus faith, aesthetics versus ethics, etc. The curious thing is that one was never swallowed by the other. Europe is neither Jewish nor Greek. In "Rome" in Christianity (e.g., the Roman Catholic Church), Jerusalem and Athens are simultaneously joined and kept apart.
>
> With the coming of Christianity the preceding cultures were not destroyed, but a new civilization was formed. As the Romans recognized that their culture was "secondary" to that of the Greeks, the Christians recognized that Judaism preceded Christianity. This understanding gave European civilization a unique openness and humility towards the enormous cultural achievements of the past. This humility has been a great strength. It fosters the awareness that you cannot simply inherit a civilizing tradition, but that you must work very hard to obtain it – to control the barbarian inside. This has given European culture the possibility of renaissances: a renewed appreciation of the sources of our culture, to correct what has gone wrong.[19]

Let us hope that what has gone wrong in our contemporary culture, especially our loss of an ability to find meaning and hope, can and will be corrected.

But to return to the discussion of secular societies, let me be clear: we are secular, democratic societies and there is rightly a separation of church and state. The question is, what does respecting that separation require?

Separation of church and state means that the state and its laws and public and social policy are not based directly on religious beliefs as occurs in, for example, Islamic societies such as Iran.[20] The doctrine is meant to protect the state from being controlled or wrongfully interfered with by a religion or religions, and to protect religions, within their valid sphere of operation, from state interference or control. For instance, the Chinese government's interference in the appointment of Roman Catholic bishops in that country contravenes the doctrine of separation of church and state. The doctrine of separation of church and state can be viewed as having division of powers or demarcation of jurisdictions functions.

Those wanting to exclude religion from the public square have created confusion among freedom *of* religion, freedom *for* religion, and freedom *from* religion. Freedom of religion means the state does not impose a religion on its citizens: there is no state religion. Freedom for religion means the state does not restrict the free practice of religion by its citizens. Freedom from religion means the state excludes religion and religious voices from the public square, particularly in relation to making law and public policy. The first two freedoms are valid expressions of the doctrine of the separation of church and state. The third is not.

This mistaken interpretation of the doctrine of "separation of church and state" has been promoted by secularists in order to win a victory for their values in the culture wars by eliminating consideration of the values of their opponents by excluding those opponents on the basis that their views are religiously based.

Should Moral Values Based on Religious Beliefs Be Excluded?

So, should moral values based on religious beliefs – as compared with religious voices or religious beliefs – be excluded from the public square, as some secularists argue?

Many people's moral reasoning is connected with their religious beliefs. To exclude them and their moral views from the public square, because of the source of their beliefs, would be to disenfranchise them. This is an issue articulated in *Chamberlain v. Surrey School District*.[21] Mr Justice Mackenzie, writing for a unanimous Court of Appeal for British Columbia, interpreted what subsections 76(1) and (2) of the School Act required.[22] They read as follows:

> ss.76 (1) All schools must be conducted on strictly secular and non-sectarian principles.
> (2) The highest morality must be inculcated, but no religious dogma or creed is to be taught in a school or Provincial school.

The respondents had challenged a resolution, passed by the board of trustees of the Surrey School District, establishing that three books not be approved as learning resources for kindergarten students. The books were about same-sex families, and the respondents claimed the resolution withholding approval of the books was based on the trustees' religious beliefs and so offended the "strictly secular and non-sectarian principles" and the "no religious dogma or creed" requirements of the act.

The court first made a "distinction between religion and morality":

> A moral proposition may originate from a religious insight, but religion is more than morality and moral positions are not necessarily derived from religion ... Religion and morality are not synonymous terms ... Moral positions [whether secularly or religiously based] taken as positions of conscience are entitled to full participation in the dialogue in the public square where moral questions are answered as a matter of law and social policy ... There is no bright line between a religious and a non-religious conscience. Law may be concerned with morality, but the sources of morality in conscience are outside the law's range and should be acknowledged from a respectful distance ...
>
> Moral positions must be accorded equal access to the public square without regard to religious influence. A religiously

> informed conscience should not be accorded any privilege, but neither should it be placed under a disability. In a truly free society moral positions advance or retreat in their influence on law and public policy through decisions of public officials who are not required to pass a religious litmus test …
>
> Today, adherents of non-Christian religions and persons of no religious conviction are much more visible in the public square than a century ago and any truly free society must recognize and respect this diversity in its public schools. "Strictly secular and non-sectarian" must be interpreted in a manner that respects this reality. That respect precludes any religious establishment or indoctrination associated with any particular religion in the public schools, but it cannot make religious unbelief a condition of participation in the setting of the moral agenda … "Strictly secular" in the School Act can only mean pluralist in the sense that moral positions are to be accorded standing in the public square irrespective of whether the position flows out of a conscience that is religiously informed or not. The meaning of strictly secular is thus pluralist or inclusive in its widest sense.[23]

On appeal to the Supreme Court of Canada, Justice Gonthier, in dissent but writing on a point of unanimous agreement for all nine judges, ruled:

> [N]othing in the [Canadian] Charter [of Rights and Freedoms], political or democratic theory, or a proper understanding of pluralism demands that atheistically based moral positions trump religiously based moral positions on matters of public policy. I note that the preamble to the Charter itself establishes that "… Canada is founded upon principles that recognize the supremacy of God and the rule of law." According to Saunders J. [of the British Columbia Supreme Court where the case was heard at trial], if one's moral view manifests from a religiously grounded faith, it is not to be heard in the public square, but if it does not, then it is publicly acceptable. The problem with this approach is that everyone has "belief" or "faith" in something,

> be it atheistic, agnostic or religious. To construe the "secular" as the realm of the "unbelief" is therefore erroneous. Given this, why, then, should the religiously informed conscience be placed at public disadvantage or disqualification? To do so would be to distort liberal principles in an illiberal fashion and would provide only a feeble notion of pluralism. The key is that people will disagree about important issues, and such disagreement, where it does not imperil community living, must be capable of being accommodated at the core of modern pluralism.[24]

The Supreme Court of Canada's judgment in the *Loyola High School* case,[25] released in March 2015 and discussed briefly in the next chapter, further affirms the spirit of this approach. It merits noting in the context of a discussion of the role of religion in the public square that the Supreme Court held that not only individuals but also religious institutions have a right to freedom of religion, because the practice of religion is both an individual and a collective or communal activity. As Chief Justice McLachlan and Justice Moldaver (Justice Rothstein concurring) write, upholding a Catholic boys high school's right to teach Catholicism from Catholic moral, ethical, and religious perspectives and not to be forced by law to teach their religion from neutral or secular ones: "The individual and collective aspects of freedom of religion are indissolubly intertwined. The freedom of religion of individuals cannot flourish without freedom of religion for the organizations through which those individuals express their religious practices and through which they transmit their faith" [94].

To summarize, to exclude from public square debates those arguments about moral values that are based on religious beliefs would cause serious harm to society, just as excluding the arguments that are based on secularist values would. Religion brings to bear important considerations that secularism does not, and vice versa. We need to hear both sides and give proper weight to each if we are to make wise decisions about the values that should take priority when values are in conflict. And, as I explained, to exclude either set of arguments is anti-democratic.

The Role of Moral Reasoning in the Public Square

So, what functions does and should moral reasoning play in the public square? Jennifer Marshall, from the DeVos Center for Religion and Civil Society at the Heritage Foundation in Washington, DC, argues that moral reasoning is foundational to democracy. Here's how she describes the link between moral reasoning and democracy:

> The Founders [of the United States] thought moral reasoning was a prerequisite for a self-governing people. In the Constitution, they designed a system that presumes we are capable of deliberating together about what is good.
>
> By appealing to shared concepts of the common good, we ensure our exercise in democratic self-rule is a matter of reasoned discourse rather than raw political muscle, the triumph of strong over weak.
>
> Morality and reasoned discourse are essential to safeguarding individual liberties and basic human rights – and make tolerance possible. Refusal to rely on reasoned discourse creates both ugly spectacle and dangerous precedent.[26]

Some politicians interpret the doctrine of separation of church and state to claim that their own personal views on what is and is not moral have no place in politics, often in order to avoid standing up for what they believe is morally right or to avoid opposing what they believe is morally wrong, when they think that will lose them votes. Thus they believe, as Michael Cook, editor of Mercatornet.com puts it, "that morality and politics have little to do with each other. In fact, [they believe] political expediency should trump moral truths."[27] Surely this is not a position that should be reassuring to the citizens these politicians represent, especially when these same politicians are making decisions about issues that affect our most important shared values.

In an obituary for the Canadian-born Father John Neuhaus, a highly respected American public intellectual, Colleen Carroll Campbell provides an excellent description of the contribution that religious voices can make in the democratic public square:

> The political liberalism that Neuhaus championed was one rooted in moral truth and open to the transcendent perspective of religious faith. When liberalism loses that foundation, Neuhaus argued, democracy falters and human rights are imperiled. Politics ceases to be the deliberation about how we ought to order our life together. It becomes instead a brutal contest in which who's weak and who's strong matter more than who's right and who's wrong.
>
> Neuhaus saw this perversion of democratic ideals dominating what he famously labelled "the naked public square," a secularized civic realm in which religious voices are unwelcome and an all-powerful state eventually arrogates to itself the authority to decide the values by which we will live. In writings that married intellectual gravitas with razor-sharp wit, Neuhaus labored to advance an antidote for the naked public square: "a religiously informed public philosophy" that respects both the religious character of Americans and the demands of a pluralistic society.[28]

Ways of Evicting Religious Voices from the Public Square

It is instructive to look at the strategies used by people who want to exclude religious voices from the public square. We could call these ways of *evicting* religious voices from the public square. They are not mutually exclusive; they overlap, and are often used cumulatively.

First, secularists suppress the voices or views of religious people by using ad hominem attacks. To "derogatorily label the person and dismiss them on the basis of that label" is an approach intentionally used to suppress strong arguments against any secularist stance and to avoid dealing with the opposing arguments.

Examples include a straight-out ad hominem attack. For instance, in a comment article published in the online *Globe and Mail* (one of Canada's national newspapers),[29] I argued for the importance of children's biological ties to their parents and doing the least damage possible to these. This argument was unpopular with people such as those who support same-sex marriage, who believe that what constitutes a family is simply a matter of adults' personal preferences. Here is one response to that article: "Any chance that Dr Somerville is a Catholic? If so, she should at least state it in her opinion pieces and not hide behind her ivory tower. Oh, and Doctor, you lost the argument on same-sex marriage. Kinda pathetic you're using this issue to re-argue it."[30]

And, in response to an article of mine in the *Ottawa Citizen* on societal factors that might favour legalizing euthanasia,[31] Joe Agnost wrote: "Why anyone would give this horrible woman a voice is beyond me! Margaret Somerville is so out of touch with reality it's pretty scary … thankfully she has NO influence beyond the occasional (deluded) article in a newspaper. I really do wish she'd shut up though!"[32] And in yet another example, in response to an opinion I was invited to contribute to the *Globe and Mail* on patients' rights to privacy and confidentiality of their medical records[33] (a topic that has nothing to do with homosexuality), someone wrote, "Montreal's shame is back! Margaret Homophobe Somerville, who should NEVER be printed in any serious newspaper."[34]

In light of such attacks, the decision of the editors of some of the world's leading medical journals to require that authors reveal their religious affiliations in their conflict-of-interest disclosures can be seen as surprising and probably not wise.[35]

Some (although not by any means all) politically correct positions conflict with some people's religious and moral beliefs. But whatever the basis for people disagreeing with a politically correct stance, they and their arguments are excluded simply by labelling them as politically incorrect. Those who challenge a politically correct stance are automatically branded as intolerant, as bigots or hate-mongers. The substance of their arguments against the politically correct stance is not addressed; rather, they themselves are attacked as being intolerant and hateful simply for making those arguments, which are dismissed on that basis. In short, political correctness operates by shutting down non-politically correct people's freedom of speech.[36] Recently, prominent people who have supported politically incorrect positions have been forced to resign from their employment; one such case is Mozilla CEO Brendan Eich, who contributed funds to the California Proposition 8 campaign to uphold traditional marriage and opposed same-sex marriage.[37]

Similarly, while intense tolerance (which derives from the now-ubiquitous moral relativism) is advocated, that tolerance is not extended to politically incorrect views. Yet the façade of tolerance masks the intolerance involved and makes it difficult to object to political correctness as a suppression of freedom of speech, and also sometimes a suppression of freedom of religion and freedom of conscience.

As an aside, it is interesting to note that in societies with largely homogenous values we used to have what can be called "universal truth" and very low levels of tolerance for any deviation from it. Now, with exceptions such as noted above, we have "universal tolerance" and very low levels of agreement on "truth."[38]

Another strategy to suppress freedom of speech as a means of evicting religion from the public square is to characterize speech as a verbal *act*. For example, speaking against abortion or same-sex marriage is not characterized as speech but rather is characterized as a sexist or discriminatory *act* against women or homosexuals, respectively, and, therefore as in itself a breach of human rights or even a hate crime. Consequently, it is argued that protections of freedom of speech do not apply.

Yet another part of the same strategy is to reduce to two the available choices of position. Someone is either pro-choice on abortion and for respect for women and their rights, or pro-life and against respect for women and their rights. The possibility of being pro-women and their rights *and* pro-life is eliminated. The same approach is taken to same-sex marriage. One is against discrimination on the basis of sexual orientation and for same-sex marriage, or against same-sex marriage and for such discrimination. The option of being against such discrimination and against same-sex marriage, as I am, is eliminated.[39]

Placing Social-Ethical Values Issues in a Moral Context in the Political Public Square

I propose that the most important task of religious voices in the public square is to place and keep social-ethical-values issues in a moral context. It is a huge challenge but crucial to maintaining ethics in general, and in particular with respect to issues such as I listed at the beginning of this chapter. A purely secular approach to establishing our collective values creates serious risks that a moral context will be lost. That is true because a secular approach is usually based on utilitarian values and moral relativism, which can lead to a loss of a sense that a given issue raises moral concerns.

John Ralston Saul calls history "human memory."[40] It is one of our main "human ways of knowing." Religion should be seen as an important holder of our "collective moral memory," which we lose or ignore at our peril.

We can see what happens when an issue loses its moral context by looking at what has happened with abortion. Abortion is always a moral and ethical issue – or it should always be. However, the former archbishop of Canterbury, the Reverend Rowan Williams, writing in the English Sunday newspaper *The Observer*, says that we have lost our sense that abortion involves a "major moral choice." Instead, it has been "normalized" – "something has happened to our assumptions about the life of the unborn child ... when one-third of pregnancies in Europe end in abortion."[41] In Canada, one-quarter to one-third of pregnancies end in abortion. Abortion has gone from being a rare exception to the norm.

So we must consider how can we place and keep issues such as abortion, euthanasia, new reproductive technologies, embryo stem-cell research, and so on in a moral context. And we must try to imagine what will happen if we fail to do that.

Jennifer Roback Morse, the president of the Ruth Institute in California, describes the impact of the loss of a moral context when we are deciding about such issues:

> I have talked with people who were adults when Roe v Wade legalized abortion in the United States. These people will usually say they did not expect there would be so many abortions. They envisioned that women would only choose abortions in the "hard cases" of rape and incest, not to the tune of a million abortions per year. These same people also admit they would never have anticipated the moral callousness that society has developed around the sanctity of human life. They thought the predictions of euthanasia, assisted suicide, infanticide, and sex

> selection abortion were hysterical fantasies of religious fanatics. But those wild-eyed religious fanatics proved to be sober-minded prophets.
>
> This back-story is worth keeping in mind as we think about the future of reproductive technology [in particular, the creation of "saviour siblings," embryos selected for development on the basis that as a child they can be used to medically treat a sibling]. Proponents of the unlimited use of ART [assisted reproductive technologies] dismiss the fears of excesses as over-wrought and hysterical. But once we decide that it is morally acceptable to do "selective reduction" of embryos [killing some fetuses in utero in a multiple pregnancy, usually resulting from IVF multiple embryo transfer, and delivering the dead fetuses with the living ones at term], why isn't it even more acceptable to eliminate non-useful embryos before implantation in the womb? We have allowed ourselves to do pre-implantation genetic diagnosis for the purpose of screening out embryos that have medical conditions we don't want to deal with. What could possibly be the problem, then, with "screening in" for a baby that has the traits we positively want, for whatever reason.[42]

We need to revalue religion, even if we are not people of faith, to see it as a store of traditional knowledge and wisdom. Access to that knowledge and wisdom is more important than ever before in light of the possibilities opened up by the new technoscience, if we are to preserve the essence of our humanness, which requires protecting our most important social-ethical values, especially that of respect for life.

Factors Precipitating Claims that Voices Based on Religious Beliefs Should Be Excluded from the Public Square: Euthanasia as a Case Study[43]

We need to place the calls for exclusion of religious voices from the public square and the implementation of these calls in a larger context to understand how and why this has occurred. The current debate on euthanasia (a term I use here to include assisted suicide) provides an instructive case study in this regard. It also shows what can happen to our individual and collective values, if we take a purely secular approach not balanced by religious views. The outcome should be of serious concern to all of us.

Let's ask the question: Why now are Australian and Canadian societies considering legalizing euthanasia? Not one of the bottom-line conditions usually linked with calls for legalizing euthanasia – that a person is terminally ill, suffering, and wants to die, and we can kill them – is new. These factors have been part of the human condition for as long as humans have existed. And our capacity to relieve pain and suffering has improved remarkably. Why, then, are we now considering legalizing euthanasia?

I suggest that the principal cause is profound changes in our post-modern, secular, western, democratic societies and their interactive and cumulative effects. As a neutral statement of fact, almost all of these changes are related in one way or another to a loss of religious voices in the public square. In saying that, I'm not proposing that religious voices *should* dominate in the public square or that secular ones should be excluded. Rather, we need both voices to be present and heard and to function in continuing and balanced interaction, if we are to make wise choices regarding our shared values.

So let's look at some of these changes in western secular societies such as Australia and Canada in relation to the current "hot issue" of euthanasia. Have they caused us to see euthanasia in a different light from in the past and, if so, in what way?

Individualism

"Intense individualism" (sometimes called "selfish individualism," or "radical individualism"), which needs to be distinguished from "healthy individualism," dominates our societies, possibly to the exclusion of any real sense of community even in connection with death and bereavement. The rise of intense individualism could be connected with the decline in religious belief. Religion involves relating to the Other and, through that relationship, to other humans.

Intense individualism is much more likely to be present in the absence of those relationships.

Intense individualism entails giving pre-eminence to personal autonomy and self-determination, which favours the acceptance of euthanasia. Almost all the justifications for legalizing euthanasia focus primarily on individual dying persons who want it and on their right to "choose what happens to themselves." Euthanasia's harmful impact on society and its values and institutions is ignored. Religious voices would rebalance this bias, which means that their absence should be of concern to everyone.

In our society, death is largely a medical event that takes place in a hospital or other institution and is perceived as occurring in great isolation. Death has been institutionalized, depersonalized, and dehumanized – and certainly despiritualized. Asking for euthanasia can be a response to "intense pre-mortem loneliness."[44] Again, religious voices have a role to play in establishing approaches to help remedy this situation.

Mainstream Media

The media are probably the most influential and important component of the contemporary public square. A major factor in the promotion of euthanasia is the mainstream media, and it is often difficult for religious voices to make themselves heard there; when they do, they are often dismissed on the grounds that they are religious.

Roger Alton, the former editor of the British national newspaper *The Independent*, speaks of the hostility in the media to religion and the growing level of intolerance: "The ceiling of respect has been breached."[45] Many journalists are highly individualistic, reject authority and what they see as paternalism, and are hostile to religion for those reasons. They identify opposition to euthanasia as a religious, "right wing," "anti-choice" conservative view, all characteristics from which they personally disidentify.

Religious voices that are anti-euthanasia have another barrier to being heard in the mainstream media. Their arguments include the harm to values, institutions, and society that legalizing euthanasia would cause to society, both present and future, and these arguments are very difficult to present visually. They do not make dramatic and compelling television. Visual images are difficult to find. Viewers do not personally identify with these arguments, which come across as abstractions. Society cannot be interviewed on television and become a familiar, empathy-evoking figure to the viewing public. Moreover, the vast exposure to death that we are subjected to in both current-affairs and entertainment programs may have overwhelmed our sensitivity to the awesomeness of death and, likewise, of inflicting it. Ironically, the most powerful way in which the case against euthanasia has been presented on television is probably through the efforts of people such as Dr Kevorkian to promote euthanasia and the revulsion they evoked in many viewers, even in many who support euthanasia.

In stark contrast, it makes dramatic, personally and emotionally gripping television to feature an articulate, courageous, forty-two-year-old divorced woman, who is dying of amyotrophic lateral sclerosis, begging to have euthanasia made available and threatening to commit suicide while she is still able – thus leaving her eight-year-old son even sooner – if she is refused access. This describes Sue Rodriguez, a Canadian woman who took her case for legal access to assisted suicide to the Supreme Court of Canada, where she lost by the narrowest possible margin.[46] The Supreme Court was then faced, in 2014–15, with a case with nearly identical facts: the *Carter* case.[47] As discussed in chapter 4, it overruled its *Rodriguez* precedent to allow "physician-assisted death" – physician-assisted suicide and possibly euthanasia – on certain conditions. It did so on the grounds that the rights to "life, liberty and security of the person" in section 7 of the Canadian Charter of Rights and Freedoms were all breached by the Criminal Code's prohibition of assisted suicide. The court ruled that the prohibition was unconstitutional because it was "over-broad": it went beyond implementing valid goals of Parliament in enacting it and could not be saved within the charter provisions allowing for such breaches to be justified and, thereby, validated as constitutional. The court also relied on changed facts, including acceptance of physician-assisted death by many Canadians, since the *Rodriguez* decision.

Medical Cloaks

Making decisions on an issue in a medical context can give those decisions a legitimacy they would not otherwise have, including securing political and social legitimacy for certain public goals. And describing euthanasia as "medical treatment," as Quebec physicians have done, makes it seem an appropriate act for physicians to undertake. I call this putting a "medical cloak" on an issue. That cloak reassures most of us that what is being done is ethical and not of concern. But when we take that cloak off, our perceptions can be very different.

In a speech on euthanasia at a national conference of the Australian Medical Association, I stated at two or three points that "we can't have physicians killing people." A pro-euthanasia palliative care physician in the audience leapt to his feet and shouted, "Margo, will you stop using that word 'killing'; it's not killing, it's VAE [voluntary active euthanasia]." Later in the speech, I addressed the issue of, if we were to legalize euthanasia, who should carry it out. I argued against physicians doing so, because fear of being euthanized could make people frightened of consulting physicians and reluctant to accept pain relief treatment. The solution, I suggested, would be to have a specially trained group of lawyers.[48] They know how to interpret laws and regulations and apply them strictly. The same physician who had objected to my using the word "killing" immediately rose to his feet and exclaimed, "Margo, are you crazy? You'd have lawyers killing people." I agree wholeheartedly that we should not allow that, and neither should we have physicians killing people. With the medical cloak on the act, it was not killing; with the cloak off, the same act was killing. The further essential question is, "If it's not killing, what is it?"

Denial of Death, "Death Talk," and Accommodating Fear

Ours are death-denying, death-obsessed societies. Those who no longer adhere to the practice of institutionalized religion have lost their main forums – churches, synagogues, temples, mosques, prayer houses – for engaging in "death talk." As humans, we need to engage in this "talk" if we are to accommodate the inevitable reality of death into the living of our lives. And we *must* do that if we are to live fully and well.

Arguably, our extensive discussion of euthanasia in the mainstream media is an example of contemporary "death talk." Instead of being confined to an identifiable location and an hour or so a week, it has spilled out into our lives in general. This ubiquitous discussion makes it more difficult to maintain the denial of death, because it makes the fear of death more present and "real." One way to deal with this fear is to believe that we have death under control. The availability of euthanasia could support that belief. Euthanasia moves us from chance to choice concerning death. Although we cannot make death optional, we can create an illusion that it is by making its timing and the conditions and ways in which it occurs a matter of choice.

Societal-Level Fear

We can be frightened not only as individuals but also as a society. For instance, collectively we express fear of terrorism or crime in our streets. But that fear, though factually based, might also be a manifestation of a powerful and free-floating fear of death in general. We used to deal with this fear individually and collectively through religion. In an areligious or anti-religion society, calling for the legalization of euthanasia could be a way of symbolically taming and civilizing death, thus reducing our fear of its random infliction through terrorism or crime; that is, legalized euthanasia might function as what social psychologists call a "terror reduction" mechanism or "terror management" device. (Note that in coining these terms, these psychologists are using "terror" in its general sense of overwhelming fear, not terrorism.)

If euthanasia were experienced as a way of converting death by chance to death by choice, it would offer a feeling of increased control over death and, thereby, decreased fear. We tend to use law as a response to fear, often in the misguided belief that we are increasing our control over what frightens us and hence augmenting our safety.

Legalism

It is not surprising, therefore, that we have to varying degrees become legalistic societies. The reasons are complex and include the use of law as a means of ordering and governing a "society of strangers," as compared with one of "intimates." The latter is governed more by ethics and morality than law. (In chapter 7, I discuss the evolving relation of law and ethics.)

Matters such as euthanasia, which would once have been the topic of moral or religious discourse, are now explored in courts and legislatures, especially through concepts of individual human rights, civil rights, and constitutional rights. Religious voices often apply for intervener status in relevant court cases with varying success, or appear as witnesses before parliamentary committees, but many politicians are frightened that they will lose votes or be publicly criticized if they appear to be in favour of the views put forward by religious voices in relation to social-ethical values issues; they therefore refrain from doing so.

Man-made law (legal positivism), as compared with divinely ordained law or natural law, has a very dominant role in establishing the values and symbols of a secular society. In the euthanasia debate, it does so through the judgments and legislation that result from the "death talk" taking place in "secular cathedrals" – our courts and legislatures.

Thus, it is to be expected that secularists who are trying to change society's values and symbols would see this debate as an opportunity to further their goals and, consequently, to seek the legalization of euthanasia.

Materialism and Consumerism

Another factor promoting calls for the legalization of euthanasia is that our societies are highly materialistic and consumerist. They have lost any sense of the sacred, even just of the "secular sacred" (a concept I discuss in chapter 3). That loss too is connected with a loss of religion. Loss of a sense of the sacred favours a pro-euthanasia position, because it fosters and supports the idea that worn-out people may be equated with worn-out products; both can then be seen primarily as disposal problems.

In contrast, most religious people see all human beings as having intrinsic human dignity, respect for which requires that we respect their lives. That is, we do not intentionally kill them, as occurs in euthanasia.

Fear of Mystery

We are frightened of mystery, because we feel we don't have control when faced with mysteries, and we no longer have religion to turn to in order to accommodate them. We convert mysteries into problems to "deal" with them, often through a technological "solution," and in so doing reduce our anxiety. If we convert the mystery of death into the problem of death, euthanasia (or, even more basically, a lethal injection) can be seen as a technological solution to that problem.

We solve problems, but we live mysteries, and in doing so we enrich our lives.

As can be seen in descriptions of death by euthanasia – for instance, a young man dying of AIDS held an extravagant, symbolic-laden party for his friends before committing suicide – euthanasia can also function as a substitute for death rituals, which we have abandoned along with religion. Possibly it can function as well to help people who fear mystery to avoid, at least partly, any sense of it.

A sense of mystery may be required also to "preserve room for hope." Hopelessness – nothing to look forward to – is strongly associated with a desire for euthanasia. Again we can see a link with the loss of religion and a belief in the hereafter, which traditionally provided hope.

Rejection of any sense of mystery often correlates with a belief that reason (logical, cognitive, rational mentation) is the only valid way of human knowing, and with a rejection of other ways of knowing such as intuition, especially moral intuition, examined emotions, experiential knowledge, and so on. Such an approach favours euthanasia; it can make logical sense, even though humans have a deep moral intuition against killing each other, and we have thousands of years of history (human memory, as a way of knowing) in all kinds of societies that it is wrong to do so, except where it is unavoidable to save human life.

And a loss of a sense of mystery is almost certainly associated with the loss of a sense of the sacred, even if it's just the "secular sacred," particularly in relation to human life and the restrictions entailed by respect for the sacredness of life, a term I use here in a non-religious sense of respect for human life.

Impact of Scientific Advances

Among the most important causes of our loss of a sense of the sacred in general, and regarding human life in particular, are our extraordinary scientific progress and the mistaken view that science and religion are antithetical, causing many people to abandon religion.

New genetic discoveries and new reproductive technologies have given us a sense that we understand the origin and nature of human life and, because we can, we may manipulate – or even "create" – life. Transferring these sentiments to the other end of life supports the view that euthanasia is acceptable.

As well, the paradigms used to structure knowledge in general have been influenced by this unprecedented new scientific knowledge. These paradigms have been the bases for new schools of thought that can be used to challenge traditional concepts – often ones based in religion – of what it means to be human and what is required to respect human life. Secular humanists are making just such challenges.

Control

The new science has created a new reality in our societies – that of the present capacity and future potential of technoscience to move us beyond what we have known as human, to make us what the transhumanists call "posthumans." Up to the present, the ethics focus on the mind- and world-altering changes that could be wrought by the new science has been on human birth and the living of human life. Now, that science and the ethics that govern it are also having impact on how we view human death and what we see as ethical conduct in relation to it. Calls to legalize euthanasia are one expression of such impact. The transhumanists' search for immortality, which is the polar opposite of euthanasia, is yet another. The feature they have in common is control over human death: in the case of the search for immortality, to avoid it, and in the case of euthanasia, to cause it.

A science-based or technological-based approach to life and death – which both euthanasia and a search for physical immortality reflect – is strongly related to taking control. In contrast, a "spiritual approach" (which may or may not be based in religious belief[49]) accepts that there are some things that we cannot or ought not to try to control, at least through certain means.

Competing Worldviews

Though immensely important in itself, the debate over euthanasia may be a surrogate for yet another, even deeper, one. Which of two irreconcilable worldviews will form the basis of our societal and cultural paradigm?

According to one worldview, we are highly complex, biological machines whose most valuable features are our rational, logical, cognitive functions. This worldview is in itself a mechanistic approach to human life. Its proponents support euthanasia as being, in appropriate circumstances, a logical and rational response to problems at the end of life.

The other worldview (which for some people is expressed through religion but can be, and possibly is for most people, held independently of religion, at least in a traditional or institutional sense) is that human life consists of more than its biological component, wondrous as that is. It involves a mystery – at least the "mystery of the unknown" – of which we have a sense through our intuitions, especially moral ones. It sees death as part of the mystery of life, which means that to respect life, we must respect death. Although we may be under no obligation to prolong the lives of dying people, we do have an obligation not to shorten their lives deliberately.

The euthanasia debate is a momentous one, involving issues ranging from the nature and meaning of human life to the most fundamental principles on which societies are based. This debate involves our individual and collective past (the ethical, legal, and cultural norms handed down to us as members of families, groups, and societies); the present (whether we will change those norms); and the future (the impact that changes will have on those who come after us). As I discuss in more detail later, I predict that future generations will look back on decisions around legalizing euthanasia, irrespective of whether they are decisions for or against, as turning-point events in societal values in the twenty-first century.

In debating euthanasia, we need to ask many questions, but three of the most important are: Would legalization be most likely to help or hinder us in our search for meaning in our individual and collective lives? How do we want our grandchildren and great-grandchildren to die? And, in relation to human death, what fundamental values do we want passed on far into the future from generation to generation?

The euthanasia debate would be not only impoverished but dangerous in the absence of religious voices. And that debate is just one example of the role that people with values based on their religion must play in all the other social-ethical values debates.

What Does Being Human Mean?

At the heart of many of the current debates on ethics, including in relation to euthanasia, is the issue of whether humans deserve special respect as compared with animals or robots, and whether we have absolute obligations to protect and preserve the essence of our humanness.[50] Many people believe we deserve special respect simply because we are human. But some people, many of them secular humanists, don't agree that there's anything intrinsically special about being human.

Rodney Brooks, a scientist specializing in artificial intelligence at the Massachusetts Institute of Technology, criticizes the idea that human beings are "special" in any important way and therefore deserve respect of a different kind from machines or robots – or, indeed, from animals, which he, like Princeton animal rights philosopher Peter Singer,[51] would not differentiate from humans in the kind of respect they are owed.[52] So, they argue that if we see it as acceptable to euthanize our suffering dog or cat, we should likewise be able to offer euthanasia to humans.

The traditional way we have expressed the belief and moral intuition that humans are special, and therefore deserve special respect, is (for those who are religious in an Abrahamic tradition) through the concept of soul. For those who are not religious, we can do the same through the idea of a human spirit – a term I use in a religiously neutral sense, in that it can be accepted by both people who are not religious and those who are, no matter what their religion.

I define the human spirit as "the intangible, immeasurable, ineffable, numinous reality to which all of us need to have access to find meaning in life and to make life worth living. It is a deeply intuitive sense of relatedness or connectedness to all life, especially other people, to the world, and to the universe in which we live; the metaphysical – but not necessarily supernatural – reality which we need to experience to live fully human lives."[53] In other words, the human spirit is the means through which we can experience transcendence and perhaps transformation; the possession of soul or human spirit is the way we establish a difference in kind, not just in degree, between humans and other living entities (wonder-inspiring as they are), and therefore establish a difference in the kind of respect owed to each.

If we do not believe in a soul or do not believe that the human spirit means humans are different from other animals and machines, there is then no basis for arguing that humans deserve special respect. In the context of euthanasia, for example, that view is expressed in the argument referred to above, often put forward by euthanasia advocates: If your dog was suffering, you would euthanize him out of compassion, so how can you justify not doing the same for another person? The short answer is, "We are not dogs."[54]

◆◆◆

In conclusion, I would first like to summarize the main points of the message that I have tried to deliver in this chapter:

- Values conflicts cannot be solved by excluding religious voices from the public square. On the contrary, doing so is likely to exacerbate those conflicts.

- To exclude religious voices from the public square is anti-democratic, just as excluding secular voices would be. Both have a right to be heard.
- Religious voices have a valid and important role in decision-making about social-ethical-legal values, the most important of which is to bring collective moral memory to bear on those decisions and, in doing so, to help keep them in a moral context and help us avoid moral callousness.

In short, both religious voices and secular voices, which often label themselves scientific, have a valid role in the public square on an equal footing. We need all the perspectives they present to interact in a dynamic tension. To implement this diversity in practice requires recognizing that religion and science are not antithetical; rather, they are different "ways of human knowing" that give us access to different forms of knowledge. The challenges are how to convince those who oppose religious voices in the public square that they are making a mistake in seeking to exclude them, and if religious voices are admitted as they have a right to be, how to structure and engage in the dialogue that needs to ensue. Those are issues for another time.

We need to extend the scope of our analyses of contemporary social-ethical-values issues beyond an intense present to consider the needs and rights of future generations. And we must hold in trust for them not just our physical world but our metaphysical one – the values, principles, beliefs, stories, and so on that create and represent the "human spirit," that which makes us human. Religious voices not only can help us to do that but also are essential if we are to achieve that goal. Nothing is more important than that we do so.

2

Are Our "Values Conversations" Sufficiently Open and Free? The University as a Test Case

As we've seen in chapter 1, there is a powerful movement to eliminate religion from the public square, and requiring compliance with the tenets of a rubric often called "political correctness" is one strategy used to achieve this. Nowhere is that strategy more prominently employed than in our universities, with the goal of promoting and inculcating so-called progressive values. "Political correctness" functions to eliminate certain values, views, discussions, and topics of conversation by suppressing the freedoms that I focus on in this chapter. These freedoms are central to maintaining and defending some of our most important values, so the challenge is how to protect them. I propose that we can best do so through understanding and applying the concept of "academic freedom."

This chapter looks at the conflict between academic freedom and political correctness and, depending on how that conflict is resolved, the likely impact on our societal values. This issue is an especially important one because the university students of today will be the leaders of society tomorrow, and consequently their values positions need to be as well informed as possible, which requires protection of academic freedom. To achieve that protection, however, we need first to understand this concept, one on which there is no universal agreement.

Although an enquiry into academic freedom might seem esoteric, in undertaking it we will encounter principles, concepts, ideas, and arguments relevant to and useful as well in considering values issues and making values-based decisions in other contexts outside academia.

Indeed, many of the examples in this chapter, such as those involving conflict among students over abortion or euthanasia, or what is required to respect human dignity, relate directly to issues addressed in other chapters.

I'm a strong believer in asking questions in the search for insights regarding issues on which we disagree. So what questions should we ask about academic freedom? I suggest they should include: What is its purpose? What rights support it? What is the scope of rights of freedom of speech, freedom of conscience, freedom of religion, and freedom of association in academia? Are these rights currently challenged or even in some cases threatened in the university? Just as we've asked how we should deal with conflicts over the valid role of religion in the public square, how should we deal with conflicts over the valid role of religion in academia? Should religion be excluded from the academy? Should we object to the use of political correctness to shut down freedom of speech? What is at the base of the conflict between the values of religious people and those with "progressive" values? And how should we respond to the longing of students for "something more" – to be part of something larger than themselves and to seek something beyond just the materialist-consumerist-sexual nexus? In addressing these questions, I share some of my personal experiences in these regards.

We cannot properly understand academic freedom unless we place it in the larger context of which it is a part. That process again requires addressing many questions, including: What is the role and purpose of a university in a society? What protections do a university and academics need to fulfill that role and realize that purpose? What are and are not valid restrictions on academic freedom and the institutional autonomy of universities? We do not all agree on what the answers should be, or even on what constitutes academic freedom. Thomas Homer-Dixon, director of the Waterloo Institute for Complexity and Innovation, puts it this way: "It's easy to argue that academic freedom is valuable. It's much harder to precisely define actions or circumstances that might threaten this freedom. Those who say there's a bright line between freedom and constraint are being either naïve or disingenuous."[1] On the issue of why it is essential to protect academic freedom, Homer-Dixon argues: "The free pursuit, creation and dissemination of knowledge is one of society's most important checks on the abuse of authority by powerful governments, corporations and other actors."[2] This warning should alert us to the dangers of what might seem at first glance to be minor or reasonable restrictions – for example, Canadian government scientists being prohibited from presenting their research results to the media in order to inform the public, without the "consent" of a government media-relations officer.[3]

This larger context in which we must view academic freedom also requires considering, in general, rights of freedom of thought, speech, and expression, of freedom of conscience, of freedom of belief and religion, and of freedom of association. All of these rights are currently being challenged in various ways and contexts and even in some cases threatened, both in academia and society.

Freedom

At an even more basic level, academic freedom requires, first, an understanding of freedom. Freedom results from respect for the right to liberty, a right enshrined in the Canadian Charter of Rights and Freedoms,[4] but liberty is never an unrestricted right. The law has long spoken of "freedom in fetters," conveying the idea that freedom must be restricted to the extent that the conditions that make freedom possible are maintained. In other words, maintaining the conditions that make freedom possible involves restrictions.

Fetters are justified because without them we would create a society in which no reasonable person would want to live. But we will not find consensus on which restrictions are justifiable and which are not. The same is true for the more precise question of what are and are not legitimate restrictions in determining the parameters of "academic freedom in fetters" in the university.

But before considering the elements of academic freedom in more detail, I'd like to introduce two more concepts that are important to our discussion: the change in the nature of trust, and social capital. These are important concepts when discussing academic freedom because this freedom should be used in such a way as to promote earned trust and to build social capital.

Blind Trust and Earned Trust[5]

Trust is essential to the formation and maintenance of all good human relationships. But not all forms of trust are the same.

In the past, individual and societal trust was a *blind trust* – that is, based on the premise "Trust me because I know what's best for you and will act only in your best interests." It was a hierarchical, paternalistic concept, and trust was accorded to trustees on the basis of their power, status, and authority.

Today, in contrast, individual and societal trust is an *earned trust*, based on mutuality and reciprocity, a principle that can be stated as "You can trust me, because I will show and will continue to show that you can trust me." This is an egalitarian-based trust, and trustees cannot take it for granted. If they don't earn it, the other person or the public will withdraw it. And that's relevant to universities and academics.

Put simply, students and the public place their trust in each of us as academics and the university as an institution, and we must continuously show that we merit that trust. Trust engenders fiduciary or trust based obligations to the beneficiaries of the trust. Academic freedom, both in general and in any given case, must be interpreted within such a matrix of trust, privilege, obligations, and rights and what they require for fulfillment.

Social Capital

There is no agreement on the definition of social capital, but "the commonalities of most definitions of social capital are that they focus on social relations that have productive benefits."[6]

A very early social capital proponent, L.J. Hanifan, explained in a paper in 1916 that "in using the term *capital*, he was not referring to 'real estate, or to personal property or to cold cash, but rather to that in life which tends to make these tangible substances count for most in the daily lives of a people, namely, goodwill, fellowship, mutual sympathy and social [exchange] among a group of individuals and families who make up a social unit' ... Hanifan argued that bringing social resources together would offer significant benefits to a whole community, and further that institutions like a school could provide such a context for that kind of connecting."[7] Fittingly for our present discussion, Hanifan used a school as his paradigm example for creating social capital.

Francis Fukuyama defines social capital as "the ability of people to work together for common purposes in groups and organizations:"[8] "Social capital can be defined simply as the existence of a certain set of informal values or norms shared among members of a group that permit cooperation among them."[9]

Ronald Inglehart, a political scientist and scholar of cultural change, links trust and social capital, defining the latter as "a culture of trust and tolerance, in which extensive networks of voluntary associations emerge."[10] Philosopher Robert Putnam describes social capital as "features of social organization such as networks, norms, and social trust that facilitate coordination and cooperation for mutual benefit," again seeing a link with trust.[11]

These definitions of social capital bring to mind the concept of the goodwill of a business, an intangible asset based on trust that is valued both in itself for the human good that it represents and also in monetary terms, which means it can be bought and sold. In other words, goodwill benefits both the community and the individual who creates the goodwill. Social capital should do the same.

So the question for us is: What are the roles and responsibilities of academia and academics in creating and maintaining social capital, not just for their own benefit but for the good of society in general? And what is the relation of social capital and academic freedom? As I argued previously, but it bears repeating, academic freedom should be used in such a way as to earn trust and create social capital.

On the other hand, if the university is "a place where dangerously divisive ideas can be safely hashed out in the respectful setting of a classroom,"[12] how should we balance the promotion of comfort (for instance, by upholding claims of a right not to be offended) and allowing conflict (for example, that generated by respect for freedom of speech) so as to maximize social capital? Answering this question is complex and requires an examination of the various freedoms that in combination constitute the basis of academic freedom or that it is necessary to respect in order to uphold the liberty rights of academics and other people.

Section 2 of the Canadian Charter of Rights and Freedoms protects a broad range of linked fundamental freedoms, all of them relevant to freedom in the academy:

> Section 2. Everyone has the following fundamental freedoms:
>
> (a) freedom of conscience and religion;
>
> (b) freedom of thought, belief, opinion and expression, including freedom of the press and other media of communication;
>
> (c) freedom of peaceful assembly; and
>
> (d) freedom of association.

Freedom of Thought

Thought is necessary to creating our beliefs and opinions and the speech we wish to use to express them. If our thoughts are not free, our speech cannot be. We hear a lot in mainstream media about freedom of speech but rarely about freedom of thought, which is a particularly relevant consideration in the context of academia. It is an area to which we should devote a great deal more attention.

So, what might impinge on our freedom of thought?

The classic consideration of this question is often undertaken in terms of examining the invasive actions of "thought police," and new ethical concerns are arising in this regard because new technologies – functional magnetic resonance imaging (fMRI), for example – might enable others to read our thoughts. But I want to take a different approach. Some recent concerns that have arisen in applied ethics are relevant to addressing this question. Consider, for instance, the *ethics of neuroscience* – the ethics of mind-altering or mind-control technologies, a field of exploration sometimes called neuroethics.

Would it be ethically acceptable, from the perspective of respecting freedom of thought, to program soldiers to kill without feeling guilty?

What about inserting a gene in human embryos for hyper-aggressivity in order to create future members of the armed forces? What about wiping out distressing memories? What about mentally programming university professors to adopt certain beliefs?

Experimental psychologists are also researching the *neuroscience of ethics* – how we make decisions about what is and is not ethical. These decisions are foundational to what we think and believe and, therefore, to our teaching and research. The dangers here include "genetic reductionism" – that we might see ourselves as nothing more than "gene machines" – or that our moral sense, our sense of right and wrong, could be manipulated.

And what about new possibilities such as "designer babies" – implementing genetic control – which affect not just our thoughts but who we are who have thoughts? Altering our foundational DNA – the germline genes passed down from generation to generation – modifies the very essence of our intrinsic being, the self itself. The vast majority of people, including ethicists, believe that such alteration is inherently wrong and that the human gene pool must not be tampered with and must be held in trust for future generations as the common heritage of humankind.[13] Very recent developments in "gene-editing" techologies are challenging this belief, because the possibility of doing good – wiping out horrible inherited diseases, such as Huntington's chorea – can overwhelm our understanding that altering the germline is ethically wrong.

Jürgen Habermas proposes that intentionally altering the human gene pool would transgress two very important values: equality, because designed persons are not equal to their designers; and liberty, because designed persons are not free in their innate being to create their selves without interference from another person, as to do so requires that they have non-contingent origins.[14]

What would designing our students mean for them? Would they be intellectually free? Would it change how their university experience affects them? Would it change our approaches to teaching them?

And what would "designing our children" mean for society and for institutions such as the university? Surely it would adversely affect democracy and democratic institutions, as the capacity to participate in the democratic process is posited on the concepts that we are all equal and all free.

Constructing "designer babies" (my use of the word "constructing" is not accidental – that is, "building better babies" with reproductive technologies) is the twenty-first century's eugenics. Relevant to this issue is the approach of the late philosopher Hans Jonas in explaining why human cloning is wrong. Jonas believed that all individuals had a right to their own unique ticket in the great genetic lottery of the passing on of human life and a right to live their life as a surprise to themselves – that is, a right not to be an intentionally created clone of another human being.[15]

If we accept that designing children is wrong, our first obligation in the exercise of academic freedom is to speak out to protect the innate freedom of those who will later become our students.

I have been challenged with the question of how teaching students is any different from interventions such as I've just described – it's alleged that teaching is equally "brainwashing," just by a different route. I think the answer depends on whether we see such interventions as different in kind from teaching or only different in degree. I believe they are different in kind. But facing that question, especially in the context of freedom in academia, should make us realize that we need to take care in how we teach and what we teach in order not to infringe upon students' rights to freedom of thought. Our role is not to indoctrinate but to open students' minds to the widest range of thought and knowledge.

We can also look to other examples that raise questions about protecting freedom of thought. Consider, for instance, whether the compelled treatment of the mental illness of a scientific researcher is ethically and legally acceptable – the issue addressed by the Supreme Court of Canada in the *Starson* case.[16] Scott Starson had been held at the Oak Ridge institution north of Toronto for a considerable time. His scientific papers had been published in major academic journals despite his having no academic degrees. He had made death threats against his psychiatrist and had most often been diagnosed as having a bipolar disorder.

The Supreme Court ruled that Starson could refuse anti-psychotic treatment that altered his thought process – the treatment deprived him of his ability to engage in scientific discovery in physics – even though that meant he would remain involuntarily committed to a psychiatric institution. Starson described the drugs as transforming him "'into a struggling-to-think drunk,' and would therefore limit his pursuits in physics"; their effects, he said, "would be worse than death for me, because I have always considered normal to be a term so boring, it would be like death."[17]

Freedom of Expression and Freedom of Speech

Nowhere is respect for freedom of speech more important than on university campuses, both for faculty and students. But freedom of speech in universities is at least equally important for society as a whole.

Freedom of speech is not an absolute right. Any speech that clearly constitutes ethical or legal wrongdoing may be restricted. Speech is no less subject than other activities to the necessity of "freedom in fetters," in order to maintain the conditions that make freedom possible. But the basic presumption of freedom of speech means the limits on it must be narrowly constructed and able to be justified, with the burden of proof of justification on those wishing to curtail free speech. In other words, the avoidance of serious risks and harms must outweigh the harm of restricting speech. Examples of legal restrictions include hate speech, incitement to commit crime, and defamation.

We can compare the right to freedom of speech to one aspect of the role the doctrine of informed consent plays in medical law and ethics: when the patient and physician disagree on what course of medical treatment to follow, the patient needs to rely on the ethical and legal requirement for informed consent, because this means the physician must not proceed with treatment that the patient refuses. Similarly, we need to rely on the right to freedom of speech when others disagree with what we say; that is, when there is conflict. Freedom of speech in a university is meant to ensure that the conflict necessary to pursuing the truth is not suppressed and can run its course. Not allowing that can result in what John Furedy, emeritus professor of psychology at the University of Toronto, calls "velvet totalitarianism."[18]

Practices such as enforcing politically correct speech codes on university campuses out of concern to avoid conflict and make people feel comfortable, while in general having laudable goals, can generate a culture that inhibits freedom of speech. In the context of University of Toronto, Furedy writes:

> Competing with academic freedom (of both students and faculty) was what I have called the "culture of comfort," according to which the essentially subjective criterion of "feeling offended" had become a valid reason not only for individuals censuring other individuals for their stated opinions, but also (and more significantly) for institutions like the university punishing and even attempting to censor those individuals. Not that the early concept of academic freedom meant "anything goes." One could not, with impunity, libel an individual or groups, but this was a matter of law arbitrated by the legal system of Canada, rather than a matter of culture arbitrated by university administrators (often advised by their equity officers).[19]

Feeling uncomfortable with conflict is itself a danger to freedom of speech in the academy. Freedom of speech allows conflict to emerge, and conflict may be an essential ingredient for the university to fulfill its proper function. The late Father John Courtney Murray, a Jesuit priest and theologian, writes of the conflict created by religious pluralism in secular western democracies,

> If the university takes its function seriously, it ought to find itself in the characteristically modern situation of religious conflict, which is at once intellectual and passionate, a clash of individual minds and of organized opinions. Any refusal on the part of the university (and the university sometimes makes this refusal) to recognize its own spiritual and intellectual situation would be a flight from reality. The university would succumb to a special type of neurotic disorder if it were to cultivate an "inflated

> image" of itself as somehow standing in all serenity "above" the religious wars that rage beneath the surface of modern life and as somehow privileged to disregard these conflicts as irrelevant to its "search for truth." The only inner disorder that would be worse than this would be a flight to the fantasy that the university is omnicompetent to judge the issues of truth involved in all the pluralism of contemporary society.[20]

An interesting issue arose in relation to freedom of expression, conscience, and religion in regard to some prospective citizens of Canada. They objected to swearing or affirming the citizenship oath because it involves swearing allegiance to the queen and her heirs. Some of them opposed hereditary privilege and consequently did not want to affirm it and wanted to be free to speak against it. For others, hereditary privilege was against their religious beliefs.[21] This incident is an example of a negative content claim based on the right of freedom of expression: a right not to be required to express certain views.

Freedom of Expression of Pro-Life Students on Canadian University Campuses

Expressing what one wishes to is broader than just words and includes other forms of communication, such as we can see in the serious conflicts over abortion on Canadian university campuses between pro-life supporters and pro-choice ones. Attempts have been made to suppress debate about abortion in Canada across the country, especially on university campuses. In November 2011, for example, pro-life students at the University of Ottawa organized a formal debate around the question "Should physicians provide, or refer for, abortion?" Their press release stated that "this question addresses some of the most pressing issues around conscience rights and medical ethics in Canadian society."[22] They reported that they contacted major pro-choice figures four months prior to the event, but none was willing to take part in the debate.

A coalition of pro-choice students and activists led by the Women's Resource Centre of the Student Federation of the University of Ottawa announced on their Facebook page that they intended picketing the event, explaining that they planned "to represent the fact that this is NOT a debatable issue."

Pro-life students at other Canadian universities have faced obstruction and intimidation in forming pro-life student clubs or setting up anti-abortion display booths on university premises. At both the University of Calgary, the other at Carleton University in Ottawa, students were charged with criminal trespass for not complying with restrictions their university had placed on their display of posters of aborted fetuses, including that the signs must face inwards so passersby could not see them. Such a restriction had never been required of any other student group. The students refused to comply, claiming a breach of their right to freedom of speech and expression.

In the Calgary case, the charges were later stayed. In the Ottawa one, they were withdrawn by the crown prosecutors involved.

The groups whose voices are most recently being targeted for exclusion from campuses and university websites, at the University of Toronto, for instance, are those focused on men's issues. These groups are unjustly characterized as being against women – sexist, patriarchal, and misogynist – and their events have been shut down by protesters, who claim the speakers engage in "hate speech." "Masculinist" has become a highly pejorative label.

A Campus Freedom Index resulting from surveys carried out by a Calgary group, the Justice Centre for Constitutional Freedom (JCCF), merits noting. In its 2012 survey it gave only three As with regard to respecting various freedoms, to thirty-six universities and student unions surveyed; an F was awarded twenty-eight times to twelve universities and sixteen student unions. In 2013, 180 letter grades were awarded to forty-five campuses. The universities and student unions received only six A grades; F grades were earned thirty-two times, thirteen by universities and nineteen by student unions.[23] A serious discrepancy was found between policy and practice: for instance, in the 2012 survey, the University of Toronto received an A for its policy on free speech and an F for its actions in implementing the policy.[24] In the 2013 survey, the F had improved to a D. JCCF president John Carpay, a co-author of the report, remarked, "Universities get [taxpayers'] money in part by claiming to be these centres of free enquiry."[25]

Emeriti psychology professors John and Christine Furedy, in their paper "From the Socratic to the Sophistic,"[26] quote James Allan, serving as guest host on *Counterpoint* on Radio National (Australia), on why defending freedom of speech in the university is so important:

> Free speech for views you agree with is what you might think of as the sitting-in-a-circle-and-holding-hands-and-singing-Kumbaya understanding of free speech. It makes the singers feel good about themselves, feel morally self-righteous, in fact. But it accomplishes nothing and delivers no good consequences. No, the reason for valuing lots of scope for views we dislike and think wrong is because such scope has such good long-term consequences for society. It creates a cauldron of competing views where over time the idiotic ones will be found out. We'll get closer to truth than when government overseers are in place to tell us what we can hear.
>
> As is the case more generally for freedom of speech, the real test cases of academic freedom usually involve opinions that are not held by the majority, and that may be outrageous or distasteful to them.[27]

With majorities in universities in western democracies now adherents of political correctness, those who are not politically correct are the real "test cases" of academic freedom.

Using Political Correctness to Shut Down Free Speech[28]

Political correctness is a serious threat to the proper functioning of universities with respect to freedom of speech. I discussed in chapter 1 how labelling persons as politically incorrect can be used as a means of evicting religious voices from the public square. Politically incorrect voices are silenced in universities through the same mechanism.

Before I continue, let me explain that I'm using the term "politically correct" as shorthand to cover a variety of identity-based social movements and the neo-liberal values (progressive values) and moral relativism philosophy that they espouse. I am not using it, as can sometimes happen, to describe people or their views or values derogatorily.

I agree with some of these views and values and disagree with others, but I strongly disagree with shutting down the freedom of speech of those who disagree with the politically correct stance.

Some examples of political correctness on university campuses are extreme. For instance, a professor at Queen's University in Kingston, Ontario, was suspended from teaching a history course because of student complaints, including that he had said in class that he hoped students would become "masters and mistresses" of the course, a characterization that was alleged to be sexist.[29] The Canadian Association of University Teachers investigated the case and found that the professor's right to academic freedom had been violated by the university administration in the way they handled the case. They recommended an apology, but the university refused to give one.[30]

More generally, as explained in chapter 1, people disagreeing with a politically correct stance are excluded from presenting their points of view and arguments simply by labelling them as politically incorrect. They are automatically branded as intolerant, as bigots or hatemongers. The substance of their arguments against the politically correct stance is not addressed; rather groups or individuals are themselves attacked as being intolerant and hateful simply for making those arguments and dismissed on that basis. In short, political correctness operates by shutting down non-politically correct people's freedom of speech.[31]

Political correctness often operates through fear of being shamed, shunned, excluded, or punished in some way. Indeed, as a person labelled politically incorrect, I had an interesting experience in this regard. Politically correct people sought to exclude me from speaking at the 2008 Federation for the Humanities and Social Sciences (Learned Societies) Congress held at the University of British Columbia. This conference is the largest annual meeting of Canadian academics, often attracting around eight thousand participants.

The custom at the congress is to invite the previous year's CBC Massey lecturer as one of two keynote speakers, and I was appearing in this capacity as a result of a postponed invitation arising from my 2006 Massey lectures. Professor Noreen Golfman, from Memorial University in Newfoundland, then the president of the federation, received complaints from people who object to some of my views and the values they reflect (in particular, about same-sex marriage and its impact on children's rights with respect to their biological parents and the family structure in which they are reared), to the effect that it was inappropriate to have invited me as a keynote speaker. (The CBC had received similar complaints for having invited me to deliver the Massey lectures, including, I understand, a complaint lodged with the Canadian Radio-Television Telecommunications Commission (CRTC), the regulatory body governing broadcasting in Canada.) When Professor Golfman was asked by a reporter from the *Globe and Mail*, a national Canadian newspaper, why she had invited me, she was reported as replying that "the Congress never got any news coverage, so she and her committee thought perhaps it might, if they had a controversial speaker." Professor Golfman also told the reporter that inviting me "shows we [the congress organizers] are not afraid of taking risk with our speakers." The next day the story was on the front page of the *Globe and Mail*.

It is very important to protect our universities as spaces where the most open dialogue possible can be engaged in and for us to be aware that those spaces are at substantial risk of being shut down on some Canadian campuses through the impact of political correctness. That risk should be of great concern to all academics, no matter what their personal values or views on the matters at issue, and to universities and societies.

Universities must be protected as "sites of discussion and discovery" if they are to fulfill their overall purpose and justify their continued existence.[32] It is sometimes said that "all movements go too far," but that might be necessary for them, including politically correct, identity-based social movements, to have any impact. However, that being the case, they need to pull back or to be pulled back at a certain point if they are not to do more harm than good.

My specific concern is that the various politically correct movements and the moral relativism that accompanies them have "gone too far," with very harmful impact on freedom of speech, freedom of association, and academic freedom in our universities. The iconic Canadian columnist Rex Murphy links the impact of political correctness with harm to academic freedom, free speech, and truth in his inimitable style:

> That so many on university campuses feel their ideas are so

> perfect that they may now go on crusade to shut or shout down the ideas and opinions of others, is a more than worrisome sign. Our higher education – at least in some of the humanities – is not what it should be.
>
> This latest episode at Carleton [where a student tore down a message board with anti-abortion statements in the university's "free speech zone"] is a reminder that some universities are in the business more of promoting attitudes than liberating young minds, and more concerned with fleeting "correctness" than lasting truth.[33]

Some commentators argue that the dangers of political correctness in our universities are being overemphasized, and that claim might be true from time to time. It has also been argued that conservative students could benefit from political correctness, because the need to deal with it could give them an advantage. Professor Amy Binder, a sociologist at the University of California, San Diego, is reported as saying that a response she "heard repeatedly in her survey of campus conservatives is that they take solace in what might be called the revenge of the nerds. Just as the high school science dork can take comfort in the prospect of a high-paying job in the future, so too does the campus conservative believe that he is getting a better education than the liberal cool crowd. Forced to hone arguments, do extra work and debate against the grain, they believe conservatives grow tough while liberals grow complacent. Campus conservatives 'think of themselves as having benefited immensely from having been conservative in a sea of liberals and moderates.'"[34]

Other Strategies to Shut Down Free Speech

As I mentioned earlier in this chapter, the same strategies used to evict religious voices from the public square (described in chapter 1) are used in universities to silence people viewed as politically incorrect.

In summary, freedom of speech is shut down through ad hominem attacks that derogatorily label someone and dismiss that person on the basis of that label, as a strategy to suppress strong opposing arguments and avoid dealing with their substance.[35] What should be dealt with as a conflict of ideas, values, beliefs, and so on is converted to a conflict of persons.

Speech is characterized as a verbal act, which in its turn is characterized as sexist or discriminatory and in itself a breach of human rights or even a hate crime, to which, it is argued, protections of freedom of speech do not apply.

The range of choices of position available is reduced. For example, one is either pro-choice on abortion and anti-discrimination against women or pro-life (anti-abortion) and pro- such discrimination. The option of being against abortion and against discrimination, that is, for women's human rights, is eliminated.

Duties of confidentiality and respect for privacy can also restrict freedom of speech. Sometimes, when conflicts between them occur, it is difficult to determine the right balance between privacy and freedom of speech.

Fear of being punished with respect to appointment, tenure, and promotion for expressing one's views is another silencer. I have had several young academics come to me and say they agree with some of my views but would never say so publicly because of such fears. This self-censorship is a tragedy and negates the concept of academics as "truth tellers" to the best of their ability, the role that academic freedom is meant to enable and protect.

That said, we can disagree on what the truth is. For instance, addressing how to deal with religious pluralism in the university, the late Father John Courtney Murray identified such pluralism as "a problem in the order of truth … [which] presents itself to the university" and articulated his concept of the role of a university in terms of truth seeking: "By the university I mean here that social institution whose function it is to bring the resources of reason and intelligence to bear, through all the disciplines of learning and teaching, on the problems of truth and understanding that confront society because they confront the mind of man himself."[36]

Whether in the academy or in society as a whole, a hard vocal minority is dominating many debates on what our shared cultural values should be, because the soft silent majority feels threatened in speaking out. This fear allows extremists to set the agenda and to characterize the larger group to which they belong, which may reject their views. One example that has been given is of Muslims with extremist views characterizing the Muslim community as a whole, as compared with those with moderate views doing so. A serious problem in this regard is that the majority seems to have much less political influence than the minority, because politicians too are afraid of them.

Freedom of Information

Information is necessary to have the capacity and opportunity to exercise freedom of thought and freedom of speech. Therefore there is a need for freedom of access to information; blocking information curtails freedom of speech and, in the university, the capacity to carry out research.

For example, abortion statistics are being withheld under the Ontario Freedom of Information Act, which has the effect of limiting both freedom of thought and freedom of speech. Effective 1 January 2012, section 65 of the Freedom of Information and Protection of Privacy Act (FIPPA) was amended to exclude records relating to the provision of abortion services. This means "individuals no longer have a right to make access requests ... to an institution for records in the custody or under the control of that institution relating to the provision of abortion services." In short, all information relating to abortion held by government institutions or departments in Ontario is now secret. We know that doctors billed for over 44,000 abortions in Ontario in 2010, but this type of information is now hidden from the public.

Because good facts are essential to good ethics, this change has ethical implications. It might also raise legal issues. For instance, a right to freedom of speech is seriously curtailed if one is prevented from obtaining the facts needed to form one's opinion. When such restrictions are imposed in non-democratic countries, we often speak of them as a breach of human rights.

The situation shows that abortion is more than a pro-life versus pro-choice conflict; it is also a pro-democracy versus anti-democracy one. It manifests a clash between pro-democracy values (pro-freedom of speech, pro-transparency, pro-accountability, and so on) and anti-democracy values (denial of these rights). Contrary to strong contemporary trends in the opposite direction, this change moves Ontario from a pro-"earned trust" position ("Trust me, because I'll show you that I can be trusted by keeping you fully informed") to a pro-"blind trust" one ("Trust me, because I know what's best for you and will decide for you, so you don't need this information").

FIPPA is meant to augment the transparency, openness, and accountability of all levels of government for their decisions and actions, and our right, as Canadian citizens, to participate in democracy and democratic decision-making. My guess is that if the same approach were taken, for instance, to information on breast cancer, people would be outraged.[37]

Transparency, especially in government, and with respect to the outcomes of the use of taxpayers' money is essential to accountability, which is essential for ethics; we learned this to our disgust, for instance, in the revelations made at the government-established Charbonneau Commission of enquiry into corruption in the construction industry in Quebec.

An example I have already mentioned, in some ways a softer one, is the restrictions on Canadian government scientists in presenting their research results to the media in order to inform the public, without the "consent" of a government media-relations officer.[38] Obviously these restrictions are politically motivated, making them even more reprehensible.

Freedom of Belief

As is true for freedom of thought, speech, and conscience, the freedom of belief should also be highly protected in a university. But, as the case of Trinity Western University makes clear, far from everyone agrees with that.

Trinity Western is a Canadian Christian university that wants to establish a law school. The university requires all faculty and students to sign a pledge – a "Community Covenant" – to behave according to Christian beliefs, including with respect to abstaining from extramarital sex, whether heterosexual or homosexual. The covenant also defines marriage as being between a man and a woman. This is considered *ipso facto* discriminatory despite the sections of the federal

Civil Marriage Act that explicitly protect the right to hold different understandings or definitions of marriage without fear of sanction.

Media coverage has been widespread and voluminous on the outrage from certain persons and sectors opposing the university being given the necessary approval and on the refusals of three Canadian provincial law societies, which govern licensing to practice law in each province, to accredit the school, thus making its graduates ineligible to practice law in those provinces.The Federation of Law Societies of Canada approved the law program of TWU as meeting academic and professional standards. The three law societies admit there is nothing wrong with the program but claim that TWU's Community Covenant discriminates against the LGBTQ+ community. The objections seem to be largely focused on the fact that the orthodox Christian belief is that homosexual acts are immoral; it could be anticipated that the course contents would reflect this belief, and that law graduates from the university would hold such beliefs and, therefore, would discriminate on the basis of sexual orientation. Yet another objection is that homosexual people would not want to attend the university, which means they would suffer discrimination from having a reduced chance of being accepted into a law school to study law.

But, as the Supreme Court of Canada has pointed out, freedom of belief is much broader than freedom of conduct. Because a lawyer believes that homosexuality is immoral does not mean he would discriminate against homosexual people. As is true for everyone, it would be ethically and legally wrong for him to do so. And many Canadian law professors, both heterosexual and homosexual, currently teach the moral acceptability of homosexuality and what flows from it, such as advocating the legalization of same-sex marriage. Whatever one's views in this regard, should challenging that stance be repressed?

The TWU proposal was in process with the British Columbia Ministry of Advanced Education and the Federation of Law Societies of Canada. In May 2013, the federation established a special advisory committee to advise it on the TWU Community Covenant. The committee's report was issued in December 2013. The committee had exhaustively examined the submissions made to it, the law, and whether, in light of TWU's Community Covenant, it would be contrary to the public interest to accredit the law school. They concluded it would not be, unless evidence of harm from doing so could be produced. In April 2014, the British Columbia Law Society gave its approval of the law school; however, a non-binding vote of Law Society members asked for that decision to be reversed. This vote was followed by a referendum of all members of the BC Law Society, which voted overwhelmingly to reverse the decision. In October 2014, the BC Law Society responded by reversing its decision to approve. In December 2014, BC's minister of advanced education revoked the ministry's consent. The litigation involving the accreditation of a TWU law school and the admission of future TWU law graduates to provincial law societies to enable them to practise as lawyers continues in BC and in other provinces.

Of the BC Law Society's 13,000 members, 3,210 voted in favour of reversing the decision and 968 were opposed.[39] It would be interesting to know why more than two-thirds of the society's members did not vote. It merits noting that the Canadian Association of University Teachers, which purports to be a defender of academic freedom and institutional autonomy,[40] has condemned Christian universities on the basis of their statements of faith.[41]

The situation at Trinity Western University came to mind in reading about an Australian case. Here is John and Christine Furedy's description of it: "In 2005, Andrew Fraser, an associate professor in the Department of Public Law at Macquarie University, was banned from teaching law students on the grounds that he had written an article on immigration that was considered to be 'racist.' In effect, it was thought that there was the danger that, by allowing him to teach students, he might 'corrupt the youth.'"[42] Might there be similar concerns about law students being "corrupted," although with respect to different values and beliefs, through studying at Trinity Western University? Such concerns have an ancient heritage. The Athenian democracy charged Socrates with "corrupting the youth" with his teaching. He defended himself by arguing that in education all opinions should be open to critical examination, that is, that academic freedom should prevail.[43]

The Furedys also provide another apropos Australian example, but in exact contrast to the situation at TWU, it involved a religious figure attacking a secular university. In July 1961, the Anglican archbishop of Sydney at the time, Hugh Gough, "gave a sermon in conjunction with a gathering of jurists, in which he attacked unnamed philosophers and psychologists, especially at Sydney University, for teaching immorality ('free love') and soul-destroying philosophies, saying that these academics helped the communist cause ... The archbishop's sermon was not well received at Sydney University even by members of his flock. The university stood together, and the vice-chancellor, Sir Stephen Roberts, even threatened legal action. The Archbishop backed off and remained silent on the matter of philosophers and psychologists and their teaching."[44]

I will just note here that the protests about establishing a law school at TWU also raise the issue of breach of freedom of association.

Freedom of Conscience

Being free to express your thoughts, beliefs, principles, attitudes, stories, and so on is only part of the necessary protection of freedom. Another part is freedom of conscience: freedom from being forced to act contrary to what one believes or being prevented from doing what one believes to be required as a matter of conscience. The freedom of conscience of health-care professionals can often be a major issue in the academy, because research universities have medical faculties and affiliated teaching hospitals.

Consider, as an example of infringing on health-care professionals' freedom of conscience, An Act Respecting End-of-Life Care, passed by the Quebec Legislative Assembly in May 2014: physicians who have conscientious objections to euthanasia must notify the executive director of the institution of a person who wants "medically assisted death," the euphemism used in the act for euthanasia, and the executive director must find a physician willing to administer it.[45] The act forces physicians and hospital administrators who have conscientious objections to euthanasia to be complicit in an action they believe to be morally wrong.

Yet another example is legislation in the state of Victoria, Australia, that "decriminalises abortion and forces doctors with a conscientious objection to refer a woman to a doctor who will do an abortion. In the event of an 'emergency' abortion … regardless of their moral qualms, doctors must do [an abortion] themselves. Victorian nurses will be in an even worse predicament. They must participate in an abortion if ordered by their boss."[46] The same scenario, in a somewhat softer version, is being played out in the United States and Canada. There, codes of professional conduct or regulations, rather than legislation, are being proposed to limit freedom of conscience rights, in particular with respect to abortion.

Consider, for example, a 2008 directive of the Ontario College Physicians and Surgeons that contemplated excluding physicians' rights to refuse to provide certain interventions because of conscientious objection.[47] The college justified this approach on the grounds that the Ontario Human Rights Commission (OHRC) had warned the college that physicians who refused to facilitate procedures contrary to their moral or religious beliefs, which patients requested, could be in breach of the patients' human rights. Here is the OHRC's startling view of a physician's obligation in the physician-patient encounter: "It is the Commission's position that doctors, as providers of services that are not religious in nature [such as abortion], must essentially 'check their personal views at the door' in providing medical care."[48]

The commission made it clear that physicians' "personal views" include their deepest and most important ethical and moral beliefs and values. In other words, this is a directive to physicians to "park your ethics and values with your car outside the surgery." The College of Physicians and Surgeons of Ontario warned that failure to do so could result in legal liability for discrimination or loss of a licence to practice medicine.[49] Obviously, that directive raises serious problems for physicians, but it also raises problems for patients: Would any of us really want to be treated by a physician who had complied with instructions to "leave your ethics and values outside the surgery"?

The commission's stance is "power speaking to truth," even if it's only the truth of some physicians' consciences. It is an exercise of power because health-care professionals who follow their conscience despite such coercion risk a variety of legal threats. Their conduct can be found to constitute discrimination under human rights codes, or professional misconduct when it would result in disciplinary proceedings and penalties ranging from reprimands to fines and loss of a licence to practise medicine or to practise as a nurse. Needless to say, this state of affairs has caused deep concern for many health-care professionals.

The problem could extend to medical students. A group called "Medical Students for Choice" has lobbied Canadian medical schools to make abortion a "required procedure."[50] That would mean that students must competently perform an abortion to graduate as physicians. The lobby group has been unsuccessful.

What has led to this situation? A major force is a political problem caused by the disproportionate influence, especially on politicians, of what are being called "vocal hard minorities," such as the pro-choice lobby, as compared with "silent soft majorities." Politicians whose personal values are not consistent with those of pro-choice advocates are frightened of them and will not support the rights of people, including health-care professionals, who oppose them. One reason is that such politicians would be derogatorily labelled in the ways I have previously described, which can be very damaging to them politically. Another probable reason is the strategy of these advocates is to paint an either/or picture that terrifies the vast majority of Canadians – for example, no restrictions on abortion at all, or total prohibition of abortion. Given only that choice, they choose no restrictions, although, as polls show, a majority of Canadians would like to see society have a more nuanced and balanced response to law on abortion.[51]

The push to abolish respect for physicians' and other health-care professionals' freedom of conscience also reflects an emerging view that physicians are mere technicians able to provide services that patients want and have a right to access. Thus, it is argued, physicians have a duty to provide these services and no right to bring their moral or ethical reservations into play; to do so is characterized as discrimination. But the physician who refuses to be involved in abortion, for instance, is not providing the service to one patient but not another, or basing his refusal on any characteristic of the patient. Rather, he is refusing the service to all patients and doing so because of the nature of the procedure, which he believes is morally and ethically wrong.

The practice of medicine always and unavoidably involves ethical and moral issues, although when we all agree on how they should be dealt with, we might not be consciously aware of them in day-to-day practice. It is only when something goes wrong or there is a conflict of values that the ethical issues flash up on the big screen. Treating physicians as mere technicians fails completely to take that omnipresent ethical aspect of the practice of medicine into account.

It is sometimes true that acting on personal views can be discrimination. For example, refusing to treat patients simply because they are homosexual is discrimination and wrong. But that is not the issue here. Rather, the problem lies in classifying as discrimination a refusal to provide or refer for a service, such as abortion, euthanasia, or artificial reproduction, that the physician believes – and many other people believe – is morally and ethically wrong. Such refusals should be treated differently from refusals of morally and ethically neutral services, such as renting an apartment or serving someone in a restaurant, on the basis of a prohibited ground of discrimination. We can all agree that such a refusal is wrong.

In Canada, having achieved a black hole on abortion law (there is no law), pro-choice advocates are not content with having the freedom to act according to their values but also want to make others, for whom it would be a breach of their values, act likewise. And they want to have their beliefs and values publicly affirmed through imposing them on others who reject them. They establish that their values should predominate as the societal norms by obtaining official rulings from human rights tribunals that physicians have no freedom of conscience protection regarding abortion. This exercise of power goes even further when coercive legislation enshrining the advocated beliefs is enacted, as in the law in Victoria, Australia, referred to above.

In short, these people claim freedom of values, belief, and conscience for themselves, but refuse to respect others' freedom. That's why they will not tolerate a respect-for-freedom-of-conscience exception. No matter what our values or views, we should all be concerned by such totalitarianism and fundamentalism.

In trying to deal with such conflicts, the authors of a recent paper in the *Journal of Bioethical Enquiry* make a useful distinction between "perfective" and "preservative" freedom of conscience. The former is exercised in the pursuit of a perceived good. This must sometimes be limited. The latter is more fundamental and cannot legitimately be coerced except in the most exceptional circumstances. Here is their explanation: "If the state can legitimately limit perfective freedom of conscience by preventing people from doing what they believe to be good, it does not follow that it is equally free to suppress preservative freedom of conscience by forcing them to do what they believe to be wrong. There is a significant difference between preventing someone from doing the good that he/she wishes to do and forcing him/her to do the evil that he/she abhors."[52]

The authors point out that the fact that individuals were coerced does not shift their feeling of moral responsibility for their actions. They give as an example the well-documented guilt and shame felt by concentration camp survivors who were forced to participate in heinous crimes, and conclude: "When it [conscience] is suppressed by coercion, the result is the kind of spiritual rape suffered by those victims of the camps who were forced to do what they believed to be wrong."[53]

"Perfective" freedom might, however, have more importance in relation to freedom of conscience in the academy than it does in other contexts, because academics have obligations – for instance, to inform the public – that others do not, which means that restrictions on "perfective" freedom could be more difficult to justify. It might also be that the line between perfective and preservative freedom of conscience is more difficult to draw in universities. Is informing the public conferring a benefit or avoiding a harm? The answer could depend on the content of the information. And when does failing to do the good of conferring a benefit become the harm of doing wrong?

With such questions in mind, we should also consider the actions of whistle-blowers and computer hackers, and consider on which side of the line any individual instance of disclosure falls. We don't agree on that, as we know from recent high-profile cases, such as those of Julian Assange/WikiLeaks and Edward Snowden. What we do know is that it can take a great deal of courage to follow one's conscience when doing so creates a risk of serious harm to oneself or those one loves. The risks to the latter need to be kept in mind: many people may be much more reluctant to cause harm to their families and friends than to themselves in following their conscience.

There has been a new development in Ontario regarding physicians' freedom of conscience, as we go to press. The College of Physicians and Surgeons of Ontario consulted on whether patients' right of access to certain procedures, such as abortion, should trump the rights of those physicians who refuse, for reasons of conscience, to provide them. Dr Marc Gabel, a college official, chaired the working group that looked at this issue and drafted a new policy, "Professional Obligations and Human Rights," approved in May 2015. The "obligations" include: "Where physicians are unwilling to provide certain elements of care for reasons of conscience or religion, an effective referral to another health-care provider must be provided to the patient. An effective referral means a referral made in good faith, to a non-objecting, available, and accessible physician, other health-care professional, or agency."[54] Clearly, the "effective referral" would be complicity in the act the physician believes to be wrongful, and as such is equally wrongful.

Dr Gabel was reported as saying that physicians unwilling to provide or facilitate abortion for reasons of conscience should not be family physicians, and it seems the college has approved that stance. Sean Murphy, of the Protection of Conscience Project, describes this position as "ethical cleansing of Ontario's medical profession … ridding it of practitioners unwilling to do what they believe to be wrong."[55]

Freedom of conscience, like the other fundamental freedoms enshrined in the Canadian Charter of Rights and Freedoms, is a fundamental pillar of democracy. So how could breaching this right be, as Dr Gabel claims, "required by professional practice and human rights legislation"? The best answer is that it is not. In fact, it is a perversion of the norms and applications of both professional practice requirements and human rights legislation to interpret them as establishing such a requirement. So why has the college done this?

Murphy explains that the "crusade for the ethical cleansing of the entire medical profession is not driven by merely practical concerns about access to services such as abortion [and now physician-assisted suicide and euthanasia] … It is driven by a markedly intolerant ideology masquerading as enlightened objectivity." This is yet another values battle in the culture wars.

In stark contrast to those "crusaders" who seek out physicians with conscientious objections and demand treatment they know they will refuse, I want the opposite. I do not want to be treated by physicians who are willing either to act contrary to their conscience or who undertake interventions I believe to be seriously ethically wrong. For example, if the Quebec law legalizing euthanasia survives any constitutional challenges to it, I don't want to be cared for by a physician who would be willing to give me – or anyone else – a lethal injection with the intention of killing me, or who would help me – or others – to commit suicide. So how might my "rights" in this regard be respected?

First, physicians with conscientious objections to supplying medical procedures that would destroy human life or contravene respect for it, including euthanasia and assisted suicide, must not be drummed out of the profession as Dr Gabel proposes. There may be rare circumstances where physicians exercising their right of conscientious objection would jeopardize patients' lives or create serious risk to their health, and there are no reasonable alternatives. The ethical and legal validity of physicians' refusals in such a situation would need to be determined on a case-by-case basis, not through steamrollering and obliterating physicians' freedom of conscience as Dr Gabel's committee proposed and the college endorsed.

Consideration should be given to creating a public list of physicians who register as having conscientious objection to providing a specified medical procedure. The list would allow people who want to be treated by a physician with such values to identify those physicians, at the same time allowing those who want such procedures to avoid those physicians.

A concern that physicians on such a list would be targets for abuse by those who oppose their values would need to be addressed. Reasonable steps would also need to be taken to ensure that sufficient numbers of physicians were available on either side to honour Canadians' choices. We should keep in mind in this regard that sometimes upholding important values, such as respect for freedom of conscience, is not cost-free, and we should be prepared to pay what is necessary to do so.

Alternatively, or in addition to the above, health-care institutions should have the right to declare themselves, for instance, "euthanasia-free" and "physician-assisted-suicide-free" zones. Patients who object to those procedures could then be confident they would not be subject to them.

Forcing physicians to act against their conscience, to do something they believe is deeply wrong against their will, harms not only them. This coercive violation of their freedom of conscience also harms society and the values that inform its culture.

Progressive-values adherents claim to give priority to respect for individual autonomy when values are in conflict, and pride themselves on their tolerance. Such claims are only tested, however, when "progressivists" do not agree with the stance that another person takes, such as a physician who for reasons of conscience refuses to participate in abortion or euthanasia. In the current controversies, the "progressivists" are not scoring well on these tests.

Freedom of Religion

In chapter 1, I explored some of the complex and multifaceted issues raised in relation to freedom of religion, many of them relevant to academic freedom, not least because secularists object to religion being brought to the fore in academia, except usually to criticize or even malign it. As has become true in many public arenas, there is hostility to input into public or social policy debates that is seen as in any way connected with religious belief.[56]

I have used the word "secularists" above, and it is important to make a distinction between a secular society and one based on secularism. Canada is a secular society; secularists want to make it one based on secularism, which is a belief form and ideology, much like a religion, a principle edict of which is excluding religion, religious people, or religious views and values from any public input, influence, or role.

As I pointed out in chapter 1, freedom of religion can have several different aspects attributed to it:

- Freedom *for* religion: there is no state religion and the state does not interfere in religious matters
- Freedom *of* religion: there is freedom to worship and practice one's religion according to one's beliefs

- Freedom *from* religion: religion is barred from the public square

Freedom for and freedom of religion are protected rights and valid components of a secular society. Freedom from religion is neither; it is a manifestation of secularism and is a form of breach of freedom of speech and of belief and, sometimes, of freedom of conscience.

As I argued in chapter 1, to evict religion, in a broad sense of that word, from the public square and debates on social and public policy, as secularists want to do, would be anti-democratic and amount to disenfranchizing religious people. Calls to do so have been rejected by Canadian courts, including the Supreme Court of Canada,[57] which has upheld the right of all people in a democratic society to have a voice in the public square, no matter what the basis of their beliefs and values.[58]

That said, the "Report of the Committee of the National Assembly of Quebec on Dying with Dignity"[59] provides an interesting example in relation to the concept and value of sanctity of life, of excluding people's stances when they are, or are assumed to be, based on religious belief. The problem for the committee was that the value of sanctity of life could not be allowed to take priority if, as the committee recommended, euthanasia were to be legalized. The committee demoted "sanctity of life," by connecting it with religion.

The committee wrote, "The value of the sanctity of life has undergone a significant transformation" relative to other values, and concluded this transformation means that now it doesn't necessarily take priority. In prioritizing conflicting values, the committee started from and took throughout their report a purely utilitarian approach and adopted, as the overriding value, respect for individuals' rights to autonomy and self-determination. They justified this ordering of priorities on the basis, among other reasons and examples, of "the decline in adherence to religion" in the Province of Quebec.

Pro-euthanasia advocates often argue that seeing life as "sacred" is a religious value and thus should not be taken into account in the public square. The Quebec report endorses this view: "In a secular state like ours, the [religious] beliefs of some [regarding sanctity of life] cannot be the basis for the development of legislation applicable to all." But although the world's major religions all uphold the principle of sanctity of life/respect for life, it is not simply a religious precept. (I prefer to use the term "respect for life," rather than "sanctity of life," to avoid religious connotations and associations.)

What Habermas calls "the ethics of the [human] species"[60] and I call "human ethics,"[61] which must guide secular societies such as Canada, also embraces this principle. Whatever one's views regarding the value of the sanctity of life/respect for life, it's a foundational value of all societies in which reasonable people would want to live, as the Canadian Charter of Rights and Freedoms recognizes in enshrining it.

As to how academics regard religion, I'd like to recount an anecdote. I was asked by the comments editor of the *Ottawa Citizen* to write an opinion article responding to the question: What is currently the world's most dangerous idea?[62] I enquired of some of my law school colleagues what they would choose and all, without exception, answered "religion." This is only anecdotal evidence, and they are law professors, but it's food for thought on the topic of the place of religion in the university. A Californian professor of the sociology of religion, with whom I discussed the response, said he was most surprised by the fact that they thought religion was just an idea. For millennia, people have viewed faith as integral to being human – of the essence of our humanness.

I have already discussed the opposition to establishing a law school at Trinity Western University because of its Christian foundations and practices.[63] Law professor Janet Epp Buckingham, a leader in the campaign to establish the TWU law school, emailed me on reading the above paragraph to say, "I was a little shocked that all your faculty colleagues identify 'religion' as the most dangerous idea. Any wonder why TWU is proposing to have a law school? But it also is an indication of why law professors are deeply opposed to it. I am just on my way back to Ottawa from our annual TWU faculty retreat. One theme that came up at the retreat was the freedom TWU faculty feel in being able to do research on religious and spiritual themes. Many come to TWU having taught first at a public university."[64]

In other words, while some see a requirement such as the TWU Community Covenant as a restriction of academic freedom, others experience it as an affirmation of that freedom and as enabling it.

Teaching about religion in universities is another disputed area. Father John Courtney Murray ventures "a few assertions of a practical kind" in that regard. He merits quoting at some length:

> First, I venture to assert that the university is committed to the task of putting an end, as far as it can, to intellectual savagery in all its forms, including a major current form, which is the savagery of the American student (perhaps also the professor?) who in matters religious and theological is an untutored child of the intellectual wilderness. Again, the university is committed to the task of putting an end to prejudice based on ignorance, by helping to banish the ignorance. Unless indeed the university wishes to commit itself to the prejudice that religious knowledge is really ignorance.
>
> The assertion I chiefly wish to venture, however, is that the university is committed to its students and to their freedom to learn. Its students are not abstractions. And whatever may be the university's duty (or right, or privilege, or sin) of non-committalism, the fact is that many of its students are religiously committed ... The university as such has no right to judge the validity of any of these commitments. Similarly, it has no right to ignore the fact of these commitments, much less to require that for the space of four years its students should be committed to being scientific naturalists within the university, whatever else they may choose, somewhat schizophrenically, to commit themselves to be outside its walls.
>
> The major issue here is the student's freedom to learn – to explore the full intellectual dimensions of the religious faith to which he is committed ... [I]t is the right of the university to require that his quest of religious knowledge should be pursued in the high university style – under properly qualified professors, in courses of high academic content, in accordance with the best methods of theological scholarship, and so on. But this right of the university should itself conspire with the student's own freedom to learn, so as to create the academic empowerment that is presently almost wholly lacking. Your college and university student is academically empowered to grow in all the dimensions of knowledge – except the dimension of religious knowledge.[65]

Another way to view the study of religion in the academy is as opening up an opportunity for students to experience transcendence – the experience of feeling that one belongs to something larger than oneself – and to seek something beyond just the materialist-consumerist-sexual nexus. In our culturally diverse societies, as reflected in the microcosm of the university, opportunities for such experiences are not always easy to find.

As I mentioned in chapter 1, in March 2015 the Supreme Court of Canada handed down an important judgment, *Loyola High School v. Quebec (Attorney General)*,[66] upholding freedom of religion. Loyola High School is a private, English-speaking Catholic high school for boys, administered by the Jesuit Order of priests. Since September 2008, as part of the mandatory core curriculum in schools across Quebec, the Ministry of Education, Recreation and Sports required a "Program on Ethics and Religious Culture" (ERC), which teaches about ethics and the beliefs of different world religions from a neutral and objective perspective. The school was willing to adopt neutrality regarding religions other than Catholicism but objected to being forced to teach its own religious beliefs and ethics from a neutral stance. It applied for an exemption, for which the law allowed with respect to Catholicism, but was refused it by the minister. All seven judges agreed that this was an unjustifiable breach of the charter right to freedom of religion, which could not be saved under section 1 of the charter, because the refusal was not "minimal impairment" of the right, that is, it was not "reasonable" or "proportional" to the objectives the legislature wanted to achieve through the law establishing the ERC program. Justice Abella (writing as well for three other judges) first noted the objectives of the law establishing the ERC program: "The ERC Program has two key stated objectives: the 'recognition of others' and the 'pursuit of the common good.' The first objective is based on the principle that all people possess equal value and dignity. The second seeks to foster shared values of human rights and democracy. By imposing this program in its schools, Quebec seeks to inculcate in all students openness to diversity and respect for others" [11].

Later in the judgment she explains the court's reasoning for striking down the minister's decision to refuse an exemption:

> The context before us – state regulation of religious schools –

> poses the question of how to balance robust protection for the values underlying religious freedom with the values of a secular state. Part of secularism, however, is respect for religious differences. A secular state does not – and cannot – interfere with the beliefs or practices of a religious group unless they conflict with or harm overriding public interests. Nor can a secular state support or prefer the practices of one group over those of another: Richard Moon, "Freedom of Religion Under the *Charter of Rights*: The Limits of State Neutrality" (2012), 45 *U.B.C. L. Rev.* 497, at pp. 498–99. The pursuit of secular values means respecting the right to hold and manifest different religious beliefs. A secular state respects religious differences, it does not seek to extinguish them. [43]

This judgment is a very welcome approach to respect for the right to freedom of religion, both in educational institutions and more broadly, as the exercise of this right and the scope of the protection it provides give rise to more and more increasingly contentious issues.

Academic Freedom and Institutional Autonomy

Why is it so critical to protect academic freedom and institutional autonomy?

Academic freedom is a privilege accorded to academics for the benefit of the public and society. Its purpose is to protect the freedoms we have been discussing by establishing a forum in which ideas and knowledge can be fully and openly discussed and tested without fear or favour.

It is not, however, an unlimited licence for proselytizing or for ideologically based advocacy, although sometimes it's difficult to determine when the line has been crossed in these regards. As Thomas Homer-Dixon puts it, "Academic freedom is a privilege negotiated with society. This privilege carries obligations and is inevitably limited."[67]

What are some of the current problems in protecting academic freedom? Paradoxically, threats can come from university administration.

The form of university governance has changed from the traditional, long-established egalitarian, collegial model to a hierarchical, top-down and corporate-style management one. Today's senior university administrators may be more concerned with protecting the institution from what they see as damage to its reputation from the public positions taken by some faculty than with protecting professors' academic freedom – although they almost always pay lip service to the latter – and act precipitously to condemn those people.

The reaction of the University of Calgary to remarks made by Professor Tom Flanagan is probably an example. In responding to a question from the audience about how people who viewed child pornography but did nothing more should be dealt with, Flanagan said he didn't necessarily agree with sending them to prison. The university condemned him and distanced itself from him.[68] The way in which Bernard Shapiro, then principal of McGill University, handled a complaint against me is in stark contrast.

Some years ago, I was asked by a reporter for the *Ottawa Citizen* why I spoke against female genital mutilation but not infant male circumcision (IMC). I explained that I thought that we should not do either, but up to that time I had refrained from speaking publicly against IMC, although I had published an academic article that *inter alia* addressed it.[69] My hesitation arose because I anticipated that many people would be upset with my views on IMC, including people for whom it was an important religious ritual of their faith.

Next morning, my comments made the front page of the newspaper and caused a furor. Principal Shapiro telephoned to tell me that he'd received a call from a major donor to McGill, who was Jewish. She had told him she would never give another cent to the university while I remained a faculty member and demanded that I be fired. I asked him, "What are you going to do?" He said, "Nothing. You have academic freedom. But I thought that you should know."

The statement on academic freedom by the presidents of Canadian universities issued in 2011 by the Association of Universities and Colleges of Canada was described by the Canadian Association of University Teachers as "an academic freedom wakeup call"[70] and an "attempt to downsize academic freedom."[71] Among the criticisms were that the statement failed to refer to extramural speech as included within academic freedom; failed to have a sufficiently broad definition of intramural freedom, including the right to criticize the institution and the administration; and failed "to acknowledge academic freedom with respect to service to our institutions, our professions and our communities."[72]

Academic freedom and protection of institutional autonomy are often linked, and sometimes the term academic freedom is used to cover both, but they should be distinguished as sometimes they can be in conflict, as the above discussion indicates.

Institutional autonomy requires that the university should remain largely independent of outside influence in relation to its functioning, academic programs, and research. It establishes and implements the requirement that the university is "not for sale."

Thomas Homer-Dixon explains that threats to academic freedom and institutional autonomy can come in the form of "carrots or sticks."[73] Carrots are offers of funding in return for influence over decision-making about research programs, or even choice of faculty. It can sometimes be difficult to say when the line between acceptable and unacceptable input has been crossed.

It is a current reality that universities must now partner with industry, governments, international organizations, community groups, and others in pursuing their missions, especially in the context of research. This reality raises challenges to both academic freedom and institutional autonomy. It also raises ethical difficulties. Jane Jacobs's book *Systems of Survival*[74] is very useful in understanding the nature of these difficulties.

Jacobs describes two moral syndromes: the "guardian moral syndrome," based on trust generated in a paternalistic, hierarchical, status-based system for ensuring ethical conduct; and the "commercial moral syndrome," based on trust generated in a process-based system, an egalitarian trading relationship. The former syndrome does not allow the stronger party to benefit at the expense of the weaker one; the latter does, provided the stronger persons act ethically and legally.

Each system has its own internal integrity and safeguards, but the internal integrity of each system can be lost, and the safeguards often fail to operate if the systems are mixed. In short, mixed systems are the most difficult ones to ensure that they function ethically.

Universities have operated traditionally under an unalloyed guardian moral syndrome, whereas corporations are governed through a commercial moral syndrome. Consequently, corporate involvement in university research creates a mixed system, with its accompanying ethical problems. These problems become even more complex when government is also involved, as it is in the government-academic-industry complex that supports much scientific research. Moreover, government, which has traditionally been subject to a guardian moral syndrome, can often find itself not only with external ethical conflicts but also with internal ones, because increasingly it functions under a combined guardian-commercial moral syndrome.

I have emphasized throughout this chapter the pivotal role of trust in all aspects of academia. The basis of trust that is applicable in a system that operates under a guardian moral syndrome can also be different from that in a commercial one. Blind trust ("trust me because I will act in your best interests") has classically been the basis of trust in universities, with respect to, first of all, students, and to the choice of research and how it is carried out. By contrast, earned trust ("trust me because I will earn your trust") is more typical of corporations – even if they sometimes fail badly to earn that trust.

The use of blind trust in academia has long antecedents that reach back to times when the general public was largely uneducated. In more recent times, it was principally explained and justified on the basis of the belief that the pursuit of knowledge was a value-free activity; consequently, for example, neither scientists nor the public needed to be concerned about the ethics of scientists' choice of research. According to this view, ethics became relevant only at the point of application or use of the knowledge gained from the research. The Declaration on Science and the Use of Scientific Knowledge, drafted at the 1999 World Conference on Science – which was organized by the United Nations Educational, Scientific and Cultural Organization (UNESCO) in cooperation with the International Council for Science (ICSU) – and later ratified by a resolution of the General Assembly of UNESCO, recognized that this approach was no longer acceptable. Ethics must be embedded in all research from its inception and therefore governs not just how the research is carried out or used but also, for example, the choice of research and who may be allowed to sponsor it. Moreover, the research enterprise must be based on earned trust, especially the earned trust of the public, which requires openness, transparency, accountability, honesty, integrity, and avoidance of conflict of interest. And all participants in that enterprise, whether individual researchers, universities, government, or industry, must be governed by those requirements and honour them (which speaks for itself about the importance of academic freedom), if this trust is to be earned.

We can also see the ethical problems created by a mixed system when we look at the nature of universities' obligations to students. In acting as an educator of students, the university is governed by fiduciary obligations and guardian moral syndrome ethics; in interacting with industrial funders of research, the university is governed by business ethics. The problem is that the boundaries between these two roles of the university – what it owes to students or even faculty, and what "business" ethics allow, and the different obligations they each create – are not clear or are nonexistent.

Moreover, the primary aims of the university in acting in one capacity or the other are not the same and can often conflict. When acting as a business, the university is concerned to maximize its resources and possibly its prestige, and may favour future benefits at the expense of present ones. When acting as a provider of education, its main goal must be to do so primarily in the "best interests" of present students. We need institutional structures that can protect students' welfare but at the same time allow the realization of goals such as efficiency and effectiveness, which are also ethically required outcomes. The same concerns and conflict can arise in relation to the university's obligations to faculty members.

We need institutional structures in academia that will help to ensure ethical behaviour, and we must eliminate those that do the opposite. In implementing such organizational ethics, we must make certain that our efforts do not detract from a feeling of ethical responsibility on the part of individuals. Organizational ethics must be in addition to, not in place of, individual ethical responsibility. Indeed, individual ethical responsibility is crucial to the practice of institutional ethics. Moreover, individuals must understand that they can play an important role in developing institutional ethics. An approach taken by the Quebec government is interesting in this regard. Instead of legislating a code of ethics for health-care institutions, it legislated that each institution, after wide consultation with its staff, must draft and adopt its own code. This approach ensures that institutions take "ownership" of ethics within their milieu. The danger is that there is not sufficient ethical expertise in any given case to ensure that ethical mistakes are avoided.

Flow-on problems that universities are facing from mixed systems include how to ensure scientific integrity and quality – in particular, how to prevent fraud in science, which is more likely when there is pressure to publish and pressure to find commercially viable results, especially when future funding depends on doing so.

An interesting case arose in 2013 at Macquarie University in Australia, where a climate-change scientist, Murry Salby, had his employment contract terminated. A newspaper article on the case said the university declared that it "supports academic freedom of speech and freedom to pursue research interests" and reported the reason for Dr Salby's termination "involved breaches of university policies in relation to travel and use of university resources." Salby said the results of his study of the evolution of greenhouse gases "contradicts many of the reckless claims surrounding greenhouse gases. More than a few originate from staff at Macquarie, which benefits from such claims." According to the reporter, Salby claimed that "presentation of the research was blocked by Macquarie, effectively silencing the release of the research … He says the university then modified his professional duties. 'My role was reduced to that of a student teaching assistant: Marking student papers for other staff – junior staff.'"[75]

It seems that environmental research is an area particularly prone to conflict and claims of failing to respect freedom to communicate research results. Scientists at Environment Canada have made such claims and have been endorsed by a very prestigious group of Canadian scientists in a public letter decrying the situation.[76]

That said, there are also responsibilities on academics in exercising their academic freedom. The "we are only philosophers" defence to justify postulating so-called post-birth abortion is a case in point.[77] Two bioethicist authors proposed in an article published in a prestigious medical ethics journal that disabled babies, who would have been aborted if their parents had known of their disabilities before birth, should be allowed to be killed after birth. Subsequent to outraged reactions from around the world, the authors claimed that they never intended their proposition to be put into practice. They said they were just engaging in philosophical enquiry, as philosophers are meant to do.

In the current cultural climate of the overwhelming dominance of radical individual autonomy and intense individualism – characteristics of all the so-called progressive values that are the focus of conflict in the culture wars – academics must take care not to abuse academic freedom by stretching its protections beyond their proper ethical limits, especially in the militant or one-sided promotion of their own values. Academic freedom is a privilege, but one that carries responsibilities to others and to society for balance in transmitting information and knowledge.

Academic boycotts are a contentious area where issues of abuse of academic freedom can be raised. Examples of boycotts include refusing to attend conferences in boycotted countries, which have included South Africa, Cuba, and Israel, or refusing to invite scholars from those countries or to publish their work. The goal is to communicate moral outrage about unethical political systems, such as apartheid in South Africa, and to bring pressure to bear on them. Questions raised in this context are whether this is an acceptable use of academic freedom by the people or institutions imposing the boycotts and whether it is a breach of the academic freedom of those on whom the boycotts are imposed. As is so often the case in relation to issues involving academic freedom, there is no agreement.

◆◆◆

To conclude, it is a great privilege to spend one's life as an academic, and academic freedom is a precious privilege meant to benefit society. We must hold it, and the knowledge that it allows us to pursue and share with others and society in general, in trust. Doing so requires us to accept certain fetters on academic freedom and to reject others. As with many important decisions, determining which fetters should be accepted and which rejected requires wise ethical restraint – prudence – courage, and wisdom.

Universities may still retain some ivory-tower characteristics, but they are not isolated from the wider culture of which they are a part.

Western secular democracies, such as Canada, are often described as involved in "culture wars," manifested as conflicts between the proponents of conservative values and so-called progressive values. The more of such conflict there is in society, the more important it is to honour academic freedom in order to create a safe space for the exploration of divisive ideas and knowledge. Creating that space requires nurturing the art of attentive listening and insightful questioning and rigorous thought processes, in a milieu of mutual respect.[78] Academic freedom is not an excuse, or a licence, or a get-out-of-jail free card – although a Canadian academic, philosopher Mark Mercer, strongly disagreed with this proposition and argued that academic freedom should be both a licence and a "no jail" card, as unrestricted "critical discussion" is central to a university's mission.[79] It is a heavy responsibility and, viewed and exercised as such, it will properly fulfill its important function of maintaining respect for liberty in our societies, whether that liberty is exercised, to cite the Canadian Charter of Rights and Freedoms once more, as "freedom of conscience and religion ... freedom of thought, belief, opinion and expression ... freedom of peaceful assembly ... [or] freedom of association."

3

Is the Concept of Human Dignity Useful, Useless, or Dangerous?

The lawyer's answer to the question, "Is the concept of human dignity useful, useless or dangerous?" is, "That depends!"

It depends on what we *mean* by human dignity, an issue on which there is no consensus. On how we *use* the concept, again, there is no consensus. On what we see as *its basis* – in particular, secular or religious or both – yet again, no consensus.

As to dangers of the concept, as I mentioned in the preface, there is an old saying in human rights, "Nowhere are human rights more threatened than when we act purporting to do only good." The reason is that when we focus only on the good we hope to do, we don't see the harms unavoidably involved. Respect for human dignity is overwhelmingly perceived as doing only good. But we need to ask, are we overlooking some accompanying harms? If so, what are they?

Use of the Concept of Human Dignity in International Instruments

Extracts from four international instruments in Appendix C show that they rely heavily on the concept of human dignity. These instruments are the Universal Declaration of Human Rights (UDHR), UNESCO's Universal Declaration on Bioethics and Human Rights (UDBHR), the Universal Declaration on the Human Genome and Human Rights (UDHGHR), and the Convention on the Rights of Persons with Disabilities (CRPD). As can be seen from the emphasis I've added in the documents, the concept is referred to a total of thirty-seven times.

The messages about dignity that these four instruments deliver expressly include that recognition of dignity means recognition of equal rights,[1] and respect for dignity affirms the worth of the person,[2] means all people are equal,[3] requires respect for cultural rights,[4] and requires access to paid work.[5] Scientific advances can threaten dignity;[6] therefore, in light of these advances, we need to promote respect for dignity.[7] Respect for culture must not be used as an excuse to infringe dignity,[8] and the provisions of the UBDHR do not ground any permission to infringe dignity.[9]

We must improve health, but only within the confines of respecting human dignity.[10] The human genome shows our unity and, as the common heritage of humankind, our common inherent dignity.[11] We all have dignity no matter what our genetic differences,[12] and that dignity means we are more than our genetic characteristics[13] – that is, genetic reductionism is inconsistent with respect for human dignity – and genetic discrimination offends human dignity.[14] The human dignity of genetic research subjects must be respected;[15] respect for dignity prohibits practices such as reproductive cloning;[16] and research on the human genome must respect dignity.[17] States must defend human dignity;[18] breaches of human dignity need to be identified.[19]

The CRPD preamble recognizes that "discrimination against any person on the basis of disability is a violation of the inherent dignity and worth of the human person,"[20] and that a comprehensive and integral international convention will "promote and protect the rights and dignity of persons with disabilities [and] will make a significant contribution to redressing the profound social disadvantage of persons with disabilities."[21] The purpose of the convention "is to promote, protect and ensure the full and equal enjoyment of all human rights and fundamental freedoms by all persons with disabilities, and to promote respect for their inherent dignity."[22] States have obligations to protect people with disabilities from exploitation, violence, and abuse and to create "an environment that fosters the health, welfare, self-respect, dignity and autonomy of the person."[23]

Yet despite the extensive use of the concept of human dignity in these instruments, nowhere is it defined. Human dignity is distinguished from human rights and from fundamental freedoms, as reference is made to each of them. The rule against redundancy in interpreting legal texts indicates that dignity must mean something not encompassed by these other terms, but what is that something? Some interventions are expressly labelled as contrary to human dignity: for example, "germline interventions" and "reproductive cloning of human beings." What is the basis for that labelling, and could knowing that help us to decide whether other interventions, actions, or omissions – for example, euthanasia – are contrary to human dignity? The order of "human dignity," "(fundamental) freedom(s)," and "human rights" varies. Does that tell us anything? Are they in different orders of priority in different situations?

In other words, none of these documents spells out what human dignity consists of or what respect for it in general requires we do or not do.

Adam Schulman, who was the senior research consultant at the United States President's Council on Bioethics, offers an interesting explanation of why dignity is not defined, focusing on the relation of dignity and human rights:

> While human dignity in [the Universal Declaration of Human Rights and, one could add, in subsequent international instruments] ... plays the role of a supreme value on which all human rights and duties are said to depend, the meaning, content, and foundations of human dignity are never explicitly defined. Instead, their affirmations of human dignity reflect a political consensus among groups that may well have quite different beliefs about what human dignity means, where it comes from, and what it entails. In effect, "human dignity" serves here as a placeholder for "whatever it is about human beings that entitles them to basic human rights and freedoms." This practice makes a good deal of sense. After all, what mattered most after 1945 was not reaching agreement as to the *theoretical* foundations of human dignity but ensuring, as a *practical* matter, that the worst atrocities inflicted on large populations during the war (i.e., concentration camps, mass murder, slave labor) would not be repeated. In short, "the inviolability of human dignity" was enshrined in at least some of these documents chiefly in order to prevent a second Holocaust.[24]

In a 2002 speech, the late Sergio Vieira de Mello, at the time the United Nations special representative in Iraq and a prominent human rights advocate, described the relation of dignity and human rights: "In the post-war [World War II] years the international community committed to a set of basic universal values: equality, dignity, tolerance and non-discrimination. We recognised, through the Universal Declaration of Human Rights, that 'the inherent dignity and the equal and inalienable rights of all members of the human family is the foundation of freedom, justice and peace in the world.' 'Freedom from fear and want' was our common aspiration."[25] De Mello proposed that "we should nurture our sense of self as part of a common humanity" and that "our common humanity is an inclusive one, built on values such as tolerance and dignity."[26]

American physician-ethicist Daniel Sulmasy describes the relation of dignity and human rights in a similar vein: "Intrinsic dignity ... can be understood as the foundation of all human rights. We respect the rights of an individual because we first recognize his or her intrinsic dignity. We do not bestow dignity because we first bestow rights. Human beings have rights that must be respected because of the value they have by virtue of being the kinds of things that they are."[27] In short, Sulmasy sees human rights as secondary to human dignity. Stated another way, human rights establish the conditions that are required if inherent human dignity is to be respected. Most importantly, all these descriptions of the relation of dignity and human rights show that if everyone's human rights are to be respected, then an inclusive definition of dignity is necessary – that is, one that recognizes that all human beings have dignity that must be respected.

Because dignity is a ubiquitous concept in bioethics, as two of the four international declarations in Appendix C show, in 2008 the United States President's Council on Bioethics issued a report on human dignity and bioethics (hereafter the *President's Council Report*).[28] Many of the eminent authors who contributed chapters and comments were responding to American bioethicist Ruth Macklin's proposal that dignity is a useless concept that should be abandoned because it cannot be defined, and that we should use instead concepts of respect for persons and respect for autonomy to guide us ethically.[29] So to begin examining the report, let's first look at how some commentators, in particular the essayists who contributed to the report, have defined dignity.

Defining Dignity

Historically, dignity was an elitist or aristocratic concept. American philosopher-physician Leon Kass puts it this way: "The very idea of 'dignity' smacks too much of aristocracy for egalitarians" and "smacks ... too much of religion for secularists and libertarians. Moreover, it seems to be too private and vague a matter to be the basis for legislation or public policy."[30]

The Greek concept of comparative dignity associated dignity with rank and status. But this changed in the nineteenth century with the spread of democracy and the Christian idea of the equality of all human beings. From this idea, the Christian concept of equal dignity evolved, and democracy required that everyone be seen as having dignity. But there was and still is no easy consensus on the nature of dignity, its basis, or what respects or contravenes it.

One reason is that dignity has a complex history in multiple religious and philosophical traditions. But those complex origins make for conceptual richness, which has both advantages and disadvantages, as we will see.[31] Political scientist Diana Schaub says "we no longer agree about the content of dignity, because we no longer share what Meilaender calls a 'vision of what it means to be human.'"[32] She's correct that the various interpretations of "what it means to be human" are at the core of our disagreements about the nature of dignity and what respect for it requires, and those disagreements are what I would like to explore by examining how some of contributors to the *President's Council Report* would answer some questions about the nature of human dignity.

Is Dignity Connected with Morality?

The American philosopher Holmes Rolston III sees dignity as the marker of the ethical and moral sense that humans have, which he sees as distinguishing them from animals, which also have consciousness. "With humans we need, somewhat provocatively, the term 'spirit' to get past the consciousness that is present in animals and capture this self-reflective inwardness ... After four hundred years of science and enlightenment, the value questions in the twenty-first century remain as sharp and as painful as ever. Not the least of such questions is how to recognize and to respect human dignity. Much in our future depends on the answer."[33]

In regard to the importance of respect for dignity for our future, lawyer and author Wesley J. Smith would concur. Starbucks Coffee, which claims that it has "always supported a good healthy discussion" in the tradition of coffee houses sparking good conversations, ran a campaign called "The Way I See It," a "collection of thoughts, opinions, and expressions provided by notable figures," which it printed on its coffee cups. Smith wrote, as quote 127: "The morality of the twenty-first century will depend on how we respond to this simple but profound question: Does every human life have equal moral value simply and merely because it is human? Answer yes, and we have a chance of achieving universal human rights. Answer no, and it means that we are merely another animal in the forest." It is a powerful warning that deciding about dignity is no insignificant issue or choice on our parts.

To return to the report, here's what other contributors to it have to say along the same lines as Smith about the relation between dignity and morality. Political science professor Charles Rubin writes that "human dignity implies that we are morally responsible beings, worthy of judging what others do and are, and of being judged for what we do and are."[34] Gilbert Meilaender, a professor of Christian ethics, proposes that we have recourse to the language of dignity in order to express moral concern or condemnation.[35]

So these commentators argue that dignity is intimately connected with morality; but is it also necessarily connected with religion? Many secular humanists argue that it is, which is the reason they label it as a useless concept at best, dangerous at worst. But are they correct that it is necessarily a religious concept?

Is Dignity Connected with Religion?

Robert Kraynak, a professor of political science, believes "human dignity is based on the mystery of the human soul."[36] Most people regard "soul" as a religious concept with a theological base. But there is a broader concept linked to that of the soul that might allow us to find greater consensus about the values we should adopt if we are to respect human dignity.

I have already spoken about this concept in chapter 1; it's what I call the human spirit,[37] which I propose is of major importance in dealing with ethical issues. As I explained, I adopt a very broad definition of spirituality and regard it as a natural, inherent characteristic common to all humans, expressed by some through religious belief and practice and by others in secular ways. I call our capacity to experience that spirituality the "human spirit." Our human spirit enables us to search for meaning and is a term I use in a religiously neutral sense, so that it is open to people who are not religious and those who are, whatever their religion. We should all be able to agree that we have a human spirit, and having that agreement gives us a starting point in searching for some shared ethics.

Because the concept of the human spirit is so central to the arguments and propositions in this book, the definition given in chapter 1 bears repeating: "The human spirit is the intangible, immeasurable, ineffable, numinous reality to which all of us need to have access to find meaning in life and to make life worth living – a deeply intuitive sense of relatedness or connectedness to all life, especially other people, to the world, and to the universe in which we live; the metaphysical – but not necessarily supernatural – reality which we need to experience to live fully human lives."[38]

Is Dignity Connected with Sacredness?

We need to enlist a concept of sacredness to protect and promote our human spirit, and I will speak about what I mean by sacredness shortly. But here I want to ask: Is dignity connected with sacredness? It has been suggested it is, which raises the question of the purpose of that connection. Might it be that there is a connection between respect for human dignity and protecting and promoting our human spirit, and that this connection is mediated through the concept of sacredness?

The late Father John Neuhaus, a theologian, writes that "it was by ideas and experiences outside the law that the concept of the dignity of the human person was enshrined in the law. The word 'enshrined' is used advisedly, indicating the sacred sources of that dignity."[39]

And David Gelernter, a professor of computer science, suggests that in order to define dignity, "we begin by looking up the word 'sacred' in (for example) the *Oxford English Dictionary*. The definitions rest on 'set apart' in many forms – 'set apart for or dedicated to some religious purpose'; 'regarded with or entitled to respect or reverence'; 'secured by religious sentiment, reverence, sense of justice, or the like, against violation, infringement, or encroachment' ... Human dignity means that humans are *set apart*" (my emphasis).[40]

British philosopher Roger Scruton provides another insight relevant to understanding the nature of dignity. What is left out of contemporary standard treatments of ethics, he says, is the requirement to "face the surrounding world with due reverence and humility," a disposition he calls piety.[41] I agree with him, although what he calls piety, I'd call respect for the *secular sacred*. It's a concept I introduced in *The Ethical Canary*;[42] everyone disliked it. Secular people thought I was trying to impose religion on them and maintained that religion had no place in the public square or public policy; religious people objected that I was denigrating the concept of the sacred. One of my students said to me, "You know, Professor Somerville, when you have everyone mad at you, you are probably on to something important," so I explored the concept further in my next book, *The Ethical Imagination*.[43]

As I explained in that book, in talking about the secular sacred I am suggesting that the sacred is not only a concept that applies in a religious or ritualized context but also one that operates at a general societal – or secular – level. I'm proposing it as a concept that, among other outcomes, might help us to find some shared ethics, including in relation to what respect for human dignity requires. It is a concept we should be able to endorse whether or not we are religious, and, if we are religious, no matter which religion we follow. Each of us needs to experience a complex interaction of knowing ourselves, relating to others, appreciating our place in the great web of all life, and seeing ourselves as part of the earth, the stars, the universe, and the cosmos. The acute and continuous awareness of such a mind-blowing web of relationships is what I mean by the "human spirit."

In summary, I propose that linking the secular and the sacred, by adopting a concept of the secular sacred, could help to unite everyone who accepts that some things are sacred, whether they see the sacred's source as religious or purely natural or secular.

If we accept the sacred, whether the religious sacred or the secular sacred, we will accept that certain aspects of life are sacrosanct. Not everything that can be done to life, particularly human life, may ethically be done to it, and certain moral and ethical principles that should be respected and should govern our conduct flow from that.

The sacred, then, requires that we respect the integrity of the elements that allow us to fully experience being fully human; in doing so, we protect that experience. The sacred is a concept that we should use to protect what is most precious in human life, starting with life itself.

One place where we might find the secular sacred operating is in the environmental protection movement, some aspects of which mirror those of a religion. The movement functions through shared "truths" and ideology and the bonding that results from sharing those beliefs; it causes people to focus on a reality external to themselves; it provides an opportunity for transcendence – belonging to and protecting something larger than oneself. Its adherents demonstrate a willingness to make sacrifices and to suffer to promote the great cause they believe in, and they are concerned for future generations and want to hand on their values and beliefs to their descendants. Religious studies scholars Paul Nathanson and Katherine Young have proposed that such movements are secular religions,[44] a concept I noted in chapter 1. If we can have a secular religion, it would seem logical that we can also have a secular sacred.

Could using the concept of the secular sacred help to promote human dignity in the context of euthanasia? What would applying the concept to human life tell us about whether legalizing euthanasia and physician-assisted suicide was a good idea?

Here's what a pro-euthenasia Australian politician, Jeff Kennett, declared: "As far as I'm concerned, when you are past your 'use by' or 'best before' date, you should be checked out as quickly, cheaply and efficiently as possible." His view is the antithesis of seeing human life as having a secular sacred element that requires respect and protection. Kennett sees us as disposable products. But we are not products to be checked out of the supermarket of life, and the values of materialism and consumerism are not the ones that should govern our dying. Euthanasia can fit with the idea that they should.

In considering whether a concept of the secular sacred could help to promote human dignity, an important question to ask is: What are our ethical obligations to future generations? What must we regard as sacred and hold in trust for them in order not to leave them worse off than we are or with fewer choices or options than we have? What do we owe them? What does an ethics of responsibility – as compared with an ethics of rights – require of us? The entities that need to be seen as secular sacred and held in trust must extend beyond physical realities to include important metaphysical realities – in particular, important shared societal values such as respect for all life.

Sacredness may also protect our physical reality, particularly that of our own bodies, and of the world around us, or what we can refer to as nature. I propose that respect for human dignity requires that we see human beings as having an element of at least secular sacredness. Science's ability to change the human body has been moving breathtakingly fast, starting with transplants and cosmetic surgery and moving on to creating chimeras (human-animal combinations) and cyborgs (human-machine combinations). For the people who promote and laud such developments, the natural essence of being human has no element of the sacred; they see nothing that must be protected and preserved through restricting what we can do in light of what we ought not to do if we are to maintain the integrity of our humanness. We will further consider such situations shortly, but for the moment let's leave the sacred and return to the President's Bioethics Council report to look at some of the other contributors' thoughts about dignity.

Nick Bostrom, director of the Future of Humanity Institute at the University of Oxford, cites Stephen Darwall's description of "two different kinds of attitude, both of which are referred to by the term 'respect.'" The first kind Darwall calls *recognition respect*: "This attitude consists in giving appropriate consideration or recognition to some feature of its object in deliberating about what to do, and it can have any number of different sorts of things as its object" – for instance, being human. The other kind he calls *appraisal respect*: "an attitude of positive appraisal of a person either as a person or as engaged in some particular pursuit."[45]

In other words, in recognition respect, we respect something because of what it is, for instance, a human being. I call this "intrinsic dignity." In appraisal respect, we confer respect on something – or withhold it – because of its qualities or lack thereof, respectively. I call this "extrinsic dignity."

Likewise, Meilaender writes about two different senses in which one might speak of human dignity. For instance, the language of dignity might be used to mark either a "floor," a kind of respect and care beneath which our treatment of any human being should never fall, or a "height" of human excellence, encompassing those qualities that distinguish some of us from others.[46]

Sulmasy distinguishes between intrinsic and instrumental values, characterizing the latter as a subclass of attributed values. "Intrinsic value is the value something has of itself – the value it has by virtue of its being the kind of thing that it is … Attributed values are those conveyed by a valuer."[47]

American philosopher Samuel Kerstein has argued elsewhere that Kant's Formula of Humanity – "So act that you use humanity, whether in your own person or in the person of any other, always at the same time as an end, never merely as a means" – could help us to define human dignity and what respecting it requires. "Treating persons as ends in themselves," says Kerstein, entails respecting "the special value inherent in persons, that is, their dignity."[48]

This Formula of Humanity ("categorical imperative") can be seen as Kant's formulation of the Golden Rule, a version of which is to be found in all major world religions. Kant's encompassed both positive and negative formulations of the Golden Rule: Don't do to others what you would not want them to do to you (non-maleficence). Do unto others as you would like them to do unto you (beneficence). But Kant's formulation is broader than the Golden Rule, because treating another as you're willing to treat yourself is not necessarily sufficient to fulfill the requirements of respect for the other's dignity or, indeed, your own dignity.

Importantly, Kerstein points out that to respect human dignity we must have respect for both the human dignity of each individual and the worth of humanity as a whole.[49] Individual consent is thus not necessarily sufficient to ensure human dignity is not being violated. Moreover, Kerstein sees treating people as means or ends as mutually exclusive categories.

Kerstein defines what he means by "an end in itself" – "an end in itself has dignity, that is, 'unconditional and incomparable worth' … The value of something with dignity … is incomparable in the sense that it has no equivalent for which it can be exchanged."[50] To treat human life or the human body as having a price or being exchangeable for some other benefit is to contravene human dignity, whether of the individual or of human life in general.

As an aside, Kerstein comes close to saying that dignity is connected with human nature being unique, a possibility I discuss shortly. I just note here that if that is true, then respect for human dignity requires respect for that uniqueness. And if dignity is connected with the natural uniqueness of individual human beings, we can see why, for example, intentional human cloning is wrong.

Kerstein's analysis resonates with that of American political philosopher Michael Sandel. In his book *What Money Can't Buy: The Moral Limits of Markets*,[51] Sandel argues that some entities, for example, human organs and tissues, must not be for sale, because commodifying them offends fairness, as these are entities that should be equally available to everyone, but only the rich can buy and only the poor sell. And these transactions corrupt important values, for instance, by diminishing the intangible worth of altruism in altruistic organ donation.

To summarize, broadly speaking, it seems there are two basic and mutually exclusive concepts of human dignity. *Intrinsic dignity* means one has dignity simply because one is human. Intrinsic dignity is a status model: dignity comes simply with being a *human being*; respect is contingent on what one is. *Extrinsic dignity* means that whether one has dignity depends on the circumstances in which one finds oneself and whether others see one as having dignity. It is conferred and can be taken away; it depends on what one can and cannot do. Extrinsic dignity is a functional, achievement, or attribute model – dignity comes with being able to perform in a certain way and to not perform in other ways. According to this concept, dignity comes with being a *human doing*; respect is contingent on what one can do.

These two definitions provide very different answers as to what respect for dignity requires. For example, if human embryos are human beings, under a concept of respect for intrinsic human dignity, their dignity must be respected. If embryos are not yet "human doings," under a concept of extrinsic human dignity they have no dignity that requires respect.

Similarly, the two definitions provide very different answers in relation to what respect for the human dignity of people with disabilities or dying people requires, and that difference matters in relation to euthanasia.

Under an inherent dignity approach, dying people are still human beings; therefore they have dignity, which means their lives must be respected. Euthanasia breaches respect for life and thereby contravenes their individual human dignity and human dignity in general. Under an extrinsic dignity approach, dying people are no longer human doings, and so they are seen as having lost their dignity, and eliminating them through euthanasia is perceived as remedying their undignified state.

Pro-euthanasia advocates decry citing the Nazis as a relevant example for consideration in today's euthanasia debates, claiming it as irrelevant and unfounded fear-mongering. Those who are anti-euthanasia avoid it for fear of weakening their case and providing an easy reason to dismiss their voice in the public debate. But an article in the *New York Times* of 8 October 1933, "Nazis Plan to Kill Incurables to End Pain; German Religious Groups Oppose Move," resonates so clearly with rhetoric and arguments in our contemporary debates, and contains such powerful warnings and, in retrospect, such a chilling example of where seeing people as "human doings" can lead, that I am including it in its entirety:

> Berlin, Oct 7. – The Ministry of Justice, in a detailed memorandum explaining the Nazi aims regarding the German penal code, today announced its intention to authorise physicians to end the sufferings of incurable patients. The memorandum, still lacking the force of law, proposed that "It shall be made possible for physicians to end the tortures of incurable patients, upon request, in the interests of true humanity". This proposed legal recognition of euthanasia – the act of providing a painless and peaceful death – raised a number of fundamental problems of a religious, scientific and legal nature.
>
> The Catholic newspaper Germania hastened to observe: "The Catholic faith binds the conscience of its followers not to accept this method of shortening the sufferings of incurables who are tormented by pain". In Lutheran circles too, life is regarded as something that only God alone can take. A large section of the German people, it was expected in some interested circles, might ignore the provisions for euthanasia, which overnight has become a widely discussed word in the Reich.
>
> In medical circles the question was raised as to just when a man is incurable and when his life should be ended. According to the present plans of the Ministry of Justice, incurability would be determined not only by the attending physician, but also by two official doctors who would carefully trace the history of the case and personally examine the patient.
>
> In insisting that euthanasia shall be permissible only if the accredited attending physician is backed by two experts who so advise, the Ministry believes *a guarantee is given that no life still valuable to the State will be wantonly destroyed.*
>
> The legal question of who may request the application of euthanasia has not been definitely solved. The Ministry merely has proposed that either the patient himself shall "expressly and earnestly" ask it, or "in case the patient no longer is able to express his desire, his nearer relatives, acting from motives that do not contravene morals, shall so request" [emphasis added].[52]

"A guarantee is given that no life still valuable to the State will be wantonly destroyed": "human doings" would not be euthanized, but "human beings" who were perceived as "useless" could be – and were.

Some pro-euthanasia advocates argue that, below a certain quality of life, a person loses all dignity. They believe that respect for dignity requires the absence of suffering, whether from disability or terminal illness, and also requires respect for autonomy and self-determination. Consequently, they argue that respect for the dignity of suffering people who request euthanasia and can give informed consent to it requires it to be an option. In other words, they equate respect for autonomy with respect for human dignity. That approach can be seen as an alternative to Macklin's proposal, referred to previously, that we should abandon the concept of dignity as useless and focus on respect for autonomy, since it results in the same outcome. This approach can be contrasted with that of Kant, who recognized autonomy as a fundamental moral principle but, in the interests of maintaining a civilized society, saw respect for human dignity as a separate requirement and more important than respect for individual autonomy when the two were in conflict.[53]

Opponents of euthanasia treat respect for human dignity and for individual autonomy as two separate requirements that can sometimes be in conflict. They believe respect for human dignity requires, above all, respect for human life and that while suffering must be relieved, life must not be intentionally ended. In other words, respect for human life takes priority over respect for individual autonomy expressed as consent to euthanasia. Taking life, except where that is the only way to save life, as in justified self-defence, offends human dignity. That is why capital punishment is wrong and why euthanasia is wrong. In fact, the original primary purpose of the concept of human dignity developed in western democracies was to ensure respect for life. It is ironic that it has been turned on its head by pro-euthanasia advocates to promote exactly the opposite outcome.

Importantly, to respect human dignity, we must have respect for both the human dignity of each individual and for that of humanity as a whole. In other words, we must have respect for each individual human life and for human life in general. Thus, even if we were to accept that individual consent could justify taking human life, that position is not necessarily sufficient to ensure that human dignity is not being violated. A French court provided an example of such a finding when it prohibited "dwarf throwing." In this "sport," people with the genetic condition of achondroplasia – very short arms and legs – were thrown by average-size men, the man who threw the dwarf the farthest being the winner. The court held that treating another human as an object was in breach of respect for human dignity and banned it, even though the people being thrown consented and protested the ban as taking away their capacity to earn a livelihood.

Dignity and Bioethics

Schulman, in introducing the report of the President's Council on Bioethics on human dignity and bioethics, explained the challenges the relation of dignity and bioethics raise and tentatively proposed "that a certain conception of human dignity – dignity understood as *humanity* – has an important role to play in bioethics, both now and especially in the future."[54]

Kass further emphasizes the relevance of dignity to bioethics: "Today, human dignity is of paramount importance especially in matters bioethical. As we become more and more immersed in a world of biotechnology, we increasingly sense that we neglect human dignity at our peril, especially in light of gathering powers to intervene in human bodies and minds in ways that will affect our very humanity, likely threatening things that everyone, whatever their view of human dignity, holds dear. Truth to tell, it is beneath our human dignity to be indifferent to it."[55]

Meilaender cites Deryck Beyleveld and Roger Brownsword, who "have distinguished three different ways in which the concept of dignity has, they believe, been used in bioethics. The first they term 'human dignity as empowerment.' The central idea here is that one's dignity is violated if one's autonomy is not respected, and this concept leads quite naturally to an emphasis upon informed consent." The second concept of dignity Beyleveld and Brownsword call "'human dignity as constraint'– that is, constraint on individual choices." For example, as noted above, dwarf throwing is prohibited as offending human dignity, even with consent. A third concept, "somewhat different from the first two, is that of 'dignified conduct.'"[56]

If one believes that respect for dignity requires respect for freedom of choice, that is, respect for individual autonomy, the idea of dignity as a constraint on autonomy and self-determination in order to preserve human dignity in general could be described as "dignity in fetters," similar to "freedom in fetters," discussed in chapter 2. As I explained, "in fetters" means that sometimes we have to restrict individuals' freedom in order to maintain the conditions that make freedom possible.

Dignity is like justice in that often it is easier to identify what constitutes a violation of it than to define what it is. Thus, in the same way we identify something as unjust without defining justice itself, it is not uncommon to speak of something as being "beneath human dignity" or sub-human without defining what dignity is. That negative-content description tells us that what is involved does not respect human dignity, a judgment that may be informed in part by moral intuition or examined emotions, not just logical cognitive mentation or reason, important as those latter ways of knowing are.

Exploring Dignity in Specific Cases

Dignity and the Sale of Organs for Transplantation

There is now a serious worldwide shortage of organs for transplantation, including in North America. Desperate people engage in desperate measures, including transplant tourism, organ trafficking, and the sale of organs across international boundaries. The vast majority of people agree that these practices are seriously unethical and must be prohibited, but to do so requires national action and international cooperation.

In April 2008, a specially convened international meeting on transplant tourism and organ trafficking was organized by the Transplantation Society in Istanbul. The resulting Declaration of Istanbul on Organ Trafficking and Transplant Tourism condemns organ trafficking, transplant tourism, and the sale of organs.

To test whether the sale of organs for transplantation offends human dignity, Kerstein[57] takes Immanuel Kant's Formula of Humanity as a basis. He approaches his analysis in two ways. First, to treat others as mere means is a failure to respect their dignity, so he considers what treating each person as ends in themselves, not "mere means" entails in the context of organ procurement. This is an individual level analysis. Second, he looks at whether any given act or omission is consistent with respect for the worth of humanity in general – "respect for the special value inherent in persons, that is, their dignity"[58] – to decide whether that act or omission contravenes respect for human dignity and therefore is morally impermissible. This is a societal level analysis. We need to maintain respect for human dignity at both levels and, consequently, require analysis at both levels.

Kerstein explains that part of what it means to have dignity is to have value that is not legitimately exchangeable for anything whose value can be fully encompassed by mere price. In other words, respecting the dignity of an entity that demands such respect requires recognizing that the entity has a value beyond what can be compensated by money – in short, that it is priceless. If selling body parts gives a general message that people and their parts are exchangeable for the "right price," those sales contravene human dignity, because respect for human dignity requires upholding the principle that they are not exchangeable. In short, all of us are dehumanized if we treat body parts as merchandise.

The sale of an organ involves using human beings simply as means rather than as ends in themselves, treating human beings and human life as objects or things, commodifying them. Doing so offends the human dignity of the "donor" and offends respect for human dignity in general. No matter how much good we might realize by the act, good ends do not justify unethical means.

Selling organs is also wrong because it breaches principles of equity and justice. In practice, desperately poor, vulnerable people with no other options are exploited as "donors" for rich, privileged recipients. Recent egregious examples include destitute refugees from the Syrian war who have fled to Beirut selling a kidney or even a cornea in order to survive. Some argue that such abuses could be guarded against. However, even if the seller were a rich, competent, free-living, consenting adult with a strong desire to sell, doing so would still violate respect for human dignity in general.

As well, only the very rich can afford to buy organs. It's one thing in terms of equity and justice that we all do not have equal access to luxury cars, for instance. It's quite another that only the very rich can buy parts of the bodies of the very poor.

But the sale of organs raises even larger issues. Central to the essence of our humanness is that we are morality-seeking and meaning-seeking beings. The *gift* of an organ affirms that essence and important shared values that include altruism, generosity, courage, and concern and care for others. These are human characteristics that manifest, implement, and promote human dignity. In contrast, the *sale* of an organ, by commodifying the human person and the human body, shifts the taking and delivery of an organ from an affirmation to a breach of this same essence and these values. In *What Money Can't Buy*, Sandel explains how the sale of what should not be for sale corrupts these values.[59]

Respect for fundamental human dignity and the special respect owed to the human body require that we preclude its sale. To do otherwise is to implement a twenty-first-century version of slavery in which instead of selling whole persons we sell their parts.

Dignity and Dying

Pro-euthanasia advocates argue that respect for human dignity requires that euthanasia be legalized. Opponents of euthanasia argue exactly the opposite, that respect for human dignity requires it remain prohibited. The two groups are using different concepts of dignity.

Pro-euthanasia advocates argue that respect for dignity requires the absence of suffering, whether from disability or illness or terminal illness, and so requires euthanasia to be an option. Relatedly, as explained previously, they also believe that respect for dignity requires respect for autonomy and self-determination. The basic approach of pro-euthanasia advocates is that euthanasia is necessary to respect a dying person's dignity: "You are in an undignified state and we will correct that by putting you out of your undignified state by eliminating you."

Opponents of euthanasia believe that respect for human dignity requires respect for human life and, if there is a perceived conflict, the latter should take priority. In fact, as mentioned previously, the original primary purpose of the concept of dignity in western democracies was to ensure respect for life. It's paradoxical that the concept of dignity has been turned on its head by pro-euthanasia advocates to promote exactly the opposite outcome.

Harvey Max Chochinov, a professor of psychiatry at the University of Manitoba, specializes in psychiatric care for dying people. He identified and defined the components of dignity and then looked at how they could be implemented to enhance dying people's feelings of dignity and being treated with respect. This approach, which he calls "dignity conserving care," encompasses a broad range of considerations that can guide care providers in preserving patients' dignity.[60] Chochinov and his colleagues also developed as a part of such care, a specific brief psychotherapeutic intervention they called "dignity therapy," which facilitates the creation of a legacy document.[61] (The table below outlines the elements of this approach.[62])

Dignity Themes, Definitions, and Dignity-Therapy Implications

Dignity Theme	Definition	Dignity-Therapy Implication
Generativity	The notion that, for some patients, dignity is intertwined with a sense that one's life has stood for something or has some influence transcendent of death	Sessions are tape-recorded and transcribed, with an edited transcript or "generativity document" being returned to the patient to bequeath to a friend or family member
Continuity of self	Being able to maintain a feeling that one's essence is intact despite advancing illness	Patients are invited to speak to issues that are foundational to their sense of personhood or self

Continued

Dignity Theme	Definition	Dignity-Therapy Implication
Role preservation	Being able to maintain a sense of identification with one or more previously held roles	Patients are questioned about previous or currently held roles that may contribute to their core identity
Maintenance of pride	An ability to sustain a sense of positive self-regard	Providing opportunities to speak about accomplishments or achievements that engender a sense of pride
Hopefulness	Hopefulness relates to the ability to find or maintain a sense of meaning or purpose	Patients are invited to engage in a therapeutic process intended to instill a sense of meaning and purpose
Aftermath concerns	Worries or fears concerning the burden or challenges that their death will impose on others	Inviting the patient to speak to issues that might prepare their loved ones for a future without them
Care tenor	Refers to the attitude and manner with which others interact with the patient that may or may not promote dignity	The tenor of dignity therapy is empathic, nonjudgmental, encouraging, and respectful

As is obvious from the broad range of considerations included in the table, this approach presents a stark contrast to the quick-fix solution of a lethal injection being seen as the best way to enhance a person's dignity.

Here's the edited abstract from the study by Dr Chochinov and his colleagues:

> The study examined a novel intervention, dignity therapy, designed to address psychosocial and existential distress among terminally ill patients. Dignity therapy invites patients to discuss issues that matter most or that they would most want remembered. Sessions are transcribed and edited, with a returned final version that they can bequeath to a friend or family member. [That is, the patient can leave a legacy, which is important in helping people to die peacefully.] The objective of this study was to establish the feasibility of dignity therapy and determine its impact on various measures of psychosocial and existential distress.
>
> ... Terminally ill inpatients and those receiving home-based palliative care services ... were asked to complete pre- and post-intervention measures of sense of dignity, depression, suffering, and hopelessness; sense of purpose, sense of meaning, desire for death, will to live, and suicidality; and a postintervention satisfaction survey ....
>
> Ninety-one percent of participants reported being satisfied with dignity therapy; 76% reported a heightened sense of dignity; 68% reported an increased sense of purpose; 67% reported a heightened sense of meaning; 47% reported an increased will to live; and 81% reported that it had been or would be of help to their family. Post intervention measures of suffering showed significant improvement and reduced depressive symptoms. Finding dignity therapy helpful to their family correlated with life feeling more meaningful and having a sense of purpose, accompanied by a lessened sense of suffering and increased will to live ...

> Dignity therapy shows promise as a novel therapeutic intervention for suffering and distress at the end of life.[63]

These results are truly remarkable. But to achieve them takes care, time, commitment, research, and expertise. In thinking about where to invest health-care and medical research dollars so as to enhance human dignity, we should keep such studies in mind.

Dignity and Reproductive Technologies: Human Dignity of Human Embryos

Does enhancing human embryos offend human dignity? Meilaender would agree that it does, because it takes away equality. "We are equal to each other, whatever our distinctions in excellence of various sorts, precisely because none of us is the 'maker' of another one of us," he insightfully maintains. "We have all received our life – equally – as a gift from the Creator."[64]

From a purely secular basis, Jurgen Habermas in his book *The Future of Human Nature*[65] argues that designed persons can no longer own themselves, which is necessary to make their being and their lives fully theirs – they are not free in their intrinsic being. They are deprived of the liberty that comes from the fact that no one has interfered with the essence of their being and as a result their genetic makeup has come into existence through chance. Moreover, because these designed people are not equal to the designer, they are deprived of equality. Respect for each individual's freedom and equality is fundamental to respect for the person's dignity and for human dignity in general.

Bostrom defines dignity as being worthy of respect, possessing qualities to be admired. Contrary to Meilander and Habermas, he argues that because enhancement improves those qualities, it adds to dignity rather than offending it, as many people believe.[66] To further support his approach, he proposes that the essence of dignity is that humans alone can choose what we want to be and that our enhanced self might be our authentic self. But an embryo cannot choose to be enhanced. And would emotional enhancement, for example, be respectful or disrespectful of an embryo's human dignity?

Does creating human embryos for research or to make products offend human dignity? And what about using "leftover" or "spare" embryos from IVF for research or to make products – does that offend human dignity? Whatever the source of the embryos, there is the ethical issue of instrumentalism in using them for research or to make therapeutic products. Instrumentalism is another way of saying we are treating something as a means not an end in itself. Embryos deserve respect in their own right. They are ends, not means.

The use of an embryo as a thing involves its objectification, reification, and dehumanization and our disidentification from the embryo. We use language to implement those outcomes: we call the embryo a "bunch of cells" or a "pre-embryo." We can compare that with the statement of fact that "we are all ex-embryos" – that being an embryo is the earliest form of each of our lives. Treating the embryo as just a thing that can be used to benefit the rest of us leads to such horrible possibilities as setting up human-embryo manufacturing plants.

Habermas writes that respect for what he calls "pre-personal human life" is necessary to maintaining our ethical understanding of what it means to be human: "There is a long-established, widely shared, deep moral intuition that human embryos are not just things or just cells like any other cell as some argue, and we breach that moral intuition at our ethical peril."[67] And, as I've argued already, respecting the essence of what it means to be human is at the heart of respecting human dignity and vice versa.

We form our most important collective values around the two great events in every human life: birth (or our perceived coming into existence, which can now be as an IVF embryo in a petri dish) and death. Human embryo research will affect values of respect for human life formed around birth.[68] Honouring the right to come into existence through natural means and to know one's biological identity and biological family is an essential part of respecting human dignity – it's the right to identity, to know through whom life travelled to us down the generations, and to whom we are biologically related.[69]

Dignity and the New Technoscience

One of the central questions in deciding what is and is not ethical in using the new technoscience is whether only humans have dignity that must be respected. Do animals also have it?

We should answer this question in one of two ways. We may view only humans as having dignity, which is probably the traditional use and limitation of the concept of dignity, linked to a religious belief that only humans have a soul – a sharing in a divine spark. Or, if we see all of creation as having dignity (a concept that I like), then humans have special dignity – human dignity.

Another way to ask this same question, one that is at the heart of some of our most important current ethical debates, is: Are humans special? Is there a discontinuity between humans and other animals? Are humans and other animals different in kind or only different in degree? Depending on how we answer these questions, our answers to the question "Do humans deserve special respect?" will also vary.

A further question: If humans do deserve special respect, is the concept of dignity the best way to implement this respect, particularly if we are to act ethically in intervening in humans with the new technoscience? Good facts are needed for good ethics, so what impact might the new technoscience have on human dignity?

As I document in chapter 5, in responding to the question of what it means to be human, some eminent scientists and philosophers do not believe humans and their humanness require special respect. Indeed, the transhumanists among them are arguing for a world in which humans as we know them will become "obsolete models."

As well as denying that humans deserve any special respect as compared with animals, questions that their "posthuman" approach is facing us with include: Should super-intelligent robots deserve more respect than natural humans? What ethics should govern our decisions about redesigning the human mind? What about manipulating human embryos' genes to create fearless soldiers? What are the ethics of extending the "normal" human lifespan to 150 years and beyond?

These are not fanciful questions; they are all currently under serious consideration. The American broadcaster and writer Charles Morris provides another example:

> German scientists have substantially deciphered the genome of Neanderthals. George Church, a genome researcher at the Harvard Medical School, recently told the *New York Times* that since modern human and Neanderthal genes are mostly the same, it should be relatively straightforward to create a living Neanderthal. He suggested splicing the uniquely Neanderthal genes into a human genome and using a chimpanzee as the surrogate mother. While the idea has ignited some controversy, Church suggested that if financing were available, "we might go along with it." Another genome specialist, however, asked whether we would place the clones "in Harvard or in a zoo."[70]

A utilitarian might contemplate carrying out such research, but a principle-based ethicist would regard it as inherently wrong, pursuant to a natural law or natural morality approach, and therefore unethical.

The new technoscience faces us with questions no humans before us have ever had to contemplate. For example, is there an essence of our humanness – "human beingness" – that we must hold in trust for future generations? Is respect for human dignity one way we can protect that essence and fulfill that trust? Do some utilitarians reject the concept of human dignity because it restricts what they want to do? Such questions raise an important new possibility, the use of science to search for human perfection, and the issue of when that process is a breach of human dignity.[71] It is often said that nowhere are we at more ethical peril than when we undertake quests such as the search for human perfection through science. The Nazi horrors showed us the dangers of a political platform or public policy approach that uses science and technology to search for perceived biological "perfection" in ourselves, individually and as a society.

Today we can seek the perfect baby through designing it using genetic and reproductive technologies – positive eugenics. We can clone perfect copies of ourselves, create the perfect athlete with drug use or gene doping, sculpt the perfect body with cosmetic surgery. And beyond our own bodies, we can carry out the perfect war – risk free, to us – with virtually controlled (disembodied) combat technologies. All these searches for perfection raise serious ethical problems.

Likewise, we can seek to eliminate those we see as imperfect through negative eugenics. We already use new technology to carry out "embryo biopsies" (pre-implantation genetic diagnosis) on in-vitro fertilized embryos to identify and discard those who are "defective." We use prenatal screening to identify fetuses with genetic or other disabilities, such as Down syndrome, and abort them. And, most recently, we have a do-it-yourself test that can be used at seven weeks of gestation to see if the baby is male or female, so that if the baby is the "wrong" sex, we can abort it and try again.

And, in a context that is relevant to all of us because we will all face death, through euthanasia and assisted suicide we can seek both to achieve the perfect death and to eliminate imperfect people.

Equating human perfection with having human dignity and seeking human perfection as a way of enhancing human dignity opens up the possibility of justifying these kinds of intervention. Why does that matter? I suggest that at least some, and perhaps many, of these interventions in search of the perfect and the elimination of the imperfect threaten the essence of our humanness – our human spirit, that which makes us human and enables us to experience wonder, awe, and the mystery of life, and through which we search for meaning. This latter search is of the essence of being human; we are meaning-seeking beings and, as far as we know, uniquely so. As I've mentioned already, those who are religious define what constitutes the essence of our humanness as the soul – the sharing of a divine spark. It is extremely difficult to define what constitutes that essence for those who reject religion, but many such people believe such an essence exists – or at least act as though it does. For instance, anybody who agrees that humans are "special" as compared with other living beings and therefore deserve "special respect" is manifesting such a belief. However, some secular humanists expressly reject "human specialness" or exceptionalism. They regard "preferencing humans" (seeing humans as special as compared with other animals or even robots) as wrongful discrimination in the form of what they call "speciesism."

A very important question we need to ask in deciding what we may and should not do with our new technoscience – that is, what is ethical or unethical – is whether any given use of it to search for human perfection could damage or destroy the essence of our humanness. Could not some imperfections be elements of that essence and of immense value as such?

If we succeed in our search for human perfection, or perhaps even engage in it, we will lose our authenticity, our human essence, our messy, old, much-touched soul. We will be like copies of masterpieces or like restored antiques: not originals, no longer unique, no longer the "real thing." In short, I'm proposing that we need a deep respect for the natural if we are to respect human dignity.

To implement that respect, I argue in my book *The Ethical Imagination*[72] that in using the world-altering powers of the new technoscience, especially in relation to interventions in life itself, and in particular in taking decisions that will affect our children and their descendants down the generations, we should start from a basic presumption in favour of respecting nature, the natural, and life. This presumption could be described as seeing the natural, whether it is we humans or other animals or our ecosystem, as having dignity – as expressing the order of creation – and starting from a presumption of the need to respect it. That premise does not mean that nature, the natural, and life must not be altered but rather that those altering them must justify doing so. It is a precautionary principle or approach.

We must ask ourselves what we owe to future generations in terms of holding nature, the natural, and life in trust for them. Applying this approach in relation to what human dignity is and requires leads to the conclusion that we should adopt a concept that having dignity should depend simply on being human, which means that all humans deserve respect and deserve equal respect.

The concept of dignity must be used to maintain respect for the integrity and authenticity of each person and respect for human life and for the essence of our humanness. The current danger is that it could be used to realize precisely the opposite outcomes.

To summarize, I would answer the three questions in the title of this chapter, "Is the concept of human dignity useful, useless, or dangerous?" as follows:

- It is useful when we can use it as a common starting point. Starting from where we can agree and moving to where we disagree is likely to help us find more agreement about ethics than would otherwise be possible. The concept of human dignity is also useful when it helps us to identify what respect for individual human dignity and for human dignity in general require us to do and not do if we are to act ethically.
- It is useless when it is of no assistance in the above respects, although we should keep in mind that just asking the question "What does respect for human dignity require?" can be a contribution to ensuring that ethics prevails. Asking it makes us aware that respect for dignity matters. The issue is not whether asking this question absolutely ensures that we will act ethically but whether we are better off asking it than not.
- Asking "What does respect for human dignity require?" is dangerous when the concept of dignity is defined in such a way that it leads to unethical answers to that question.

All of which means that, in speaking of dignity, we always need to proceed with great care.

◆◆◆

I would like to conclude by quoting the late physician and ethicist Edmund Pellegrino, chairman of the President's Council on Bioethics at the time of its report on dignity. In his concluding chapter to the report, he writes:

> Two contrary, but not necessarily contradictory, world views will dominate the discourse in our post-secular civilization. Two images of human dignity compete for moral authority. One is the scientific, the other the religious. Neither is likely to capitulate to the other. Is a productive dialogue and dialectic between these two world views possible, and how is it to be conducted?
>
> Extremists on both sides, militant atheists and intransigent

> dogmatists, insist there can be no common ground. More responsible proponents of both views hope for a productive dialogue and appeal to the necessity of a common ground in the public arena, even while metaphysical foundations remain disputed.[73]

May we engage in the necessary dialogue with courage, wisdom, and mutual respect.

4

Legalizing Euthanasia: Evolution or Revolution in Societal Values?

Killing as Kindness: The Problem of Dealing with Suffering and Death in a Secular Society

In the previous chapter we explored the concept of dignity. Recently, courts have been equating suffering to the loss of dignity, and vice versa. They define dignity as requiring that persons have control over what happens to them and, consequently, also equate a loss of autonomy and self-determination with the loss of dignity. This approach is consistent with American physician Eric Cassel's definition of suffering as having a sense of our own disintegration and a loss of control over what happens to us.[1] Often, claims with regard to what respect for a person's dignity and autonomy requires are framed as respect for a right to choice. In short, allowing "choice" regarding what happens to us is put forward as the remedy for a loss of dignity and an appropriate means to relieve suffering.

At present, physician-assisted suicide and euthanasia are the most prominent and contentious issues in relation to maintaining a person's dignity, relieving suffering, and the proper approach of the law in dealing with suffering. The law already seeks to uphold or restore dignity by giving terminally ill, suffering persons who want to die control over the treatments they receive. Requirements for informed consent – which, from the perspective of giving control over their treatment to patients, can be characterized as a "suffering reduction mechanism"[2] – and rights to refuse life-prolonging treatment are examples. However, pro-euthanasia advocates argue that the necessary and only sufficient control of suffering is to be able to choose death.

Pro-euthanasia advocates see euthanasia principally as a way to relieve people's suffering. They view suffering as the greatest evil and the relief of it as trumping almost all other values; respect for individual autonomy is the major exception. One of the challenges in responding to this argument in the euthanasia debate is that it is not easy to give meaning to suffering other than through religion, which was how many people dealt with suffering in the past. But today, many people are not religious. When suffering cannot be given any worth or meaning and people do not believe that there is anything inherently wrong in inflicting death on a suffering person – at least one who requests and gives informed consent to it – it is very difficult to convince them that legalizing euthanasia is a bad idea.

Considering how we should respond to suffering, especially as a society, also raises the philosophical claim that it is not the job or proper role of medicine or the law to relieve all suffering and that in trying to do so, physicians and law-makers are unjustifiably crossing boundaries that should be respected.[3] And that leads to the question: How, then, does and should the law deal with suffering? First, let's look at how some law students view it.

How Suffering Is Perceived

I used to teach a course, Ethics, Law, Science and Society, to upper year and graduate law students at McGill University, and one of the topics we discussed was euthanasia. I've researched euthanasia, physician-assisted suicide, the ethics and law of palliative care and pain relief treatment, decision-making at the end of life, and related topics, for nearly three decades and published a 433-page book, *Death Talk: The Case against Euthanasia and Physician-Assisted Suicide*.[4] Yet I came away from the class feeling that I had completely failed to communicate to most of my students what the problems with legalizing euthanasia were – that I was hitting a steel wall. This was not due to any ill-will on their part; rather, they seemed not to see euthanasia as raising major problems, at least any beyond preventing its abuse – a reaction I found very worrying.[5]

So, I emailed my students explaining I felt "that I had not done a good job in presenting the euthanasia debate ... [and] decided to see if I could work out why not by writing about it." I attached an early draft of my article setting out my thoughts in that regard and asked for comments; I received several, very thoughtful replies.

One student explained that she thought I was giving far too much weight to concerns about how legalizing euthanasia would harm the community and our shared values, especially that of respect for life, and too little to individuals' rights to autonomy and self-determination, and to euthanasia as a way to relieve people's suffering. She emphasized that individuals' rights have been given priority in contemporary society, and they should also prevail in relation to death. Moreover, she said, legalizing euthanasia was consistent with other changes in society, such as respect for women and access to abortion.

I had suggested in my article that, among other causes of the move to legalize euthanasia, the vast exposure to death that we are subjected to in current-affairs and entertainment programs might have overwhelmed our sensitivity to the awesomeness of death and, likewise, of inflicting it. But one of my students responded, "If anything, I think many of our reactions come not from an overexposure to death, but from an aversion to suffering, and an unwillingness or hesitancy to prolong pain."

The *Carter* Case

The *Carter* case[6] shows a judge at the trial level,[7] Justice Lyn Smith of the British Columbia Supreme Court, articulating, in great detail, both the same approach taken by the students and the reasoning on which they based their approach. She ruled that prohibiting physician-assisted suicide is unconstitutional, because it is necessary medical treatment for the relief of the suffering of people with disabilities who are unable to commit suicide without assistance. The British Columbia Court of Appeal overruled Justice Smith's judgment on the grounds that it was contrary to the then-binding precedent of the Supreme Court of Canada's ruling in the *Rodriguez* case,[8] in which a narrow majority held that the Canadian Criminal Code's prohibition of assisted suicide was constitutionally valid.[9] The plaintiffs in the *Carter* case appealed to the Supreme Court of Canada, which in effect, although not explicitly, overruled its previous precedent in the *Rodriguez* case and allowed the appeal, relying on and strongly endorsing Justice Smith's findings of both law and fact.[10]

At 355 pages and 137,000-plus words, the trial court judgment of Justice Smith in the *Carter* case[11] is rightly described as a tome. But it is one with ground-breaking impact for Canadian society, because it has been upheld on appeal by the Supreme Court of Canada. Leaving aside abortion, it constituted the crossing of the line in the sand, thousands of years old, that established that we must not intentionally kill other innocent human beings (the only exception being where that is the only way to save human life, as in justified self-defence) or help them to kill themselves.

In striking down the prohibition of assisted suicide in section 241(b) of the Canadian Criminal Code[12] as unconstitutional, Justice Smith took the first step in legalizing physician-assisted suicide in Canada and, where the person is incapable of committing suicide because of physical disability, euthanasia. One of the plaintiffs, Gloria Taylor, a woman suffering from ALS (Lou Gehrig's disease), wanted to have a physician assist her in committing suicide at a time and a place of her choosing. Justice Smith legitimized and granted Ms Taylor's wish. Ms Taylor subsequently died of natural causes. In reaching its conclusion that an absolute prohibition on "physician-assisted dying" was in breach of the Canadian Charter of Human Rights and Freedoms,[13] the Supreme Court of Canada relied heavily on this first-instance judgment. (Without meaning any disrespect, one could say the Supreme Court hid behind the skirts of the trial judge, especially with regard to questions of fact.) For this reason, the trial court decision merits close analysis.

Read as a whole, Justice Smith's judgment gives a strong impression that she is far from neutral about physician-assisted suicide and euthanasia; rather, she favours these interventions in certain circumstances. In particular, with respect, the judgment seems to give undue weight to the evidence of witnesses in favour of legalizing physician-assisted suicide, while massively devaluing that of those who oppose it. But the Supreme Court of Canada expressly found the contrary: "The trial judge's findings were based on an exhaustive review of the extensive record before her" [3].[14] Moreover, the Supreme Court at its hearing refused to allow the admission of evidence that would have corrected this imbalance in Justice Smith's assessment of the evidence [109]. As well, the trial judge's emphasis on the relief of suffering – the words "suffer" and "suffering" appear 212 times in her judgment – gives rise to what appear to be philosophical and social biases being imposed by her upon the wealth of evidence submitted by both parties.

Thus, one can question Justice Smith's conclusions from the evidence she accepted, that physician-assisted suicide is not inherently unethical and that availability of legalized physician-assisted suicide is necessary "medical treatment" for some, and the validity of the lengthy legal justification she constructs to allow her to implement her rulings to these effects. That justification was largely based on a selective application of Canadian Charter of Rights and Freedoms jurisprudence[15] and was established by distinguishing the precedent set by the Supreme Court in the *Rodriguez* case,[16] which found the prohibition of assisted suicide to be constitutional in a fact situation very similar to Ms Taylor's.

A majority of the Court of Appeal of British Columbia overruled Justice Smith by holding that the *Rodriguez* precedent applied. But the Supreme Court reinstated Justice Smith's finding that she was not bound by *Rodriguez* on two bases: since that case, the law had changed, and there were new facts. With regard to the change in the law, after agreeing with Justice Smith that the Criminal Code's absolute prohibition of assisted suicide breached all section 7 Charter rights – rights to life, liberty, and security of the person – the Supreme Court ruled that she was also correct that the test for compliance "with the principles of fundamental justice" that section 7 allows to render such breaches constitutional had changed. It now required that to be constitutionally valid, legislation must not be overbroad – that is, must not breach the rights of people who do not fall within the legislature's object in enacting the legislation:

> [*Rodriguez*] did not apply the principle of overbreadth as it is currently understood, but instead asked whether the prohibition [of assisted suicide] was "arbitrary or unfair in that it is unrelated

> to the state's interest in protecting the vulnerable, and that it lacks a foundation in the legal tradition and societal beliefs which are said to be represented by the prohibition" (*Rodriguez*, at p. 595). By contrast, the law on overbreadth, now explicitly recognized as a principle of fundamental justice, asks whether the law interferes with some conduct that has no connection to the law's objectives (*Bedford*, at para. 101). This different question may lead to a different answer. [46]

And, with regard to the change in the facts, "The matrix of legislative and social facts in this case also differed from the evidence before the Court in *Rodriguez*. The majority in *Rodriguez* relied on evidence of (1) the widespread acceptance of a moral or ethical distinction between passive and active euthanasia" [47]. The Supreme Court ruled that distinction was no longer accepted, which meant that many Canadians now agreed with allowing "physician-assisted death."

I now examine in more detail some of the issues raised in the *Carter* judgment and how the Supreme Court endorsed the way they were dealt with by Justice Smith.

The Primary Goal of Prohibiting Physician-Assisted Suicide

Central to the judgments of both the trial court and the Supreme Court is whether protecting vulnerable people is the only purpose of the prohibition on physician-assisted suicide. Justice Smith rejects the attorney general of Canada's argument that the purposes are more extensive, including upholding respect for human life and the integrity of the medical profession, and "preventing negative messages about the value of human life, particularly the value of the lives of individuals with disabilities" (1187). Likewise, the Supreme Court of Canada rejects the attorney general of Canada's argument "that the object of the prohibition [of assisted suicide] should also be defined more broadly as simply 'the preservation of life'" [75]. It rules: "Section 241 (*b*) is not directed at preserving life, or even at preventing suicide – attempted suicide is no longer a crime … The direct target of the measure is the narrow goal of preventing vulnerable persons from being induced to commit suicide at a time of weakness" [78].

The Supreme Court also held that rights to refuse life-support treatment, including artificial hydration and nutrition, show that there is no overriding goal of "the preservation of life." That is correct, but this overriding goal or object should have been argued as maintaining "respect for life," including at the societal level, and emphasis should have been placed on the argument that there is a difference in kind, not just a difference in degree, between justifiably *allowing someone to die* of natural causes and *killing them* with a lethal injection or helping them to kill themselves. Both the trial judge and the Supreme Court expressly rejected this distinction.

If the prohibition of assisted suicide were meant to uphold "respect for human life" in general at the societal level, then in all probability it would not, in stark contrast to these rulings, be found to be unconstitutional on the grounds on which both courts relied, which focused very strongly on individuals' rights. Justice Smith ruled, and the Supreme Court agreed, that the prohibition was overbroad because of its harmful impact on people with disabilities, such as Ms Taylor, who want to commit suicide but need assistance to do so, in that it was absolute, with no exceptions for people such as Ms Taylor. Consequently, the prohibition impaired her charter rights to "life, liberty and security of the person"[17] more than was necessary for the state to achieve its legitimate goal of protecting vulnerable people. In other words, limiting the goal of the prohibition on assisted suicide to the protection of "vulnerable people" is essential to the reasoning that the prohibition is unconstitutional because it is overbroad.

This ruling raises the issue of whether Parliament should include in any legislation it passes to implement the Supreme Court's decision (as the court invited it to do) a provision that the object of the legislation is also to uphold respect for human life at both the individual and societal levels. I would strongly recommend that it do so, as even if completely banning physician-assisted suicide is not possible without using the charter's section 33 "notwithstanding" clause, this would enable Parliament to severely restrict access to assisted suicide.

In light of the object identified for the prohibition of assisted suicide, it is not surprising that Justice Smith's conclusions, and those of the Supreme Court, do not give substantial weight to institutional or societal protections or needs, but are focused principally at the individual level and on giving individuals' claims priority, which in Ms Taylor's case was her claim of a right to access assisted suicide for the relief of suffering. In other words, the rulings accept an individual's suffering as the principal justification for euthanasia; the presence of suffering means an individual's request for "assisted death" trumps other claims and considerations. Here's how the Supreme Court opens its judgment: "It is a crime in Canada to assist another person in ending her own life. As a result, people who are grievously and irremediably ill cannot seek a physician's assistance in dying and may be *condemned to a life of severe and intolerable suffering*. A person facing this prospect has two options: she can take her own life prematurely, often by violent or dangerous means, or she can suffer until she dies from natural causes. *The choice is cruel*" [1] (emphasis added).

The last four words tell us what the decision will be. And the Supreme Court turns to the stories of individuals' suffering and difficult deaths to support this outcome: "The stories in the affidavits vary in their details: some witnesses described the progression of degenerative illnesses like motor neuron diseases or Huntington's disease, while others described the agony of treatment and the fear of a gruesome death from advanced-stage cancer. Yet running through the evidence of all the witnesses is a constant theme – that they suffer from the knowledge that they lack the ability to bring a peaceful end to their lives at a time and in a manner of their own choosing" [14]. We must listen to and take into account such stories, but they are not all that we need to hear and to take into account.

There is also a paradox here in that the focus on individual persons' suffering and, hence, vulnerability, a focus meant to protect vulnerable people, is being used to place them at risk from assisted suicide by legitimizing it. The same reversal of an initial protective goal has occurred with the concept of quality of life. Initially "quality of life" was developed as a concept intended to protect and promote life through the argument that everyone had a right to the resources, especially health-care resources, needed to maintain an acceptable "quality of life." Now the concept is often used to achieve the exact opposite outcome, namely, that persons' "quality of life" is so poor that they are better off dead or at least don't merit the expenditure of resources needed to keep them alive.

Having decided that the ban on assisted suicide is intended primarily to protect vulnerable persons, Justice Smith then concludes, and the Supreme Court agrees, that an absolute ban on it is not necessary to implement that goal and, moreover, that an absolute ban infringes Ms Taylor's charter rights as a disabled, suffering person, and, by extension, those of other and similarly situated "vulnerable persons." Justice Smith holds, "In this case, I have found that the infringement [of the charter] arises from the preclusion of physically disabled persons who are grievously ill and *experiencing intractable suffering* from ending their lives. Thus, it is the *absolute nature* of the prohibition against assisted suicide that requires justification, not the prohibition overall. In other words, the real question is whether the defendants have demonstrated justification for criminalizing the rendering of assistance in suicide to persons such as Gloria Taylor" (1171) (emphasis added).

In reaching this conclusion, Justice Smith takes into account Ms Taylor's own views that she does not need protection from assisted suicide as helping to establish that she does not. In other words, the judge gives priority to the value of individual autonomy in relation to a decision to commit suicide to avoid suffering. She rules that a safeguarded exception should be allowed and sets out the conditions for such an exception. Justice Smith envisions that the cases in which physician-assisted suicide or euthanasia is acceptable will be rare. But it is important to note that the method she sets out in her exception is broad and without the safeguards that might assure its application only in very restricted cases. Exactly the same observations are true of the Supreme Court's ruling in this regard.

I wish to note here, because it is so unusual, and especially because it was adopted by the Supreme Court, the way in which Justice Smith interprets the right to life enshrined in section 7 of the Canadian Charter of Rights and Freedoms: "[The prohibition on assisted suicide in section 241(b) of the Criminal. Code] infringes Ms. Taylor's right to life (13) ... The legislation affects her right to life because it may shorten her life. Ms. Taylor's reduced lifespan would occur if she concludes that she needs to take her own life while she is still physically able to do so, at an earlier date than she would find necessary if she could be assisted" (17).

To say the least, this is a novel way to construct a breach of Ms Taylor's charter right to life. In effect, this reasoning converts the right to life to a right to death by physician-assisted suicide or euthanasia. The Supreme Court endorsed this approach:

> [W]e do not agree that the existential formulation of the right to life *requires* an absolute prohibition on assistance in dying, or that individuals cannot "waive" their right to life. This would create a "duty to live," rather than a "right to life," and would call into question the legality of any consent to the withdrawal or refusal of lifesaving or life-sustaining treatment. The sanctity of life is one of our most fundamental societal values. Section 7 is rooted in a profound respect for the value of human life. But s.7 also encompasses life, liberty and security of the person during the passage to death. It is for this reason that the sanctity of life "is no longer seen to require that all human life be preserved at all costs" (*Rodriguez*, at p. 595, per Sopinka J.). And it is for this reason that the law has come to recognize that, in certain circumstances, an individual's choice about the end of her life is entitled to respect. [63]

It merits noting the lengthy reasoning the Supreme Court uses here to reach its conclusion that "an individual's choice about the end of her life is entitled to respect": it has eight separate steps. But as mentioned previously, while it's correct "that all human life [need not] be preserved at all costs," that does not mean that it can be intentionally taken. Not preserving human life and taking it are not commensurable and are not the same ethically or legally. Provided it can be justified in any given circumstances, not preserving life can be ethical and legal; intentionally taking life has never been, except when it is the only reasonable way to save innocent human life, as in self-defence.

With respect to who are the suffering persons who may have access to physician-assisted suicide, in speaking about palliative care services in British Columbia, Justice Smith refers to "the end-of-life population"

(692). She does not define this term, which in the Royal Society of Canada Expert Panel report *End-of-Life Decision Making* encompasses a continuum beginning with a serious diagnosis or injury.[18] This expansion of a term that traditionally is used for those in the last days or weeks of life to all with chronic conditions resulting from illness and injury presages precisely the dangerous expansion along a "slippery slope" from the "limited" exception the judge proposes. Likewise, the Supreme Court did not require a person to be terminally ill to have access to "physician-assisted death."

There is something chilling about Justice Smith's construction of an "end-of-life population" that is not present when we speak of "dying people," "vulnerable people," "terminally ill people," or even "the terminally ill." First, we do not know to whom the term refers. But if, as seems plausible, Justice Smith has accepted the approach of the Royal Society Expert Panel report, to which the Supreme Court also refers with approval [7], it may be all those with a serious diagnosis or injury that might be fatal in the course of time. And, of course, it is notoriously difficult to predict with any certainty the timing of death in relation to even obviously terminal illnesses for which no clinical treatment is possible.[19]

Just as troubling is the dropping of the word "people" or "person." That omission is dehumanizing and depersonalizing and allows easier disidentification from the person or people concerned. "End-of-life population" marks off the people labelled as such from the general population. They become "them," in contrast to the "rest of us." It brings to mind Susan Sontag's metaphor of the "two kingdoms," the kingdom of the well and the kingdom of the sick – but, if physician-assisted suicide or euthanasia is legalized, with even more alienating and frightening connotations: "Everyone who is born holds dual citizenship, in the kingdom of the well and in the kingdom of the sick. Although we all prefer to use only the good passport, sooner or later each of us is obliged, at least for a spell, to identify ourselves as citizens of that other place."[20]

Justice Smith's depersonalized and undefined generalization of an "end-of-life population" also brings to mind the dystopic world imagined by P.D. James in her novel *The Children of Men* in which elderly persons' duty to die is enacted through a form of mass suicide called the Quietus (that is, quiet us).[21] This disposal of fragile persons through a "duty to die" was famously argued as policy by Colorado Governor Richard Lamm in the 1980s[22] as well as, in a modified form, by ethicist and Hastings Center Fellow Daniel Callahan in the 1990s.[23]

The point, yet again, is that despite the promise of very restricted relaxation of the current legal prohibitions protecting persons, implicit in Justice Smith's decision is the invitation to expansion of physician-assisted death to many people not dying but diagnosed with a serious illness, or disabled, or simply suffering. The same is probably even truer with respect to the Supreme Court's ruling: "Section 241 (*b*) and s. 14 of the *Criminal Code* unjustifiably infringe s.7 of the *Charter* and are of no force or effect to the extent that they prohibit physician-assisted death for a competent adult person who (1) clearly consents to the termination of life and (2) has a grievous and irremediable medical condition (including an illness, disease or disability) that causes enduring suffering that is intolerable to the individual in the circumstances of his or her condition" [147].

The Supreme Court explicitly requires that informed consent to "physician-assisted death" (physician-assisted suicide and euthanasia) be obtained. But informed consent is not possible unless all reasonable alternatives to the proposed "treatment" are offered;[24] fully adequate palliative care must be available before a patient's consent to "physician-assisted death" would be valid. We know, however, that only 16 to 30 percent of Canadians who need palliative care have access to it, which is appalling. We also know that many patients who ask for euthanasia change their minds when given good palliative care.[25] And, because the Canadian Medical Association was proposed as one of the main advisers to the government about the steps it should now take in response to the *Carter* judgment, it is immensely worrying that in their factum as an intervener in the Supreme Court of Canada appeal, they expressly said that the non-availability of palliative care should not be a reason to refuse "physician-assisted death."

Suicide Is Not a Crime

Justice Smith focuses on Canadian Parliament's repeal of the suicide and attempted suicide offences in 1972 and accepts, as she is bound to do by the precedent established by the Supreme Court of Canada in the *Rodriguez* case,[26] that this was not done to give priority to a personal choice to die: "As to the objective underlying Parliament's repeal ... the majority [in *Rodriguez*] held that the objective was not to recognize a consensus that the autonomy interest of those who might wish to kill themselves is paramount to the state interest in protecting the lives of citizens; rather, it was to recognize that attempted suicide did not mandate a legal remedy" (926).

In the same vein, the Supreme Court notes that "Section 241 (*b*) is not directed at preserving life, or even at preventing suicide – attempted suicide is no longer a crime" [78]. With respect, I would explain the matter differently: the crimes were abolished to try to save the lives of suicidal people. It was hoped that if they were not threatened with the possibility of being charged with a criminal offence in seeking medical help to treat suicidal ideation, they and their families would be more likely to seek such assistance.

In coming to her conclusions about the acceptability of legally permitted assisted suicide, Justice Smith relies heavily throughout the judgment on the fact that it is not a crime to commit or attempt to commit suicide, and asks: Why then is it a crime to assist it? She opines: "[T]he law does not prohibit suicide (15) ... The plaintiffs ... argue that there is no ethical distinction between the laws that permit suicide and those that prohibit physician-assisted suicide (176) ... What is the difference between suicide and assisted suicide that justifies making the one lawful and the other a crime, that justifies allowing some this choice, while denying it to others?" (1010). The answer is, as explained above, that decriminalizing suicide and attempted suicide is intended to protect life; decriminalizing assisted suicide does the opposite. We try to prevent suicide and, importantly, there is no *right* to commit suicide. If there were such a right, we would have a duty not to treat people who attempt suicide, in order to try to save their lives, and to let them die.

The difference between suicide and physician-assisted suicide is fundamental. Suicide is a solitary act that we may try to prevent but is carried out by the individual, usually in despair. Physician-assisted suicide is a social act in which medical personnel, licensed and compensated by the state, are involved in the termination of the life of a person with the approval of the state. Allowing assisted suicide asks not that we attempt to preserve life, the normal role of medicine and the state, but that we accept and act communally upon a person's judgment that his or her life is unworthy of continuance.[27] Allowing assisted suicide is to see the infliction of death as an ethical, appropriate, and justified response to suffering. This is exactly the message that those trying to prevent suicide want to negate totally.

Assisted suicide thus involves a separate ethical enquiry that distinguishes it from suicide, an enquiry not undertaken in either the trial or Supreme Court judgments: this enquiry is about the ethics of both society's and a physician's complicity in helping persons to kill themselves. Society is complicit in legalizing the procedure, and a physician, licensed by society and in Canada compensated by society for undertaking it, is complicit in carrying it out.

For this reason, assisted suicide's impact on the value of respect for life, especially at the societal level of respect for human life in general, is different from that of suicide. The former contravenes this value, particularly at the societal level, in a way that the latter does not.

Justice Smith relied on the dissenting judgment of Chief Justice Lamer of the Supreme Court of Canada in the *Rodriguez* case to find that

> s. 241*(b)* of the *Criminal Code* creates an inequality by preventing persons physically unable to end their lives from having the option to choose suicide, while other members of the public have that option. He [Chief Justice Lamer] found that the inequality is imposed because of a physical disability, a personal characteristic among the grounds of discrimination listed in s. 15(1) [of the Canadian Charter]. He concluded, at 549–50, that the inequality constitutes a burden or disadvantage since it limits the ability of persons who are subject to the inequality to take and act upon fundamental decisions regarding their lives and persons; for them, "the principle of self-determination has been limited." Differing from the majority, he found that the infringement of s. 15 was not justified under s. 1 [of the charter]. (1014)

But Justice Smith fails to mention that, in order to rule to this effect, the chief justice recognized a *right* to choose to commit suicide.

The way in which the chief justice's ruling is summarized in the head note to the *Rodriguez* case throws a different light on the passage from his judgment upon which Justice Smith relies: "This inequality – *the deprivation of the right to choose suicide* – may be characterized as a burden or disadvantage, since it limits the ability of those who are subject to this inequality to take and act upon fundamental decisions regarding their lives and persons" (emphasis added).[28]

Does such a right mean that we would have correlative obligations not to prevent people making that choice? Certainly, hospital emergency rooms and health-care professionals faced with a patient who has attempted suicide do not at present act on that basis. And psychiatrists who fail to take reasonable care that their patients do not commit suicide, including by failing to order their involuntary hospitalization in order to prevent them committing suicide, can be liable for medical malpractice (negligence), unprofessional conduct (they lose their medical licences), and even, in extreme cases, criminal negligence.

The Supreme Court avoided addressing the issue of discrimination. In responding to the question "Does the prohibition on assisted suicide violate Section 15 of the *Charter*?" it ruled: "Having concluded that the prohibition [of assisted suicide] violates s. 7, it is unnecessary to consider this question" [93].

Weighting the Evidence Disproportionately

Consistent with focusing on the risks and harms to individuals, the vast majority of the evidence to which Justice Smith gives credibility is empirical evidence. Correlatively, she dismisses or gives short shrift to evidence she labels as non-empirical, including evidence of risks and harms to existential realities such as important shared societal values. In fact, *empirical* appears with great frequency in the judgment – twenty-eight times in all. (It is paired with the words *studies*, *research*, *evidence*, *knowledge*, *data*, *foundation*, *work*, *proof*, and *precision*.) Suffering can be empirically established, although the evidence that demonstrates it is to a large extent subjective. In the *Carter* case, it was introduced in evidence by witnesses who described either their own circumstances of illness and disability, and explained why they wanted the option of physician-assisted suicide to be available, or the circumstances of loved ones, who had also wanted that option. The Supreme Court emphasizes this evidence, focusing on individual cases and the suffering they manifest, starting with Gloria Taylor's situation [12] and continuing by referring to witnesses' descriptions of horrible diseases and suffering, the agony of treatment, and the fear of a gruesome death [14]. As mentioned previously, at the very beginning of its judgment the Supreme Court summarizes how it sees the situation of these people: "A person facing this prospect has two options: she can take her own life prematurely, often by violent or dangerous means, or she can suffer until she dies from natural causes. The choice is cruel" [1].

In contrast to the weight she gives to the plaintiffs' evidence, Justice Smith dismisses or gives little weight to most of the defendants' expert witnesses' testimony on the grounds that it is not empirically based. (See, for example, such references by the judge to the evidence of Dr Jose Pereira, Baroness Ilora Finlay, and Dr Herbert Hendin (664)). The problem here is that many of the serious risks and harms of legalized physician-assisted suicide and euthanasia, at levels other than that of the individual, are not physical risks and harms but metaphysical ones (to values, beliefs, attitudes, norms, and so on) not necessarily assessable through empirical research, especially those that will occur in the future. The strong emphasis on empirical evidence, to the exclusion of other valid and accepted research methodologies, means that what cannot be measured or counted is treated as unimportant or ignored.

That said, there are also serious risks of legalized physician-assisted death, particularly its abuse, especially with regard to vulnerable people, which can be and have been empirically established in jurisdictions that allow it. Justice Smith gives little weight to the evidence of these abuses. The Supreme Court allowed the attorney general of Canada to present an affidavit from one expert witness providing testimony about such abuses in Belgium, but refused to admit further evidence that would have corrected Justice Smith's factual errors in this regard. Indeed, as mentioned previously, the Supreme Court affirmed her findings of fact.

The Supreme Court's refusal is consistent with the rules governing appeals, namely that evidence that was available at the time of trial and not presented cannot be introduced on appeal; that there must be great deference to a trial court's findings of fact; and that appeals must be on questions of law, not fact. However, with respect, Justice Smith's findings on the basis of the evidence before her in regard to abuses of euthanasia in the Netherlands and Belgium and its ongoing expansion in those countries to more and more people in more and more situations were so manifestly wrong that I would have hoped that the Supreme Court justices would have wanted to ensure that the evidence on which they based their decision was as accurate as possible. The question of whether legalizing euthanasia leads to its abuse is such a critical issue in the decision of whether to legalize it, and legalizing it is such a landmark change for Canadian society's collective values and for medical practice, that it is imperative that the evidence on which such a decision is based is correct, complete, and accurately interpreted. With respect, I do not believe that is true of Justice Smith's findings which the Supreme Court endorsed. Indeed, in my respectful opinion, many of those findings are clearly wrong.

In summary, almost all of Justice Smith's analysis, in particular of the risks and benefits of physician-assisted suicide, is at the level of the individual suffering patient who wants physician-assisted suicide. By focusing her analysis at this level and treating empirical evidence as the only relevant or credible evidence, Justice Smith in effect uses an exclusionary mechanism to eliminate the evidence of the defendant government's experts against legalizing physician-assisted suicide. In doing so, she weighs the balance heavily in favour of the relief of suffering as the overriding value and a strong justification for permitting physician-assisted suicide and euthanasia.

After refusing to allow the attorney general to bring further evidence to clarify the problems with Justice Smith's rulings on the evidence (although allowing an affidavit from a Belgian expert witness on abuses of legalized euthanasia in that country), the Supreme Court then examined these rulings in relation to Justice Smith's finding that section I of the charter's requirement of "minimal impairment" of charter rights was not fulfilled. If fulfilled, section I "saves" a law that would otherwise be unconstitutional. The Supreme Court concluded:

> This question [of whether an absolute prohibition of assisted suicide is required] lies at the heart of this case and was the focus of much of the evidence at trial. In assessing minimal impairment, the trial judge heard evidence from scientists, medical practitioners, and others who were familiar with end-of-life decision-making in Canada and abroad. She also heard extensive evidence from each of the jurisdictions where physician-assisted dying is legal or regulated. In the trial judge's view, an absolute prohibition would have been necessary if the evidence showed that physicians were unable to reliably assess competence, voluntariness, and non-ambivalence in patients; that physicians fail to understand or apply the informed consent requirement for medical treatment; or if the evidence from permissive jurisdictions showed abuse of patients, carelessness, callousness, or a slippery slope, leading to the casual termination of life (paras. 1365–66). [104]
>
> ... As to the risk to vulnerable populations (such as the elderly and disabled), the trial judge found that there was no evidence from permissive jurisdictions that people with disabilities are at heightened risk of accessing physician-assisted dying (paras. 852 and 1242). [107]
>
> ... The evidence, she concluded, did not support the contention that a blanket prohibition was necessary in order to substantially meet the government's objectives [of protection of vulnerable people]. We agree. A theoretical or speculative fear cannot justify an absolute prohibition. [119]
>
> ... We find no error in the trial judge's analysis of minimal impairment [of section 7 rights, required under section 1 of the Charter for the impairing law to be constitutionally valid]. We therefore conclude that the absolute prohibition [on assisted suicide/physician-assisted death] is not minimally impairing. [121]

Underlying Assumptions and Principles

Both Justice Smith and the Supreme Court of Canada make assumptions that assisted suicide or euthanasia is not inherently wrong and, moreover, that access to such an intervention is morally required in certain circumstances, in particular to relieve suffering. In all probability, they are doing the same as we find in the Royal Society Expert Panel Report[29] and the Quebec Legislative Assembly one,[30] both admitted in evidence at trial against the defendants' objections, and both referred to by the Supreme Court [7]. They thus assume, without justifying doing so, that individual autonomy is the value that always takes priority. Like both the reports, Justice Smith's entire judgment, as well as that of the Supreme Court, is also consistent with the adoption of a philosophical base of moral relativism and an approach of utilitarianism that favour seeing relief of suffering as an overriding justification for physician-assisted suicide or euthanasia.

In addressing the question of whether the principle of preservation of life has exceptions, Justice Smith first finds that it does, and then accepts the evidence of one of the plaintiffs' expert witnesses, Canadian philosopher Wayne Sumner, to the effect that death is not a loss or bad if there is no benefit in a continuing life – in other words, that a poor quality of life and suffering can justify such an exception. Here is her reasoning:

> With respect to the first question [does a physician have an overriding duty to support the inviolability of life and refrain from intentionally causing death, or can it be ethical, in an individual case, for a physician to assist a competent and informed patient who requests hastened death?], I think that the real difference of opinion is not about the value of human life; no-one questions that the preservation of human life has a very high value in our society. Rather, the difference of opinion is about whether the preservation of human life is an absolute value, subject to no exceptions (350).
>
> Professor Sumner explores this point:
>
>> Normally we assume that death is one of the worst fates that can befall us, which is why in both ethics and law the causing of death is taken to be such a serious matter. But what makes death such a bad thing in the normal case is what it takes away from us – the continuation of

> a life worth living. The disvalue of death is therefore a direct function of the value of the life thereby lost. This is the *deprivation account* of the badness of death: death is bad for us by virtue of depriving us of the goods of continued life. On this account showing that death would be bad for a person requires a comparison between two possible futures for that person: the one in which he dies and the one in which he lives on. If the goods of further life would outweigh the evils then it would be better for the person to continue living, and death would therefore be a harm to him since it would deprive him of this good future [emphasis in original]. (351)

On the other hand, if the "evils" of continued life outweigh its goods, death is not a harm as nothing good is lost. This is a *quality of life* argument couched in different terms, those of non-deprivation. The persons' quality of life is seen as being so poor that they are not deprived of any benefit – indeed, they are benefited – by their life being taken.

Although Justice Smith speaks of this approach applying "in an individual case," this same reasoning could readily be applied to disabled babies, people with dementia, and so on. Justifying the taking of or not maintaining the lives of such people on the basis of their poor quality of life and the suffering continued life involves is usually supported on the grounds that they are "individual cases." The cumulative effect of the decisions taken in those cases is ignored, yet the cumulative effect is to wipe out the people with a specified characteristic as a group. For instance, in North America around 85 percent of Down syndrome babies are now aborted. And, as mentioned in chapter 2, two bioethicists caused an international furor in 2011 when they published a paper in a highly respected journal proposing "post-birth abortion": parents who have a Down syndrome child, whom they would have aborted if they'd known of the condition, should be allowed to have the child killed after birth (legalized infanticide).[31] In this respect, it is relevant to point out that the Groningen protocol in the Netherlands allows the parents of severely disabled newborn babies to request that they be euthanized.[32]

It merits noting in the context of exploring the cumulative effect of legalizing physician-assisted suicide and euthanasia that the reports of the Royal Society panel[33] and the Quebec Legislative Assembly Committee[34] raise the issue of whether euthanasia should be available for mentally incompetent people, for instance, those with Alzheimer's disease. Neither report comes out against it being allowed; rather, they leave the question open, stating that it is an issue to be examined further at a later date. However, if physician-assisted suicide is medical treatment meant to relieve suffering, as its supporters argue, then it would be discriminatory to offer it to mentally competent people and not to incompetent ones.

The "No Difference" Argument

The essence of the "no difference" line of pro-euthanasia argument, accepted by Justice Smith and the Supreme Court and central to their judgments, is that we already accept and practise interventions such as withdrawal of life-support treatment or the provision of necessary pain management that result in death or could shorten life, respectively; there is no ethical or moral difference between these and physician-assisted suicide and euthanasia,[35] and there ought to be no legal difference. The argument is that the latter are of the same kind as the former, and legalizing them is just a further incremental step along a path we have already taken and regard as ethically and legally acceptable. Justice Smith puts it this way: "That spectrum [of acceptable interventions at the end of life] already encompasses decisions where the likely consequence of the decision will be the death of the patient" (1240).

I call this strategy "legalizing euthanasia through confusion."[36] It depends on a misleading and, I argue, false analogy. The issue in the "euthanasia debate" is not *if* we die – we all die eventually – but the ethics and law of *how* we die. People who oppose physician-assisted suicide and euthanasia believe these are unethical ways to die and can be validly distinguished from the other ways in which life may be shortened; consequently, the former should remain prohibited. The difference can be summarized as that between allowing a person to die a natural death and killing the person.

The essential ethically and legally relevant differences between the two kinds of interventions do not include that between an act and an omission, on which pro-euthanasia advocates, such as Canadian law professor Jocelyn Downie, allege anti-euthanasia proponents rely.[37] Like the *acts* of physician-assisted suicide or euthanasia, an *omission* – for example, withdrawal of life-support treatment that results in a person's death – can be (but, unlike physician-assisted suicide or euthanasia, is not necessarily) ethically, morally, and legally culpable. The relevant differences between these two kinds of interventions lie in the primary intention with which they are undertaken and in causation of death.

The distinction between pain relief treatment and euthanasia hinges on the physician's primary intention in giving the treatment and the patient's need for the treatment given. Pain relief treatment given with a primary intention to relieve pain and reasonably necessary to achieve that outcome is not euthanasia, even if it shortens the patient's life (a rare occurrence for correctly titrated treatment). Any intervention, including the use of pain relief drugs, carried out with a primary intention of causing the patient's death and resulting in that outcome, is euthanasia.

Acting with a primary intention to kill is a world apart from acting with a primary intention to relieve pain. And this approach is not novel or exceptional; the law recognizes the relevance of such distinctions in intention daily. If we accidentally hit and kill a pedestrian with our car, it is not murder; if we deliberately run him down with our car intending to kill him, it is. It's the same act, but different intentions make the difference.

People in pain are among the most vulnerable persons, so the issue of pain management has special application in relation to them. As Albert Schweitzer said, "Pain is a more terrible Lord of mankind than death itself." A person in pain can want to die by any means rather than go on living in pain. Consequently, as I argue in chapter 7, we have serious ethical obligations – and I would argue legal obligations – to offer everyone who needs it fully adequate pain management.

An adverse consequence of equating pain management to euthanasia is that it can make people who reject euthanasia reject adequate pain management for ethical or religious reasons, or because of fear that if they consent to it, they will be euthanized. Experience in the

Netherlands shows that the latter is not unjustified. It has been alleged that Dutch physicians have interpreted patients' consent to pain management as consent to euthanasia.[38]

The *primary intention* is also different in withdrawing life-support treatment, on the one hand, and physician-assisted suicide and euthanasia, on the other. In withdrawing life-support treatment, the primary intention is to respect patients' right to refuse all treatment, or to remove medically futile treatment or treatment where the burden for the patient outweighs any benefits. In physician-assisted suicide or euthanasia, the *primary intention* is to help patients to kill themselves or to kill them, respectively. The former intention is ethically and legally acceptable; the latter intentions are not.

Patients have a right to refuse treatment, even if that means they will die. Such a refusal is an exercise of their right to autonomy and self-determination, but the content of that right in such situations is a right not to be touched without their consent – a right to inviolability – not a right to die.

Pro-euthanasia advocates use recognition of the right to refuse treatment, even when it results in death, to argue that, likewise, patients should be allowed to exercise their right to autonomy and self-determination to choose death through lethal injection. Advocates say that there is no morally or ethically significant difference between these situations, and there ought to be no legal difference. They found their argument by wrongly characterizing the right to refuse treatment as a "right to die," and then generalize that right to include euthanasia and physician-assisted suicide. But the right to refuse treatment is not a "right to die" and does not establish any such right, although death results from respecting the patient's right to inviolability. The right to refuse treatment can be validly characterized as a "right to be *allowed* to die," which is quite different from a right to be killed, which legalized euthanasia establishes.

This particular pro-euthanasia line of argument is just one more example of promoting euthanasia through deliberate confusion between interventions that are not euthanasia, such as acting on valid refusals of treatment, and interventions that are euthanasia.

This brings us to the issue of causation, which also differentiates refusals of treatment that result in death from euthanasia. In refusals of treatment that result in death, the person dies from her underlying disease – a natural death. The withdrawal of treatment is the occasion on which death occurs, but not its cause. If the person had no fatal illness, she would not die. And, moreover, sometimes patients who refuse treatment and are expected to die do not die. In contrast, in euthanasia, death is certain, and the cause of death is the lethal injection. Without that, the person would not die at that time from that cause.

The fact that the patient dies both in refusing treatment that results in death and in euthanasia is one of the reasons for confusion between the two situations. If we focus only on that outcome of death, we miss the real point of distinction between the two situations.

Here's how Justice Smith articulated the plaintiffs' expert witnesses' "no difference" arguments, which she endorsed (see, for example, at 335, 339, 349) and which the Supreme Court not only accepted but also used as a central rationale for distinguishing (overriding) its previous decision in the *Rodriguez* case:

> [T]he plaintiffs argue that the current line drawn between permissible and impermissible end-of-life care is based upon distinctions that in reality have no practical ethical or moral force. They also argue that there is no ethical distinction between the laws that permit suicide and those that prohibit physician-assisted suicide (176) ... One of the main arguments for the proposition that physician-assisted death can be an ethical practice is that physician-assisted death is ethically indistinguishable from conventionally ethical end-of-life practices such as withholding or withdrawing treatment or administering palliative sedation (186) ... However, as set out in my review of the evidence with respect to safeguards, in the opinion of a number of respected ethicists and practitioners, physician-assisted death *in an individual case* is not ethically distinguishable from currently legal and ethically accepted end-of-life practices (1369) [emphasis added].

The Supreme Court described Justice Smith's formulation of this "no difference" argument as follows:

> The trial judge began by reviewing the current state of the law and practice in Canada regarding end-of-life care. She found

> that current unregulated end-of-life practices in Canada – such as the administration of palliative sedation and the withholding or withdrawal of lifesaving or life-sustaining medical treatment – can have the effect of hastening death and that *there is a strong societal consensus that these practices are ethically acceptable* [emphasis added] (para. 357). After considering the evidence of physicians and ethicists, she found that the "preponderance of the evidence from ethicists is that there is no ethical distinction between physician-assisted death and other end-of-life practices whose outcome is highly likely to be death" (para. 335). Finally, she found that there are qualified Canadian physicians who would find it ethical to assist a patient in dying if that act were not prohibited by law (para. 319). [23]

It is interesting to speculate why Justice Smith yet again[39] limited her statement to "an individual case." Read in relation to the judgment as a whole, it is probably because she requires justification for physician-assisted suicide in each case, and that would require that the person be "grievously ill" (1271), that is, suffering. But it could also be taken to mean that such interventions are not able to be justified as a group or on the whole, because of their cumulative impact on important shared values, in particular respect for life, or at institutional and societal levels – issues that she does not consider in any depth or at all. Or it could be that Justice Smith wants to avoid setting a precedent that people with a certain disability are automatically identified by that disability as having a claim – or even a right – with respect to having access to physician-assisted suicide or euthanasia.

The Supreme Court adopts a "no difference" approach and expands on Justice Smith's reasoning in analyzing what respect for the section 7 charter rights to "liberty and security of the person" require, making these rights protective of a very broad scope for the exercise and dominance of individual autonomy and, concurrently, more easily breached by any restriction on a person's "choice":

> We agree with the trial judge. An individual's response to a grievous and irremediable medical condition is a matter critical to their dignity and autonomy. The law allows people in this situation to request palliative sedation, refuse artificial nutrition and hydration, or request the removal of life-sustaining medical equip-

> ment, but denies them the right to request a physician's assistance in dying. This interferes with their ability to make decisions concerning their bodily integrity and medical care and thus trenches on liberty. And, by leaving people like Ms. Taylor to endure intolerable suffering, it impinges on their security of the person. [66]

This broad interpretation of section 7 rights to liberty and security of the person and, likewise, the section 7 right to life, combined with a very narrow interpretation of the valid object of prohibiting assisted suicide, allowed the Supreme Court to find, respectively, breaches of all section 7 rights and a lack of justification for those breaches.

The Supreme Court also opined that requiring respect for "the principles of fundamental justice" if breaches of section 7 rights are to be constitutionally valid is connected with respecting people's dignity: "In *Re B.C. Motor Vehicle Act*, [1985] 2 S.C.R. 486 (the '*Motor Vehicle Reference*'), Lamer J. explained that the principles of fundamental justice are derived from the essential elements of our system of justice, which is itself founded on a belief in the dignity and worth of every human person. To deprive a person of constitutional rights arbitrarily or in a way that is overbroad or grossly disproportionate diminishes that worth and dignity" [81].

In considering the impact of legalizing physician-assisted suicide on physicians, patients, and palliative care, Justice Smith recognizes there will be both positive and negative effects but concludes the positive ones will outweigh the negative: "For physicians who see no ethical distinction between assisted death for grievously ill patients and certain current legal end-of-life practices, the law draws an arbitrary line and promotes a kind of hypocrisy. Removing it would permit physicians a more open relationship with their patients and support intellectual honesty in the ethical debate. Indeed, evidence from other jurisdictions suggests that physicians are able to provide better overall end-of-life treatment to patients at the end of their lives once the topic of assisted death is openly put on the table" (1271).

As mentioned previously, Justice Smith considers in her judgment the personal stories of people who recount serious suffering because physician-assisted suicide or euthanasia was not available. Personal stories of those who oppose these interventions, while submitted, apparently were not a factor in her deliberations.

Yet, in contrast to the rulings cited above, Justice Smith notes that the Supreme Court of Canada recognized in the *Rodriguez* case that there is a valid distinction between refusing life-support treatment and euthanasia: "*Rodriguez* also summarized and clarified the law regarding the common law right of patients to refuse consent to life-sustaining medical treatment, and to demand that such treatment be withdrawn or discontinued. As I have earlier described, the majority [of the Supreme Court] accepted that there is a valid distinction between the role of physicians in those situations and the role of physicians in assisted suicide or euthanasia, based on the intention of the physician" (929). Clearly the Supreme Court is no longer of this view.

In the context of considering the "no difference" line of reasoning, it merits noting that a common thread among all end-of-life interventions, and their goal, is the avoidance or relief of suffering. The pro-euthanasia argument is that such relief is the overriding priority and an end that justifies any necessary means of achieving it, including assisted suicide and euthanasia. While people who are anti-euthanasia are also anti-suffering, they strongly disagree that outcome should be realized through the infliction of death.

Dismissing Slippery Slopes

Justice Smith's rulings regarding the practical and logical slippery slopes in jurisdictions that had legalized "physician-assisted death" are of major importance, because they were accepted by the Supreme Court, which, as noted previously, refused Canada's request to bring evidence to show they were wrong.

In assessing the practical slippery slope – the risks of abuse if an absolute ban on physician-assisted suicide is not maintained and is permitted under certain conditions – Justice Smith considers "life ending acts without explicit request" (acronym: LAWER) and the presence of mental illness in people wanting physician-assisted suicide. She extensively reviews "medically assisted dying" legislation in Oregon, the Netherlands, and Belgium and notes that prohibiting physician-assisted suicide and euthanasia does not prevent them from being carried out (see, for example, 523). And she again conflates pain relief and withdrawal of treatment with euthanasia (525).

The judge's reassuring conclusions about the effectiveness of safeguards in the jurisdictions she examines are, however, far from universally shared. In fact, evidence for the existence of both practical slippery slopes and logical slippery slopes – the expansion of justifications for physician-assisted suicide and euthanasia – is very convincing. Justice Smith's findings in this regard were expressly rejected by the High Court of Ireland in *Fleming vs. Ireland and others*,[40] after the court extensively reviewed the evidence on which Justice Smith relied. Here's how their finding is summarized:

> In that case [the *Carter* case at trial level], the Canadian court reviewed the available evidence from other jurisdictions with liberalised legislation and concluded that there was no evidence of abuse. This Court also reviewed the same evidence and has drawn exactly the opposite conclusions. The medical literature documents specific examples of abuse which, even if exceptional, are nonetheless deeply disturbing. Moreover, contrary to the views of the Canadian court, there is evidence from this literature that certain groups (such as disabled neonates and disabled or demented elderly persons) are vulnerable to abuse. Above all, the fact that the number of LAWER ("life-ending acts without explicit request") cases remains strikingly high in jurisdictions which have liberalised their law on assisted suicide (Switzerland, Netherlands and Belgium) – ranging from 0.4% to over 1% of all deaths in these jurisdictions according to the latest figures – without any obvious official response speaks for itself as to the risks involved.

Yet the Supreme Court of Canada held that Justice Smith "made no … error":

> The trial judge then turned to the evidence from the regimes that permit physician-assisted dying. She reviewed the safeguards in place in each jurisdiction and considered the effectiveness of each regulatory regime. In each system, she found general compliance with regulations, although she noted some room for improvement. [25]

> The trial judge made no palpable and overriding error in concluding, on the basis of evidence from scientists, medical practitioners and others who are familiar with end-of-life decision-making in Canada and abroad, that a permissive regime with properly designed and administered safeguards was capable of protecting vulnerable people from abuse and error. [Headnote]

The problem is that the error is Justice Smith's heavy reliance on the evidence of the plaintiffs' experts to the effect that there was little or no evidence of abuse and her failure to give weight to the evidence of the defendants' experts to the contrary.

A chilling example of the logical slippery slope is the euthanizing in December 2012 of forty-five-year-old twins in Belgium. Deaf since childhood, Marc and Eddy Verbessem were facing the additional disability of blindness. Accepting that they were irremediably suffering, their physician euthanized them.[41]

Justice Smith rules that the nature of the risks of "medically assisted death" is no different from that of other end-of-life decisions. In other words, she again adopts the "no difference" approach outlined previously to reject the dangers of physician-assisted suicide opening up slippery slopes, accepting the plaintiffs' suggestion "that the very same risks exist with respect to current end-of-life practices [as with physician-assisted suicide]. A patient who chooses to withdraw from life-sustaining treatment may present exactly the same challenges to caregivers, who need to know if the patient is truly giving informed consent, is not suffering from untreated depression, or is acting under some kind of duress or coercion" (1237).

Justice Smith does not look at the slippery slope in the Netherlands constituted by the expansion of justifications for euthanasia, and she does not mention the major increase in the use of terminal/palliative sedation (patients are sedated until they die) in Belgium.[42] Some uses of deep sedation are euthanasia, others are not. Sedation is "slow euthanasia" (terminal sedation) where it is used to continuously sedate patients until they die from lack of food and fluids, in circumstances where it is not the only reasonable way to relieve serious pain and suffering. Palliative sedation is where sedation is the only reasonable way to relieve serious pain and suffering and is not used with a primary intention to shorten life. Whether sedation is terminal or palliative depends on all the circumstances, including the patient's medical situation, the medication used and its dosage, the alternative treatments available, and the intention of the physician in administering it.

We can ask why terminal sedation is now being favoured over "classic" euthanasia methods (lethal injections) used up to the present, for instance, in the Netherlands. Might palliative sedation make the patient's death seem more like a natural death? Might it reflect a moral intuition that there is something wrong in intentionally killing another human being and the killing is less obvious when a lethal injection is avoided? Might it be less psychologically traumatizing for physicians? Or might it just be that administrative requirements, such as the requirement to report cases of euthanasia, do not apply to terminal sedation?

Prioritizing Autonomy and Choice

At its simplest, the euthanasia debate can be seen as a clash between the value of "respect for life" and the value of respect for individual autonomy, usually backed up by a "relief of suffering" argument, and disagreement as to which should take priority.

People who oppose euthanasia give priority to respect for life and point out that pain and suffering can be relieved without killing the person who suffers, including, where warranted, by palliative sedation. In contrast, the value of "choice" or individual autonomy and self-determination is central to the pro-euthanasia argument, and because it gives the person a sense of control, it is seen in itself as reducing suffering. Justice Smith expresses that argument in her judgment: "No-one should be deprived of liberty, or *forced to suffer*, without adequate cause. Failing to respect an autonomous choice to die risks paternalism" (emphasis added) (315). For people with liberal values, paternalism is always a major harm. Then Justice Smith rules: "In my opinion, the law [prohibiting assisted suicide] creates a distinction that is discriminatory. It perpetuates and worsens a disadvantage experienced by persons with disabilities. *The dignity of choice* should be afforded to Canadians equally, but the law as it stands does not do so with respect to this ultimately personal and fundamental choice [to die]" (emphasis added) (1161).

But even assuming that there is such a legally relevant distinction, in view of the fact that no one has a right to commit suicide and, where possible, people who attempt it will be prevented from doing so, one can query whether it is the law that creates a discriminatory distinction as would be required for the law to be struck down as discriminatory. The Supreme Court takes a complementary but different approach: it identifies a lack of access to "physician-assisted death" – a lack of that choice – as a cause of suffering, saying, as cited previously: "Yet running through the evidence of all the witnesses is a constant theme – that they suffer from the knowledge that they lack the ability to bring a peaceful end to their lives at a time and in a manner of their own choosing" [14].

I also note here Justice Smith's use of the phrase "the dignity of choice," which I have not encountered before. As I discussed in chapter 3, dignity is a complex and controversial topic in bioethics; choice is a neutral concept in the sense that some choices will enhance human dignity, others will harm it. It is *what* we choose that makes a choice ethical or unethical, not just the presence of choice itself.

Justifying Physician-Assisted Suicide and Euthanasia through Relief of Suffering

As noted already, respect for individual autonomy and choice is one of the primary values for supporters of legalizing euthanasia; the other is the relief of suffering. Justice Smith links these values and also gives priority to the relief of an individual's suffering over risks of harm to other individuals from the precedent set by the means used to relieve that suffering. She states: "My review of all the evidence shows that the ethical and practical arguments *in favour of* making physician-assisted death available to the limited category of patients described [include that] ... it is unethical to refuse to relieve the suffering of a patient who requests and requires such relief, simply in order to protect other hypothetical patients from hypothetical harm (315(l)) ... It must not be overlooked that what is at stake for someone in Gloria Taylor's situation is not merely autonomy, nor is it simply autonomy with respect to physical integrity. It is the *autonomy to relieve herself of suffering*"(emphasis added) (1156).

The attorney general of Canada argued that "the Court must address whether the autonomy interests and suffering of some individuals are outweighed by the public benefits of promoting the value of every life, preserving life, protecting the vulnerable, preventing abuses, maintaining the physician-patient relationship and promoting palliative care"(1247). But Justice Smith rejects arguments that harm to society can outweigh individuals' rights to autonomy, although she requires the presence of suffering for those rights to extend to physician-assisted suicide and euthanasia. In doing so, she limits the scope of a person's autonomy to choose death by requiring the presence of suffering. In other words, the presence of suffering is functioning as a limiting device on the exercise of a legal right to autonomy with respect to self-willed death and the assistance of a physician in implementing that goal.

The Supreme Court addressed the attorney general's arguments that allowing "the permissive regulatory regime ['physician-assisted death'] accepted by the trial judge 'accepts too much risk,' and that its effectiveness [to prevent abuse of physician-assisted death] is 'speculative' (R.F., at para. 154)" [118], and, therefore, the prohibition of assisted suicide was justified under section 1 of the charter. The Supreme Court responded: "The burden of establishing minimal impairment [in order to justify a breach of a constitutional right under section 1] is on the government." It continued:

> The trial judge found that Canada had not discharged this burden. The evidence, she concluded, did not support the contention that a blanket prohibition was necessary in order to substantially meet the government's objectives. We agree. A theoretical or speculative fear cannot justify an absolute prohibition. As Deschamps J. stated in *Chaoulli*, at para. 68, the claimant "d[oes] not have the burden of disproving every fear or every threat," nor can the government meet its burden simply by asserting an adverse impact on the public. Justification under s. 1 is a process of demonstration, not intuition or automatic deference to the government's assertion of risk (*RJR-MacDonald*, at para. 128). [119]

Justice Smith also sees the presence of suffering at the end of life as differentiating suicide in that context from it in other contexts, and as a justification for the former: "[The attorney general of] Canada mistakenly presumes that Canadians do not see a difference between assisted death in response to intolerable suffering at the end of life, and suicide arising out of mental illness or transitory sadness" (1262). The judge does not consider that many suicidal people also experience what they perceive as "intolerable suffering" and the likely impact of the message that this passage gives that suicide is an appropriate response to suffering, at least in some circumstances. The Supreme Court does not address the issue of the impact of legalizing "physician-assisted death" on legitimating suicide in general.

Suffering is a very difficult reality to deal with in postmodern secular democracies such as Canada. Traditionally, we have accommodated suffering in our lives by finding meaning in it, but we largely did that through traditional religion. In secular societies, it is much more difficult for many people to find such meaning. Yet it can be found, as many stories of deep suffering and bravery that move us profoundly attest.

Accepting Physician-Assisted Suicide and Euthanasia as Medical Treatment

Justice Smith appears to accept the argument that legalizing euthanasia could enhance palliative care (see, e.g., 584, 585, and 721), and the Supreme Court notes this finding [26 and 107]. This goes some way, at the least, towards treating euthanasia as, as some have termed it, "the last act of good palliative care." The argument is also consistent with the "no difference among them" approach to a spectrum of end-of-life medical interventions that include euthanasia and physician-assisted suicide, discussed above. But my colleague Donald Boudreau, a specialist physician, and I adamantly reject that euthanasia can ever be medical treatment, as it is fundamentally incompatible with the healing role of physicians.[43] It merits noting that as a result of palliative-care physicians in Quebec protesting the inclusion of "medical aid in dying" in the definition of palliative care in article 3(3) of An Act Respecting End-of-Life Care, the definition was amended, although not to their satisfaction. It now reads: "'[E]nd-of-life care' means palliative care provided to persons at the end of their lives, including terminal palliative sedation, and medical aid in dying."

Apart from other considerations, whether euthanasia is medical treatment matters in Canada for jurisdictional reasons. Governance of medical treatment is a provincial, not a federal, jurisdiction, one reason why both the Quebec Legislative Assembly Committee's report "Dying with Dignity"[44] and the Quebec College of Physicians and Surgeons argue that it is medical treatment. The Supreme Court has recognized it as such, ruling in the *Carter* case:

> Health is an area of concurrent jurisdiction; both Parliament and the provinces may validly legislate on the topic: *RJR-MacDonald Inc. v. Canada (Attorney General)*, [1995] 3 S.C.R. 199, at para. 32; *Schneider v. The Queen*, [1982] 2 S.C.R. 112, at p. 142. This suggests that aspects of physician-assisted dying may be the subject of valid legislation by both levels of government, depending on the circumstances and focus of the legislation. We are not satisfied on the record before us that the provincial power over health excludes the power of the federal Parliament to legislate on physician-assisted dying. [53]

This ruling means the Quebec government has the right to pass laws to regulate these physician-assisted death "treatments" and physicians administering them to patients.

But, if, as we are told, society wants physician-assisted suicide and euthanasia legalized, should physicians or some other professionals carry them out? In other words, should we clearly separate those interventions from medical treatment? It's a controversial suggestion, but I propose that the "medical cloak" – the "white coat" – must be taken off legalized physician-assisted suicide and euthanasia; that is, physicians should not be the ones to carry them out. One reason, among many, is that to do so causes people to fear physicians and to fear accepting pain relief treatment and hospice and palliative medicine and care.

As well, placing a medical cloak on physician-assisted suicide and euthanasia yet again causes confusion. It makes these interventions seem safe, ethical, and humane, because those are the characteristics we associate automatically with medical care, when, in fact, we all need to question the ethical acceptability of legalizing physician-assisted suicide and euthanasia and physicians being authorized to carry them out.

One suggestion for alternative practitioners, which has shocked even people who are euthanasia advocates, is to consider having specially trained lawyers, a proposal that I discussed in chapter 1.[45] The justification put forward for this choice is that lawyers understand how to interpret laws properly and to strictly apply them, and for pro-euthanasia advocates preventing abuse is their major concern, not euthanasia itself.

Justice Smith turns to the British Columbia prosecutorial policy on assisted suicide for definitional assistance with respect to whether physician-assisted suicide is medical treatment: "In the policy, 'palliative care' is defined as 'a qualified medical practitioner, or a person acting under the general supervision of a qualified medical practitioner, administering medication or other treatment to a terminally ill patient with the intention of relieving pain or suffering, even though this may hasten death.' The policy states that that conduct, 'when provided or administered according to accepted ethical medical standards, is not subject to criminal prosecution'" (303). In other words, the policy can be expansively interpreted as placing physician-assisted suicide and euthanasia in the same category as other end-of-life treatment interventions that "may hasten death." This "no difference" reasoning, which I have discussed already, is central to both the trial judge's and the Supreme Court's decisions.

Justice Smith was deeply impressed with the evidence given by an expert witness for the plaintiffs, the American philosopher and bioethicist Margaret Battin, a prominent advocate of legalizing physician-assisted suicide and euthanasia. The judge extensively reviewed and endorsed Professor Battin's views about "the core principles central to the [assisted suicide and euthanasia] debate: liberty (also referred to as freedom, self-determination or autonomy) and mercy (compassion, or the right to be free from pain and suffering) … [and] a third core value for physicians, non-abandonment" (239).

The judge also extensively reviewed research by Battin and her colleagues on euthanasia in the Netherlands and the State of Oregon and endorsed their findings that abuses are within acceptable limits.[46] She approvingly quotes Battin: "Those who oppose physician aid in dying must show that the principles of liberty and *freedom from suffering* that are basic to an open, liberal and democratic society should be overridden"(emphasis added) (241). In short, a reversal of the burden of proof is justified on the basis of respecting liberty and implementing freedom from suffering.

Balancing Autonomy and the Common Good

I would like here to summarize how I see the Supreme Court of Canada's judgment in regard to the central issue in the *Carter* case – striking the balance between upholding respect for individual autonomy and protecting the common good.

By adopting a very expansive interpretation of the section 7 charter rights – the rights to life, liberty and security of the person – with respect to the scope of their protection of individuals' rights to autonomy, the Supreme Court was able to find that they were all violated. In stark contrast, the court adopted a very narrow interpretation of what was required to protect the common good, in effect eliminating this consideration as a valid objective of the prohibition of assisted suicide. This combination of both these expansive and narrow approaches allowed the court to rule, respectively, first, that all the section 7 rights were breached by an absolute prohibition of assisted suicide and, second, that these breaches could not be justified under the "saving provisions" of the charter, and therefore the absolute prohibition was unconstitutional.

The court was able to reach this conclusion through three main steps in its reasoning, all of which, in my respectful opinion, raise problems. To summarize: first, as examined already, at the heart of the *Carter* judgment are the "no difference" arguments, which are in error when based on false analogies and failures to distinguish between differences of degree and differences of kind, or indeed expressly rejecting such distinctions, as the court did in ruling there was "no difference" between withdrawing life-support treatment to allow a person to die a natural death and inflicting death (helping a person to kill herself or, even, killing her). Second, the court focused on the requirements for upholding the value of "preservation of life," as the relevant value in determining whether an absolute prohibition on assisted suicide was justified. In ruling that it was not justified, the court relied heavily on its finding, which is correct, that the value of "preservation of life" is not absolute, citing once again the acceptance of the withdrawal of life-support treatment as legal and ethical as showing this. The problem, in my opinion and as I have explained previously, is that "preservation of life"is not the correct value against which to test whether an absolute prohibition on assisted suicide is justified. Rather, the value of "respect for life" and what is required to uphold this value are the relevant considerations in this instance, and, I propose, do require an absolute ban. And, third, the court accepted several other "no difference" arguments, including that there is no difference between suicide and assisted suicide and therefore if suicide is not a crime, assisting suicide should not be a crime.

Values Related to Human Life

Finally, in analyzing the *Carter* case, I wish to briefly note the large number of values related to human life that Justice Smith identifies in her judgment (some of them also found in the Supreme Court judgment) and that inform her decision.

The concepts of *right to life*, *respect for life*, *preservation of life*, *inviolability of life*, *protection of life*, *sanctity of life*, and *quality of life* are all referred to by Justice Smith. They are all related, not least by their connecting thread of dealing with life, and some are used interchangeably, including by Justice Smith. There can be, however, differences among them, which, despite sometimes being nuanced, are important to understand for two reasons: such understanding can lead to different conclusions about ethics than would otherwise be the case, and it can provide insights that would be otherwise unavailable.

I want to note here the legal rule of statutory interpretation against redundancy, namely, that when a different word or term is used in the same statute, it is meant to refer to something different from a synonymous word or term used in the same statute. Although that rule does not apply to the *Carter* judgments because they are not legislation, the wide variety of words and terms used in them to describe the same realities raises questions in this regard, which are relevant to how the judgments should be interpreted in some instances.

Right to Life

As discussed previously, both Justice Smith and the Supreme Court ruled that the prohibition of assisted suicide affected Ms Taylor's right to life because it might shorten her life. "Ms. Taylor's reduced lifespan would occur if she concludes that she needs to take her own life while she is still physically able to do so, at an earlier date than she would find necessary if she could be assisted" (17). This reasoning converts the right to life to a right to death by physician-assisted suicide or euthanasia.

Respect for Life

Justice Smith links *respect for life* with *protection of life*, which I discuss shortly, and interprets it through that latter lens, which radically alters how the requirements of the former are defined. She writes:

> Canada says that the preservation of human life is a fundamental value in Canadian society and that respect for life transcends individual, religious and diverse cultural values. Canada does not assert a state interest in the absolute protection of all human life. It says, however, that respect for this fundamental value is reflected in the state's interest in not condoning the taking of human life, and embodied in the criminal law (168) …
>
> For the purposes of both its s. 7 and s. 1 [charter] analyses, the majority [of the Supreme Court of Canada in *Rodriguez*] held that the objective of s. 241(b) is the protection of the vulnerable who might be induced in moments of weakness to commit suicide. It held that objective to be grounded in the state interest in protecting life, and in the state policy that human life should not be depreciated by allowing life to be taken. (926)

Limiting the purpose of prohibiting assisted suicide to the protection of vulnerable people means that if in a given case they don't require this protection (as Justice Smith rules Ms Taylor does not), abandoning it does not contravene respect for life. This limiting creates a large unprotected population, in Justice Smith's vague phrase the "end-of-life population," for whom the protections promised to the population at large will not hold. They are excluded by judicial fiat.

Compare this with the reverse order of analysis, which starts from respect for life: respect for life requires protection of vulnerable people as members of the human community – indeed, it requires protection of all human lives – and failure to provide that protection contravenes respect for life. As this comparison shows, starting points of analyses and basic presumptions are not neutral with respect either to decisions based on them or to outcomes.[47]

As well, Justice Smith looks at respect for life only at the level of the individual person or at least primarily through that lens. She does not consider what might be required if we are to maintain respect for human life in general and at institutional and societal levels. Those analyses could result in different conclusions as to what is required.

But focusing the analysis of the risks, harms, and benefits of physician-assisted suicide at the level of the individual patient is inevitable when the analysis is directed through a charter lens, as is true in the *Carter* case. The charter's main purpose is to protect individuals from wrongful exercises of state power that unjustifiably interfere with their rights. Any competing claims of society, including what is required to avoid harm to institutions or to important shared societal values, are taken into account mainly at a secondary justificatory analytic stage under section 1 of the charter. As can be seen in the *Carter* case, these latter claims can be downplayed by the judiciary. The *Carter* judgment, at both the trial court and Supreme Court levels, contains little in-depth consideration of the impact on societal values and on the institutions of law and medicine of legalizing physician-assisted suicide. It merits noting that the same failure to give sufficient weight to societal claims and needs, and unwillingness to uphold those claims, is manifested in Parliament's enormous reluctance to use the charter's "notwithstanding clause," which allows Parliament to validate legislation that the courts have found to be unconstitutional.[48]

The charter makes available so many tests for assessing whether legislation is in compliance with its provisions that it can be used by a court to "analyze to death" any legislation. (See an example of such analysis by Justice Smith at 1358.) This can have wide implications, including that individuals can use the charter, in effect, to overrule democracy. For instance, the April 2010 vote in Parliament of 228 "against" and 59 "for" a private member's bill that would have legalized physician-assisted suicide and euthanasia, which is noted by Justice Smith (112), is in practice if not in theory overruled by the *Carter* judgment. Yet it is hard, especially for politicians, to criticize court rulings based on the charter, without running the risk of being labelled in a stigmatizing way.

Preservation of Life

As discussed earlier in this chapter, *preservation of life* is another term used in the *Carter* judgment. It can be distinguished from *respect for life* in that the former is not always required, ethically or legally, and the latter is. Not preserving life by justifiably allowing a person to die a natural death does not contravene the requirements of respect for life. For instance, in certain circumstances, withdrawing life support treatment when a competent patient gives an informed refusal of such treatment, either at the time or through "advance directives," is not only justified but ethically and legally required.

In addressing the question of whether the principle of preservation of life has exceptions, Justice Smith finds that it does, a finding endorsed by the Supreme Court. Then, as discussed previously, she accepts the evidence of one of the plaintiffs' expert witnesses, Professor Wayne Sumner, to the effect that death is not a loss or bad if there is no benefit in a continuing life – in other words, that a poor quality of life can justify such an exception.

Inviolability of Life

Justice Smith uses the term *inviolability of life* (350), a concept not in everyday use, at least in Canada. It seems that she employs it to mean a belief, which she does not share, that life must never be intentionally taken. The right to inviolability is, however, frequently spoken of in the context of medical ethics and law and encompasses the right not to be touched without one's consent, a right that protects a person's physical and mental integrity. It is a negative-content right (a right against unconsented-to interference) not a positive-content right (a right to something).

The doctrine of informed consent, explored at length by Justice Smith, is linked to inviolability. One's right to inviolability is not breached by interventions to which consent has been given. And consent protects one's rights to autonomy and self-determination. But just because one consents to an intervention does not mean that it is ethical or legal as, for instance, the Criminal Code of Canada provides: "No person is entitled to consent to have death inflicted on him, and such consent does not affect the criminal responsibility of any person by whom death may be inflicted on the person by whom consent is given."[49] As a result of the *Carter* case, this provision will no longer apply to "physician-assisted death" carried out in accordance with the requirements specified by the Supreme Court [147].

Protection of Life

Justice Smith also refers to *protection of life* as a valid goal, for instance in this passage: "To reiterate, the purpose of the prohibition against assisted suicide is the protection of vulnerable persons from being induced to commit suicide at times of weakness, a purpose grounded in the respect for and the desire to protect human life"(1362).

One question this statement raises is the difference, if any, between protection of life and respect for life. Intentionally taking human life can be justified when that is the only reasonably possible way to save human life, as in justified self-defence or "just war." These actions involve taking the life of an aggressor in order to protect the lives of the persons placed in serious danger by the aggressor. But the judge is not speaking of such a situation here. She speaks of protecting the lives of vulnerable people, not taking life to protect life, and of respect for and protection of life in general. Her interpretation of the "right to life" could, however, help in interpreting what she contemplates by protection of life: she views the right to life as requiring that physician-assisted suicide be allowed in certain circumstances, because when disabled people know that they can have assistance to commit suicide, they will wait longer to do so. Might the judge also see this as protecting life for the same (misguided) reason?

Sanctity of Life

Although many people use the terms *sanctity of life* and *respect for life* interchangeably, they can be distinguished in some regards. The former tends to be used by people whose values are primarily based on religious beliefs and who can have even more stringent requirements with regard to what is required to respect human life than those who are anti-euthanasia and use the term *respect for life* to describe the basis for their opposition.

Because the concept of *sanctity of life* is often associated with religion, that association is commonly used to dismiss claims based on it. In contrast, the existence of a "societal consensus" is often argued in support of a claim for legalizing euthanasia. The following passage from the trial judgment is one example that manifests both approaches: "[T]he plaintiffs say that if the purpose of the law is to uphold a particular religious conception of morality [sanctity of life] (about which there is not a consensus in Canadian society), it is an invalid purpose. They suggest that there is a societal consensus supportive of their claim (177) ... [to legalize physician-assisted suicide, namely] that the current line drawn between permissible and impermissible end-of-life care is based upon distinctions that in reality have no practical ethical or moral force" (176). As to a societal consensus alone ethically validating a claim, we should keep in mind that just because a majority supports a certain position does not mean that stance is ethical: democracy is only as ethical as the people who vote. And it is interesting to contemplate that the etymology of "religion" is *religare*, to bind and re-bind together through shared belief – that is, societal consensus.

In assessing the relevance of "the principle of sanctity of life," which Justice Smith finds was "espoused in the *Rodriguez* decision" (300), she takes into account the British Columbia prosecutorial policy for the crime of assisted suicide. This policy sets out the conditions for initiating such prosecutions, which has the effect of limiting them overall. She rules that the policy is relevant for three reasons:

> First, the policy may shed some light on social consensus about the ethics of assisted suicide or euthanasia. Second, the British Columbia policy incorporates by reference accepted medical ethical standards. Finally, the plaintiffs suggest that the prosecution policy marks a significant change since *Rodriguez*. The plaintiffs characterize the B.C. policy as "remarkable" because, they say, it appears to allow for the exercise of discretion not to prosecute a person who has violated the assisted suicide provision and thus to contradict the principle of sanctity of life espoused in the *Rodriguez* decision. (300)

It's important to point out that, as the BC prosecutorial policy accurately states, recognizing "society's interest in protecting the sanctity of human life ... does not require life to be preserved at all costs" (307). In other words, "the prohibition of euthanasia does not imply a commitment to vitalism, namely the doctrine that life should be prolonged at all costs."[50] But not adhering to a value of preserving life no matter the cost is not the same as intentionally inflicting death.

In referring to "sanctity of life" Justice Smith writes that the plaintiffs argue there is "no societal consensus supporting a principle of the absolute sanctity of human life but that there is a societal consensus supporting the principle of a person's autonomy over his or her own body" (167). She accepts this argument and finds that personal choice (autonomy) trumps sanctity of life. In doing so, as pointed out previously, she echoes the assumption on which the reports of both the Royal Society Expert Committee[51] and the Quebec Legislative Assembly[52] are based.

The report of the Committee of the National Assembly of Quebec on "Dying with Dignity" is especially interesting with respect to the concept of sanctity of life. Like Justice Smith, the committee starts from and takes throughout its report a purely utilitarian approach, and as the overriding value, it adopts respect for individuals' rights to autonomy and self-determination, justifying this stance on the basis, among other reasons, of the decline in adherence to religion. The committee writes that "the value of the sanctity of life has undergone a significant transformation"[53] relative to other values, which means that now it doesn't necessarily take priority.

As mentioned above, pro-euthanasia advocates often argue that seeing life as sacred is a religious value and thus should not be taken into account in the public square. The Quebec committee report endorses this view: "Rappelons cependant que dans un État laïque comme le nôtre, les croyances de certains ne sauraient servir de base à l'élaboration d'une législation applicable à tous." I translate this as "However, note that in a secular state like ours, the beliefs of some cannot be the basis for the development of legislation applicable to all." Compare that with the official translation: "Nevertheless, we feel that in a secular society such as ours, the beliefs of some cannot form the basis for broad-based legislation" – which seems to be a less powerful dismissal of religious beliefs.[54]

Although the world's major religions uphold the principle of sanctity of life/respect for life, it is not simply a religious precept. I noted previously that what German philosopher Jurgen Habermas calls "the ethics of the [human] species"[55] and I call "human ethics"[56] also embraces this principle, which must guide secular societies such as Canada. Whatever one's views regarding the value of the sanctity of life/respect for life, it is a foundational value of all societies in which reasonable people would want to live, as the Canadian Charter of Rights and Freedoms recognizes in enshrining it. As is true of the Quebec committee report, the Royal Society report, and the *Carter* judgment, pro-euthanasia advocates dismiss the harm to the value of respect for life, especially respect for human life in general, that legalizing euthanasia would necessarily entail at the societal level.

Justice Smith concludes that "sanctity of life is a principle that is not absolute in our society (it is subject to exceptions such as self-defence) and, while it is central to the value system of a number of religions, that does not settle its place in a secular society" (315). As observed already, the exception of self-defence that the judge mentions does indeed inform the scope of what the value of respect for life requires. The only justification for intentionally taking human life in self-defence is when that is the only reasonably available way to save human life. (The same requirement that human life may only be justifiably taken to save human life is true for "just war"; traditionally for abortion, which was only justified when necessary to save the mother's life; and for capital punishment, which was justified as preventing the condemned person from killing again.[57]) Physician-assisted suicide and euthanasia do not fulfill that requirement.

However, the Supreme Court of Canada opines that while the "sanctity of life is one of our most fundamental societal values [and] Section 7 is rooted in a profound respect for the value of human life ... s. 7 also encompasses life, liberty and security of the person during the passage to death. It is for this reason that the sanctity of life 'is no longer seen to require that all human life be preserved at all costs' (*Rodriguez*, at p. 595, per Sopinka J.). And it is for this reason that the law has come to recognize that, in certain circumstances, an individual's choice about the end of her life is entitled to respect" [63].

In this passage the Supreme Court commingles respect for human life, the value of human life, sanctity of human life, and the preservation of human life; it gives priority to individual autonomy in relation to all of these concepts; and it espouses a moral relativist philosophy in deciding "that, in certain circumstances, an individual's choice about the end of her life is entitled to respect."

Quality of Life

I have already mentioned the concept of *quality of life*, often spoken of as in opposition to *sanctity of life*. One difference between these two concepts is that quality of life is based in moral relativism and utilitarianism (it depends on the circumstances whether life is worth living, and if not, physician-assisted suicide and euthanasia are ethical), and sanctity of life/respect for life is principle based, a belief that all human life has dignity and must not be taken, because it is inherently wrong to do so.

As discussed previously, paradoxically, "quality of life" was initially developed as a concept intended to promote life through the argument that everyone had a right to the resources, especially health-care resources, needed to maintain an acceptable quality of life. Now the concept is used to achieve the opposite outcome: that is, if individuals' quality of life is very poor, they are better off dead or at least do not merit the expenditure of resources to keep them alive.

Although assessment of quality of life is often treated as an objective exercise, we know there is a great deal of subjectivity and discretion involved. Research has shown that health-care professionals assessed patients' quality of life as lower than the patients themselves assessed it;[58] we grade a negative event such as going blind as much worse when we have not experienced it than when we do; and our decisions about hypothetical traumas are not the same as the ones we make when we are faced with those traumas in real life.

To conclude this section, "Values Related to Human Life," both ethics and the law operate on the basis of a presumption in favour of life. This does not mean that life must be preserved at all costs, but it does mean that if our acts or omissions will have an effect of shortening life or not sustaining it, we must be able to justify what we do. In short, the default position in both ethics and law is a presumption in favour of life. Justice Smith's judgment does not reflect that position, and her interpretations of many of the concepts I have discussed show a similar approach. It is an open question whether the same can be said of the Supreme Court's judgment, but it is relevant to recall that the Supreme Court strongly endorses Justice Smith's reasoning and findings.

Looking beyond the Intense Individualism of the *Carter* Case

There is a radical difference between valuing only what we want in relation to our own life and valuing the lives of the generations to follow and deciding what we owe to them and acting accordingly. Legalizing physician-assisted suicide or euthanasia in order to allow personal preferences concerning death to prevail, as Justice Smith and the Supreme Court do in the *Carter* case, is an example of the former. Rejecting physician-assisted suicide or euthanasia because of the harm we believe it would do to individuals, our shared values, societal institutions, society, and future generations is an example of the latter.

Before we legalize assisted suicide or euthanasia, we need to ask ourselves, "If we do that, how might our great-grandchildren die?" and answer honestly.

Physicians and nurses must be sensitive to patients' pain and suffering and meet it with great compassion, but they must do so without intentionally inflicting death. Reducing suffering and inflicting death must never be equated. Physicians' and nurses' absolute rejection of intentionally inflicting death is necessary to maintaining both people's trust in their own physicians and society's trust of the profession of medicine as a whole. This is true in part because physicians and nurses have opportunities to kill that are not open to other people.

Physicians and nurses need to continue to have a clear line that powerfully manifests to them, their patients, and society that they do not inflict death. Both their patients and the public need to know with absolute certainty – and to be able to trust – that is the case. Anything that blurs that line, damages that trust, or makes physicians or nurses less sensitive to primary obligations to protect and respect life is unacceptable. Legalizing physician-assisted suicide or euthanasia does all of these.

Moreover, it is a very important part of the art of medicine to sense and respect the mystery of life and death, to hold this mystery in trust, and to hand it on to future generations – including future generations of physicians. We must consider deeply whether legalizing physician-assisted suicide or euthanasia would threaten this art, this trust, and this legacy. I believe it would.

The "euthanasia debate" is a momentous one. It involves our individual and collective past (the ethical, legal, and cultural norms handed down to us as members of families, groups, and societies); the present (whether we will change those norms); and the future (the impact that this would have on those who come after us). We need a much broader analysis and a great deal more thought before we go down the path that Justice Smith and the Supreme Court of Canada map out in the *Carter* case.

Essential and important as the consideration of individual suffering is, the central issue in the *Carter* case is not just what compassion for Ms Taylor and others in her situation might lead people to recommend

– people who do not have ethical or moral problems with physician-assisted suicide or euthanasia, who, it appears, include Justice Smith and the nine judges of the Supreme Court. The central issue is whether we will abandon some of the foundational values of our Canadian society. If we are going to do that, at the least we should explicitly recognize that is what we are doing. At both the trial stage and in the Supreme Court, the *Carter* judgments are, with respect, a total failure in that regard.

◆◆◆

In this chapter I have explored the interaction of ethics, law, and suffering by focusing on the *Carter* case and how it deals with the issues of physician-assisted suicide and euthanasia. I have taken this approach because I believe that what our societies decide about legalizing these interventions will be for them a defining event of the first half of the twenty-first century.

In making those decisions, to repeat yet again an important warning, we need to keep in mind an old saying in human rights: "Nowhere are human rights more threatened than when we act purporting to do only good." The good that we hope to realize can blind us to the harms and risks also unavoidably involved in doing that good. When the good we seek is the relief of serious suffering, our moral intuition that it is wrong to intentionally kill another human being can be overwhelmed. Such intuitions are important guides in making good ethical decisions.[59] And while we ignore our feelings at our ethical peril,[60] our emotional reactions to an individual's suffering need to become "examined emotions," if we are to avoid the danger of their misleading us ethically.[61] In other words, we need to be careful that legitimate feelings of empathy and compassion for suffering individuals don't trump facts about the risks and harms of legalized euthanasia.

By arguing against physician-assisted suicide and euthanasia, I am proposing that there are and should be ethical and legal limits to our freedom to alleviate suffering and that these interventions are not legitimate means of doing so. Just as the concept of "freedom in fetters" tells us that we must restrict freedom to some extent to protect and maintain the conditions that make freedom possible, so we must restrict what we do to relieve suffering to ensure that we protect and maintain the shared values that are necessary if we are not to risk creating a society in which no reasonable person would want to live.

These limits mean that within bioethics and biolaw we must position our moral and legal obligations to relieve suffering so that they are consistent with upholding respect for human life, at the level of both the individual person and human life in general at the societal level. Fortunately, we have new tools to relieve suffering that will help us to achieve that balance. The unprecedented powers of the new medicine and science often face us with additional serious ethical difficulties; in relation to relieving pain and suffering, the opposite is true. Research is providing us with means never before available to help those who need our help to relieve their pain and suffering.

For millennia, our kinds of societies have prohibited euthanasia and assisted suicide. Why then, now, when there is nothing new about the circumstances in which these interventions are called for and there is so much more we can do to relieve suffering, do we think that intentionally inflicting death is a good response to suffering? A wise answer to that question requires much thought.[62] What would be the long-term impact of death by euthanasia becoming the norm? How would that normalization affect the way in which we view and treat people who are old and vulnerable, or have disabilities? We must address these and many other questions before changing the law to allow the intentional infliction of death.

I hope that my analysis of the *Carter* case in this chapter has served to show that we cannot overemphasize the gravity of the situation we now face as a result of the Supreme Court of Canada's decision. What this decision represents is not an evolution in the foundational values that bind us together as a society, but a revolution, a radical departure from upholding the value of respect for life. That value implements the belief and practice that we must not intentionally kill another human being. To allow it constitutes radical change, not only for individual Canadians but also for the institutions of both law and medicine: the law is changed to allow killing, and physicians are authorized to carry it out. In a secular society such as Canada, law and medicine carry the value of respect for life for the society as a whole. Their capacity to do so in Canada is seriously damaged by the *Carter* decision, which is primarily focused on what individuals want: that is, on individual autonomy and self-determination.

Making euthanasia and assisted suicide part of medical practice is not, as pro-euthanasia advocates claim and the trial judge and Supreme Court agreed, a small incremental change consistent with interventions that we accept as ethical and legal, such as honouring patients' refusals of life-support treatment that allow them to die. Allowing physicians to inflict death on their patients is different in kind, not just different in degree, from other interventions we accept as ethical and legal. Moreover, legalizing euthanasia represents a seismic shift in our fundamental societal values, not just another step on a path we've already taken. For 2,400 years, consistent with the Hippocratic Oath, euthanasia has never been characterized as a medical treatment. It should not be now. Indeed, if it is legalized, it should be kept out of medicine.

To repeat my warning in the preface, just as we now realize that our actions could destroy our physical ecosystem and we must hold it in trust for future generations, we must likewise hold our metaphysical ecosystem – the collection of values, principles, beliefs, attitudes, shared stories, and so on that bind us together as a society – in trust for them. In this regard, there is no more important value than respect for life. That value requires that we always react to pain and suffering with deep compassion and assistance to relieve it, but that we kill the pain and suffering, not the person with the pain and suffering.[63]

It bears repeating: we must consider the values that we should hold in trust for future generations if they are to inherit a world in which reasonable people would want to live. I believe that history will see what we decide about "physician inflicted death" as a defining ethical-legal-societal event of the twenty-first century.

5

Is Every Life Beautiful?

When I was invited to speak at the University of Toronto, Crystal Mason, the communications officer for the Current Affairs Exchange Forum (CAFEX), one of the student groups sponsoring the event, suggested that in my remarks I should address the question, "Is every life beautiful?" My first response was along these lines:

"Is every life beautiful? My concern is that my answer might be 'no,' but that doesn't mean that every human life does not deserve respect or that any human life lacks dignity. And it really depends on how we define what constitutes beauty."

For a person who is experiencing deep suffering, life is certainly not beautiful in the usual sense of the word. But while I recognize that we must not romanticize suffering and the serious dangers of doing so, the suffering person can remain beautiful, and beautiful outcomes can result from suffering, as many people who have suffered and even those who still are suffering try to explain to us.

I then wondered whether John Keats's closing lines of "Ode on a Grecian Urn" might give us a clue to understanding this: "'Beauty is truth, truth beauty' – that is all / Ye know on earth, and all ye need to know." Perhaps suffering can put us in touch with deep truths and thereby with a form of beauty. Certainly, I think suffering is the most difficult reality to deal with in terms of giving it worth or meaning, at least in the absence of religion, and something that is very traumatic and in which we can find no meaning is difficult to characterize as beautiful. While musing on the conundrum of suffering and beauty, I came across some words of Confucius (551–479 BC) that might provide insight regarding whether every life, even a suffering life, can be beautiful – that is, could help us to reconcile suffering with beauty, to see that beauty can be present despite suffering. Confucius said: "Everything has beauty, though not everyone sees it."

If beauty and truth are linked (as Keats says), might Confucius be saying that everything (including suffering) can help us to see the truth? And, moreover, if we see as beautiful everything (especially truth) that can help us to find meaning in life, might everything have beauty in that sense? And in "not everyone sees the beauty," might Confucius be saying that not everyone finds the truth and meaning present in everything, whether through positive or negative experience?

The thoughts of the Swiss Jesuit Hans Urs von Balthasar who wrote on theological aesthetics (a theology based upon contemplation of the good, the beautiful, and the true) might also lead us to relevant insights with regard to whether all life is beautiful. One of von Balthasar's most-quoted passages is: "Before the beautiful – no, not really *before* but *within* the beautiful – the whole person quivers. He not only 'finds' the beautiful moving; rather, he experiences himself as being moved and possessed by it."[1]

It seems that von Balthasar sees beauty as part of the essence of God and therefore the experience of beauty as a spiritual one. Moreover, if one believes that God is also the source of all life, one could conclude that all life is beautiful, as God would not create life contrary to his own nature.

Seeing life as beautiful is extremely important, because whether we do or do not affects our attitudes and values, which in turn affect what we see as ethical or unethical in relation to, for instance, dying people and euthanasia and assisted suicide, people (especially old people) with disabilities, the transmission of human life through reproductive technologies, the taking of human life with abortion, and so on.

Whether we see life as beautiful also depends on what factors we take into account in assessing beauty. Very often physical beauty is the predominant or even the only consideration. In that case, especially in a culture that is overwhelmingly youth oriented, it's easy to understand why elderly people and those with disabilities can be characterized as not beautiful, even ugly.

On the contrary, if we see wisdom, intellectual curiosity, openness of mind, excitement in learning and understanding, courage, wise ethical restraint, generosity of spirit, a sense of humour in its meaning of balance, and so on as characteristics that mark out the beautiful person, who we see as beautiful will be quite different.

Beauty is also linked to value and respect. What we see as beautiful we regard as valuable, and probably vice versa, and we respect what we see as beautiful and valuable. This explains our outrage at the willful destruction of priceless works of art, especially if that art also has deep religious significance, as, for instance, in the case of the sixth-century Bamiyan Buddhas carved into the cliffs in the Hazarajat region of central Afghanistan, which were intentionally destroyed by the Taliban.

The linking of beauty, high value, and respect raises the question of what human characteristics we value. Does recognizing people's value and respecting them, in particular their right to life, depend on seeing them as beautiful? In other words, is respect for the person contingent on seeing them as valuable and beautiful? A positive answer to that question is an extremely dangerous idea, which I will shortly explore further. Here, I'd like simply to make the point that even if we don't see a person as beautiful, that does not mean that they lack value or dignity or that they don't deserve respect.

In the rest of this chapter I'd like to look at some examples in which the idea that "all life is beautiful" is under serious challenge. These examples will be familiar, as they have all been in the news lately. They include the issues I have already mentioned: abortion, euthanasia, prenatal screening, reproductive technologies, health-care costs, an aging population, and so on. I suggest that the common feature linking people with values on one side of these issues, and distinguishing them from people with values on the other side, is whether or not they believe that "all life is beautiful" – in the sense that all human life has intrinsic dignity and must be respected.

But first let us look at an approach that those who do not believe that all human life is beautiful, in the sense I have just defined, are putting forward to promote their view.

What Is Presently the World's Most Dangerous Idea?

The greatest evil is not recognizing other humans as humans.
– comment on PBS *Frontline* on the tenth anniversary of 9/11

I mention in previous chapters being asked by a newspaper editor for an article responding to the question "What do I believe is presently the world's most dangerous idea?" My answer was, "The idea that there is nothing special about being human and, therefore, humans do not deserve 'special respect,' as compared with other animals or even robots." This response might seem anodyne and a cop-out, but I would like to try to convince you otherwise.

Whether humans are "special" – a concept sometimes referred to as human exceptionalism or uniqueness – and therefore deserve "special respect" is a controversial and central question in bioethics, and how we answer it will have a major impact on many important ethical issues.[2] In short, not seeing human beings and human life as deserving of "special respect" has broad and serious impact for individuals, institutions, and society. It could affect matters ranging from respect for human rights to justifications for armed conflict, the way we treat prisoners, the way we run our health-care and aged persons' care systems, what we will allow or prohibit with respect to euthanasia or reproductive technologies, the ethical and legal tones of our societies, and so on.

Although all living beings deserve respect, which certainly excludes cruelty to animals, traditionally, humans have been given "special respect," which brings with it special protections, especially of life. In practice, we have implemented this special respect through the idea of personhood, which embodies two related concepts: all humans are persons, and no animals are persons. But the concept of "universal human personhood" – the idea that all humans deserve special respect simply because they are human – and the exclusion of all animals from personhood are both being challenged.

Some philosophers are arguing that humans should be regarded as just another animal, which results in a loss of special respect for human beings. Others argue that at least certain animals should be regarded as persons in order to give them the same rights and protections as humans, which results in the same outcome, a loss of special respect for human beings.

Humans Are Just Another Animal

Peter Singer, a Princeton philosopher, takes the former approach. He believes that distinguishing humans from other animals and, as a result, treating animals differently from humans, is a form of wrongful discrimination he calls "speciesism."[3] In short, he rejects the claim that humans deserve special respect. Rather, he believes the respect owed to a living being should depend only on avoiding suffering to it, not on whether or not the being is human.[4]

That means that what we do not do to humans in order not to inflict suffering on them, we should not do to animals; and what we do to animals to relieve their suffering and regard as ethical, we should also do for humans. We don't eat humans; therefore we shouldn't eat animals. We allow euthanasia for suffering animals; therefore we should allow it for suffering humans. This is the informing principle of the pro-euthanasia argument "You love your dog and euthanize it to relieve its suffering, so you should do the same for people you love."

Animals as Non-Human Persons

To implement this "equal treatment" of humans and animals, other philosophers have proposed that at least some animals should be regarded as persons. They do this on the basis that the attribution of personhood should not depend on being human but on having certain characteristics or capacities to function in certain ways. They argue that animals that are self-conscious and intelligent and that have free will and emotions comparable to those of humans should be treated as non-human persons.[5]

Correlatively, these philosophers argue that some humans who lack the characteristics on the basis of which some animals are designated as persons should not be characterized as persons. They propose that for humans to be considered persons, they must be self-aware, have a sense of their history and, perhaps, of a future, and possess a capacity to relate to others.

Consequently, it is a logical application of this approach that these philosophers believe that humans who lack these characteristics – for instance, disabled babies with no potential to develop them, and seriously mentally disabled adult humans – humans who are among the most vulnerable and most in-need members of our societies, are not persons; therefore they are not entitled to the protections that personhood brings, such as respect for their right to life. We could ponder whether such thinking has been adopted in the Netherlands where the Groningen protocol sets out the conditions on which parents of disabled newborn babies can give consent to their child being euthanized in the first year of life. It certainly applies to the two bioethicists who created a storm of outrage around the world by arguing that infanticide, which they called "post-birth abortion," can be justified.[6]

In summary, both the "humans are just another animal" camp of philosophers and the "animals are non-human persons" camp believe that humans are not special and do not deserve special respect simply because they are human, and that some animals could deserve greater respect than some humans.

One way to gain insights into these philosophers' approach, and to contrast it with that of those of us who disagree with them, is through the lens of the question "Is all life beautiful?" As I observe above, what we see as beautiful we see as valuable and meriting protection, and we are appalled by its intentional destruction. If we see each human life as beautiful and valuable, as having intrinsic dignity just because it is human, we will protect all human lives on that basis.

However, if we require human life to exhibit certain characteristics before we see it as beautiful and valuable, if we see it as not having dignity in itself but only if we confer that dignity, we will not protect human life that does not have the characteristics we demand.

Wider Impacts of Loss of Human Exceptionalism

Vulnerable humans are placed in serious danger by this idea that simply being human does not mean one deserves special respect but rather that the respect owed to a "being" depends on its having certain attributes. The concept could lead to situations of robots being seen as deserving of greater respect than humans, or the ethical restrictions on what we may do to change human life becoming inoperative.

People who believe that the kind and degree of respect owed to an entity depends on its intelligence argue that some super-intelligent robots will deserve more respect than humans. They define intelligence narrowly as logical, cognitive mentation, and for them these robots are more "intelligent" than any humans. This approach has far-reaching and serious implications well beyond the degree of respect that should be shown to an individual human as compared with an individual robot.

If there is nothing special about being human, there is no "essence of our humanness" that we must hold in trust for future generations. That means we are free to use the new technoscience, as the transhumanists advocate, to alter humans so that they become "posthuman," that is, not human at all, as we know it. In other words, there would be many less or perhaps no ethical barriers to seeking the transhumanists' "utopian" goal, that "humans will become an obsolete model." This goal would be achieved through our redesigning ourselves using technoscience – or perhaps robots doing so; instead of our designing them, they would redesign us. It is interesting to note that Francis Fukuyama believes that transhumanism is the world's most dangerous idea.[7]

Implementing and maintaining special respect for humans requires that we recognize, as I've discussed (in chapter 3), that all humans have innate human dignity which must be respected and that we regard as unethical interventions on humans that contravene that dignity. Such interventions include designing our children, making a baby from artificial sperm or ova or from two same-sex people, creating human-animal hybrids, cloning humans, using human embryos as a "manufacturing plant" to produce therapeutic agents for the rest of us, euthanasia, and, with the new neuroscience, perhaps most worrying of all, designing or controlling our minds or intervening in them in certain ways. The field being called neuroethics, which is emerging in response to the new neuroscience, is just at its beginnings.

Can Life Be Beautiful in the Context of Suffering?

I turn now to a very difficult question: Can life be beautiful in the context of suffering? Our answer will depend on whether we can find meaning in suffering. Those who can find meaning will answer "yes"; those who cannot will answer "no." The two examples that I will explore briefly in relation to this question are abortion and euthanasia.

I suggest that euthanasia and abortion are perceived as appropriate responses to suffering – in the case of euthanasia, when the life of the suffering person is seen as "not beautiful," because no meaning can be found in its continuance; in the case of abortion, when the life of the fetus is seen as "not beautiful" for causing the woman's suffering, and no meaning can be found in the unborn child's preservation. The common feature in euthanasia and abortion is that eliminating a life is seen as an appropriate response to eliminating the ugliness of suffering and the distress and fear it engenders.

Is There a Connection between Euthanasia and Not Seeing Life as Beautiful?

In our youth-obsessed culture, old people are often perceived as losing their beauty. This loss is frequently connected with an emphasis on physical beauty. It is also linked to materialism and consumerism, with old people being equated to worn-out products, a phenomenon discussed in previous chapters. The same can be true for people with disabilities. All these people are vulnerable members of society, and vulnerable people are most at risk from euthanasia, were it to be legalized.

Language matters in determining what we perceive as beautiful or ugly, and that perception can affect what we see as ethical or unethical and, as a result, how we treat people. For example, when we speak of "the aged," as compared with "old people" or "elderly people," we dehumanize them. And we can think of other intentionally demeaning terms for old people such as "crumbles," "the grey tsunami," and even "geezers." We only drop the word "person" or "people" when we are using a denigrating characterization; for instance, we speak of "mental incompetents" but not "mental competents"; rather, we speak of "mentally competent people." Likewise, we speak of criminals, juvenile delinquents, the dying, the terminally ill, or, most recently, the "end-of-life population." In French, we use the horrible word *sidatiques* to refer to people with HIV infection or AIDS (SIDA, *le syndrome d'immunodéficience acquise*).

We need to consider why we use such language. I propose it is to distance ourselves from what we see in the old person that we can't accept in ourselves – our own fragility and vulnerability. We identify with the old person and think "This could be me" or, "This will be me," and we disidentify from them through labelling language that places them in a different category of human beings from us. Then we can treat them in a way we would never want to be treated ourselves, without, we believe, setting a precedent that could apply to us. It is to implement the double-negative formulation of the Golden Rule: Do not do unto others what you would not want done to yourself.

To the extent that we see terminally ill people as having lost their dignity and that state as a form of loss of beauty, indeed, of ugliness, then euthanasia can be seen, as it is by its proponents, as putting people out of their undignified, ugly state of existence. Euphemizing language is often used to describe euthanasia in this context. It is characterized as a "merciful act of clinical care," not "doctors killing their patients." The former phrase elicits a certain sense that a beautiful act is involved; the latter does the opposite. The language used in the context of death and dying affects how we see the ethics of end-of-life decision-making, especially euthanasia.

I have addressed elsewhere the question of why western secular societies now think that legalizing euthanasia is a good idea and necessary, when they have rejected it for millennia.[8] I have argued that we must identify the factors that give rise to people's calls for euthanasia and address these. The other way to describe such an enquiry is: What can we do to make life as beautiful as possible in the context of dying and death so that euthanasia is rejected by dying persons and those who love them?

Dying alone or unloved seems to be a universal human fear. In democratic western societies, many people have a sense of loss of family and community: relationships between intimates have been converted into relationships between strangers.[9] That loss has had a major impact on the circumstances in which we die.

As I noted in chapter 1, death has been professionalized, technologized, depersonalized, and dehumanized. Life is not experienced as beautiful when facing those realities that make euthanasia seem an attractive option. Euthanasia can be seen as a response to "intense premortem loneliness."[10] Yet a powerful way to remedy such a reality is to provide easily accessible, good palliative medicine and care. To do so benefits not only the dying person but also their loved ones, in that it assuages the suffering of everyone. The death of the person is much more likely to be seen as a "good death," even in some cases as beautiful.

This possibility leads to a question of whether the strongest argument against euthanasia might relate not to death but to life: that normalizing euthanasia would destroy a sense of the unfathomable mystery of life and seriously damage our human spirit, especially our capacity to find meaning in life. Euthanasia pulls the plug on the potential to grow in deeply human ways that dying people and those who love or are caring for them can experience.

Death itself is not beautiful, but we can find meaning, value, and respect in the context of dying. In that sense, the last great act of life – dying – can be experienced as beautiful by both the dying person and those they love and who love them.

Is There a Connection between Not Seeing Life as Beautiful and Selecting and "Deselecting" Our Children through Prenatal Testing and Abortion?

An area where there is intense conflict as to whether or not "all life is beautiful" is in relation to unborn children and abortion. Fortunately, in my view, it seems that there is increasing moral discomfort among young people about abortion, always an explosive topic. Let's look at prenatal testing undertaken in order to allow a woman to decide whether or not to have an abortion. Do certain test results cause the pregnant woman to see the unborn child as "not beautiful," such that it should be killed?[11]

Prenatal testing and screening

A headline in a Danish newspaper boldly announced "Plans to Make Denmark a Down Syndrome-Free Perfect Society."[12] The accompanying article reported: "Denmark has decided not to listen to people who may complain of human selection and have put their foot on the ground to promote increased abortion of foetuses suspected of having Down syndrome. As such, if progress [*sic*] continues at this rate, the last case to be born with the illness will be around the year 2030, according Danish newspaper Berlingske."

It continued: Niels Uldbjerg, an Aarhus University bioethicist, "describes it as a 'fantastic achievement' that the number of newborns with Down syndrome is approaching zero." The article continues: "'What's next? Is the child born with diabetes ... [to] be discarded?' asks Ulla Brendstrup, the mother of a child with Down syndrome." Lillian Bondo, a member of the Denmark Ethics Committee and also chair of the Danish association of midwives, told Berlingske she "wants to help as many people as possible to discuss how society should draw the line. I do not want a society in which sorting by [testing] is the norm."

Whatever our views on this issue, at least the Danes are bringing it into the open and being more honest about it than we are in Canada. Current estimates are that in North America over 85 percent of unborn babies with Down syndrome are aborted. Importantly, the Danes are also recognizing that "deselecting" Down syndrome children – or any other group who, likewise, are chosen for elimination – raises issues for society and is not just a matter of private decision-making by individuals.

Riots involving very large numbers of people, such as those in England and France in recent times, provide an analogy: a very large number acting aggressively or rioting is different in kind, not just degree, of one person or a very small group of people doing so, although both situations may raise many similar ethical and legal issues. The same is true of individuals "choosing" their children. So what limits should we place on their doing so in the interests of society and the harmful impact it would have on our shared values? Should there be any legally imposed limits?

The ethics issues raised by prenatal screening will only become more prevalent as the range of tests expands, as they become safer for the pregnant woman and cheaper and easier to use, and as many are presented as routine precautions in medically managing a pregnancy. Prenatal testing can now identify a baby's sex at seven weeks of pregnancy,[13] raising fears of sex selection (discussed below), which many people regard as unethical, at least when not carried out for serious medical reasons. Widespread publicly endorsed and paid-for prenatal screening to eliminate people with certain conditions, for instance, Down syndrome, implicates among other values those of respect for individual human life and for human life in general and respect for people with disabilities, both as individuals and as a group. The implementation of negative eugenics with respect to people with disabilities is the unavoidable collective impact of these screening-based decisions. As harsh as the language is, we can describe screening as a "search and destroy" mission to wipe out certain groups of people whose lives or existence are seen as "not beautiful."

And where might supporting such screening lead a society? For instance, what would endorsing a belief that a society without people with disabilities can be considered "perfect" say about us? What kind of society might it result in? History teaches us that the use of science in the search for human perfection has been at the root of some of the greatest atrocities in terms of respect for human life, individual humans, and human rights.

Offering prenatal screening as a routine procedure communicates a message that a woman is conditionally pregnant until she is told there is "nothing wrong" with the baby – until the fetus is certified as "normal" – or it is the "right sex," or perfect, or beautiful. This approach contravenes our concept of parental love – that it is unconditional, that we love our children simply because they are our children.

The societal-level message we will unavoidably be delivering is "We don't want you in our society unless you measure up to a certain genetic or other standard. You are only a potential member until you've passed the admission test that we are willing to pay for with our tax dollars and implement. You are not beautiful enough for us!"

And what about the "everyday ethics" involved in screening? Certainly not all physicians are competent to obtain informed consent to these tests and carry out follow-up genetic counselling. Physicians tend to be pessimistic in predicting the impact of, for instance, Down syndrome on the child and to see no benefits from having such a child. They can be astonished to learn of the joy, bonding, and love that such a child can bring to a family.

And, how will women who refuse screening be regarded? What will be the impact on families who "choose" not to abort when "abnormalities" are discovered? Will they be seen as socially irresponsible? That belief in itself creates a climate of coercion not to proceed with the pregnancy.

One cause of their and our ignorance is that the people who could inform them and us otherwise are not listened to or silenced. Audrey Cole, a remarkable Canadian who advocates for the rights of people with disabilities and who is the mother of a fifty-year-old man with Down syndrome, wrote to me: "Our voice [against eliminating people with Down syndrome] will, inevitably, be dismissed as the whinings of a 'special interest' group. I have never been able to understand why my feelings as a parent of a wonderful, caring, gentle man can be so easily dismissed as 'special interest.' I am frightened of the times that seem to be coming."[14]

Perhaps in deciding about the ethics of prenatal screening and the law that should govern it, we should recall that with contemporary medical diagnostic technology it is true for all of us that "the well are only the undiagnosed sick" and be thankful that no one "deselected" us.

Sex-Selection Abortion

Sex-selection abortion focuses on the fetus. In the vast majority of cases, it involves unborn girl babies being seen as not beautiful and unborn boy babies being seen as beautiful. In other words, perceptions of an unborn child's beauty or otherwise can depend on its sex.

Over 100,000 abortions take place each year in Canada, which, uniquely among western democracies, has no law restricting access to the procedure. Abortion is legal throughout pregnancy, although the vast majority of physicians will not carry it out after viability of the fetus (the time at which the fetus has a chance of living outside the womb, which the Canadian Medical Association sets at twenty weeks gestation), except for serious medical reasons. Other exceptions to the twenty-week limit do occur, however, and are probably not uncommon. If a woman wants an abortion, she may have an abortion, whatever her reason for her decision. And pro-choice advocates argue that that's how it should be, as women have the right "to absolute reproductive freedom." That right means that abortion is a private matter between a woman and her physician, just another medical decision; it is nobody else's business and certainly not society's or the law's. The fetus is "just a bunch of cells," part of the woman's body, not a separate being, a "parasite" she is entitled have removed.

The one exception some feminist pro-choice advocates used to allow to the absolutist pro-choice position – namely, that there should be no law recognizing the existence of a fetus or unborn child – was a legal prohibition on sex selection. They agreed to this because the vast majority of fetuses aborted on the grounds that they were of the "wrong" sex were female. Feminist pro-choice advocates labelled this "female feticide" or "gendercide." But more recently, because they do not want to endorse the legitimacy of any restriction on abortion in order to give "a woman's right to choose" absolute priority without exceptions, some of these advocates have adopted the position that sex selection should not be illegal. The absence of any restrictions not only makes abortion more accessible but sends a message and establishes a cultural value that having an abortion is "no big deal," as one woman expressed it, which is consistent with pro-choice ideology.

In stark contrast, the Parliament of the Council of Europe passed a resolution on 3 October 2011 urging its member states to prohibit sex selection "in the context of assisted reproduction technologies and legal abortion, except when it is justified to avoid a serious hereditary disease." In its resolution, the Council of Europe, which includes forty-seven countries on the European continent, cited sex selection as "a huge problem" in some Asian countries, and said it had reached "worrying proportions" in the European member states of Albania, Armenia, and Azerbaijan. Georgia was also cited as a country that should be investigated for such practices by the UN Committee on the Elimination of Discrimination against Women. The results of a September 2011 telephone poll of two thousand

Canadians carried out by Environics Research reflect the same rejection. In their analysis, the pollsters noted "an astonishing 92% of Canadians thought sex selection abortions should be illegal in Canada."

Why is there this huge fuss about sex-selection abortion? If a woman can have an abortion for any reason or none, why not because a baby of the opposite sex is strongly preferred? The reason is, as sex-selection abortion most clearly demonstrates, that abortion is not just a private matter. The issue involves shared societal values, cultural norms, and clashes of cultural values and shows that the cumulative impact of abortion has societal consequences.

Pro-choice advocates have long proposed that women having unfettered access to abortion should be the litmus test of whether a society has respect for women and their rights. They argue that this access is required to protect women's rights to autonomy and self-determination, and to protect their dignity. Ironically, however, sex-selection abortion is overwhelmingly the expression of a lack of respect for women in cultures where sons are highly valued and daughters are massively devalued.

Sex-selection abortion also shifts the analytic, ethical, and legal spotlight from the pregnant woman (who is the basis of the pro-choice case) to the unwanted fetus (which is normally ignored in the pro-choice analysis). This shift happens because in sex selection, unlike probably most other abortions, the woman wants a baby, just not a girl baby. With this change of focus to the fetus, we see abortion in a different ethical and legal light.

As is true in all ethical decision-making, our choice of language in relation to abortion is also important, because it can affect our moral intuitions and emotional responses, which factor into how we see abortion's ethical acceptability. As mentioned already, sex-selection abortions are often referred to as "female feticide" or "gendercide" – both emotionally evocative terms. But all abortions are feticide: why don't we refer to them as such? Consider also that seeing someone or something as beautiful or ugly is also an emotional response and perhaps an intuitive one; it too affects how we see the ethics involved.

And sex-selection abortion makes most clear that, cumulatively, abortion decisions have an impact on society and are not just a private matter. It is estimated that there are at least 160 million missing girls in India and China as a result of sex-selection abortion and female infanticide.[15] In one Indian study in which 7,000 consecutive abortions were followed, 6,997 were of female fetuses. In some areas of China, there are 160 young men for every 100 girls. The practice is harmful to both sexes: women are devalued, treated as objects, abused, and harmed, and men cannot find wives.[16]

An editorial suggestion in the *Canadian Medical Association Journal* that the way to handle sex-selection abortion in Canada is to withhold information on the sex of the baby until thirty weeks gestation is neither feasible nor ethical.[17] A baby's sex can be determined at seven weeks of gestation with a blood sample from the mother, and in general people have an ethical and legal right to know the information a physician generates about their condition.

Moreover, testing unborn children for sex is only the tip of the prenatal testing iceberg. Tests for many other conditions are available and more are coming fast. Much as some politicians, including the Canadian prime minister, Stephen Harper, protest against doing so, Parliament must start discussing abortion. How may prenatal tests be used and how should they not be used? What law governing abortion should be put in place to ensure that the values we want to enshrine regarding the use of these tests are respected? These issues affect some of the most important values on which we base our Canadian society. And they are not going away.

Is There a Connection between Seeing Life as Not Beautiful Enough in Its Natural State and Designing Our Children?

Assisted Reproductive Technologies

Many assisted reproductive technologies are used to repair nature when it fails. Such uses are not my focus here. And I have raised elsewhere questions that include what designing a child means for that child and the experience of living his or her life. I've pointed out that such a child is neither free to create an authentic self nor equal to the designer,[18] that the use of such technology contravenes the value that parental love is unconditional and converts the child to the status of a product and an object. If cloning were involved, the ethical issues would multiply exponentially, as they do with the use of technologically manufactured gametes (sperm and ova) to enable two men or two women or more than two parents to have a shared genetic baby.

Here, however, I want to look briefly at the use of reproductive technologies as enhancement technologies to create "super children" in a search for the "perfect child," a process that reflects an attitude that life is not beautiful enough in its natural state. What is the link between perfection and beauty, or between the searches for them? How perfect do we want to be? Let's look at the transhumanists' answer.

Transhumanism

Transhumanists believe that the info-bio-nano-robotic-AI (artificial intelligence) technology revolutions will converge to alter the fundamental nature of being human. We and all our most important values and beliefs will be changed beyond recognition. For transhumanists, being human is not the end of evolution but the beginning. Technoscience provides them with a strong "No" to the existential question, "Is this all there is?" Transhumanists are techno-utopians. They want to do good – as they put it, to expand technological opportunities for humans to live longer and healthier lives and to enhance their intellectual, physical, psychological and emotional capacities.

That sounds fine. But the ultimate goal is articulated more fully in a transhumanist website, Incipientposthuman.com, which speaks of "unprecedented physical, intellectual, and psychological capacity," of being "potentially immortal" and "a person who no longer can be classified usefully with homo sapiens" as a result of having "undergone sweeping modifications to inherited genetics, physiology, neurophysiology and neurochemistry." Transhumanists and I have completely different and contradictory views of what it means to be human and what obligations that entails.

We must have profound respect for the natural, especially for human nature. And we must have strong justification for interfering with it. We must not radically change natural human nature so as to destroy its essential essence. The "science without limits" camp will dismiss this view as anti-science. It is not; rather, it works from a premise that we must be able to justify what we do with science. Not everything can be justified, even when it might do great good.

That said, humankind is already taking incremental steps toward what some people might characterize as a posthuman future. We used to see ourselves as an integral whole from birth to death (perhaps missing a few parts from accidents or surgery). With transplants, we accepted a modular theory of human identity: Interchangeable Parts 'R' Us. Technology has changed our perceptions of our bodies. For example, older people see cellphones as items to be used; younger people see them as an extension of the ear. Enhancing our bodies through cosmetic surgery and our psychology through mood-altering drugs is now regarded as routine, normal, and beneficial. The transhumanists argue that what they envision are just the next steps down these same paths – yet another justification for radical change based on an incrementalism argument.

Transhumanists are great optimists: they foresee physical immortality. They currently propose that it is possible to prolong human life to around 150 years – including by retarding the aging process at early and mid-life stages. Needless to say, it is difficult to persuade people not to seek such a goal. We all want to live with a high quality of life for as long as we can. But no lesser person than physician-philosopher Leon Kass, a former chair of the US President's Commission on Bioethics, has argued against radical life extension. "Human life without death would be something other than human," he says; consciousness of mortality gives rise to our deepest longings and greatest accomplishments.

The issue of prolonging the human lifespan is intentionally front and centre on the pro-technology agenda, because if, as we will be sorely tempted to do, we accept radical life extension, then why not cloning? Why not designing our children, reproducing entirely by artificial means. enhancing our intelligence with computer chip implants – even eventually being superceded by robots infinitely more intelligent and durable than we are?

Whether or not we agree with the transhumanists, they are doing us a major service in making us aware of the enormity the new technoscience could effect. They see no reason why the future development of human nature should be limited to traditional humanistic methods like education and culture. They want us to use technology to discover and create our authentic (technological) selves. You and I, flawed natural humans, are what the posthumanists will call "un-debugged humans," unmodified by technology to improve us. The transhumanists assure us that we will be able to get these upgrades at an affordable cost (or for free).

But, inevitably, the affluent and educated will be more able to avail themselves of such choices. Also disquieting is the fact that more men than women seem interested in such offers. Not only are the members of the board of the World Transhumanist Association mostly men, but 90 per cent of the members of the world's various transhumanist organizations are male. Many are American, white, highly educated, and under forty-five years of age. What new divides does this portend, not only between the sexes but between rich and poor, North and South?

In chapter 1 I argued that people in postmodern societies tend to be uncomfortable with mystery, even frightened by it. We respond by converting mysteries to problems and seeking technological solutions. Men might do so more than women, because many men dislike just talking about problems; they want solutions, and often prefer technological ones. From this perspective, as I also proposed previously, euthanasia – say, by lethal injection – can be seen as a technological response to the mystery of death converted to the problem of death.

Transhumanism might function in the same way with respect to the mystery of life. Will it prove to be a lethal injection to our deepest sense of what it means to be human and our ability to find meaning in life? In seeking immortality and other godlike attributes, we risk our very humanity.

The Search for Perfection in our Children

What would we lose in the search for perfection? The quest for perfection in our children, if not in ourselves, is flawed, especially when pursued through technological means.[19] Technology can eliminate many human imperfections, but we risk losing that messy quality that is the essence of our humanness.

When I went to school, all children wore school uniforms that included a sweater. It was navy blue with two narrow stripes – one red, the other gold – in a band around the V-shaped neckline. Most of us had working-class parents, and most wore sweaters hand-knitted by their mothers. Mine was made by my aunt.

Then machine-knitted sweaters became available. They were more closely woven, smoother, immensely more fashionable, and much more expensive than the old hand-knitted ones. They were perfect. I wanted one, but my mother refused. I envied my sweater-privileged friends and felt humiliated to be so ill-attired.

Today, mass-produced sweaters are relatively inexpensive, whereas anything hand-knitted costs hundreds of dollars. The latter often carry a small ticket saying that imperfections are part of the art and character of the garment; that is, these imperfections are desirable and valued because they make it unique. They are evidence that the sweater is the time-consuming, painstaking, often loving, authentic work of human hands. They give it its "soul."

My musings about sweaters were prompted by thinking about the use of science in the search for human perfection. It is often said that nowhere are we at more ethical peril than when we undertake such quests. As I wrote in chapter 3 in exploring the concept of human dignity, the Nazi horrors showed us the dangers of a political platform or public policy approach that uses science and technology to search for perceived biological "perfection" in ourselves and in society as a whole. I also pointed out the augmented ethical dangers opened up by new technoscience when it is used to search for "human perfection" through positive and negative eugenics. Further, I suggested that the calls to legalize euthanasia and assisted suicide could be linked to seeking both to achieve the perfect death and to eliminate imperfect people.

A very important question we need to ask in deciding what we may and should not do with our new technoscience (that is, what is ethical or unethical) is: Does the proposed use of this science in search of human perfection damage or destroy the essence of our humanness – our human spirit, our human beingness? That question leads to another, of whether some imperfections are elements of that essence and of immense value as such. Like the imperfections in the hand-knitted sweater, are they part of what makes each of us unique?

I have written elsewhere on why seeing the original of a famous painting is not only different from but much more exciting than seeing an exact copy – at least to me. (It turns out that some people prefer the copy. For instance, the Australian government built a replica of part of the Great Barrier Reef to reduce the number of tourists to the real reef in order to better protect it. Tourists from Japan preferred the replica to the real thing.) Or we can think about how antiques lose their value if they are refinished – when the many human hands that have touched the antique and the marks they have left have been erased, we consider that the object is no longer authentic, that its priceless intangible essence is gone. We value such antiques less because in our later touching of them to alter them, they can no longer touch our imagination with the same profundity. They are no longer as beautiful, although in one sense they are more perfect.

If we succeed in our search for human perfection – or perhaps even just engage in it – we will lose our authenticity, our human essence, our messy, old, much-touched soul. Just as we changed our minds about which was the most valuable sweater, the perfect machine-made or the "imperfect" hand-knitted one, perhaps the same will happen with respect to our natural, untampered-with, imperfect human selves. Or is prizing authenticity an old-fashioned value that has been abandoned by younger generations?

Damage to trust and integrity in the search for perfection

Many people were angered by the Chinese deception during the opening ceremonies of the 2008 Beijing Summer Olympic Games because they believed it represented a breach of trust. The deception involved footage of "footprint" fireworks being digitally inserted into the TV coverage of the opening ceremony and one adorable child miming the "Ode to the Motherland" as another child's lovely voice floated over the 90,000-person crowd and was transmitted across the world. The atmospheric conditions at the time of the ceremony did not result in fireworks as beautiful as those set off under ideal conditions. Seven-year-old Yang Peiyi wasn't pretty enough, and nine-year-old Lin Miaoke's voice wasn't pure enough; neither young girl alone was beautiful enough to satisfy the games organizers.

So what's wrong with a combination that results in the best of both worlds? Why did this story make front-page headlines in western democracies and elicit so many strong negative reactions? Did we overreact? I propose that our immediate reaction was based on a strong moral intuition that something was wrong. It is difficult, however, to fully identify what that is. To do so, we need to explore the ethical and values issues implicated in this incident. They include deception, integrity, authenticity, trust, and the search for perfection.

But, first, a word of warning: there was almost certainly a cultural miscommunication in this situation. My guess is that it never occurred to the Chinese how their approach would be seen by people from other cultures. Western democracies are intensely individualistic cultures. Indeed, the highly individualistic western approach is manifestly obvious in the media stories reporting this incident, whether in the *New York Times* or a local TV news report. Much of the focus was on Yang Peiyi and how cruel it was to tell her she wasn't pretty enough and how hurt she must have felt at being excluded – which, I hasten to add, the journalists were right to recognize as a wrong.

In stark contrast, Chinese culture is an intensely collectivist one – if two girls are more "perfect" than each alone, and that benefits the collectivity, the Motherland, then go for it. That difference means we need to cut the Chinese some slack in regard to the incident, not just to be fair to them but also in our own long-term interests of trying to cross the divides between us, and certainly not to make them wider.

Deception is the central issue involved, and deception is always ethically suspect. But does this deception really matter? Leaving aside the hurt to Yang Peiyi from being dumped and her voice still being used (it's hard to imagine that the issue of her consent was even considered), seeing the opening ceremony as grand theatre would have given the organizers permission to use techniques that allowed the world audience to suspend its disbelief. So why were we shocked?

Unlike the situation that prevails in relation to theatre, we the audience did not agree to be deceived. The ethical problem is that something that was not real was presented as real. The opening ceremony incidents might also have shocked us to a degree beyond what at first glance seems reasonable, because of their context. Deception contravened the very spirit of the Olympic Games – the inspiration generated by the gathering of the "youth of the world," the noble aspirations, the no-cheating-with-drugs, the "spirit of sport" ethos and its espoused values. It came across as cheating, as a breach of trust. Breaches of trust are often experienced as a betrayal; this was a betrayal of the Olympic spirit as its promoters present it.

The word "integrity" frequently arises in discussions of trust. In 2005, it was the most frequently searched word in *Webster's* online dictionary. The *Oxford English Dictionary* defines integrity, in a moral sense, to include "soundness of moral principle; the character of uncorrupted virtue, esp. in relation to truth and fair dealing; uprightness, honesty, sincerity." This definition could be used as an advertisement for the spirit meant to inform the Olympics, cynical as we might sometimes be about the authenticity of such a statement in relation to a mega-event with enormous commercial spin-offs.

Integrity is at the core of ethics and ethical conduct, an essential condition precedent to implementing all of our most important personal and communal values. And integrity is the beating heart of democracy, justice, and respect for human rights. These are the values and principles on which in western democracies we build organizations, institutions, and the state itself. Without integrity, these values and principles cannot be implemented, and they and the institutions built on them die. The fact that much of the world is worried about justice, respect for human rights, and ethical conduct in China, and hopes one day to see democracy in that country, might also help to explain why there was such a powerful negative reaction to what were, on its face, minor deceptions.

Acting with integrity is also linked to maintaining social trust, a central component of what is being called "social capital," discussed in chapter 2 – the accumulated common good that we need to maintain a healthy society of the kind that most of us would want to live in. A culture of social trust is difficult to establish, fragile, and easy to destroy. The espoused goal of the Olympics is to build worldwide social trust and certainly not to damage it, as the opening ceremonies incidents might have done.

In general, we trust what we can perceive directly with our senses – what we can see or hear or touch. But virtual reality means that things that are not real can seem real to our senses and so have resulted in an overall loss of trust in society as a whole. If that loss is to be halted, it is especially important that we are able to trust the media not to deceive their audiences. The incidents of both the miming and the "footprints" fireworks need to be examined from this perspective – although again, as at first glance with the former, the latter seems a minor liberty to have taken.

I've mused in this chapter about why seeing the original of a famous painting is different from and more exciting than seeing an exact copy and how antiques lose their value if they are refinished. We consider them no longer the "real thing." The priceless intangible essence is gone, they can no longer touch our imagination and emotions with the same power. Seeking the "perfect" little composite girl means the same is now true of the Beijing Opening Ceremony.

Then there is the question of authenticity: what is required for the Olympic Games to be authentic in their essence, without which that essence is lost? An important element is that athletes must compete only on the basis of their own natural talent, unenhanced by prohibited means such as drugs. But the games, as a whole, must also be authentic. In other words, individuals, institutions, and societies must all uphold the values that are important to us, if those values are to survive and prevail. The opening ceremony faced the Chinese authorities with a choice between authenticity and perfection, as they saw it. Their choices were to go with authenticity at the expense of the perfect; to choose the "perfect" but to be transparent about it and disclose this choice; or to do what they did, choose perfection but hide the deception involved. Ethically, it was the wrong choice. The search for perfection is often just that.

Speaking of authenticity in relation to antiques brings to mind that contemporary interior designers are telling us that antiques are out of fashion, *depassé*, too large for postmodern living spaces. Their history is not appreciated as being of worth, and they have been drastically devalued, in their case, in monetary terms. Might the same kind of changes be true, *mutatis mutandi*, of our traditional values and might future generations see that as a serious error and a major loss for them? A recent arts report story on an emerging pop star FKA Twigs seems to be giving us a very different message in this regard: "Twigs pulls this [performance] off far more professionally than most independent acts and with more integrity than most superstars. Her show is more than music because she's more than a musician. To mention 'integrity' feels square – it smacks of the old attitude that sees the well-presented as phony and the phony as impure."[20]

So What Can We Do to Make It More Likely We Will See All Life as Beautiful?

Whether or not we see all human life as beautiful has profound and far-reaching implications. So what can we do to make it more likely we will see all life as beautiful?

Being Open to Amazement, Wonder, and Awe

Yet another editor, this time the managing editor of the Canadian student newspaper the *Prince Arthur Herald*, Rebekah Hebbert, sent me a rather daunting request: "If you had one message/piece of advice/warning for students, what would it be?"

What on earth could be important enough to be that "one message"? I decided that what we all know to be important – family, friends, love, trust, loyalty, honesty and so on – should not be the focus of my message. I thought long and hard, but then, as I always do when faced with a complex and difficult decision, decided to "trust my unconscious" – to put the issue at the back of my mind and wait. (To do that, by the way, was my first piece of advice, so I disobeyed Ms Hebbert's instructions and gave two pieces of advice.) Here's the message for students my unconscious came up with: "You should be open to experiencing amazement, wonder, and awe, in as many situations and as often as possible."

What I hope will result from such experiences is that we will open ourselves to re-enchantment with the world, recover a sense of the sacred, for some a "religious sacred," for others a "secular sacred." For me, an experience of amazement, wonder, and awe can occur in a myriad of settings: on a calm, freezing winter night on seeing the staircase to the full moon reflected in the Fleuve Saint Laurent, for example, or, in early spring, a sparkling, dew-encrusted spiderweb on my front terrace. It can emerge slowly in musing on how beautiful my cats' movements are, or in an instant when watching a video resulting from pointing the Hubble Space Telescope at a seemingly blank patch of sky and detecting over three thousand galaxies at the edge of the universe, each one containing billions of stars.

Experiencing amazement, wonder, and awe can enrich our lives, help us to find meaning, and change how we see the world. It can change the decisions we make, especially regarding values and ethics, and how we live our lives. It can put us in touch with the sacred – whether the religious sacred or the secular sacred – that to which we must not lay waste but hold in trust for future generations.

I suggest that experiences of amazement, wonder, and awe can also elicit an existential perception that differentiates those who have that experience from those who do not in terms of what they regard as ethical or unethical. For instance, it would affect how we see the transmission of human life and what respect for that transmission requires. If we see it as a mystery and requiring the utmost respect, we are unlikely to agree that it is ethical to create human embryos with the intention of killing them for the production of stem cells to be used as therapies. Or, if we perceive the coming-into-being of a unique new human being with amazement, wonder, and awe, we are likely to see it also as involving a mystery that must be respected, which will usually exclude abortion and certainly exclude infanticide. If we do not look at both the unborn child and the born one with amazement, wonder, and awe just because they exist and do not perceive that mystery, we are much less likely to see abortion, or even infanticide,[21] as morally and ethically unacceptable.

In the same vein, as I've explained, being uncomfortable with mystery makes it more likely we will convert the mystery of death to the problem of death and seek a technological solution to that problem, which makes it more likely we will see a lethal injection, euthanasia, as an ethical response.

Valuing experiences of amazement, wonder, and awe, and sometimes having them, can also cause us to choose differently, to rearrange our priorities on an everyday level, for instance, in relation to choosing our area of work. When we have a choice between taking a job in an area to which we are passionately committed – one where our heart is – and one in an area to which we are not committed but pays much more money, we will be more likely to choose the former if we want to maximize our chances of experiencing amazement, wonder, and awe. We can't manufacture these experiences, but our choices can make them more – or less – likely to occur.

To speak from personal experience, I often marvel that I have been so lucky as to have fallen into the work that I do. I count it as one of the major blessings in my life that, even after more than thirty-five years in the "same job," almost every morning I walk into my office wondering what "exciting" experiences I will have that day. I place the words "same job" in quotes because in many ways my work is never that; it continues to evolve in unexpected, challenging, and fascinating ways. The possibility for such evolution is something to look for in making a commitment, at any stage of our life, to a vocation or calling or just an activity, whatever it might be, while keeping in mind that we cannot just sit back and expect that evolution to happen by itself. To allow it to occur, we must be alert to opportunities and open-minded about exploring them. And we need to take calculated risks and not expect up-front guarantees that all our endeavours will reward us as we might hope.

I have found that the requests I receive to participate in various projects or events that I anticipate will be the most exciting are often not so, and some events that I reluctantly participate in out of a sense of obligation are often the most rewarding intellectually and emotionally. As a result, I have on occasion advised young people to consider accepting a position that does not fit exactly what they believe they want – or deserve – and to see where they can direct it so as to create new opportunities for themselves. The results are sometimes very surprising and rewarding. I would give exactly the same advice to "old" people – those who are retiring, as so many now are.

I also placed the word "exciting" in quotes, because I am using it to cover a broad range of both positive and negative experiences, both our successes and our mistakes and failures, whether personal, professional, intellectual, emotional, or spiritual. We can learn and grow as persons from all of them.

I like Thomas Jefferson's advice: "It's not your failures that count; it's what you do with them." We should not be surprised or depressed by our failures, although, as I well know, it can sometimes be difficult not to be. This is no way meant to say that we should not take our mistakes seriously and try to avoid the same ones in the future.

To have your heart, mind, and soul engaged by your work, to be excited and fulfilled by what you do, is indeed an extraordinary gift. To be hopeful at the end of the day that you might have made a tiny contribution to others and a better world is a true privilege. To have had a small, personal experience of the axiom that "one person can make a difference" gives meaning to life and work. And, to repeat a point made earlier, finding meaning is of the essence of being human: we are meaning-seeking animals. It's what differentiates us from all other animals. And speaking of finding meaning leads to my next point.

I was not sure in what order to place the words "amazement, wonder, and awe," and in thinking about that I realized they were not necessarily a linear progression but three different (although connected) entryways into an experience of transcendence – the feeling that you belong to something larger than yourself and that what you do or do not do matters more than to just yourself. Such experiences of transcendence can be powerful antidotes to cynicism, particularly about whether values and ethics matter or will be implemented in practice. Such cynicism is extremely dangerous, what I would call a "secular mortal sin." It could result in a future world in which no reasonable person would want to live.

The antithesis of cynicism is hope, the oxygen of the human spirit. Without hope, our human spirit dies; with it, we can overcome seemingly insurmountable obstacles. Hope requires a sense of connection to the future, whether or not we will be physically present in that future; consequently, leaving a legacy is related to generating hope. Hope and realistic optimism are also related. And seeing life as beautiful even despite serious difficulties, even despite suffering, is a component of all these states of being.

A further insight into the impacts of experiencing amazement, wonder, and awe came to mind as I was recounting this story of my advice to young people. A thread linking many chapters in this book is consideration of the ethics that should govern contemporary scientific discoveries, especially those in the biosciences that give us unprecedented powers to intervene in the physical essence of life and manipulate and change it. Might experiencing amazement, wonder, and awe about this new knowledge gained through science be a condition precedent to its conversion to wisdom, and that in turn a condition precedent to the wise govermance of scientific discoveries?

Some time ago I gave a speech I called "Spacing-Out and Spacing-In: Searching for the Purple-Pink Middle." Purple-pink is the colour of the imagination and, as I have emphasized previously, we need to use all our "human ways of knowing," of which imagination is an important one, in making decisions about the ethics that will govern new scientific developments. Our exploration of deep outer space with cosmology, astrophysics, and spacecraft, and of deep inner space with molecular biology and genetic research, has enormously expanded the spectrum that represents our knowledge. Researching for a speech I gave recently at an International Conference on Global Space Governance[22] made me aware that we can gain insights into how each of these areas should be governed, especially ethically, by asking what the parallels between them are.

For instance, issues of appropriate ethical behaviour – especially what we should not do – are being raised in both contexts. Both raise questions around conflict between "individual autonomy" and the "common good," including questions of who constitutes the "common" whose good must be protected and what constitutes that "good."

I suggested that in deciding about the ethics that should govern our new scientific discoveries, it matters how we view what we learn from science. We can see science as our sole source of valid knowledge, believing that eventually it will be able to explain everything – this is scientism. Or we can stand in amazement, wonder, and awe at what we now know and, with epistemological modesty, experience the insight that as the radius of knowledge expands, the circumference of ignorance increases. The more we know, the more we know that we do not know. I believe that experience of amazement, wonder, and awe in the face of the mystery of the unknown that new scientific discoveries open up changes how we see science and the ethics needed to govern it. This is especially true of the science that involves biotechnology and intentional intervention in life itself. At a subsequent conference on biotechnology and ethics, speaking this time about the ethics of intervening on the human germline to alter the genes passed on from generation to generation, I concluded that

I sincerely hoped that the latter approach, which I made clear is not necessarily associated with religion, would prevail.[23]

To return to the advice that I gave to the students, I told them that a word that comes to mind is "gratitude" for the capacity to experience amazement, wonder, and awe. As far as we know, this is a uniquely human characteristic and, it can be argued, of the essence of our humanness. As such, we have obligations to future generations to hold that capacity and the situations that foster it in trust for them and, correlatively, obligations to avoid what would harm it.

As I have explained, just as we now recognize that our physical ecosystem is not indestructible and that we have obligations to future generations to care for it, we must recognize that same is true of what we can call our metaphysical ecosystem – the values, principles, attitudes, beliefs, shared stories, and so on, on the basis of which we form our society. Holding our metaphysical ecosystem in trust will require wisdom, wise ethical restraint (prudence), and courage on all parts, young and old. Our elders must take up an ancient role that has been abandoned in our youth-obsessed, postmodern culture, that of being the "keepers of our values." They must look back seven generations and look forward seven generations to decide what constitutes the wisdom that should be held in trust for future generations. Young people, decision-makers of the future, need to learn from them in order to become the keepers of our values. Everyone should be involved in exercising the enormous privilege and obligation to hold in trust our values for future generations. There is no more worthwhile, important, or exciting challenge.

Learning from Jean Vanier

Musing about whether all life is beautiful and what we can do to make it more likely we will see it as such brings to mind Jean Vanier. This remarkable man, the founder of L'Arche, a refuge and life-long home for people with intellectual disabilities, conveys a powerful message that all life is beautiful. We can learn from the profound wisdom, humanity, and humanness of his approach. He shows us the opportunities that disability can provide both to people with disabilities and to those without (at least without obvious ones) to "become human."

Some years ago I was asked to write a blurb for a then-forthcoming book by Vanier, *Our Life Together*.[24] This collection of his letters, written over many decades, reflects his worldwide work and travels in establishing L'Arche. The wisdom to be found in it has immediate relevance to the approach we need to take in seeing all life as beautiful and if we hope to prevent the acceptance of values, attitudes, beliefs, and conduct based on the opposite presumption – namely, that some life is not beautiful and therefore has no value and is undeserving of respect or being treated with dignity.

As you read my comments about Vanier's book, each time I say "person with disabilities," think also of any vulnerable person, for instance, a dying person or an unborn child threatened with abortion.

But first, a warning is in order, and it relates to a topic with which we began: suffering. There is a grave danger in romanticizing any form of suffering, which is not the same as respecting the mystery it can contain or with which it can allow us contact. The latter requires looking squarely at the tough realities that suffering involves, struggling to live with them, and finding meaning in doing so. Jean Vanier is an outstanding model in this respect. He does not romanticize disability, but he shows us how one can find hope, joy, and love despite it – or perhaps, in part, because of it.

Here's my blurb:

> As we move through Jean Vanier's letters to his and L'Arche's friends and supporters, increasingly he signs off with just "Love, Jean" – the most simple and profound salutation. This book is a love story of a different kind. It shows the extraordinary flourishing of the human spirit that can occur when a certain kind of love – a truly unselfish, non-self-centred love – is made central to ordinary daily life.
>
> Jean Vanier's radical, counter-contemporary-culture message is that we "non-disabled" people are the losers in refusing to accept people with disabilities and rejecting the unique gifts they have to offer us as individuals and societies. He writes: "It's

not a question of going out and doing good to them; rather receiving the gift of their presence transforms us."[25] This unfashionable belief in the enormous value of what people with disabilities can contribute was summed up for me by a L'Arche assistant (a non-disabled person living in a L'Arche community) who said: "You have to understand, Margo, we're not martyrs, saints or heroes; we do this because of the fullness of life it brings us."

Jean Vanier's letters gently show that among the many gifts people with disabilities can offer us are lessons in hope, optimism, kindness, empathy, compassion, generosity and hospitality, a sense of humour (balance), trust and courage. But, as Jean Vanier recognizes, to do that they must be treated justly; given every person's right to the freedom to be themselves; and respected as members of our community. That requires us to accept the suffering, weakness and fragility we see in them, which means, as Jean Vanier emphasizes, we must first accept those realities in relation to ourselves. Most of us find that an enormous challenge and flee.

The ethical tone of a society is not set by how it treats its strongest, most privileged, most powerful members, but by how it treats those who are weakest, most vulnerable and in need. This book is testament to an amazing example in the latter respect and, as such, deserves to be widely read and deeply contemplated.

Jean Vanier's remarkable, uncommon "common humanity" shines through these letters. Not everyone will share his Christian tradition, but everyone can learn from him how to enrich themselves, others and our world through developing, experiencing and celebrating the "gifts of the heart" and putting into practice a "little sign of love in the world."[26]

What are the "gifts of the heart" and what does putting into practice a "little sign of love in the world" require of us in relating to vulnerable fellow humans? We need, for instance, to recognize the importance to dying people of leaving a legacy. People die more peacefully if they belive they are leaving something for those who remain. And those gifts must be accepted and valued by the receivers. Euthanasia advocates recognize this and speak of the dying person's gift of furthering the euthanasia cause by dying by choice. Likewise, in the context of pregnancy and abortion, we need to support the pregnant woman, so that she feels she really has a choice to continue with the pregnancy, that her doing so is a courageous decision and a valuable gift to the rest of us.

◆◆◆

A major challenge for those of us who hope to promote the idea that all life is beautiful is how we can communicate, both to individuals and to society in general, the unique and precious value of each human life, especially the lives of people who are vulnerable. We cannot do this as an isolated event, or just in words, certainly not by pious statements. We need, as Jean Vanier did in relation to radically changing how at least some of us now see the lives of people with disabilities, to see the vulnerable person's act of living their life as best they can in courage and hope despite their suffering, as beautiful and valuable, a gift from that person to the rest of us that helps us to find meaning in life. We need to learn how to accept that gift and to articulate and communicate its immense and irreplaceable value.

We have obligations to hold the future in trust for the generations to follow, and nowhere is that more important than in the context of human life, birth, and death. The challenge is to find meaning, especially in difficult circumstances and in the face of suffering, and, most importantly, to learn how to pass meaning on to others. Seeing all life as beautiful can help us to do this and can allow us to create and leave a legacy of meaning. If we do not regard all life as beautiful – if we fail to nurture an approach of amazement, wonder, and awe about life – we seriously risk being unable to find meaning in life.

And that would be the ultimate tragedy for individuals and societies, present and future.

6

How Might a Problem – a Crisis Pregnancy – Be Converted to a Mystery, the Gift of Life?

I spoke in the previous chapter of how some people deal with their fear of mystery by converting it into a problem and then seeking a technological solution for it. In this chapter I want to explore whether converting a problem – an unwanted pregnancy – to a mystery – the coming into being of a new and unique human life – could change what pregnant women might decide regarding continuing their pregnancy.

Let me start with the message I received from Lola French, the executive director of the Canadian Association of Pregnancy Support Services (CAPSS), when she invited me to give a speech at the CAPSS's 2014 national conference: "As you know," French wrote, "our centres are the 'pastoral arm' so to speak of the pro-life spectrum; meeting women where they are at and sitting with them to listen to their stories and reason with them, offering them information so that they can make a well informed decision. I would like you to address some of the ways we can reason with our abortion-minded clients, and with our communities and even our media, as you describe in your article which I cut and pasted below."

Here's the passage that Ms French was referring to:

> To find some common ground, we have to stop allowing people with views at the far ends of either the pro-choice spectrum or the pro-life spectrum to dominate the debate, as they now do, especially in the mainstream media. For too long, the battles between those on each extreme have prevented the nuanced

> discussion with which most Canadians can identify. We need to work together and build on the existing consensus, rather than focus just on differences. In short, we need to start our discussions from where we. agree, not where we disagree.

What starting from where we agree does is to allow us to have an experience of sharing a common morality. That gives a different tone to our discussions and, very importantly, to our disagreements.

Ms French goes on to further quote me:

> Allowing an early period in pregnancy, when women can seek unbiased counseling without fear of criminal prosecution, could help them to decide against having an abortion. That requires we ensure there are facilities readily available for crisis pregnancy counselling, which are not abortion clinics.
>
> The most relevant analogy here is to the decriminalization of suicide to try to prevent it, because suicidal people and their families would be more likely to seek help, if they were not threatened with criminal prosecution.
>
> And, just as we have supportive, non-coercive suicide prevention programs, we need to consider supportive, non-coercive abortion prevention programs. For instance, a woman with a crisis pregnancy should know that, if she decides against abortion, she will be offered fully adequate psychological and social support. Such an offer is required, if for no other reason, to obtain a valid – non-coerced – informed consent to abortion, should that be the woman's decision.[1]

Ms French then continues:

> I believe that the last statement you made here describes our pregnancy centres outreach. We would like you to bring a message that will encourage and equip our leaders to be wise in their presentations and encouraged in their work.
>
> Many of our centres are under attack in the media. At times there are journalists going to our centres presenting themselves

> as clients and secretly taping the sessions, cutting and pasting them to give a negative story via TV news broadcasts.
>
> Just recently, CBC Radio has been broadcasting petitions that have been to keep our centres out of the schools, [to keep us from] sharing about abstinence based sexual health programs, which is part of the school curriculum, but there are radical people who feel that we have no right to teach simply because we are a faith based organization. We do not bring our religion into the conversations at all in public school class rooms, but to them that is beside the point.[2]

The issues that Lola French raises here include media ethics, the place of religion and the voices of religious people in the public square, and the requirements for upholding respect for democracy – not a small agenda.

I've structured my comments in this chapter in three parts. I start by recounting a personal experience of interacting with a woman who had experienced a crisis pregnancy and passing on what she hoped others could learn from her experience. I then explore the need for ethics and law to catch up with science to inform us appropriately when we engage in the abortion debate, and the need for us as a society to consider the impact on the wider community of our decisions about abortion. Finally, I recount some thoughts about how we should handle the situation in which we find ourselves in Canada in the absence of any abortion law, and where we should go from here.

Interacting with Women with a Crisis Pregnancy

A case in which I became personally involved is a good example of the profound complexities of obtaining informed consent to abortion. Anna (not her real name) came to see me in my role as a professor researching and teaching in the area of medicine, ethics, and law, to discuss the research she was doing on abortion. We talked about the articles she'd read, and I asked her, "How did you become interested in the topic?"

She hesitated, then said, "I've just had an abortion, and I'm terribly upset and I'd like to tell you about it."

Her story is tragic. Anna explained, "Everyone in Quebec thinks that abortion is normal, nothing to fuss or be upset about, the obvious and easy solution to an unplanned pregnancy." But when she unexpectedly found herself pregnant, she didn't feel that way and sought support to continue the pregnancy. All the people she approached, however, told her to "get on with it" – have an abortion.

Anna first asked her mother whether she would help her if she had the baby. Her mother flatly refused, saying, "I do not want to waste my life babysitting and I want to be free to travel." Anna's male partner, the father of the unborn child, said he "wasn't interested in a kid," and their relationship has since ended. She tried to see her gynecologist to discuss her options, but the first available appointment was two months away. She then contacted an abortion clinic, which gave her an appointment in two weeks, at which time she was nine weeks pregnant. She said, "I went to them to get information on abortion, to know more about my options, the consequences of an abortion. I was open to getting an abortion, because that was what everyone around me recommended I do. I saw abortion as an option but was really not sure. I was hoping for some answers."

Anna met first with a nurse for a "consent interview." She said, "The nurse told me that at this stage of the pregnancy the fetus is just a bunch of cells. I also asked her if the abortion would have any impact on my health, my future pregnancies, and so on. She said abortions had no impact at all, no consequences at all, that all that I had read [to the contrary] were myths. The nurse said, 'In two weeks, it will be as if all this never happened.'"

Anna changed into a hospital gown and was taken into an examination room where a technician proceeded to do an ultrasound. Anna asked what the fetus looked like and requested to see the ultrasound. She said, "The technician told me she was not allowed to show me the images and I was unable to see the screen" which showed the fetus. At nine weeks gestation, it would have had a beating heart. The technician picked up the printout of the ultrasound but dropped it on the floor. She scrambled to gather it up quickly, saying, "You don't want to see this." But that's exactly what Anna did want.

Anna says she was left "waiting alone in a little room in the blue gown," before a nurse took her to the operating room, "where they gave me the sedative injection. At that point I was just crying, I was just thinking of all the reasons people told me I had to get the abortion, and that I did not have any help anyways, so I was crying. The doctor asked me if I was here on my own will and I said, 'Yes,' while crying. So they gave me a double dose of sedative to calm me down. At that point, I felt it was pointless to protest further and that I couldn't back out at that stage and would just have to go ahead." She closed her eyes and let the abortion proceed.

"The attitude in Quebec, that 'of course you should have an abortion, it is of no consequence,' is not true," Anna said. "I feel terrible. I can't go to work. I've started seeing a psychologist. I feel guilty." She mused, "I wonder why Quebec is like this."

So, what ethical and legal issues does this case raise?

First, whether we are pro-choice or pro-life, we should all agree that women do not have a free choice unless there are easily accessible, adequate support systems for continuing a pregnancy, as Anna says she wanted to do. She explained that she is thirty-two years old and believes having a child is a fundamental life experience for a woman, and now she may not have that experience.

We discussed how she felt that her choice was between the baby losing its life or her "losing her life:" without any support to enable her to complete her studies and start a professional career, she "just couldn't do everything that would be necessary alone."

We should consider whether Anna is an emotionally abused woman. Finding Hope,[3] an initiative of Life, the largest pro-life organization in the United Kingdom, is relevant in this regard. The group's research for this initiative showed that many women who had repeat abortions were victims of abuse and had lost hope. As I have said before, hope is the oxygen of the human spirit. Without hope, our spirit dies; with it, we can overcome even seemingly insurmountable obstacles.[4]

Anna queried why, each year, we spend so much taxpayers' money on bringing 50,000 immigrants to Quebec but not on supporting the pregnant women among the 30,000 who have an abortion, who, with support, would choose to have their babies. It's a serious fault on our part as a society not to provide such support, which should include easy access to free counselling independent of abortion facilities, as is being proposed in Britain and as CAPSS provides to the best of its ability. The concern about abortion clinics acting in this capacity is that they have a conflict of interest, because they are a for-profit undertaking selling a "service."

The next issue Anna and I discussed was whether she gave her free and informed consent to an abortion. Ethically and legally, as the Supreme Court of Canada has ruled, informed consent requires that a person be given "all the information that would be material to a reasonable person in the same circumstances" in making a decision whether to undergo a given medical procedure.[5] The ruling requires that the harms, risks, and benefits of the procedure, and its alternatives, including doing nothing, are disclosed. The law in some American states requires that women contemplating an abortion must be shown or at least be offered the opportunity to see an ultrasound image of their fetus, as part of the information necessary to obtain their informed consent. Anna's request to see the ultrasound image is relevant in this respect. Informed consent is not present if the information is inadequate – indeed, a health-care professional's failure in that regard is medical negligence (medical malpractice). Even non-material information must be disclosed if a person's questions indicate its relevance to her, and those questions must be answered honestly and fully.

Consent is never present where intentionally false information is given, especially when it involves consequences and risks – indeed, such information can even give rise to the legal wrongs of battery and assault. In this regard, consider the nurse's unqualified reassurance regarding risks. Anna believes, as I do, that her experience at the abortion clinic raises issues with respect to possible breaches of all of these requirements.

Informed consent also requires that the consent be voluntary, that is, not affected by coercion, duress, or undue influence. To help ensure the consent is "free," some American states legally require a "cooling off" period between deciding to have an abortion and its being carried out. Anna's experience is far from that. She went to the clinic for information but was given an abortion.

Because consent is an ongoing process, not a one-time event, even assuming that Anna's consent was present initially, the voluntariness of her continuing consent is questionable in the circumstances existing from the point at which she was given sedation. Consider, as an analogy, if Anna had consented to sexual intercourse in similar circumstances. Would her initial consent have been sufficient to avoid a charge of sexual assault (rape)?

Anna speaks about her consent in this way: "In that time of my pregnancy I had a lot of nausea and was on a real hormonal roller coaster. The difference between my decision process in my 'normal' state and that state are two worlds. I think that when a woman is pregnant, from my experience, she is much more vulnerable, and thus can be pushed around more easily. This should be taken into account when a clinic is looking to have consent from a pregnant woman."

While protecting Anna's privacy and with her consent, I shared my experience in her case with Kathleen Gray from the Centre for Reproductive Loss in Montreal. She responded, "Anna's story is so familiar, as we have heard many similar tragic stories over twenty years of counselling post-abortive women. These elements could apply to hundreds of women, especially the serious problems concerning the information they are both given and denied. Sadly, Anna's story is not unique."

One of the most pernicious myths propagated in relation to abortion, which we see in the nurse's reassurance to Anna that in two weeks she will have forgotten about all of this, is that abortion will restore the woman to a situation as if the pregnancy never occurred. That is impossible, as many women like Anna come to realize too late. As this case shows, abortion is not the simple quick-fix solution to an unplanned pregnancy that it is often presented as being. It is a life-affecting decision in more ways than one.

Anna's comment on reading the article about her case, which I published in a Canadian newspaper with her permission, was, "Thank you for that. I hope [the loss of] a life and my own suffering will help others."

Ethics and Law Must Catch Up to Scientific Advances in Divisive Debate about Restrictions on Abortion

Scientific progress that now makes it possible for increasingly younger premature babies to survive has made for more acrimonious debate as to the legal restrictions that should apply to abortion. Although

Canada has no legal restrictions on abortion, in practice the vast majority of physicians will not undertake it, except for the most compelling reasons, after viability of the unborn child, which the Canadian Medical Association's "Policy on Induced Abortion" sets at twenty weeks gestation.

Before looking at some of the incidents that have stimulated renewed public debate about abortion and related issues, and the arguments raised in these debates, I want to set out some general analysis of how we can perceive pregnancy and unborn children/fetuses. This analysis is relevant because our perceptions affect what we see as ethical, which in turn affects our views on what we believe the law should be in this context. Indeed, the alternative characterizations of unborn human beings as unborn children, as compared with fetuses, reflect such a difference implemented through a choice of terminology.

Two Different Focuses to Consider

In shining a spotlight on the issue of abortion, we can choose one of two different focuses as the primary one: the unborn child or the pregnant woman. The fundamental difference between the pro-life supporters and the pro-choice ones is their radically contrasting focuses on what an abortion involves. Pro-life advocates look to the intentional destruction of a new human life; they see a beating human heart and "ten little fingers." In stark contrast, pro-choice supporters ignore or dehumanize and depersonalize the fetus, seeing it as an object and obstacle – even a "parasite" – to be removed in effectuating the woman's decision to rid herself of an unwanted pregnancy. Let's examine these approaches in greater detail.

In focusing primarily on the unborn child, pro-life advocates adopt what American lawyer Richard Stith calls a "development approach"[6] to inform their assessment of the ethical acceptability of abortion. The embryo is the earliest stage of every human life. (As I have said before, we are all ex-embryos.) It is fully human, not "less than human," as Canadian journalist Chris Selley has unscientifically claimed;[7] and its entire potential to develop throughout its life, however long that might be, is fully present from conception. The unborn child is not a potential human being but a human being with the present potential to develop throughout a natural human lifespan. There is no bright line that can be scientifically justified between conception and natural death. Therefore, pro-life people believe that a fetus deserves the same respect for its life as the rest of us. An arresting manifestation of such a view occurred in the listing of the victims on the World Trade Centre 9/11 Memorial on the occasion of the tenth anniversary of the attacks: "Ten women who died on September 11, and one in the February 1993 bombing, were known to be pregnant. [With their families' consent] their names … [were] listed on the memorial with the phrase 'and her unborn child.'"[8]

Sometimes the authenticity and credibility of the pro-life position is challenged on the basis that survey results on attitudes to abortion show that not all pro-life supporters would legally ban all abortion. Care needs to be taken to distinguish between ethics and law in interpreting these results. Pro-life adherents can believe that abortion is always ethically wrong, but that in certain cases, such as a pregnancy presenting a serious threat to a mother's life, it should not be a legal wrong.

Some pro-choice advocates are absolutists who will not tolerate any restrictions on abortion. They view the unborn child as having no moral status and not meriting any protections and certainly not rights. Their characterization of the embryo as "just a bunch of cells" manifests this approach. In this regard, we should keep in mind that not seeing humans as humans – dehumanizing other humans – is at the base of much evil. Also relevant is a Chinese proverb: "The beginning of wisdom is to call things [and living beings] by their right names."

In short, these pro-choice advocates deal with unborn children/fetuses by either ignoring them or by denying they have any intrinsic worth. Indeed, they argue that an unborn child exists only as part of the woman's body and has only the value she chooses to give it.

This view is reflected in the current legal position in Canada, which has arisen by default rather than direct intention. Since 1988, when in the *Morgentaler* case[9] the Supreme Court of Canada struck down as unconstitutional the provision in the Criminal Code governing abortion, there has been no law restricting abortion. Consequently, as noted above, abortion is legal throughout pregnancy even though the vast majority of physicians will not abort a viable fetus except for serious medical reasons. Despite such reluctance on the part of physicians, the Canadian Institute for Health Information (CIHI) reports that in 2008 there were 556 known abortions past twenty weeks in Canada ; for over 68,000 abortions (which represents more than half the total number of abortions in 2008), the gestational age is not known. Accurate statistics in this regard have been unavailable for some time because – even prior to the CIHI taking over the collection of statistics on abortion – Statistics Canada was instructed to discontinue asking reporting hospitals for gestational age at the time of abortion. And clinics (which accounted for almost 50,000 abortions in 2008) are not required to report information about the abortions they perform.

Some pro-choice advocates are not absolutists but take what Stith calls a "constructionist approach." They view the fetus as "under construction" by the woman and up to a certain point in gestation not sufficiently developed to merit protection or respect for its life against her wishes. They see the unborn child as having some moral status, but not yet the same status as the rest of us and therefore not deserving of the same protections. This position can be described as seeing the fetus as "potential human life," as compared with the pro-life position of seeing it as "human life with potential."

An above-the-fold, front-page headline in the *Globe and Mail* provided a striking example of a constructionist approach to fetuses in a context other than abortion. An article by journalist Carolyn Abraham on "genetic technology that soon could allow [parents] ... to customize their kids ... [by] selecting for gender, height or brains" is entitled "Building a Better Baby."[10]

Many pro-choice activists have passionately defended the current vacuum in the law and vociferously oppose any efforts to pass a new law governing abortion (as the Supreme Court of Canada stated in the *Morgentaler* case it was open to Parliament to do), or any other law that would give some legal recognition or protection to an unborn child or that might help a woman to choose not to have an abortion. For instance, pro-choice advocates adamantly condemned a Conservative private member's bill, C-484, the Unborn Victims of Crime Act, which would have made it a separate criminal offence to injure or kill a fetus when the offender attacked a woman knowing she was pregnant and intending to harm the fetus.

This bill passed on second reading in March 2008, but never got to third reading because in September 2008 Parliament was prorogued and an election was called, meaning that all pending legislation died on the Order Paper. Prior to the election being called, however, in August 2008, then Minister of Justice Rob Nicholson went on national television distancing his government from the bill and promising to introduce an alternative bill "that leaves no room for the introduction of fetal rights."

Another Conservative private member's bill meant to protect pregnant women from being coerced into having unwanted abortions (An Act to Prevent Coercion of Pregnant Women to Abort [Roxanne's Law]) was likewise condemned by pro-choice advocates and defeated on second reading in the House of Commons on 15 December 2010. This bill was a response to the horrific murder of a young Canadian woman who refused to have an abortion. Roxanne Fernando, from Winnipeg, was murdered by Nathanael Plourde, the father of her unborn child, after he failed to convince her to end her pregnancy. In February 2007, Plourde and two friends beat Roxanne brutally and dumped her in a snowbank to die, thereby also killing her unborn child.

The political cost, especially to conservative politicians, of indicating any concern about abortion, or of recognizing or seeking to protect unborn children, seems to figure strongly in many politicians' calculations about winning or losing votes. They clearly fear the power of the pro-choice lobby, which does not hesitate to brand them with having a "secret agenda" to restrict abortion if they indicate any such concerns. It's an instance of a very vocal "hard minority" being able to rule a largely silent "soft majority," as surveys show that around two-thirds of Canadians believe there should be some legal restrictions on abortion. (The figures on what Canadians believe in this regard can be difficult to obtain because different claims can be made depending on the survey, the nature of the questions asked, and how the results are interpreted.)

Pro-Life Advocates' Objections to Taxpayers Funding Abortion

This soft majority is becoming more strategic, however, in challenging the impact of the absence of any legal restrictions on abortion in Canada. One way is to object to the funding of medically unnecessary abortions with taypayers' money, as presently occurs. A "Defund Abortion" rally was organized in Toronto on 22 October 2011 by Campaign Life Coalition Youth to send a strong message to the newly elected minority Liberal government of Ontario. "Stop using our tax dollars to pay for an elective procedure that is not medically necessary," rally organizer Alissa Golob, the coordinator for the Campaign Life Coalition Youth, said in a statement, which continues: "The Defund Abortion Rally shows a growing movement of young people who acknowledge that pregnancy is not a disease, injury or illness and that abortion is not a medical necessity and, therefore, should not be covered by the Ontario Health Insurance Plan. Every year, at least $30 million of taypayer money funds elective abortion surgery in Ontario, while genuine areas of health care such as elder care, doctor shortages, life-saving equipment and treatment for autistic children are neglected."[11] It merits noting that an increasing number of young, vocal, pro-life advocates, many of whom characterize themselves as "abortion survivors," were born after the Canadian abortion law was struck down in the *Morgentaler* case; they could, therefore, have been legally aborted simply at their mother's request.

For absolutist fundamentalist pro-choice advocates, however, support for unrestricted, freely provided access to abortion throughout pregnancy and for a complete absence of any legal recognition of unborn children is not just an issue relevant to abortion. It is the foundation of their ideology and their litmus test of whether a person or a society respects women and their rights.

Suppressing the Abortion Debate

We have also seen the phenomenon of attempts to suppress the abortion debate itself, especially on university campuses across Canada,[12] in order to avoid any new law that might restrict access to abortion.

Similar attempts are going on outside of Canada as well. For instance, in the summer of 2011, Nadine Dorries, a Conservative Party member of the British House of Commons, introduced an amendment to the Health and Social Care Bill seeking to ensure that women considering an abortion were offered independent counselling away from the "abortion providers" who profit from carrying out abortions. Abortion providers in Britain receive £60 million a year from the National Health Services (NHS) for their services. The amendment had pro-choice supporters demonstrating against it in the streets of London.

A headline in *The Telegraph* newspaper read: "A modest proposal by MP Nadine Dorries to offer independent advice to women seeking an abortion has led to angry protests, death threats – and the stifling of a once-in-a-generation debate. How did it come to this?" The *Telegraph* article explains that it is one aspect of the "culture wars." "The polarisation is manifest," it goes on to say: "The pro-choicers divide the public arena into 'us' (for whom abortion is always a right, end of story) and 'them' (everyone else)."[13]

Scientific Advances Are Changing the Debate

However, the article continues, "What the acrid smoke of the battlefield disguises is a big shift in the terms of the debate. Yes, most Britons are pro-choice, but this support is qualified: allowing a termination at 24 weeks when babies survive outside the womb at even 20 weeks fills most (57 per cent) women with misgivings."[14] As a result of scientific progress and 3D ultrasound scans making it possible to see the unborn child, and younger and younger premature babies surviving, many people are increasingly uneasy with abortion, especially after twenty weeks gestation. They – especially young people and, in particular, many medical students – are moving away from accepting it. Counselling from independent facilities can result in women recognizing the existence of the unborn child in a way that causes them to change their minds and decide against abortion. Pro-choice supporters can experience that outcome as a rejection of their values and ideology.

Risks of Abortion and Informed Consent

I have spoken about informed consent to abortion in relation to Anna's case, but it merits noting that it is also an issue associated with the absence of unbiased counselling in that, worldwide, women undergoing abortion are not being told of its risks, including mental health risks that have been recognized through research.

Psychiatrist Priscilla Coleman, in an article titled, "Abortion and Mental Health: Quantitative Synthesis and Analysis of Research Published 1995–2009,"[15] establishes that abortion is associated with a "moderate to high" increased risk of mental health problems. Other research findings are being interpreted to dispute such claims, but at the least, one can say that there is no consensus on this question. Apart from other concerns, failure to disclose the possibility of such risks raises the issue of a lack of informed consent to the abortion procedure.

A very contentious area regarding the risks associated with abortion – and the required risk disclosure to women in order to obtain their "informed consent" to the procedure – is whether it increases the risk of breast cancer. Pro-choice advocates declare that there is no credible evidence of such a causal link and adamantly resist any mention of that possibility. Others who have researched the issue present convincing arguments in support of such evidence.[16]

Another controversial issue related to informed consent are laws such as those enacted in some American states requiring abortion providers either to show and "medically describe" the fetus to women contemplating an abortion or offer them an opportunity to see an ultrasound image of their fetus, as part of the information necessary to obtain their informed consent.

Which Is More Accurate: The Constructionist or Developmental Approach?

Which of the two approaches fits best with the reality of what occurs in pregnancy – the developmental or the constructionist one? I propose it is the developmental one. The unborn child comes into living existence at conception, just as other living entities do, not at some later date. Stith gives the example that we see as the same tree the five-year-old pear tree and the seedling it grew from which we planted. Likewise, the unborn child is the same person he or she will become over his or her life.[17] In comparison, the constructionist approach is more appropriate for inanimate objects – we can think of building a house, which is not sufficiently constructed to be called a house until a certain point. Moreover, at any point the builder can decide not to proceed, and the house will not construct itself.

Furthermore, in deciding whether the developmental or the constructionist approach fits best with the reality of what occurs in pregnancy, it is relevant to note that so far we haven't been able to create – to "construct" – artificial life. Life is necessary to beget life; it travels down the generations, whether from a bacterium to a bacterium or a human to a human. It is not created; it is passed on. And the new life "develops" in an unbroken process from its beginning to its end; in its turn, during its existence, it may pass on life.

Pro-life adherents believe that abortion is inherently wrong; that is, they could never justify it for themselves, although many would accept that the decision about justification should be left to the pregnant woman when there is a serious threat to her life from continuing the pregnancy – a rare situation.

Some pro-choice people believe that no justification is needed, apart perhaps from that it is what the pregnant woman wants (hardly a justification, because it is entirely subjective with no objective element). Some pro-choice people, for instance, journalist Chris Selley in the *National Post* article mentioned previously, seem surprised that there are pro-choice supporters who articulate a need for a justification. That felt need might result from a moral intuition that abortion is not a morally neutral act and that it raises serious ethical concerns. Consequently, they feel a need to justify it. As I've pointed out in this book, we have many ways of human knowing – among them, emotions, imagination, creativity, as well as moral intuition – not just reason in a narrow sense of that term. We ignore our "feelings" at our peril, as they can alert us to ethical dangers.[18]

Interesting in this regard is a widely commented-upon story in the *New York Times*, "The Two-Minus-One Pregnancy" by Ruth Padawar, about Jenny, the woman who "selectively reduced" a twin pregnancy to a singleton. (In selective reduction, one fetus or more – but not all – is killed. The dead fetus is delivered with the live child at term.) In the article, Jenny is reported as saying, "If I had conceived these twins naturally, I wouldn't have reduced this pregnancy, because you feel like if there's a natural order, then you don't want to disturb it. But we created this child in such an artificial manner – in a test tube, choosing an egg donor, having the embryo placed in me – and somehow, making a decision about how many to carry seemed to be just another choice. The pregnancy was all so consumerish to begin with, and this became yet another thing we could control."[19]

Jenny employs here the justification of blaming the technology, not herself, for creating a situation that resulted in an outcome she was possibly experiencing as involving ethical wrongdoing on her part. We place the technology between ourselves and the outcome and see the technology as the cause of that outcome in order to disconnect ourselves from our moral distress regarding it.

A striking example of this is the approach taken by the Australian pro-euthanasia advocate Dr Philip Nitschke in administering euthanasia. Dr Nitschke is adamantly in favour of making euthanasia widely available. Largely as a result of his advocacy, it was legal in the Northern Territory of Australia for eleven months in 1997. But Dr Nitschke did not administer the lethal injections in the cases he carried out, even though it was legal for him to do so. Rather, he designed a "death machine," which involved his attaching the patient to a computer-controlled intravenous drip through which the lethal dose would be administered at the press of a button by the patient. The technology allowed euthanasia to become suicide and functioned to distance Dr Nitschke from the direct infliction of death on the patient.

Defining the Fetus Frames the Debate

Yet another "justification" for abortion is to define unborn children/fetuses out of the protections accorded to the rest of us, particularly respect for our lives. One such approach is to distinguish between human beings and persons, arguing that only the latter deserve such respect and that unborn children are not persons.

Peter Singer, the utilitarian Princeton philosopher whose views I've discussed in previous chapters, is a prominent advocate of this approach. He believes that not all human beings are persons. He proposes as the requirements for personhood that one must be self-aware, have a sense of the future, and be able to relate to others. He divides human beings into two categories, persons and non-persons, according to whether or not they possess these attributes – and also argues that some animals that manifest them are "non-human persons." According to Singer, only persons, as defined, deserve full respect, including respect for their lives. Unborn babies do not fulfill these criteria, and hence abortion is acceptable to him, as is infanticide – and as is euthanasia in general for those who do not fulfill these personhood requirements. As he admitted in a 1999 *Newsweek* interview, and has repeatedly stated in his academic writings, he sees no moral difference between abortion and infanticide in relation to such human beings.

A 2011 Canadian criminal case is of interest in this regard. The accused, Katrina Effert, at the time a nineteen-year-old Alberta woman, gave birth secretly in her parents' downstairs bathroom and then later strangled the newborn baby and threw his body over a fence. She was found guilty of second-degree murder by two juries, but both times the judgment was thrown out by the appeals court. The Alberta Court of Appeal overturned her murder conviction and replaced it with the lesser charge of infanticide. For this crime, she received a three-year suspended sentence from Justice Joanne Veit of the Alberta Court of Queen's Bench, which meant she was able to walk out of court without serving any time in prison.

While the judge did not treat infanticide as a form of abortion from a legal point of view, she did use current Canadian abortion practice and the absence of any legal restrictions on abortion in Canada to justify the lenient – one could say token – sentence. She ruled that Canada's lack of an abortion law indicates that "while many Canadians undoubtedly view abortion as a less than ideal solution to unprotected sex and unwanted pregnancy, they generally understand, accept and sympathize with the onerous demands pregnancy and childbirth exact from mothers, especially mothers without support."[20] She applied this same sentiment in determining an appropriate sentence for infanticide.

In short, the judge viewed abortion and infanticide as comparable, a stance with which most pro-life advocates would agree and most pro-choice advocates would adamantly disagree. The problem for pro-life advocates is, however, that the judge sees infanticide as meriting a similar "compassionate" response to that taken by Canadian law to abortion, which is a total absence of protection of the unborn child. The alternative would be to see abortion as calling for the more protective legal response in favour of the life of the child established by infanticide (which is a form of homicide), as it has been understood, at least up until this case. But that response would require Parliament to act to pass some law on abortion, which, as discussed previously, many politicians are deeply afraid of doing and have refused to contemplate or even discuss.

I discussed in chapter 5 the proposition of some philosophers that some animals merit the same respect as humans or even more respect than some humans, and I pointed out that humans have traditionally been given "special respect," which brings with it special protections, especially of life. In practice, we have implemented this special respect through the idea of personhood, which embodies two concepts: all humans are persons, and no animals are persons. But, as I also explained, the concept of "universal human personhood" (the idea that all humans deserve special respect simply because they are human) is being challenged, along with the exclusion of animals from personhood. This is the challenge I describe in that chapter as currently the world's most dangerous idea.

If one sees definitions of personhood as a spectrum, the movement to include all human beings in personhood from the moment of their conception, in order to give them the same protections as human beings presently legally recognized as persons, is the polar opposite of defining some human beings out of personhood, as described above, in order to deny them any protection. In the US state of Mississippi, an initiative to recognize embryos and fetuses as persons through a state constitutional amendment – the so-called personhood amendments – was defeated in a referendum in November 2011, when 55 percent of voters rejected it. Similar initiatives are emerging in other states, including Florida and Ohio. Not only pro-choice supporters oppose such developments but some pro-life ones do also, although for very different reasons. The latter fear that the amendment could backfire and ultimately result in less legal protection overall for unborn children. This could occur if the inevitable challenges to the constitutionality of any such amendment ended up in the United States Supreme Court and opened up reconsideration by the court of *Roe v. Wade* and subsequent cases, and the court ruled that the law currently governing abortion should be less protective of unborn children.

So, to summarize, language, definitions, and concepts are very important in the abortion debate, and we must think deeply about the consequences of the language, definitions, and concepts we choose to adopt or reject in this context. I suggest that because personhood is an attributed characteristic and (no matter where we fall on the spectrum of when we believe personhood should be attributed), recognition of another as a person is discretionary, we should not use this concept to decide what respect for unborn children requires. Rather, the fact that they are living human beings should be the informing principle that guides us ethically in this regard.

Questioning Justifications for Not Restricting Access to Abortion

Pro-choice advocates focus on the woman's right to control her body as the justification for having no legal restrictions on access to abortion. But their giving absolute priority to her "right" to evacuate her uterus – to be unpregnant – raises several issues.

The first issue involves the very controversial question of whether abortion carries a "right" for the woman to have the fetus/unborn child killed, or only a "right" to evacuate her uterus when that can be achieved without killing the fetus. Before viability, abortion necessarily involves killing the unborn child; after viability it does not. If instead of being killed *in utero*, the child is delivered by induced premature labour, it has a chance of survival, although it is placed at serious risk by its premature birth. In other words, does legal abortion confer not only a right to evacuate one's uterus but also a right to kill the unborn child when that is avoidable? I've called this the "evacuation versus destruction" issue, and argued that there is no right to kill the child when this is avoidable.[21]

This is not to ignore the ethical problems raised by delivery of a post-viability unborn child other than for medical reasons. But if

Canada is to continue with no legal restrictions on abortion, these ethical problems are the lesser of two evils and, moreover, could be pre-empted in the vast majority of cases by strictly limiting abortion after viability, as countries other than Canada have done.

I've been consulted as an ethicist on two Canadian cases where this issue was relevant. In one, an unmarried graduate student from a Middle Eastern country was thirty-four weeks pregnant with a healthy unborn child and wanted an abortion to save her from "disgracing her family." In the other, a married couple learned at thirty-two weeks gestation that their unborn child had a cleft palate – correctable with routine surgery – and "didn't want a defective baby." In both cases, the unborn child was killed *in utero* and delivered dead, making the intervention that of abortion and not first-degree murder, as it would have been had the killing taken place after birth.

Later-term abortions, especially post-viability ones, raise the issue of fetal pain during abortion. Some researchers argue this can occur as early as nine to thirteen weeks gestation, but whether or not that is correct, there is solid evidence for it at twenty weeks. One response is to require that the fetus be given anaesthesia prior to being killed. The other is banning abortion after the time at which it is clear the fetus can experience pain, with very limited exceptions when abortion is necessary to save the woman's life or to avoid a serious threat to her health.

The American states of Idaho, Kansas, Alabama, Indiana, Oklahoma, and Nebraska have passed laws banning abortions after twenty weeks on this basis.[22] However, a lawsuit was filed by an Idaho woman against that state's newly passed Pain-Capable Unborn Child Protection Act, challenging, as a pro-life lawyer phrased it, "the right of the state to protect these [unborn] children from the excruciatingly painful death of abortion." A federal appeals court has since struck down the legislation.[23]

"Selective reduction" also faces pro-choice advocates with problems regarding their justification of abortion on the basis of a woman's right to evacuate her uterus, because with this procedure she does not become unpregnant with respect to the remaining living fetus(es) or the dead one(s), so this justification for abortion is unavailable. As well, selective reduction focuses on the fetuses that are not wanted, which takes the spotlight off the woman and her body, and abortion as relating only to her, and shines it on those fetuses that are intentionally rejected and destroyed. This focus makes abortion much less of a "nothing event" ethically and more of a "something event," even for those who believe it should be freely available.

Another problem with "selective reduction" is that for the mother the birth of the live baby is linked to the delivery of the child she destroyed. It is therefore very difficult to maintain denial of its prior existence, and the live child is a powerful image of what the dead child might have been. Moreover, the intentional or random selection of which fetuses to kill adds a chilling dimension to this procedure. Sometimes it is just the one most accessible to the obstetrician's lethal injection.

Selective reduction has been around since the early 1980s. At that time, a report in the *New England Journal of Medicine* described the delivery of one healthy, living twin of a normal birth weight and its dead, shrunken, calcified twin, "selectively reduced" because it had Down syndrome. The report was illustrated with a graph of the wanted twin's upward growth line and the unwanted one's downward shrinkage line from the date of the intervention.[24] Other cases have involved women who did not want twins and said they would abort both babies unless a selective reduction was performed – a self-imposed Sophie's choice.

As I have observed already, one of the most pernicious myths propagated by the pro-choice advocates is that abortion (and the same applies, in part, to unborn children lost through "selective reduction") means that the pre-pregnancy status quo can be restored, that the woman can return to her life as it was, as if the child never existed. That is impossible, even for women who do not in the least regret their choice to have an abortion or selective reduction.

Unpacking the Labels in the Abortion Debate

An email made me ponder what the labels "pro-choice" and "pro-life" really mean, particularly regarding people's stance on using law to govern abortion. In Canada this debate is very much alive because there are no legal restrictions on abortion. If a physician is willing to perform an abortion just before birth, he would not be legally prohibited from doing so, although most physicians refuse to carry out abortions, other than for a very serious reason, when the unborn child is post-viability.

My email correspondent, an articulate, politically engaged, professional woman, wrote: "I spoke to a very successful and intelligent entrepreneur at an event on Saturday, who described himself as pro-choice, who explained, 'I just have come to the conclusion that abortion is a woman's choice.' So I asked two questions: 'How would you feel if she was six months along in her pregnancy and the physician would make sure the baby was not born alive?' And, 'What if the mother wanted an abortion because the baby was a girl and not a boy?' To both questions, he answered quite adamantly, 'No, I would never agree.' And he concluded, 'I just have never thought about it in those terms.'"

Is he really pro-choice? He clearly doesn't agree with the 28 percent of pro-choice Canadians, who, one survey showed, reject any legal protection for human life prior to birth. The same survey found only 6 percent of Canadians would legally prohibit all abortions, while 60 percent believe there should be some law protecting unborn children, at the latest at viability (twenty weeks gestation). Are only the 6 percent pro-life?

The 28 percent and 6 percent are the two poles in our abortion debate, but their disputes dominate in the public square. Two-thirds of Canadians fall somewhere on a spectrum between them – they are not absolutists, in either direction, about using law to govern abortion. For them, abortion law (in comparison with abortion itself, for pro-life people) is not an either-or issue; many are uncertain where to stand, and their voices are rarely heard. Adding two new positions to the survey, "modified pro-choice" and "modified pro-life," to test public opinion more accurately, could remedy that. These terms would indicate basic presumptions rather than absolutist positions. People who accepted a "modified pro-choice" position would allow women to choose abortion, although legal restrictions would apply in certain situations. People who accepted a "modified pro-life" stance would favour legally restricting abortion, but with some exceptions to comply with the Canadian Charter and to avoid unenforceable law. This modified approach might also allow us, although we start from different bases, to identify where we agree, or are closer to agreement than we have recognized, about what the law on abortion should be.

Sixty percent of Canadians agree that abortion on demand should be legally limited after twenty weeks gestation. Their moral intuitions warn them that unborn children capable of living outside the womb should have some legal protection. They also find it horrendous to think of inflicting excruciating pain on the fetus in dismembering it in utero, to ensure it is born dead to avoid legal liability for killing it.

So should abortion on demand be legally limited before twenty weeks? In a country such as Canada, where there is no law restricting abortion, I propose that we should start by applying law at thirteen weeks gestation. This is an incremental approach that could obtain the support of many Canadians and is not wrongful complicity in abortion. When it is not possible in reality to save all unborn babies, we must save as many as we are able.

Such an approach is not to approve first trimester abortion, as some pro-life advocates argue it is. I reject the pro-choice dogma that the embryo or fetus is "just a bunch of cells" with no intrinsic value, or respect for human life is not involved in abortion, or that early abortion is not a major ethical issue. Abortion is always a very serious ethical issue, but from a practical and even an ethical point of view, if we hope to reduce the number of abortions to the minimum achievable in Canada (in view of the facts that, presently, there is no law and abortion will not be completely legally prohibited), it is only feasible to argue that it should become a legal issue after thirteen weeks gestation. There is precedent for such an approach in European countries, including Scandinavian ones usually regarded as espousing "progressive" social values, which makes it more likely to be accepted by more Canadians, whether they self-identify as pro-life or pro-choice.

As a practical reality, Canadian legislators will not legally restrict early abortion. Moreover, the law will not prevent abortions in the first trimester, especially in light of chemical abortifacients. Having a law that is ineffective and ignored could do more harm than good, as it brings the law into disrepute and could send a message that all law on abortion can be ignored. And in respect to reducing the number of abortions overall, it could also do more harm than good. Let me explain.

If early abortion is not illegal, a woman with a crisis pregnancy is more likely to seek counselling and learn of its risks and harms, and its alternatives, and perhaps change her mind. Some women might choose to keep their child if they know that fully adequate support is available. The relevant analogy is the decriminalization of suicide to try to prevent suicide, because suicidal people and their families are more likely to seek help if they are not threatened with criminal prosecution. We need abortion prevention programs, with counselling and other support systems, just as we have suicide prevention programs. Moreover, as I explained earlier in this chapter, this approach would give women the widest possible range of choices, which, apart from other considerations, is a necessary prerequisite for obtaining informed consent to abortion, if that is the woman's decision. Helping a woman to feel that she will not lose control of her life by going through with an unplanned pregnancy can help her to decide against abortion. Eliciting that feeling and informed choice require readily available facilities for crisis pregnancy counselling that are not abortion clinics, which are in a conflict of interest position as they profit financially from carrying out abortions.

We need some law on abortion in Canada in order to recognize publicly and as a society that abortion is always a serious ethical decision and that, as all the judges of the Supreme Court of Canada ruled in the *Morgentaler* case,[25] the lives of unborn children, at least at a certain point in pregnancy, merit legal protection. The court also explained in that case that it is the role of Parliament to decide and legally establish what that point of the protection of unborn children is.

To the contrary, Justin Trudeau, the leader of the federal Liberal Party, recently took a very public and highly controversial position that all politicians in his party must vote pro-choice on abortion or they were not welcome in the party. That is, they would have to vote against enacting any law on abortion. Here is Trudeau's edict: "The policy going forward is that every single Liberal MP will be expected to stand up for a woman's right to choose." Let's complete that statement: "The policy going forward is that every single Liberal MP will be expected to stand up for a woman's right to choose to kill her unborn child, even if, were it delivered, it would have a chance of surviving or if she seeks an abortion only because of the sex of the fetus."

Choice itself is neither moral nor immoral. Rather, it is what we choose that determines that, as these examples show. Trudeau and his MPs should note that facilitating immoral choices is complicity in the immorality involved.

And I haven't yet even mentioned the contravention of rights that this edict represents – rights to freedom of conscience, freedom of religion – and politicians' obligations in a democracy to those they represent and so on. The vast majority of religious people, for instance, all Catholics and Muslims (or at least those who follow their conscience), most other Christians, and many Jews, are thereby excluded from running for elected office in the Liberal Party. In the future, that exclusion might even apply to members of the party, as Trudeau initially extended his policy not just to MPs but to members.

I hope that, no matter what their position on abortion, most Canadians will feel appalled by Trudeau's action. Such an edict by a leader of a political party on a matter of conscience relating to one of our most fundamental values, respect for human life, violates the basic principle that MPs are primarily their constituents' voice in Parliament on such matters, not their leader's. Trudeau's pronouncement thwarts Parliament's role and functioning in implementing democracy in practice in deciding on our values; "stacking" Parliament in this way on a conscience issue is anti-democratic. Moreover, who wants an MP willing to contravene his or her own conscience for political gain? As a woman whose prestigious Catholic family had been active Liberal supporters for generations expressed it in her signature on an email to me the day after the edict: "Card-carrying Liberal until yesterday."

Impact of Abortion on Societal Values

In Europe and North America, between one in three and one in four pregnancies ends in abortion – that is, in these societies, abortion has both been normalized and become part of the norm. What will that mean for future generations, and, with hindsight, how will they view present practices and attitudes regarding abortion? My prediction is that they will see abortion as having been a human tragedy for individuals and society.

I predict that our descendants will characterize our current approach to abortion as symptomatic of a time when a "culture of despair" threatened to overwhelm a "culture of hope" but people, especially young people, became aware of the wider and longer-term implications and took steps to ensure that it didn't happen.

The current situation around abortion is one more example where we look only to the wishes of the individual involved and not to the impact on society, especially on its foundational values – and look only to present effects and not to future ones. That approach leads us to a simple, certain, but wrong response – namely, abortion – to the very complex issue of an unwanted pregnancy, a situation that often generates agonizing, unavoidable uncertainty.

Dealing with such uncertainty by converting it to a false certainty – for instance, the woman believing that abortion is the only feasible "right" response – is a frequent cause of ethical mistakes. Research shows that women with unwanted pregnancies commonly feel that they have lost control of their lives and, like Anna, that they must face a choice between their life and that of the unborn child; in making this choice, they are tormented by uncertainty, and its accompanying fear. Our response as a society, especially our sole response, should not be to propose to them that they should resolve that uncertainty by destroying their unborn child. Rather, at the very least, we should give them the support they need to feel that they have a real option that will allow them both to go on with the pregnancy and to maintain control of their lives.

Canada continues to be a living laboratory on social values issues, with some consequences that I predict it will one day seriously regret. However, on a more optimistic note, there are signs that more and more young Canadians are realizing that possibility, especially in relation to abortion, and working effectively to help change the current situation.

That said, I am often asked why Canadians don't speak out more forcefully about such issues as Justin Trudeau's edict. Many who regard completely unrestricted access to abortion as unethical have been bullied into thinking they have no right to "impose" what they believe is right or wrong on someone else, especially when they are told it is a breach of human rights to do so. Pro-choice advocates rely heavily on the Canadian Charter of Rights and Freedoms as justification for having no law on abortion. For example, Carolyn Bennett, a physician and a federal Liberal MP, speaking with Anna Maria Tremonti, radio journalist and host of CBC's national current affairs program *The Current*, argued in support of Trudeau's decree that all Liberal candidates must be pro-choice (meaning they must accept that women have a right to legally unrestricted abortion throughout pregnancy), because the Canadian Charter requires this. That argument, endlessly repeated by pro-choice advocates, is legally incorrect. As the Supreme Court of Canada made clear in the *Morgentaler* case, the charter does not prohibit legislating on abortion, much as Trudeau might wish it did.

The silent Canadians, among whom are many law students, are also frightened they will be shamed, and labelled as socially conservative, and black-listed if they speak against so-called progressive values. Recently, I heard a Supreme Court of Canada judge refer to socially conservative values as "restrictive values," which is not reassuring for social conservatives.

Relevant and important insights could be generated by seeing Justin Trudeau's stance as a powerful example of "adolescent progressivism" – the view that change is always beneficial and necessary, accompanied by a knee-jerk rejection of traditional values and views – and of "totalitarian utopianism" – the espousing of a primary ideology of choice and tolerance, while rejecting any values or views seen as interfering or inconsistent with the envisioned utopia. A reaction to the latter is summed up in an email I received from a woman adamantly opposed to Trudeau's declaration : "Just as it is not acceptable in the Canadian context to say that abortion is wrong because God says so, we cannot accept that it is right no matter what because Justin Trudeau says so." She added, "I personally found Mr. Trudeau's declaration to be patronizing and incongruous with the Canadian tradition of dialogue and debate in the crafting of law and policy."

So Where Do We Go from Here?

In chapter 5, I wrote about the importance of engendering experiences of amazement, wonder, and awe to help us to act ethically. I suggest that we've lost that experience in relation to the transmission of human life and we need to find it again, both individually and as a society. Consequently, it merits repeating some of what I wrote in that chapter, because it is especially relevant to the issues raised in this chapter:

- Experiencing amazement, wonder, and awe enriches our lives, can help us to find meaning, and can change how we see the world and what decisions we make and how we live our lives, especially regarding values and ethics, including in relation to the value of respect for life and abortion.
- It can put us in touch with the sacred – for some people, a "religious sacred," for others a "secular sacred" – that to which we must not lay waste but hold in trust for future generations. We must not lay waste to human life.
- Experiences of amazement, wonder, and awe can also elicit an existential perception that differentiates those who have those experiences from those who don't in terms of what they regard as ethical or unethical.

If we perceive the transmission of human life, the coming into being of a unique new human being, with amazement, wonder, and awe, we are likely to see it as involving a mystery that must be respected, which will usually exclude abortion and certainly excludes infanticide. If we do not look at both the unborn child and the born one with amazement, wonder, and awe just because they exist and if we do not perceive the mystery in their existence, we are much less likely to see abortion, or even infanticide, as morally and ethically unacceptable. Experiences of amazement, wonder, and awe can also cause us to choose differently, to rearrange our priorities, including in deciding about abortion when faced with a crisis pregnancy.

So, one question we must address, as both individuals and societies, is: In what way can we communicate with a woman with a crisis pregnancy so that she comes to regard her participation in the transmission of human life, the creation of a new unique human being, her unborn child, with amazement, wonder, and awe? How can we make it more likely that she will move from hopelessness – a feeling that there is nothing to look forward to, a feeling connected with a desire for death – to hope, which is generated by having a sense of connection to the future? To repeat yet again what is for me a mantra: Hope is the oxygen of the human spirit. Without hope, our human spirit dies. With it, we can overcome even seemingly insurmountable obstacles.

◆◆◆

In conclusion, having set out the many ways in which we disagree with each other in relation to abortion, I believe we can nevertheless start from agreement and that it is important that we do so, as it gives a different tone to our debates and disagreements. The vast majority of us, whether we are pro-life or pro-choice, agree that we want to have the fewest number of abortions possible. How to achieve that needs and merits authentic, in-depth, honest discussion carried out with the utmost integrity on the part of all participants.

7

How Might the Involvement of "Applied Ethics" in Law Affect Our Societal Values? Ethics as "First Aid" for Law

The relation of law with morality and ethics is as old as the law itself. Yet even today not everyone agrees on what that relation is, or whether ethics is beneficial or harmful to the law. To decide, we must address questions that include: Why does the relation of law and ethics matter? What is its history? Why did "applied ethics" and its practitioners emerge in the 1970s? And what is the contemporary interaction of law with applied ethics, especially in courts and legislatures?[1]

Before exploring such questions, it merits pointing out that the relation of law, morality, and ethics is still the focus of much sophisticated, analytical scholarship. For instance, Princeton University law professor Robert P. George and Oxford University professor of legal philosophy John Finnis have developed "new natural law" theory and legal scholarship which has impacted jurisprudence. However, I do not address their valuable theoretical work here; rather, my focus is on the emergence of bioethics in the last third of the twentieth century and its relation with and impact on law in practice.

Twentieth-Century Interactions of Law, Medicine, and Ethics in Courts

Emergence of Bioethics

A judicial observation describing the relation of law and medicine in the early 1970s – "law, marching with medicine but in the rear and limping a little" – can give us a window on how ethics came to the aid of the law to help it to keep up with medicine. It can help us to understand in particular the relation of law and bioethics.

This quotation comes from the judgment of Justice Windeyer of the High Court of Australia in *Mount Isa Mines v Pusey.*[2] In this early case – 1970 – the judge recognized that the law was clearly not keeping up with advances in medical science, in this instance, advances in psychiatry. With hindsight, in this litigation we can see ethics coming to the law's aid, informing and supplementing it when the law was having difficulty coping, in the sense of justice prevailing – although at the time ethics would not have been perceived as playing that role.

The case involved an engineer, the plaintiff, who was employed in a powerhouse at Mount Isa Mine in Queensland, Australia. Two electricians working in the powerhouse negligently caused an explosion that generated an electric arc of intense heat. The two men were horribly burnt. The engineer came to the rescue of one of the electricians. He was intensely distressed by seeing him with his clothes burnt off, his skin peeling, obviously grievously hurt. After some days, with the added knowledge that both men had died, the shock of the event began to tell. He became depressed and suffered a severe schizophrenic reaction, with acute depression and an acute anxiety state. He was unable to work for considerable periods and was under psychiatric treatment.

The legal issue for the court was whether the seriously psychiatrically injured plaintiff could recover damages for negligently inflicted "pure nervous shock," that is, mental injury unaccompanied by physical injury. Historically, the Anglo-Australian Common Law did not allow recovery for such injury on the basis that it did not qualify as legally recognized "damages." At the time of the High Court's hearing of this case, however, the issue of whether such damages were legally recoverable was being inconsistently handled in case law and much debated in doctrine. The fears of allowing compensation were that once this happened, there would be a flood of cases overwhelming the courts, and fraudulent claims would be presented.

The judge first took note of many recent psychiatric advances in recognizing and diagnosing mental illness. It is a truism in ethics, but no less important for being so, that "good facts are necessary for good ethics." That means that as the facts, especially medical and scientific facts, change, so do the ethics. And, consequently, so sometimes should the law. Changing the law to allow an award of damages for "pure" mental injury when that was ethically required was an early example of a court incorporating ethics into law in order to deal with advances in medical science, a practice that was to become common with unprecedented advances such as genetic and reproductive technologies, as discussed later in this chapter.

In arriving at his conclusions, Justice Windeyer cited Lord Wright in *Bourhill v. Young*:[3] "The lawyer likes to draw fixed and definite lines and is apt to ask where the thing is to stop. I should reply it should stop where in the particular case the good sense of the jury or of the judge decides."[4] Justice Windeyer went on to add,"That perhaps does not reckon with courts of appeal, and varying judicial opinions of where in good sense the proper stopping-place is."

It can be argued that the "good sense" to which Lord Wright and Justice Windeyer refer is moral intuition, which guides our sense of what is and is not ethical and which, as the judge recognizes, can vary from person to person. But that variation is not a valid reason to exclude it as an important "human way of knowing" or, likewise, to exclude our emotional response to a situation. It is sometimes said that "we ignore our feelings at our ethical peril."[5]

Rather, as I have proposed in earlier chapters, these ways of knowing need to be safeguarded, in particular by using reason as a secondary but essential verification mechanism to check if we've been led astray.[6] It might also be that these "other ways" function to bring ethics to bear in our decision-making. Because that process would be no less true of judges than other people, it might be another way in which ethics is brought into law.

And Justice Windeyer's description of the law as "in the rear and limping" is an articulation of a disconnect that he perceived between what ethics required in terms of compensating the plaintiff for his serious psychological injuries, and the law, which as it stood would not allow that.

It is probably no coincidence that this judgment was handed down in 1970. This was the era when the field of practice, research, and scholarship that we now know as "applied ethics," of which bioethics is the prime example, was just beginning to develop. Its emergence was being precipitated by unprecedented advances in science and medicine with which the law had no experience and for which it had no precedents; yet physicians, scientists, politicians, policy-makers, and the public were turning to the law, in both courts and legislatures, for guidance in relation to the development and use of these advances.

Emergence of Applied Ethics and Ethicists

Prior to around 1970, there was a tacit assumption within western democracies that we more or less agreed on the collective values on which our societies were based – that is, what was and was not moral and ethical – and that the law reflected, implemented, and upheld these values. In the late 1960s, as traditional shared values were challenged and conflict erupted as to what they should be, many societies realized that this assumption was no longer valid.

The causes included the loss of a largely shared Judeo-Christian religious tradition to which people would turn for guidance on values. Many people were no longer religious or, if they were, they followed an increasingly wide variety of religious traditions. Another cause was a lack of agreement on the values that should govern the mind- and world-altering breakthroughs being realized in the new science.

Science fiction was rapidly being converted to science fact: the previously impossible, and even unthinkable, was becoming reality, and we had no precedents for what values should govern these extraordinary developments. A seminal event in the emergence of what became the new field of applied ethics was the first heart transplant in 1967 by Dr Christiaan Barnard in South Africa. A person was now walking around with a beating heart, the primary indicator of life, of a dead person.

The law was confronted with new questions: Was it murder to have taken the donor's heart? When was a person dead so that their organs could be taken for transplantation?[7] Should organ transplants be prohibited? If not, under what conditions were they acceptable? Today we view organ transplantation as such a routine medical procedure that we forget how shocked and deeply concerned the world was to learn of Dr Barnard's feat.

A second seminal event was the birth of the first "test-tube baby," Louise Brown, in 1978. Once more, the world was shocked at a procedure that involved conception other than through sexual intercourse and outside a woman's body – again, routine today. Questions that emerged in this context included: Was it acceptable to freeze human embryos? What about using them for research? Should embryo donation be permitted? Should a surrogate mother be allowed to keep the baby to whom she gave birth but was not genetically related? And so on.

Science was moving too fast for the law and the courts to keep up with the unprecedented issues it was presenting. The number of such issues exploded through the 1980s and into the 1990s – and, of course, has continued to do so. Courts – and, indeed, legislatures – coped by turning to ethics as an "add-on" to the law. They would first look to the law, and if this did not provide a clear or satisfactory answer, turn to ethics, which was growing exponentially. The first clearly identified uses of ethics in law and the emergence of the disciplinary field known as "applied ethics" and of its practitioners, "ethicists," was initially largely in the area of bioethics. Later "applied ethics" analysis was expanded to other areas, especially professional practice, where concerns about ethics arose, bioethics becoming used as a model for addressing them.

Anecdotally, it is said that in 1970 there were seven articles published in the world in English in the field we would now call applied ethics. By 1980 there were fourteen specialty journals in the field. And by 1990 there were over two hundred ethics centres, many of them in universities, undertaking teaching and research in the field. Moreover, ethicists, in particular bioethicists, who were starting to be recognized as professionals in applied ethics, were more and more called upon as expert witnesses before official enquiries,[8] courts, and parliamentary committees. The question of what credentials should be required in order to be regarded as such an expert remains to this day a contentious one.

Chief Justice Robert French of the High Court of Australia, discussing this question in an interesting article published in 2003,[9] begins by recognizing the by then well-established interaction of law and applied ethics in relation to issues raised by scientific and medical advances. He notes "an increasing reliance on ethicists as public policy life coaches to guide us on our way."[10] Those ethicists, he proposes, must be honest, objective, independent, competent, and diligent in providing "transactional advice in the formulation of administrative practice and public policy and in the development of the law."[11] In other words, the chief justice clearly contemplates a valid role for ethics – and ethicists – in the law's future. Rightly, however, he warns, "Any tendency to commercialization or commodification of ethics as a product is damaging to the whole of society. So too is the corruption of ethics to a form of politically convenient certification of proposed actions, practices or laws."[12] He goes on to note that there "may be a need to develop ethics for ethicists,"[13] a sentiment with which I'm sure all ethicists, and many others, would concur.

To return to the history of the development of applied ethics, it's arguable that in the early 1990s the order of analysis changed from analyzing from law to ethics (law first, ethics second) to first looking at the ethics and then assessing whether the law accorded with the ethics (ethics first, law second).[14] This change might seem of minor importance and largely irrelevant, but its effect was far from neutral on the outcome of decisions that involved both ethical and legal analysis. Law-informing-ethics does not necessarily result in the same outcome as ethics-informing-law. This is easily seen in relation to physicians' decisions about offering adequate and effective pain-management treatment to patients. In the past, many physicians interpreted the criminal law as prohibiting them from giving necessary pain relief treatment if they believed there was any chance it might shorten the patient's life (or in the case of some physicians, that it might cause addiction), and would thus withhold such treatment. Yet it is unethical for a physician to unreasonably leave a person in serious pain; ethics requires that all reasonably necessary pain-relief treatment be offered.

When the order of analysis was changed, the law was correctly seen by physicians and others as not prohibiting the provision of such treatment. Indeed, we now recognize it as a breach of human rights for a health-care professional to leave a person in serious pain, and it can also be argued there is a legal duty to offer adequate pain management to patients who need it. (This approach is articulated and implemented in the 2010 Declaration of Montreal, discussed below, which provides a paradigm example of the interaction and relation of law and bioethics.)

Finally, the American Medical Association's *Opinion 1.02 – The Relation of Law and Ethics* merits noting in the context of the current discussion:

> The following statements are intended to clarify the relationship between law and ethics.
>
> Ethical values and legal principles are usually closely related, but ethical obligations typically exceed legal duties. In some cases, the law mandates unethical conduct. In general, when physicians believe a law is unjust, they should work to change the law. In exceptional circumstances of unjust laws, ethical responsibilities should supersede legal obligations.
>
> The fact that a physician charged with allegedly illegal conduct is acquitted or exonerated in civil or criminal proceedings does not necessarily mean that the physician acted ethically.

Contemporary Examples of the Interaction of Bioethics and Law

Ethics Informing Law: Mandating Pain Management

The Declaration of Montreal,[15] shepherded to fruition by the International Association for the Study of Pain (IASP), establishes that people in pain have a "fundamental human right" to have reasonable access to pain management and that unreasonable failure to provide such access is a breach of their human rights.

Why turn to human rights?

The language of human rights is a language common to ethics and to law; as such, it can bridge gaps between them. It is also very persuasive: it is is difficult to imagine any reasonable person saying, "I don't care about human rights or if they are breached."[16] Recognition of human rights, whether in domestic or international law or, indeed, in ethics, tries to ensure the rightness or ethics of our interactions with each other at the most basic level of our humanness, at the level of its essence, that which makes us human – which is not easy to define. As French philosopher Hélène Boussard writes, "Both human rights law and bioethics aim to protect human dignity, from which human rights values stem."[17] Intentionally leaving someone in serious pain is a complete failure to respect their human dignity and it is therefore appropriate to bring both human rights law and bioethics to bear to try to prevent such situations from occurring.[18] That is exactly the goal of the Declaration of Montreal.

The Nature of Human Rights

Through the use of the concept of human rights, the Declaration spans and connects law and bioethics, because both are closely connected with human rights in the context of suffering.

While human rights are often legally enacted, the law does not create them; rather, they exist independently of being recognized by any human agency. For that reason, no one can opt out of respecting them. What we do is *articulate* human rights, which is why statements of them are called declarations. This non-contingent feature of human rights also means that private actors can proclaim them, as is true in regard to the Declaration of Montreal.

In speaking of other declarations dealing with ethics in scientific and medical contexts, such as UNESCO's Declaration on Universal Norms on Bioethics, Boussard explains well the nature of such declarations: they "are legal instruments but they are not legally binding. Their originality lies in their aim, which is to translate ethical standards into legal terms in order to protect human rights in scientific research and medical interventions …[19] Bioethics and law strengthen each other to give teeth to fundamental human rights values …[20] They are ethically inspired legal instruments."[21] This last sentence, which articulates and emphasizes the symbiotic relation of bioethics and law, particularly deserves to be strongly endorsed.

One way to understand the term "human rights" is as shorthand for a tripartite concept that consists of human rights, human responsibilities (or obligations), and human ethics. Sometimes we need to focus on one of these limbs, sometimes on another, and sometimes on all of them. Figure 1 below explains this tripartite concept diagrammatically and explains how I see these limbs interacting. As it shows, human rights, human responsibilities, and human ethics can be viewed as three different entry points into the same reality, situation, or issue. The figure also illustrates why we can speak of human ethics, which can later be translated into legally recognized human rights, before that legal recognition occurs.

An advantage of such an approach is that, as Boussard states, recognizing the "interdependence between human rights law and bioethics leads us to move from a static image of existing or positive law in favour of a more dynamic concept in which views on law as it is and views on law as it should be are continually merging into views on law as it is becoming."[22] So, for instance, recognizing a human right to reasonable access to pain management means that health-care professionals and health-care institutions have ethical and sometimes legal obligations to offer patients such management.

The Nature and Impact of the Declaration of Montreal

Although human rights obligations exist whether or not we declare them, declaring them and, even more potently, formally enacting them as law help to ensure that they are honoured. The Declaration of Montreal is not just a piece of paper but what we call a "verbal act"; that is, its words will change reality, just as a judge's verdict is not just words but changes reality. The hope is that the Declaration will help to change the horrible reality of people being left in pain.

The Declaration will be an ethics guide in relation to pain management, and an educational tool for health-care professionals and trainees. It will sometimes function as evidence to justify giving necessary pain relief treatment when others would prevent it. In particular, it will help to overcome the harmful beliefs of some health-care professionals who withhold pain management because they fear legal liability or patients becoming addicted. It will deliver a strong message that it is wrong *not* to provide pain management.

Provisions in the Declaration could become case law if adopted by courts. Failure to live up to its requirements could then constitute medical malpractice (medical negligence) or unprofessional conduct, which can be cause to revoke a physician's license to practice medicine.

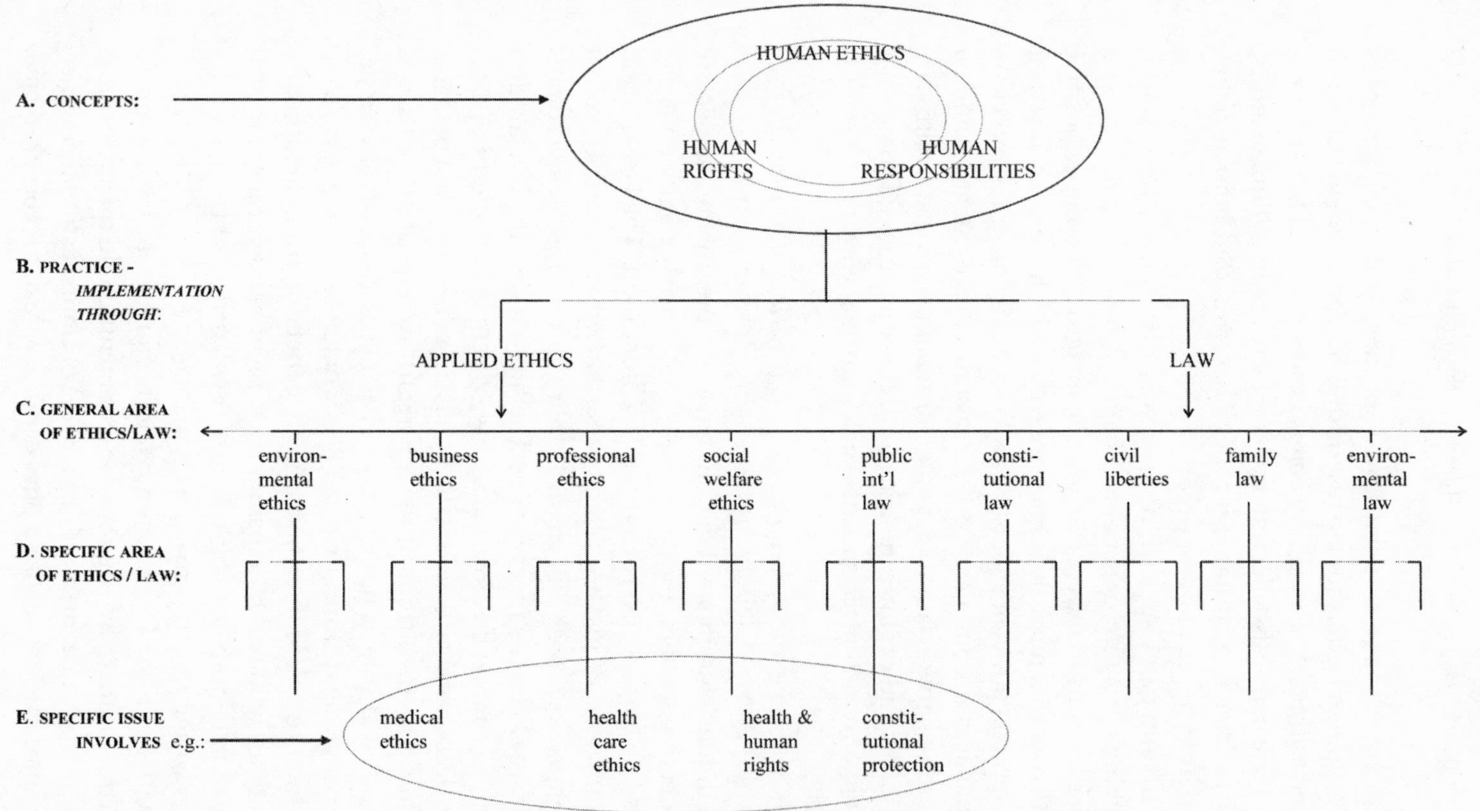

Figure 1 The relationship of human rights, human responsibilities, and human ethics

The Declaration will inform and, one hopes, guide institutions and governments in formulating health policy and law with respect to pain management. It will help governments to understand that they have both domestic and international obligations not to unreasonably hinder, at the very least, their own citizens' or other people's access to pain management.

It is an outrage and a human tragedy that in developing countries many people in serious pain do not have access to opioids, including as a result of the conditions relating to narcotic drugs some countries attach to their foreign aid to these developing countries. A Human Rights Watch report documents an egregious example of a lack of access to pain management in a developing country: in Kenya the vast majority of children dying from HIV/AIDS die with no pain-relief treatment.[23] This is clearly an area where ethics must inform law and practice.

One of the most ancient and universally accepted maxims could be applied to ensure that everyone who needs pain management receives it: "Do unto others as you would that they would do unto you" – the Golden Rule. The Declaration of Montreal spells out what those "others" have a human right to expect when they are in pain.

A beautiful Sanskrit salutation, *Namaste*, can be roughly translated as, "The Light in me recognizes the Light in you." It affirms our common humanity across all barriers and borders. It could also be rendered as "The pain in me recognizes the pain in you, and that recognition causes me to respond to relieve your pain" – which is another way to express the insight communicated in the concept of the "wounded healer."

The Declaration of Montreal is a very important step forward in making sure that as many people as possible, and especially health-care professionals, recognize others' pain and see it as their privilege and obligation to do what they can to assuage it.

The Wider Impact of the Declaration of Montreal on Human Rights

Finally, the Declaration of Montreal could raise our sensitivity to the horror of breaches of human rights in general. Fortunately, most of us don't experience such breaches of our rights in our everyday lives, and consequently we don't personally identify with many of them, much as we might abhor them. But because pain is a universal human experience which we all want to avoid, wrongful failure to manage it is one of the rare breaches of human rights with which we can all personally identify and thus better understand what breaches of human rights in general feel like. It is a lesson we should all heed.

Ethics Informing Law: Governing Reproductive Technologies

The governance of assisted human reproductive technologies (ARTs) is another context in which both ethics and law have important roles to play, and, as with pain management, whether we consider the law first and ethics second or vice versa can make a difference to our decisions about the use of ARTs. It is also a context in which the language of human rights can function as a bridge between ethics and law. And, as discussed in previous chapters, it is an area that gives rise to situations in which we need to consider the ethics of our decisions at levels other than just the individual one, the cumulative impact of decisions by individuals, and what the law that governs these decisions should be. Below I discuss each aspect in turn.

Child-centred Decision-Making

Ethics requires that decisions about the development and use of reproductive technologies must be primarily child-centred, not primarily adult-centred as they most often are at present. Indeed, the law itself can promote adult-centred decision-making in this context – for instance, when it is interpreted to require that, in order to avoid discrimination against adults, or to respect their rights to autonomy and self-determination or privacy, access to these technologies or particular uses of them must be allowed, even though they are not in the "best interests" of the resulting children. This interpretation can give rise to unethical or at least ethically questionable outcomes such as creating children who, intentionally, are unable to trace their biological parents and other family members, or who have three genetic parents, or a single parent, or two same-sex ones.

On the other hand, the law could also help to incorporate ethics into judicial decisions. For instance, the extent to which the courts view legal instruments that enact constitutional rights, such as the United States or South African Bill of Rights, or the Canadian Charter of Rights and Freedoms,[24] as a legal articulation and embedding of fundamental ethical norms and principles in a country's constitution could affect the extent to which judges are willing to interpret constitutional rights, either broadly or restrictively, so as to achieve ethical outcomes. The late American legal philosopher Ronald Dworkin called such an approach to interpretation of a country's constitution a "moral reading" of these laws, which has the effect of incorporating ethics into the law they promulgate.[25] As Dworkin points out, what given judges consider moral will vary depending on whether they espouse liberal or conservative values. Such moral readings have been responsible, Dworkin says, for the best and worst decisions of the United States Supreme Court.

Ethical Impact of Legal Charters of Rights

The more a charter of constitutional rights is seen by judges as intended to ensure that state actions are ethical, not just legal, the more likely it is that its provisions will be interpreted by courts in a way that incorporates ethics into their judgments in the interests of ensuring justice.

In the same vein, it should come as no surprise that litigants whose perceptions are that their claims have a strong ethical component are enlisting such constitutional bills of rights or charters to promote their claims.

Insofar as they resulted from seeing a need to articulate in a legal document society's shared values and ethics, legal instruments such as the Canadian Charter, enacted in 1982, or the South African Bill of Rights (1994), can be seen as yet another outcome of the realization back in the 1970s that we could no longer assume that we all bought into the same shared societal values or that the law reflected, implemented, and upheld those shared values. It merits noting that, as in all statements of principle on which a wide societal consensus is sought, such charters and bills of rights are couched in broad, general language. Variance and disagreement enter at the level of the interpretation and application of their provisions.

One of the criticisms of seeing such instruments as legally enacted "shared ethics" is that it is the proper function of the courts to implement the law, not ethics, and that their undertaking the latter task confuses and harms the law. But that is to forget a major historical feature of at least the courts in jurisdictions that have their origins in the English common law system. The Courts of Equity applied a "gloss on the common law," when strict application of that law by the king's common law courts caused unconscionable outcomes for unsuccessful litigants. They were the "courts of conscience" and acted *in personam* to prohibit victorious parties from enforcing such judgments. Although operating in a very different way legally, constitutional charters of rights can be viewed as allowing twenty-first century judges to realize goals of the same nature.

The trial judgment in the *Pratten* case[26] shows a court – the British Columbia Supreme Court – squeezing ethics into its decision through the funnel of constitutional law, but nevertheless using a conventional approach to charter interpretation and application to do so. Such a conventional approach in using the charter is arguably not true of the Supreme Court of Canada's judgment in the *Insite* case,[27] discussed shortly.

Olivia Pratten, a young woman who was conceived by anonymous sperm donation, wanted to know the identity of her biological father. The physician who carried out the artificial insemination of Pratten's mother resulting in Olivia's birth refused to release the medical records on the grounds of respecting the sperm donor's privacy.

The British Columbia Adoption Act gives adopted children, when they turn nineteen, rights to have access to information about their birth parents. Ms Pratten challenged these provisions as being discriminatory and therefore unconstitutional under the Canadian Charter of Rights and Freedoms, because they did not give children conceived from sperm or ova donations the same legal rights of access to such information as adopted children. Justice Elaine Adair of the British Columbia Supreme Court agreed.

The judge suspended her ruling striking down the offending provisions in the Adoption Act for fifteen months to allow the British Columbia Legislature time to amend the law to give donor-conceived people the same rights as adopted ones. The British Columbia government appealed the ruling, arguing that the trial judge erred in law in her finding. The province's attorney general, Barry Penner, explained:

"The B.C. government is appealing the Pratten decision because it raises important constitutional principles that extend beyond this particular case." The government's concern was that they could be limited in their "ability to provide programs that respond in tailored ways to particular groups of individuals." He continued, "Governments need the flexibility to develop programs that respond to the needs of British Columbians, such as programs that support seniors, social assistance, and other programs."[28]

One possible interpretation of the attorney general's statement is that he was concerned that affirmative action – positive content discrimination to assist historically disadvantaged groups – could be limited by Justice Adair's ruling, because governments could take it to mean that if they cannot provide everyone who can claim equivalence to the disadvantaged group with the same benefits, their only legal option is not to provide *anybody* with these benefits, as to do otherwise would constitute discrimination. Certainly, in many cases at least, ethics would not endorse that outcome.

Justice Adair's ruling was the right result, but, from a wider social and public policy and precedent point of view, as the British Columbia government recognized, the fact that it is based in discrimination is worrisome – although not legally incorrect. The only way the difference between adopted children's rights of access to their biological identities and donor conceived children's rights to the same information would be legally valid under Canadian constitutional law would be to prove the different treatment was not discrimination within section 15(1) of the Canadian Charter of Rights and Freedoms, or was justified affirmative action within the exemption in section 15(2) allowing for that, or, if it were found to be discrimination, it was justified state action within the requirements of section 1 of the charter. Establishing the latter would require the British Columbia government to show that the breach of Ms Pratten's constitutional rights resulting from the under-inclusivity of the Adoption Act are "reasonable limits prescribed by law [such] as can be demonstrably justified in a free and democratic society."[29]

Ms Pratten also argued that she was deprived of her constitutional "right to life, liberty and security of the person"[30] under section 7 of the charter. She claimed that the failure of the legislature to pass laws requiring that medical records of her biological parentage be kept was such a deprivation and was not "in accordance with the principles of fundamental justice," which section 7 allows as a justification for contravening these rights. The trial court rejected this argument on the basis that it was a claim to a positive-content right (a right *to* something) and, without deciding conclusively on the limits of the protection that section 7 could provide, ruled that the section's primary function was to protect people's negative-content rights (rights *against* something) to life, liberty, and security of the person from infringement by the state. It also ruled there was no state or governmental action infringing section 7 rights as required for the protection provided by section 7 to apply; a failure to pass legislation requiring that records be kept was not such action.

On hearing the appeal by the attorney general of British Columbia, the British Columbia Court of Appeal overturned Justice Adair's decision.[31] The court ruled that offspring have no legal or constitutional right to know their biological past, and requiring that such information be provided would amount to state intrusion into many people's lives. Ms Pratten sought leave from the Supreme Court of Canada to appeal but was refused, thereby allowing the Court of Appeal's decision to stand.

As I explained previously, if a state action were present in any given situation, the way in which section 7 rights to "life, liberty, and security of the person" would be interpreted by Canadian courts, with respect to implementing ethics in their decisions, could depend on the extent to which they view the Charter of Rights and Freedoms as a legal articulation and embedding of fundamental ethical norms and principles in the Canadian constitution and as intended to ensure that state actions are ethical. If judges see the charter as intended to promote ethics, they might be more likely to interpret section 7 rights accordingly, and, similarly, what is required to protect and respect those rights. In contrast, if they view the charter strictly legalistically, their interpretation of what section 7 requires could be quite different.

Many people welcomed the outcome at the trial level of the *Pratten* decision, although there was concern about its basis in discrimination law for yet another reason. If adoptees had not had a legal right of access to their records, as they did not until quite recently, donor offspring might not have acquired the right either, at least not on the basis of finding a breach of a constitutional protection against discrimination by way of comparison with a similarly situated group of people.

This possibility shows one difference between using law and using ethics, and between judge-made law (case law) and legislation, to deal with a social or public policy issue. An ethical analysis can take into account a much wider range of considerations than can an analysis based only on the existing law, and the same is true for politicians in enacting new legislation, as compared with judges in creating case law.

Judges must find a legal basis for their decisions, but they can and do take into account the morality and ethics of deciding one way or another. Legislators can – and many people believe they should – first look at the morality and ethics of the laws they could pass and then decide on what should be the content of those laws in light of the relevant ethics.

Ethics Informing Law and Social and Public Policy on Fundamental Rights

The ethics and law that should govern reproductive technologies is a very contentious area of social and public policy. The judgment of the British Columbia Supreme Court in the *Pratten* case is an example of law being used in this area to "inform" – implement – ethics. But if and when the British Columbia legislature deals with this issue, ethics should inform law. The proper question in the *Pratten* case was an ethical, not a legal, one: is it ethically wrong to intentionally prevent any person from knowing through whom life travelled to them? There are good arguments that it is.[32]

Supporting such arguments is a rapidly increasing recognition in many societies that to intentionally make those who are adopted or donor-conceived "genetic orphans" by not giving them access to identifying information about their biological parents is ethically wrong and ought to be legally prohibited. If we assume, for the sake of exploring the issue, that gamete donation is ethically acceptable (debatable in the eyes of some, including a growing number of donor offspring), then donor anonymity is wrong. Apart from people's right not to have knowledge of their biological heritage and relationships intentionally wiped out, people born from gamete donation need to know their medical histories for health reasons; they need to know their social histories in order to properly form their sense of identity.

Those opposing the prohibition of egg and sperm donor anonymity include the assisted reproductive technology (ART) industry (the "fertility industry") and groups claiming to represent would-be parents, who fear that ending anonymity will lead to a drop in the number of donors and thereby limit their ability to have a child. To the contrary, the United Kingdom, which banned donor anonymity in 2005, has seen an increase in the number of donors.

As can be seen in the *Pratten* case, while the immediate focus may be a legal challenge to, for instance, gamete donor anonymity, the issues raised in such social-ethical-legal values cases can be equally about the proper interaction of ethics and law in relation to forming social and public policy, and about the legitimate respective roles of the courts and legislatures with respect to that task.

Other situations where the law and ethics interact and the legitimate respective roles of the courts and legislatures are brought into question include governance of prostitution, allowing clean-needle exchanges for people with drug addiction, legalizing marijuana, and so on. Depending upon whether one gives priority to "use reduction" or to "harm reduction" in dealing with such situations, what is indicated as ethical or unethical and therefore should arguably be legal or illegal can be quite different. Difficulties arise when courts disagree with legislatures on how such situations should be handled, and interpret the law in such a way that the court overrides a government's policy decision. The judgment of the Supreme Court of Canada in the *Insite* case[33] demonstrates such a situation.

This case involved a medically supervised clean-needle exchange and medically supervised safe injection site in Vancouver's downtown eastside, which has high rates of illegal drug use and drug addiction, HIV and Hepatitis C infections, homelessness, and prostitution, constituting a public health crisis. The Insite clinic was one response to this crisis. In order to grant the professionals operating the clinic immunity from prosecution for breach of the federal Controlled Drugs and Substances Act[34] (CDSA) provisions prohibiting drug possession and trafficking, the federal minister for health had in 2003 given the clinic an exemption under section 56 of the act, which allowed "for an exemption for a medical or scientific purpose or [which] is otherwise in the public interest."

In 2008, however, the minister decided the exemption should no longer apply and revoked it, which meant the clinic would have to close. The claimants, who included drug users, challenged the revocation of the exemption as unconstitutional and the case ended up on appeal to the Supreme Court of Canada.

The Supreme Court, in a unanimous judgment, ruled that the CDSA provisions on possession and trafficking were constitutionally valid. It held, however, that the minister's exercise of his discretion under the act must comply with charter requirements. The court ruled that the minister's failure to grant an exemption under section 56 CDSA was a breach of the claimants' section 7 charter rights to life, liberty, and security of the person, because it put drug users' health and life at risk and was not in accordance with the principles of fundamental justice. The court reached this conclusion on the grounds that the failure was "arbitrary" because it undermined the purposes of the CDSA, the protection of health and public safety. It was also "grossly disproportionate," as the clinic "was proven to save lives with no discernible negative impact on the public health and safety objectives of Canada." The court also noted that the prohibition could not have been justified under section 1 of the charter, which was not argued.

The harm of the refusal to the people Insite served was found to far outweigh any benefits it would engender. Consequently, the minister's refusal did not comply with the charter requirement that any deprivation of a section 7 right must be in accordance with the "the principles of fundamental justice"; it was therefore unconstitutional. This approach can be viewed as an example of the Supreme Court of Canada using the charter to implement ethics at an individual case level, while, in upholding the CDSA provisions as constitutionally valid, thereby keeping the law intact at the general level.

The judgment met with a very mixed reaction. It was criticized by some as a court wrongfully overriding the government's policy decision and interfering in the exercise of executive discretion, thus introducing uncertainty into whether or not a law applies. Some saw it as opening up possible legal challenges to a wide range of executive decision-making and, perhaps a wider range of bases, such as social and economic considerations, on which courts may overrule legislation. Others criticized it as bad ethics. Just because a court considers ethics does not mean what it decides is necessarily ethically correct. And, as we know, we do not all agree on ethics. On the other hand, this example can be seen, as I earlier suggested was possible, as a court using the law in a legally complex and sophisticated way to reach an ethically acceptable outcome in a given case, when the law had been used by a government in a manner that prevented that from happening.[35]

Human Rights Bridging Ethics and Law to Implement Child-Centred Assisted Reproduction Decision-Making

I previously discussed how using the language of people having a human right to have reasonable access to pain management helped to make such access a reality. More recently, I have proposed that a human right to be born from natural human biological origins is necessary and should be recognized.[36] If this were the case, in passing laws to govern the use of reproductive technologies, we should work from a basic presumption that, ethically, children have an absolute right to be conceived from an untampered-with ovum from one identified, living, adult woman and an untampered-with sperm from one identified, living, adult man. This human right could be said to be the most fundamental of all. In the past we did not need to contemplate recognizing a right to come into being from natural human origins because there was no possibility of coming into being in any other way. That, of course, is no longer true, which is the reason we need such a law based on deep ethical analysis.

Each of the words in the human right articulated above is included for a reason. Requiring a sperm and ovum means transmission of human life must be through sexual reproduction, as compared to, for example, asexual replication (cloning). The words "man" and "woman" – rather than references to a sperm and an ovum – are intentional. They preclude creating an embryo with the genetic heritage of two women or two men. And "one" man and "one" woman prohibits making an embryo with multiple genetic parents.

"Untampered-with" means that an artificially constructed sperm or ovum must not be used and also excludes reproduction between a same-sex couple – for instance, the future possibility of making a sperm from one woman's stem cell and using it to fertilize another woman's ovum. "Natural" excludes an opposite-sex couple using technology to make an artificial sperm from an infertile man or artificial ovum from an infertile woman.

Requiring "adult gametes" pre-empts using gametes from aborted fetuses. It prevents children being born whose biological parent was never born. And requiring "living" donors excludes using gametes for postmortem conception. Children have a right to a chance, when being conceived, of meeting their biological parents.

And "identified" means that offspring can trace their biological parentage and through them other close biological relatives.[37]

Here's what one anonymous reviewer wrote about the above proposition: "I would urge the author to say more about this, as I'm sure she recognizes that it is this position that has made her seem like an enemy to the gay community. For example, there does not seem to be any "right" to be born at all – since nonexistent entities can't have rights – so how can there be a right to be born in any particular manner?"

To deal with the last point first: I am arguing that there is a *right not to be born* – not to come into existence – in a particular way, rather than a *right to be born* in any particular manner. And arguing that people have duties *not* to transmit human life in certain ways – for instance, through cloning – and passing laws to prohibit that from happening does not involve legally recognizing a non-existent human being. Moreover, one need not be a human being or have rights in order to have legal protection. The criminal prohibition of cruelty to animals is a good example of that.

Second, the provisions I propose apply to everyone, although the gay community might be the most affected by them, which can be a basis for a claim of discrimination. The situation is one of a conflict between adults' claims to use reproductive technology to have a child and the child's claim not to be "designed" or manufactured or not to come from non-natural origins. The ethical principle of adopting a preferential option in favour of the weakest and most vulnerable person in such conflicts indicates that the child's claim should prevail.

Third, much discussion and a large divide is emerging around the issue of whether presently non-existent persons can have rights or even claims. It is an important issue, and some new thinking is needed. I mentioned above that duties not to bring human life into existence in certain ways can be established, which can be seen as giving such "future persons" a right not to be created in that way. The concept of anticipated consent might also be useful: would the person, if alive and able to decide, on the balance of probabilities consent to being created in this way? If the answer is no, then there are obligations not do so. Finally, in a broader context, if there is no recognition that obligations are owed to future, presently non-existent persons, then neither are there obligations to hold the physical and metaphysical ecosystems in trust for them – that is, obligations not to lay waste or do irreversible damage to those ecosystems.

It can also be proposed that children have valid claims to be reared, if at all possible, by their own biological parents within their natural family, and valid claims to have both a mother and a father, unless an exception can be justified (as in adoption, including by some same-sex couples) as being in the "best interests" of a particular child.[38]

Society should not be complicit in intentionally depriving children of any of these rights. Therefore, the ethics must be considered of deliberately creating any situation that is otherwise, and this is an important context in which using the language of human rights can help to ensure that ethics informs the law, as it should.

The proposed approach applies the ethical principle of acting to favour the most vulnerable, most in need, weakest persons when claims or rights are in conflict – as, for example, in same-sex marriage, where adults' wishes to found a family may be at odds with children's rights regarding their coming into existence and the family structure in which they are reared. Ethics requires favouring children, and the law should reflect that.

Such proposals have been the source of enormous controversy and conflict, especially with advocates of same-sex marriage, who claim that to deny same-sex marriage is wrongful discrimination.[39] It is true that legal recognition of same-sex marriage constitutes a powerful statement that discrimination on the basis of sexual orientation is a serious wrong, and this is a strong argument in support of it. But marriage is a compound right – the right to marry *and* to found a family. Giving same-sex couples the right to found a family necessarily abrogates children's human rights with respect to their biological origins and family structure, and the dangers of that abrogation are amplified by reprogenetic technoscience.

If we believe that, ethically, there should be limits on the use of reproductive technologies, we now need the respect-for-natural-procreation symbolism established by opposite-sex marriage more than in the past. To recognize same-sex marriage unavoidably eliminates this symbolic function of marriage. But same-sex civil unions do not raise this problem, because they do not entail the right to found a family. Therefore, in contrast to same-sex marriage, legally recognizing civil unions does not create a conflict between ethics and law.

I recognize that my opposition to same-sex marriage has hurt some people who support it. I have chosen to advocate for children's human rights in this context with "moral regret." This ethical concept requires that when, for reasons of ethics, something we do or stand for hurts others, we should still regret the hurt it causes. While I believe that from an ethical perspective I must stand by my views on same-sex marriage, I genuinely regret the hurt that inflicts.

It should also be noted here in relation to the ethics and law that should govern reproductive technologies that, quite apart from the concerns raised by same-sex marriage, there is a need for much more in-depth discussion of children's human rights in this context. As mentioned previously, decision-making with respect to the law that should govern these technologies usually makes only a token bow to children's needs and rights and in practice has been almost entirely adult-centred. Using an ethical analysis to inform the law enacted can help with regard to both understanding why a child-centred approach is necessary and to implementing it.[40]

Levels of "Doing Ethics" in Relation to Reproductive Technologies

The case for unrestricted access to all reproductive technologies, sometimes referred to as "rights to absolute reproductive freedom," is made almost entirely at the individual level – the right of individuals to decide how and when they will or will not reproduce. This stance focuses on individual persons' rights to autonomy and self-determination and rights to decide for themselves. While there are also strong arguments at this level against such unlimited freedom to decide, especially from the perspective of resulting children, strong arguments against it exist also at the institutional and societal levels, which so far have not been given the consideration they deserve.

In short, almost all the justifications for unrestricted access to reproductive technologies focus primarily on the infertile people who want to use them, whether their infertility problem in founding a family is medical or social (that is, lack of an opposite-sex partner). The harmful impacts of such access on society and its values and institutions are ignored. We need, however, to look at their impacts not only at the micro or individual level but also at the meso or institutional level, the macro or societal level, and the mega or global level. There can be conflict at the different levels as to what is ethical, and individual decisions can have a cumulative impact at other levels – factors that need to be taken into account in decision-making about the ethics that should govern reproductive technologies. In chapter 5 I discussed impacts at these other levels in relation to the ethics of prenatal diagnosis and selecting and deselecting our children, whether on the basis of a disability or being the "wrong" sex.[41] The use of reproductive technologies is yet another context in which those broader considerations are relevant and at which ethics must inform law. One effect of the Canadian Charter of Rights and Freedoms has been that claims at the individual level have been given precedence over those at other levels, which are treated as secondary. While this ordering can be justified in some situations, it is not necessarily always the case.

Why Ethics in Medicine and Science Matter More Generally, Especially to the Law

To reprise points made already but relevant here: what our shared societal values should be is currently a source of conflict in North America – some call it "culture wars" – and medicine, medical science, and health care collectively constitute the forum in which many of the public square debates that will determine the values that govern us as a society are taking place. Anyone who reads the newspapers, listens to radio documentaries, or watches the TV news is aware of numerous reports on issues, some of them mentioned already in this book, that lie at the intersections of science, medicine, ethics, and law.[42] These issues involve some of our most important individual and collective social-ethical-legal values. Very often they are connected with respect for life, and with birth or death, the two events around which humans have always formed their most important individual and collective values. Medicine (a term I use in a broad sense) has taken increasing control, if not over birth and death themselves then over their attributes and the contexts and circumstances in which they occur; that is, life and death have been medicalized. Consequently, medicine has become an important societal forum for creating, affirming, challenging, and destroying shared values. These values, together with our principles, attitudes, beliefs, myths, and so on, make up the societal-cultural paradigm on which secular, democratic western societies are based – that is, the "shared story" that members of a society tell each other in order to form the glue that binds them.

Religion used to be the context in which moral and ethical issues were explored and in which shared values were created and communicated. Importantly, it was also the context in which those values were handed on to future generations. It is not possible to use religion in that way today in multicultural, multi-religious, multi-ethnic, postmodern, secular, democratic societies such as in the West. Moreover, unprecedented medical-scientific developments face us with socio-ethical values issues that no humans have ever before had to address; collectively, they form the most prominent and important contemporary context for the formation of a society's foundational values linked to life and death and respect for human life and dignity. As a result, what we decide with regard to the values that are honoured or breached in this context – which values we choose to respect, create, or destroy – matters well beyond that context. In short, ethics in medicine, medical science, and health care matter with respect to societal values in general, and because it is the role of law to uphold a society's most important shared values, ethics in these areas matter to law.

As I have pointed out throughout this book, extraordinary advances in medical technoscience in the last twenty-five years have opened up possibilities unimaginable in the past. We are no longer limited by nature or to repairing nature when it fails; we can now do what is impossible in nature. Assisted human reproductive technologies are a prime example.

But ethics and law in this area are also important for much more mundane reasons, for instance, in order to govern the huge "fertility industry" that has developed with the advent of assisted reproductive technologies. It is now around a $5 billion per year business in the United States alone and is rapidly expanding globally.[43] The law needs to be informed by ethics in regulating this industry for many reasons, but especially because it often involves exploitation of poor, vulnerable women in developing countries. Very large amounts of money are involved (the global industry is now estimated to be worth at least US$12 billion and possibly as much as US$60 billion annually); moreover, infertile people are often desperate to have a child, which can generate very strong pressures not to restrict the industry on ethical grounds.

The ethical questions that the industry raises are very broad and diverse. They include questions such as whether we should prohibit young women from selling their eggs to pay their way through university. Is egg donation ethically acceptable? As discussed above in relation to the *Pratten* case, what are our obligations to "donor-conceived" children with respect to knowing their genetic heritage and biological parents? Should women be able to freeze ovarian tissue when they are young and most fertile to use when they want to have a child at fifty-five or sixty years of age, when they retire? Should parents be allowed to choose the sex of their child or design the child's characteristics or genetically match it to a sibling in order to treat a disease from which that sibling suffers? Is it ethically acceptable to create human embryos in order to set up "human-embryo manufacturing plants" to produce therapeutic materials to be used to benefit the rest of us?

In short, there has been an exponential increase in the powers of medical science and its practitioners. In the past, all a physician could do was hold a person's hand, wipe their fevered brow, and give them an aspirin or narcotic. Today medical scientists can redesign life itself. With such powers come enormous responsibilities, not just towards present generations but also to future ones. The wise accommodation of ethics in law is essential to fulfilling those responsibilities.

The impact on societal values in general of the values endorsed in the "birth debates" is mirrored in those being contested in the "death debates." In chapter 1 I explored the debate around the legalization of euthanasia and physician-assisted suicide taking place in many western democratic societies, including in Canadian courts and legislatures – our "secular cathedrals."[44] In chapter 4 I looked in detail at the *Carter* case in which the Canadian Supreme Court struck down the prohibition on assisted suicide as unconstitutional opening up access to "physician-assisted death." Judgments rendered up to the present in various other jurisdictions indicate that courts are likely to rule that the law prohibiting physician-assisted suicide is discriminatory with respect to those unable to commit suicide without assistance. Depending on the judges' views on the ethics of allowing assisted suicide, the legal prohibition will be either struck down as unconstitutional or upheld, even though considered discriminatory in the way alleged, as being a necessary protection – a reasonable limit that "can be demonstrably justified in a free and democratic society – of vulnerable people. Both ethics and law need to uphold the value of respect for human life in general and for each individual human life. We can all agree on that, but where we disagree is whether, for instance, euthanasia breaches the required respect. People who reject euthanasia believe that intentionally killing another person, other than to save human life (as, for example, in justified self-defence) does so, no matter how compassionate the motives of those carrying out these interventions.

The euthanasia debate can also help us to see the kinds of questions we need to ask when deciding on issues in medicine that will affect social-ethical-legal values. As I have pointed out previously, they include exploring our obligations to future generations to hold in trust for them not only our physical world but also our metaphysical world – our shared values, attitudes, principles, beliefs, stories, and so on.

The issues also require taking into account the impact of our decisions not just on individuals but also on institutions, in particular, law and medicine; on our society, as a whole, especially its values; and, in our twenty-first century world, on our global reality. In short, we need comprehensive, sophisticated ethical and legal analysis at all the levels mentioned above: at the micro (individual), meso (institutional), macro (societal), and mega (global) levels, and in the interfaces among these levels.

In undertaking that analysis in order to find the ethics needed to guide us and to inform the law, we must be conscious of at least three dangers. The first is that of *false certainty*. To deal with that danger, we have to build into our decision-making structures an "ethics of uncertainty." To do so requires, especially if one is a social and public policy decision-maker such as a politician, having the courage to admit "I don't know the answer" when that is the case. It also requires eschewing the "do something" syndrome, in which doing something to respond to a problem is seen as better than doing nothing, even if the latter is the best response, including because it is not obvious what that response should be. The second danger is that of being simplistic; avoiding this requires building an "ethics of complexity" into decision-making structures and procedures. The dangers of being uncomfortable with uncertainty and of being simplistic are linked. Comfort with uncertainty makes being simplistic (which must be distinguished from being simple when that is appropriate) much less likely. The third danger lies in not considering the impact of our decisions in the future and on future generations; in other words, in addition, we must build in an "ethics of potentiality." What building in those elements will require is a topic for future exploration and research.

I also suggest that medicine, medical science, and health care are particularly important to societal bonding and finding some shared ethics[45] in secular democracies such as Canada with very diverse populations, because they are the societal institutions to which everyone personally relates. Indeed, medicine might be functioning as yet another example of a "secular religion."[46]

In secular western societies, the search for health (and for at least delayed mortality, if not immortality as in traditional religion) has become the basis of one of the new "secular religions." We could call it "healthism." Indeed, it is arguably the most universal of those religions, probably because, uniquely in terms of societal institutions, as pointed out already, everyone personally relates to medicine.

Everyone wants to be healthy and likewise wants the same for those they love.

Canada provides an interesting example in this respect. Medicare, our highly socialized system for health-care delivery, has become a sacred cow. Politicians are frightened to change it, which does not necessarily result in the best health-care system we could obtain for the taxpayer money we spend to support it. Under the Canada Health Act, the Canadian federal government transfers Medicare funds to each of the provinces for support of their health-care systems. The conditions the act attaches to these funds are that the provincial health-care system must be publicly administered, comprehensive (cover all insured services), universal (cover all insured persons), portable (insurance is transferable from province to province), and accessible (there must be reasonable access to services unburdened by fees). Despite the breadth of these provisions, there are limitations, sometimes serious ones, on timely access to health care. However, for the Canadian population as a whole, the health-care system contrasts dramatically with that of its big neighbour to the south, the United States, in which, at least until the advent of the Affordable Health Care Act (Obamacare), around 50 million people had no health-care insurance. As a result, Medicare has become a symbol of Canadian identity that Canadians use to distinguish themselves from Americans and show that they have different societal values.

Traditionally medicine and religion have been closely linked, and it is not a new development that health is often equated to goodness and sometimes virtue. What is relatively new, however, is that we no longer speak of sin and even less so of evil; rather, we speak of illness or disease. Many people who do wrong are seen as sick and needing treatment, not bad and meriting punishment. With the advent of genetic medicine, we are even seeing a defence emerging in criminal law of accused persons pleading that they are not responsible for their actions because "my genes made me do it."

And with health functioning as a secular religion, we can see the emergence of secular sins and, with the creation of new "diseases," new sins – for example, obesity or smoking. A twenty-first century version of the connection of illness and sin has emerged: illness is not seen as punishment for sin, as happened in the past; some illnesses are seen as sin itself.

"Healthism" requires a definition of health. Is health a state of total well-being – physical, mental, and social – as the World Health Organization's definition states? Is there a difference between well-being and health? Is health the absence of disease, or "pre-disease" (a neologism for detecting the precursors of disease or who is at risk for disease)? If so, what is the impact of new diagnostic techniques such as total body scanning with MRIs and, in particular, genetic screening? And if, as suggested above, illness is linked with sin, are such tests a secular form of examination of conscience and "absolution" in the sense of a hope for prevention or cure – that is, secular confession?

In the past we considered ourselves healthy until we were diagnosed as sick or obviously became so. The basic presumption was that we were well and being sick was an exception to our normal healthy state. But a while ago, a physician colleague remarked to me, "You know, Margo, the well are just the undiagnosed sick." That assumes that we are sick until the contrary is established. Might that approach have contributed to so many of us in North America becoming health obsessed? The "worried well" reassuring themselves that they don't have some "dread disease" is a thriving industry.

If the institution of medicine can be seen as a quasi-religion (a secular religion), then it's not surprising that physicians can be regarded as quasi-clergy (secular priests, a role that bioethicists are often accused of adopting), and the places in which medicine is practised and developed – hospitals and research laboratories – as quasi-churches (secular cathedrals). It is no accident that we speak of "modern miracle medicine"; this choice of language is telling.

However, there is also what could seem at first glance to be a countervailing trend to this "secular deification" of medicine and its practitioners, one mentioned in chapter 2. That is the trend to treat physicians as mere technicians, in that it is being argued that patients' wishes must prevail over the freedom of conscience of health-care professionals – in particular, of physicians. This trend is, however, consistent with medicine being a prime forum in democratic western societies for creating, affirming, challenging, and destroying shared values. The advocates of coercion of health-care professionals are seeking to destroy long-standing values and replace them with an ideology – "progressive" values – that espouses and implements intense individualism and moral relativism (there are no fixed moral truths and morality is more or less a matter of personal preferences). Recent examples include the various movements advocating the legalization of euthanasia.

One of the major current divisions in ethics and law is whether there is a natural law or natural morality that should inform our decisions about what is right and wrong, or whether those decisions are simply up to us; that is, should concepts of legal positivism, utilitarianism, and moral relativism be used? An overwhelming impression at the Freiburg Symposium on the Ethicalization of Law held in Germany in 2011 was that a large majority of participants did not accept any concept of natural law or natural rights. The starkest expression of this stance was a question from a member of the audience in response to my suggestion that everyone has a fundamental human right to come into being from natural human origins. The questioner asked, with an air of incredulity, "How can a non-existent human, an unborn child, have a right? There is no one to be the holder of the right and one can't have a duty to a non-existent entity." This very legalistic approach seems to be based in positivist legal philosophy and doctrine, which is used to deny any such right. Applied generally, it would mean that we cannot have legal obligations to future generations, a stance that would contradict current approaches in environmental law and ethics.

Some people see natural law as having a divine source, and such a view is probably the reason some others reject it. But it can also be seen as just innate to being human and as upholding and protecting that which is of the essence of being human – that which manifests the "kind of entity we are." These characteristics might even have some genetic substrate. Jürgen Habermas's concept of an "ethics of the [human] species," referred to in chapter 1, seems to reflect such a view.[47]

◆◆◆

To conclude, as we have seen with trying to ensure that people are not wrongfully left in pain, bringing ethics and human rights considerations to bear on a situation can influence for the good the law that should govern that situation. The same is true with respect to the law that should govern assisted human reproduction. More generally, the new science has opened up unprecedented powers and will continue to do so, and we need ethics to help us to answer questions such as what those powers could mean for individuals and societies, and what limits, if any, the law should place on their use. This science faces us with questions that go to the very essence of what it means to be human, that no humans before us have faced. We must constantly ask ourselves – especially as legislators, bureaucrats who make public policy decisions, judges, jurists, and lawyers, and ethicists – what acting ethically, wisely, and courageously with respect to these immense powers requires of us in terms of the laws that we choose to govern them.

My goal in this chapter has been to show that ethics is not only necessary but also beneficial to law, and that law needs to march with it as an equal partner and not be in the rear and limping. Ethics can function as "first aid" for law, enabling it to achieve that equality, especially in novel situations where the law is most likely to have difficulty keeping up with ethics. Ethics must inform our choices; science, ethics, and law must march forward together.

8

What Questions Are We Asking in Contemporary Cultural Values Conversations, and What Messages Are They Communicating?

It is sometimes said in ethics that the questions we ask can be more important than the answers we give in helping us to identify ethical issues and having insight into how we should address those issues. A common cause of ethical mistakes is a failure either to ask questions, or to ask the right questions, when that results in not recognizing that an ethical issue is present. Sometimes such an issue is identified as a public-relations or communications problem and sent off to professionals with expertise in those fields. The result can be spin-doctoring that only augments the ethical problems present.

Questions are not neutral; they structure our answers. And questions communicate messages, particularly messages about values. With these thoughts in mind, in this final chapter I address some questions that raise ethics and values issues I have been asked by editors to ponder and which I subsequently used as elements of speeches I delivered.

In chapter 5, I addressed the question of what I believe to be presently the world's most dangerous idea. My answer was: Not seeing human beings as unique and exceptional, as different in kind not just different in degree, from other living beings. The questions I now address are: What lessons could we learn from two films, *Amour* and *Never Let Me Go*, and from the documentary *End Credits*? How might the human race end? What will future generations see as the defining event of the first decades of the twenty-first century?

Does Old Age Have Any Honour Left? The Film *Amour*

Michael Haneke's 2012 film *Amour* (Love) is relevant to our current values discussions because it subtly transmits the message that if we are to act compassionately, as both individuals and a society, we need to legalize euthanasia. As I discussed in previous chapters, that position challenges upholding the value of respect for human life in relation to each individual person and of respect for human life in general at the societal level.

To drastically understate the reality, Haneke's film is harrowing and heartbreaking to watch. I sat there just wanting it to be over (I will return to that emotion shortly), yet I couldn't leave. I felt like an animal caught in a hunter's spotlight, unable to move, mesmerized.

The film is insightfully and accurately described by critics such as Francine Prose on the *New York Review of Books* blog as "a masterpiece you might not want to see."[1] This warning is merited; the film is intensely distressing. Paula Span in the *New York Times*, under the banner of the "new old age," calls *Amour* "the brutal truth."[2] Some people will see it as a clarion call for the legalization of euthanasia. I'd suggest, however, that it is equally, if not more so, a clarion call for our responsibilities as families and a society to change and remedy the circumstances in which many old and vulnerable people find themselves.

Anne (played by Emmanuelle Riva) and Georges (Jean-Louis Trintignant), the film's two main characters, are such people and live in such circumstances. They are financially secure, upper middle class, retired musicians, living in an elegant apartment in Paris. They have one child, Eva (Isabelle Huppert), who is around fifty years old and visits them occasionally. Eva has two young adult children who have left home; she is in a troubled marriage, and preoccupied with her own problems. The acting is superb: it is difficult to believe these are not real life events, which adds to the emotional distress the film elicits.

In the opening scene, firemen and a plain-clothes detective break into an apartment and find the decomposing body of a clothed dead woman, a crucifix on her chest. She is laid out on a bed, surrounded by flower heads that have seen better days.

The story then shifts to a concert hall, where Anne and Georges are attending a performance of a Schubert piano concerto by Alexandre (the French pianist Alexandre Tharaud, who plays himself), who, as a twelve-year-old, was Anne's pupil. They are delighted by the performance, but come home to find an attempted break-in to their apartment. Anne suggests calling the police, but Georges refuses. This is the beginning of Haneke's brilliant portrayal of what proves to be their increasing vulnerability and the unavailability of help, and of their (especially Georges') refusal to accept assistance or lack of capacity to seek it.

Next morning as Anne and Georges are eating breakfast, Anne temporarily loses consciousness and is unresponsive to Georges' questions about what is wrong. She regains consciousness, but has no memory of the incident. She pours tea, spilling it because she cannot control her movements. The rest of the film documents in graphic detail her physical and mental decline as a result of failed carotid artery surgery, strokes, and dementia, and Georges' efforts to care for her almost entirely without assistance.

We learn that Anne's physician, Dr Bertier, and a hairdresser come once every two weeks. A nurse, whom Georges hires, comes three times a week; a second nurse is incompetent and abusive, and Georges fires her. The janitor helps him carry in groceries, and the janitor's wife vacuums the rugs. Both offer further help; however, Georges does not take up their offer. They are obviously curious about Anne's condition and try to linger and talk, but Georges always promptly ushers them out. Such behaviour is described by neuroscientist Dr Tiffany Chow, author of *The Memory Clinic: Stories of Hope and Healing for Alzheimer's Patients and Their Families*. Chow is quoted in an article in the *Globe and Mail*: "The number one mistake that caregivers make is thinking 'I can do all this myself.' That's a guaranteed recipe for burnout. Caregiving has to be done with some allies, whether it's your personal friends, neighbours, other family members or professional care providers."[3]

Eva pays occasional visits to her parents, once accompanied by her husband, Howard, who suggests that Anne be placed in a nursing home. Georges adamantly refuses. He has promised Anne, who is frightened of doctors and hates hospitals, to keep her at home. The only other visitors are Alexandre and a stray pigeon that flies in through an open window.

Meanwhile, we see in great detail Georges helping Anne in and out of bed and her wheelchair, off the toilet, and, eventually, checking her diapers when she is bedridden. He tries to get her to take water from a sipping cup and food from a spoon, both of which she refuses; he reads to her and tries to sooth her when she screams "*Mal!*" (hurt) over and over.

Finally, Georges tells Anne a story from his childhood, about being sent away to a summer holiday camp and letting his mother know through a prearranged signal of drawing stars on the weekly postcard he sent home that he was desperately unhappy there. In part this was because, like Anne now, he refused to eat – in his case, rice pudding. He completes the story, takes the pillow from his side of their bed, and suffocates Anne, whose struggles to escape slowly subside.

Georges goes out to buy flowers from which he cuts the stems and then chooses a dress from Anne's closet. Our thoughts flash back to the opening scene of what we now realize was Anne's body on the bed. We then see Georges in the living room using wide tape to seal the doorway into the bedroom.

In a following scene, the pigeon returns, and the viewer cannot be sure whether Georges smothers it, as he did Anne, in the blanket in which he catches it, or whether he cuddles and strokes it and then releases it. In a letter we subsequently see him writing, which we presume is a suicide note, we learn that he released the pigeon. This comes as a tiny affirmation of hope and respect for life – a hugely welcome one in this unrelentingly depressing and joyless film, which resonates with a "culture of death" in that it makes death seem vastly preferable to life.

What can we learn from this film?

First, *Amour* shows us the impact not only of the presence of love but also of its absence.

It captures Georges and Anne's romantic love for each other, and Georges' love as portrayed in his care for Anne. Flowers and music are often associated with love, and they appear frequently in the film, which is rich with symbolism, allusion, and innuendo – for instance, in looking at the family photo album, Anne seems to look only at photos in which she is present. Haneke makes powerful use of silence, sometimes to express positive emotions and closeness, at other times negative ones and alienation. When Anne and Georges are listening to the recording that Alexandre has given them of the concert they had attended, Anne abruptly says, "Stop the CD," which Georges does. Music seems to represent the thread of life for this couple.

In contrast, the stark absence of love is seen in the almost total lack of any loving support from family, friends, or community. Eva sums up her feelings in this regard: "I can't believe that these days there's no way of handling this [situation] efficiently." Efficiency is a bureaucratic, emotionally detached value. From this perspective, the film can be viewed as a tragic commentary on the dissolution of families and the values of mutual support and responsibility for family members, especially when they are vulnerable because they are old, sick, and dying.

Likewise, the film can be seen as an indictment of the failure of communities and societies to provide palliative and hospice care and other support, including respite care, for those who try to look after loved ones at home, where most people want to die but cannot because of lack of support for their carers.

When Anne is bedridden and her dementia has become very advanced, she constantly cries out, repeating the one word, "*Mal!*" It seems reasonable to interpret this as an indication of pain. Yet we do not see her being given any pain relief treatment, and the doctor visits only once every two weeks. Inadequate pain management, or fear of being left in pain, is a reason people ask or advocate for euthanasia. Another reason, and one of the main ones, is that they see themselves as a burden on others, especially their families. A further reason is a loss of control and, as a result, seeing themselves as lacking dignity. They confuse being independent with having dignity (discussed in chapter 3) and therefore perceive dependence as the loss of dignity. The presence of each of these aspects is piercingly and powerfully communicated in *Amour*. But what can be done to address and correct the conditions giving rise to them is nowhere to be found in the film.

The book *Intimate Death*[4] by French psychologist Marie de Hennezel, who specializes in the care of dying people, could not be in starker contrast. Through moving and poetic vignettes about dying people, and without denying suffering or romanticizing or glamourizing it, de Hennezel allows us to see that dying can be the last great act of living.

Essential ingredients for that to be the case are the presence of hope, the sense that our life had and can still have meaning even when we are dying; that we can perhaps still learn and even teach; and that we have something to give others, a legacy to leave. None of these features of a "good" death is present in Anne and Georges' situation in *Amour*.

Early in the film, when Anne is wheelchair bound but not demented, a friend, Pierre, dies and Georges attends the funeral without her. When he returns, she asks him about the service, and he responds, "It was rather bizarre. The priest was an idiot. Then one of Pierre's co-workers made a speech that was embarrassingly emotional. His old secretary came with a radiocassette player and after the speech she put on 'Yesterday' by the Beatles. You can't imagine. Everybody turned round to look at her. Apparently it wasn't planned. His grandchildren were there. Of course they giggled as soon as the music began. Then the urn was put on a huge stretcher that was obviously designed for a coffin, and out we went into the rain. They placed the urn on a small electric cart that crawled along for what seemed like an eternity to the tiny hole they had dug. A lot of people had to stifle their laughter. It must have been terrible for Jeanne [Pierre's widow]."[5]

Georges' description of the funeral sums up the absence of solemnity and respect, the trivialization of the momentousness of death and the losses it involves, the failure to express grief and to mourn and, consequently, no opportunity for healing. And the secular music, the Beatles' song "Yesterday," represents the antithesis of hope. Hope requires a sense of connection to the future; the song powerfully communicates that all that is possible is a sad connection to the past.

Having a sense of connection to the future when one is dying does not have to involve religion, although of course it can. Another way is to be aware of leaving a legacy. In chapter 3, I discussed the research of Canadian psychiatrist Dr Harvey Max Chochinov and his colleagues into how to help dying people. Their development of "dignity therapy"[6] involves helping dying people to see what they can leave as a legacy to those they love and to other people. Anne's legacy was in her students, represented by Alexandre, yet she refused to listen to the CD he gave her of his critically acclaimed concert. She refused to allow hope to creep in, to have a moment of joy. In fact, a dominant feature and message of *Amour* is that there are no moments of joy in such circumstances.

Earlier in this chapter I said that I sat through *Amour* wanting it to be over. Both dying people and those who love them can also feel that way about death. But wanting the experience of dying to be over is very different from wanting to be killed; moreover, the impact of each – that is, allowing death to happen as compared with administering it – is very different, not only for the person and her loved ones but also at institutional, societal, and even global levels.

Some people will see *Amour* as making the case for legalizing euthanasia, because it exclusively focuses at the level of the individual person who is suffering and dying and wants to die, which makes the strongest case for it. But we must also consider the effect on other people of legalizing euthanasia, especially its use to abuse old people; on the medical profession and medicine's millennia-old guiding principle, "curing where possible, caring always, never killing"; on other health-care professionals and health-care institutions; on the law as a primary institution upholding the societal value of respect for life; and on society's most important values, especially that of respect for life.

Amour brings to mind lines from Alfred Lord Tennyson's poem "Ulysses": "The long day wanes: the slow moon climbs: the deep / Moans round with many voices." The poem leaves us, however, with a sense of profound meaning that is utterly absent from the film:

> Old age hath yet his honour and his toil;
> Death closes all: but something ere the end,
> Some work of noble note, may yet be done,
> Not unbecoming men that strove with Gods.

How Does Our View of a "Good Death" Affect How We See Euthanasia? The Documentary *End Credits*

I turn now to a documentary film dealing expressly with euthanasia. *End Credits* (2013), directed by Alexander Decommere and written by Marc Cosyns, focuses a lens on the practice of euthanasia in Belgium a decade after it was legalized. It allows us to recognize that pro-euthanasia and ant-euthanasia proponents have radically different reactions to suffering and views on how it should be dealt with.

In mid-November 2013 I received an invitation to fly to Calgary to attend the North American première of *End Credits* at the Marda Loop Justice Film Festival. I was asked to lead a post-screening conversation with the audience and was given access to a copy of the film with English subtitles, which I viewed once. My access was then blocked and my invitation to attend the festival withdrawn. The scenes from the film, which I describe below, are accurate to the best of my recollection. (I was later offered access to the film by its producers.)

End Credits follows the dying and death of two people; according to the filmmakers' description, "Adelin, 83, and Eva, 34, two very different people, who are at the dawn of the end of their lives, [and] ask for help with and care for a decent passing away." The most striking commonality shared by the old man, Adelin, and the young woman, Eva, is that both are profoundly lonely.

We meet Adelin in the nursing home where he lives. He is physically fragile and cognitively impaired. At one point, he describes his life as a "dead life" – a powerful phrase that must be heard by those caring for him and which should raise questions of how to improve his situation. It brings to mind the words of lung specialist Dr Donald Boudreau in speaking about euthanasia: "These euthanologists – if they have their way – will create a moral ecosystem where we will all be traversing through a sort of 'living death'. Life is the qualifier. Death is the unshakable and primary reality." At a certain point, death becomes the norm or basic presumption, living the exception.

Adelin has given his consent to euthanasia in an advance directive executed when he was competent. His physician is speaking to him, trying to determine whether Adelin still wants to go ahead with the procedure. Adelin's nephew, a middle-aged man, is sitting beside Adelin's bed. He urges the physician to administer a lethal injection, because, he says, his uncle is no longer mentally competent and so cannot validly change his mind about euthanasia. The physician continues to try to clarify with the old man whether he wants euthanasia.

Suddenly, Adelin has a burst of energy and seeming lucidity, and shouts, "You want to kill me!" – clearly horrified by the thought. He is not euthanized, and some time later dies a natural death.

Eva, a young Belgian woman who suffers from mental illness (probably severe depression), wants to be euthanasized and subsequently to donate her organs. Medical journal articles report organs being taken from euthanized people in Belgium for transplant. In at least one of these cases, a donor was mentally but not physically ill. However, Eva is refused permission to donate by the relevant authority; still, she chooses to go ahead with euthanasia.

We see shots of Eva with her beautiful dog and learn that her brother is in the house, but not with her when she dies, which says so much. Eva says to the physician, "Let's get on with this." Wearing sweat pants and a jersey, she lies down on her living room couch and rolls up her sleeve, as though she is going to have her blood pressure taken.

Watching the physician euthanizing her is a chilling experience lacking any human warmth. There is no sense of the momentousness of what is being done – one human being, and a physician at that, intentionally killing another human being who is his patient. The mundaneness of it all is reinforced by scenes of the physician sitting at Eva's kitchen table after he has killed her, routinely filling out the necessary reporting forms.

I was puzzled by what stance on euthanasia the filmmakers were taking, but my overall impression was it was probably one of neutrality, and I thought the film might function as a very powerful *cri de coeur* against euthanasia.

So I tried, although unsuccessfully, as the filmmakers ignored my emails, to get permission to show the film to others, particularly, the students in my Comparative Medical Law class at McGill University where I am a faculty member. I recommended to the Quebec National Assembly legislative committee holding hearings on Bill 52, the purpose of which was to legalize euthanasia in Quebec, that they try to see the film to understand why they should reject euthanasia and Bill 52.[7]

To my absolute astonishment and distress, I subsequently learned from Belgian colleagues that the film is intended to promote euthanasia and was funded by Recht op Waardig Sterven, a pro-euthanasia movement comparable to "right to die with dignity" movements in Canada, and that its writer, Dr Marc Cosyns, is a strong supporter and practitioner of euthanasia in Belgium. How could I have been so confused?

The explanation is the different ways in which pro- and anti-euthanasia adherents would view the two deaths featured in this film.

We see Adelin gradually deteriorating and dying over a period of time. This process is difficult to watch, but he is empathetically and compassionately attended by those caring for him until he dies naturally. The carers manifest the virtue of patience in their "death-watch." We all want Adelin's dying to be over, but that is very different from making it be over with a lethal injection. I see his human dignity as being respected and his death as a "good death." He, not someone else, completes his life cycle, and neither the mystery of life nor that of death is violated.

Pro-euthanasia advocates would regard Adelin's dying trajectory as an unacceptable loss of autonomy and control on his part. They would see him as having lost his dignity and his state as making him less of a person or even a non-person – an incomplete, diminished, even faulty, decaying, tarnished human being – who should be put out of his undignified state through euthanasia.

I saw the physician's relationship with Eva as cold, clinical, and overly rational (which can be a characteristic of a failure of good ethical judgment), and her death as horrifying and unethical. Pro-euthanasia advocates would see it as respecting her right to autonomy and thus her dignity, and putting her out of her mental misery.

A comparison between Adelin's dying and Eva's provides a "real-life" example of an insightful perspective of literary scholar Paul Yachnin that could be used to argue against legalizing euthanasia, although he himself does not reject euthanasia in all circumstances. Dr Yachin, who is Tomlinson professor of Shakespeare Studies and director of the Institute for the Public Life of Arts and Ideas (IPLAI) at McGill University, believes that each person's life has a narrative arc and that the interweaving of those narratives creates the rich tapestry of humanity on which we found our societies.[8] Euthanasia truncates those narratives, and in doing so it harms both individuals and society.

End Credits provides an opportunity to understand some of the ways in which people who are pro-euthanasia and those who are anti-euthanasia differ radically in how they view dying and death and what euthanasia involves. And those differences reflect profound differences in what we believe it means to be human and what respect for both individual human life and upholding the value of human life in general in our society requires that we not do. One is left with the strong impression after watching *End Credits* that, through legalizing euthanasia in Belgium, death has become the norm and living the exception. Societies cannot safely ratify such a presumption. To do so will place them in ethical peril.

What Warnings about the Harms and Risks of the Unethical Use of Avant-Garde Technoscience Might We Glean from Science Fiction? The Film *Never Let Me Go*

I turn now to a film that links intentional interference in our coming into being – the transmission of human life, the creation of a new human being – with intentional interference in our leaving life – our death.

What ethics lessons can we learn from Kazuo Ishiguro's spine-chilling, heart-wrenching dystopian novel *Never Let Me Go*[9] which we need to apply now if we are to ensure that our amazing scientific advances do not end up creating a world in which no reasonable person would want to live? Both Ishiguro's book and the film based on it, also titled *Never Let Me Go*, hold searing lessons in bioethics that we must heed if we are to avoid dehumanization with new technoscience.

Imagine yourself as a cloned child created from the genome (DNA) of a wealthy person who wants to have your organs available for transplant when he later needs them. The only life you know as a child is as one of a large number of other clones who are kept in the setting of an isolated English boarding school, Hailsham, where none of you has any contact with the outside world. Initially, you have no idea of your origins or intended destiny as an organ donor.

At age eighteen, you leave Hailsham for other supervised accommodation, where you will live until you become an organ "donor," usually in a sequence of "retrieval operations," finally being killed when an unpaired vital organ is taken.

In the 2010 film of Ishiguro's book directed by Mark Romanek from a screenplay by Alex Garland, we watch this dystopic and unethical example of a rapidly developing field called "regenerative medicine" (which, used ethically, offers great hope) played out against a tragic love story that involves three of these young people. Through this love, we understand how fully human they are in contrast to the immense dehumanization to which they are subjected.

Reviewers have commented that the film is unusual in being a science-fiction story set in the past, from the 1950s and '60s up to the 1990s. But what makes it so chilling is that we come to realize that our present world is the future that Ishiguro imagined. Many scenarios the film portrays, such as organ transplantation, and genetic and reproductive technologies, unknown in the 1950s and '60s, are now science-fact. The film delivers a powerful message that we need to become much more sensitive than we currently are to the ethics issues that twenty-first-century technoscience raises.

Here are some of the lessons we can take from it.

The cloned children are regarded by the people who run their school as repositories of organs rather than as individual persons, as objects, not human subjects. This dehumanization is inflicted both through the way in which the children are treated and through language. They are monitored with electronic bracelets like animals are with computer chips. One supervisor, obviously meaning to be empathetic, remarks, "You poor creatures." "Creatures" is a word we use to refer to animals, usually when we are differentiating them from humans. And someone queries whether they have a soul. What is clear to the viewer is that in dehumanizing the children, these people dehumanize themselves more. A major current example of dehumanization through language involves human embryos and fetuses. As I have discussed in previous chapters, human embryo research is justified by describing the embryos as "just a bunch of cells" and, in abortion, fetuses are characterized as "just unwanted tissue, part of the woman's body, not a child."

The physicians and nurses responsible for keeping the children healthy, so that their organs can later be used, also dehumanize them. In medically examining them, they act as though they are mechanics making sure a car is in good running order, not health-care professionals caring for patients. Most horrific in this regard is the scene showing surgeons undertaking a vital-organ-retrieval operation that kills the "donor." They carefully take the anaesthetized young man's heart, then "pull the plug" on both the life-support technology and any engagement with the "patient," simply walking out, leaving the dead body bleeding on the operating table, not even bothering to suture the wound. Even in death, the person is not respected as human.

Who are these physicians and nurses? How could they be in involved in such evil, such appalling violation of medical ethics? That same question has often been asked by scholars in relation to the Nazi doctors in the death camps. How could society have allowed this to happen? Why wasn't it prohibited and severely punished? Or was the society in *Never Let Me Go*'s imaginary world complicit in the evil by funding the technoscience that made the abuses possible without ensuring that technoscience was used only ethically?

Are comparable unethical operations taking place in some countries today, for instance, using executed prisoners as organ "donors," as has happened in China? Might some Canadians be recipients of these organs? And what about in the western world – in Belgium, with the authorization of a special committee, organs are being taken for transplantation after euthanasia. On first learning of this practice, I, like others to whom I spoke, were so shocked by it that we doubted the truth of the reports. But they are correct.

One article in a reputable medical journal reported that five people in Belgium were euthanized and their organs used for transplantation.[10] As I mentioned previously, one of the five was a woman who was suffering from mental, not physical illness; the other four had neurological disease but might not have been terminally ill. We presume that these people were euthanized (killed) and then their organs were taken for transplant, whereas in the film death was inflicted by taking organs for transplant. But these are closely related procedures. And might Belgium consider the *Never Let Me Go* approach if, as could readily be argued, it would result in organs that were more viable?

To return to the questions the film raises, who are the scientists who made the clones and what ethical requirements should have governed them? And where are society's watchdogs, the medical and scientific bodies responsible for ensuring ethics in the professions? Or is it a situation where the legislated safeguards are inadequate or inoperative?

It is clear in Ishiguro's book that "farming" these children is a lucrative commercial industry. This brings to mind the "fertility industry" (see chapter 7) that markets assisted-reproductive technologies, bringing in $5 billion annually in the United States alone, and probably around $60 billion globally. It is an area that needs very close ethical supervision, yet it is common to hear it referred to as the "Wild West of human reproduction." Note also the unethical international organ transplant industry (referred to in chapter 3), which the Declaration of Istanbul seeks to eliminate.[11]

Another warning sign comes from the intentional use of euphemistic or obfuscating language by those involved in the "cloning-transplant project." Euphemisms can skew our perceptions about ethics, probably by suppressing our moral intuitions and distorting our emotional reactions that clear language would elicit, intuitions and emotions that would function as ethical red alerts to warn us of ethical dangers.

The person cloned in *Never Let Me Go* is referred to simply as the clone's "original." The clones go looking for their "originals"; they describe sighting a person who might be such as seeing a "possible." Especially in the book, Ishiguro captures, exactly as I have personally heard donor-conceived people express it, their anguish at not knowing, but longing to know, their biological antecedents. The case of Olivia Pratten, discussed in chapter 7, comes to mind here.

The word "kill" is never used in the film, and even the word "death" is avoided, as I have explained is often true of pro-euthanasia advocates' choice of language. Rather, the final fatal surgery is referred to as a "completion." A nurse remarks that "some donors look forward to completion," which, from one perspective, is not surprising in light of the immensely debilitated state of the young people who have already made multiple "donations." Towards the end of the film, the former headmistress of Hailsham, now retired and in a wheelchair, remarks, philosophically, "We all have to complete sometime." That's true, but *how* we "complete" is the critical ethical issue, as we can see in the present euthanasia debate.

That brings us to interventions that only become possible through the convergence of separate technologies. *Never Let Me Go* is a story of the convergence of genetic and reproductive technologies – cloning, in-vitro fertilization, and surrogate motherhood – and organ transplant technologies. Each technology, taken alone, raises serious ethical issues, but combined they raise ethical issues of a different order. And we might be closer to facing such issues in real life than most of us realize.

I have raised the question of whether it is ethical for people who are euthanized, in countries where this is legal, to become organ donors. Here is another presently possible scenario of convergence, which advocates of human embryo research have argued should be allowed for "therapeutic purposes": create an in-vitro embryo and take one cell, when all cells are still totipotential (can form another embryo) to make a second embryo. Transfer the first embryo to a woman's uterus and freeze the second embryo. If, as a born child or adult, the first embryo needs an organ transplant, transfer the second embryo to a surrogate mother, abort the fetus at a late stage of gestation, and use its organs. The only element of this scenario presently illegal in Canada is the cloning of embryos.[12]

Finally, a statement from the wheelchair-bound ex-head mistress of Hailsham merits noting with respect to the philosophy and values on which we should base our ethics. It shows her exclusively rational approach to the horror of what she helped to inflict on the children in her charge. Two of them, now adults and in love, come to her seeking a deferral of the "completion" organ retrieval surgery on the young man so that they can have some time together before he is killed. She tells them that is not possible and enquires, rhetorically, "Would you ask people to return to lung cancer, heart failure and other terrible diseases?" *Never Let Me Go* is a searing lesson about the "ethics outcomes" that can result from pure utilitarianism and moral relativism, when they are used to govern the new technoscience by people without a moral conscience or moral intuition.

The most frightening aspect of the scenes portrayed in *Never Let Me Go*, taken as a whole, is that in one way or another they all involve the use of technology to intervene on humans, and we see how doing so can involve the depersonalization or dehumanization of the people on whom the interventions are carried out. This insight is another way to answer the question explored in chapter 5, "What is currently the world's most dangerous idea?" For me it is the idea that it is ethically acceptable to use new technoscience in ways that depersonalize or dehumanize others, an outcome that will inevitably result from a failure to see all human beings as having dignity and being "special" and deserving of "special respect."

And that leads to the next question an editor asked me to address: How might the human race end?

How Might the Human Race End?

Being an incurable optimist, I do not believe the human race will end, but if that were to happen, my short answer to "how?" is through human intervention in human life with avant-garde technoscience. Interventions resulting in that outcome could be either intentional with respect to that goal as in the case of the transhumanists, or unintentional as could happen with, for example, xenotransplantation. Yet another possibility, which has a precedent and would result from a failure of humans to intervene, is that we could go the way of the dinosaurs in that a huge asteroid could hit the earth and wipe us out.

I've already briefly outlined the transhumanists' philosophy and goals in chapters 1, 3, and 5. They believe that humans – and human experience, as we know and treasure it – should and will become obsolete, and are working towards achieving that goal. They predict a posthuman future in which humans will be redesigned through technology, especially robotics and artificial intelligence, to become cyborgs, human/machine combinations. According to transhumanists, the physical, mental, emotional, and even moral capacities of cyborgs will far outstrip those of "unmodified humans" – but not, they fail to note, the capacity of cyborgs to be human. They have a techno-utopian vision – one that I and others see as dystopian – of a posthuman future in which people like us, whom transhumanists call "unmodified (natural) humans," are obsolete models.

In a nutshell, as I have explained, transhumanists describe a "human, transhuman, posthuman" continuum. They believe that revolutions now occurring in info-, bio- nano-, robotic-, and AI- (artificial intelligence) technologies will converge to alter the fundamental nature of being human, and with that our concepts of what it means to be human. We and all our most important values and beliefs will be changed beyond present recognition. For them, "human" is not the end of evolution; it is the beginning. Eventually, the transhumanists propose, we will reach the nirvana of a posthuman future: we will not be human at all.

A major danger of transhumanists is that they want to do only good. It is much more difficult to see the risks and dangers involved when we have an overwhelming desire to do good. As I discussed in chapter 5, in their own words, transhumanists "seek to expand technological opportunities for humans to live longer and healthier lives and to enhance their intellectual, physical, psychological and emotional capacities."[13] At face value, most of us would endorse those goals. But the overall and ultimate goal of transhumanism is that superior beings will be created by redesigning *Homo sapiens* with technoscience to become *Techno sapiens*.[14]

The benefits of the new technologies, as transhumanists describe them, are deeply seductive. It is no accident that they present the issues of life-prolongation and age-retardation front and centre on their pro-technology agenda. Probably rightly, they believe that these issues will appeal to many people and in doing so will generate support for transhumanism and posthumanism. Life-prolongation involves using technology to extend our "natural" lifespans by repairing or replacing our "parts" as they wear out. The implications of age retardation are far more radical. The technology involves reprogramming, at the embryonic stage, the genes that control aging so that we would reach puberty at around forty years of age, early middle age at eighty years, and old age much later, if ever. Transhumanists speak of ultimately achieving immortality.

Xenotransplantation is another technoscience that creates a remote but real possibility of wiping out the human race, in this case as an unintentional outcome. Xenotransplantation is the transplantation of organs between different species – for instance, from pigs to humans. At first glance it seems a very attractive option, because it could create an unlimited supply of organs. But what does it involve?

When a human organ is transplanted from one person to another, the recipient's body will, to a greater or lesser extent, reject that organ because the donor's genetic makeup (genome) does not exactly match the recipient's (unless they are identical twins). But when we transplant an organ from an animal to a human, an additional, very powerful rejection reaction – a hyperacute rejection reaction – occurs, minutes or hours after the transplant. To overcome this reaction, scientists are working to modify the genome of the pigs to be used as a source of organs for transplantation to humans.[15] One approach is to insert human complement inhibitor genes in the genomes of pig embryos, which, when they reach adulthood, will be used as the source of transgenic organs. These genes trick the organ recipient's immune system, overcoming the hyperacute reaction. That is, the recipient's immune system reacts more as though the organ comes from a human than a non-human species.

This technology poses a risk not only to transplant recipients, their sexual partners, and families but also, possibly, to the public as a whole. An animal virus or other infective agent might be transferred across the species barrier to humans, with potentially tragic results for the person who received the organ and for other people, including the community at large, who could subsequently be infected. There might be a very remote possibility that it could wipe out the human race.

Such concerns about xenotransplantation have been raised by eminent scientists. For example, an article in *Nature Medicine*[16] in 1997 (its lead author, Fritz Bach of Harvard University, is one of the world's leading immunologists) surprised many people with the strength of its suggestion that given the risks to the public of performing xenotransplantation, there should be a moratorium until the public was better informed and consulted. The authors stressed, however, that this suggestion was not intended to be anti-xenotransplantation or anti-science in any way.

People who oppose xenotransplantation often cite "mad cow disease," or new variant Creutzfeldt-Jakob disease, nvCJD, which came from giving cattle feed made from the carcasses of sheep infected with a prion (an infectious protein) as an example of the dangers of "tampering with nature." Other concerns about xenotransplantation include pig retroviruses being introduced into the human population, and such novel possibilities as that sequences of viral DNA in the pig genome (which are harmless to the pig) could combine with sequences of viral DNA in the human genome (which are harmless to the human) to form a totally new virus. (These viral sequences come from the ancestors of pigs and humans who respectively survived their exposure to the viruses and who subsequently had offspring who inherited the viral DNA.) Research has indicated that as few as three hundred genes may form a new living organism. Could the inactive viral sequences from the pig and from the human combine to form such an organism? Or infectious agents in the pig organs might combine with innocuous human retroviruses to form chimeric agents. (Such a combination is believed to have caused human influenza epidemics.) We cannot know in advance what the mortality and morbidity of such new infectious agents would be in humans.

Or humans might develop serious illnesses from an infective agent to which pigs are immune or which causes them little trouble. This is the case in some primates with the human immunodeficiency virus (HIV). Research on HIV indicates that it may be a virus that crossed from animals (green monkeys) into humans with the disastrous results that we have seen in the HIV/AIDS pandemic.

Therefore, in answering the question of whether we are ethically justified in creating unknown risks with xenotransplantation or any other technology, the allocation of the burden and standard of proof will be crucial. Those who wish to undertake xenotransplantation have the burden to show that, at least on the balance of probabilities, and possibly to the standard of clear and convincing evidence, it is both reasonably safe and ethical. It will also be crucial to consult the public if they are placed at risk, especially if that risk includes the possibility of ending the human race.

And now to the final question.

What Will History See as the Defining Development of the First Decades of the Twenty-First Century?

From the perspective of my research on challenges to cultural values and changes in them, my answer to the above question was, "What each society decides about euthanasia." So, further to the detailed discussion of the *Carter* case in chapter 4, let's look at the debate on euthanasia and efforts to legalize it in Canada as an example of such a development.

In May 2009, the Bloc Québécois MP Francine Lalonde introduced a private members bill into Parliament that sought to amend the Canadian Criminal Code[17] to legalize euthanasia and physician-assisted suicide. The bill was soundly defeated, 228 votes to 59, in June 2010.[18]

But the issue of legalizing euthanasia has remained very much alive in Canada, especially, at least initially, in Quebec. In December 2009, the Quebec Legislative Assembly had authorized the Health and Social Services Commission of Quebec to carry out a "Consultation on the Question of Dying with Dignity." The public consultation phase of this enquiry was undertaken by a special committee of the Quebec Legislative Assembly, which issued a report in 2012.[19] This report recommended legalizing euthanasia, despite the fact that over 60 percent of the witnesses who appeared before the committee opposed it. In January 2013, a legal committee appointed by the Quebec government reported on how the Legislative Assembly committee recommendations could be implemented in practice in the province.[20] Bill 52, An Act Respecting End-of-Life Care, was introduced into the Quebec Legislative Assembly and, after legislative committee hearings on it and a roller-coaster ride on its passage, was enacted in May 2014.[21]

Surveys show that Quebecers are the Canadians most in favour of legalizing euthanasia (a word I use to include physician-assisted suicide). And it's clear that the Quebec government believes it has a claim to jurisdiction with respect to legislating to allow euthanasia, for which the act uses the term "medical aid in dying" as code.[22]

Subject to Parliament's response to the Supreme Court of Canada's judgment in the *Carter* case (see chapter 4), at present, euthanasia is prohibited, at least until 6 February 2016, as murder under the Canadian Criminal Code, which is federal jurisdiction.[23] But Quebec challenges the Criminal Code's prohibition as trespassing on provincial jurisdiction with respect to "health and social services," arguing that euthanasia is "medical treatment," a description used by the Quebec College of Physicians and Surgeons and endorsed in the two Quebec reports referred to above.[24] The Quebec law has been challenged in the courts as unconstitutional by opponents of legalizing euthanasia, but, now, as a result of the Supreme Court's judgment in the *Carter* case, it is uncertain whether those challenges will continue. Moreover, even if the Quebec law were found to be unconstitutional, euthanasia could be allowed in practice in Quebec if the attorney general of Quebec were to instruct crown prosecutors not to criminally prosecute doctors who complied with certain guidelines in carrying out euthanasia. The legal committee also proposed such an approach.

As I have emphasized throughout this book, we have always formed our most important shared values around the two great events in each human life, birth and death, and the euthanasia debate will decide whether we will change some of the most important and fundamental of these shared values, in particular respect for human life at both the individual and societal levels. This change would not be incremental, as pro-euthanasia advocates argue, but would constitute a seismic shift in our values. Legally authorizing physicians to kill their patients is to cross a clear and bright line: "You must not kill." That is the reason the debate is such a momentous one.

I have also explained that we need to place and keep death in a moral context, not just a reasoned or legal one, important as the latter is. Legalizing euthanasia would seriously threaten our capacity to do that, as we can see by looking at the expansion of the conditions in which euthanasia is available and the documentation of its use outside the law in the Netherlands and Belgium, where euthanasia is legal. Maintaining death and dying in a moral context is particularly crucial in light of an aging population and scarce and increasingly expensive health-care resources, which will face us with many difficult decisions about who lives and who dies.

I propose that the best answers to the three central questions posed about euthanasia in chapter 1 – "Would legalization be most likely to help us or hinder us in our search for meaning in our individual and collective lives? How do we want our grandchildren and great grandchildren to die? And, in relation to human death, what kind of values and culture do we want to pass on?" – all strongly indicate that we should not legalize euthanasia.

So in line with the theme of this chapter, "asking questions," what questions might help us to become fully aware of the risks and harms of legalizing euthanasia? Here are some I asked with that goal in mind about Quebec's Bill 52 immediately after its passage into law. Similar questions should now also be asked about the Supreme Court judges and their decision in the *Carter* case discussed in chapter 4:

- Why did Quebec politicians fail to give sufficient weight to the dangers and harms of legalizing euthanasia, especially to vulnerable people – those who are old and fragile or disabled, and whose lives are denigrated by euthanasia's message that they are not worth living?
- Why did their ethical imaginations, human memories (knowledge of history), and examined emotions fail to warn them that they are on the wrong path? Did they fail to distinguish between obligations to kill people's suffering through good palliative care and pain management and the act of killing the person with the suffering? Did they fail to heed the old warning, "Nowhere are human rights more threatened than when we act purporting to do only good"? A desire to do good can blind us to the harms.
- Are Quebec politicians so focused on giving priority to individual autonomy – "choice" – that they don't see the harm to the value of respect for human life at the societal level that legalizing euthanasia unavoidably causes?
- How will legalizing euthanasia affect the capacity of law and medicine to carry the value of respect for life for society as a

whole? They are the main institutions carrying this value in a secular society.

- Has the media's almost exclusive focus on heart-wrenching cases of suffering individuals asking for euthanasia blinded us to the larger-picture consequences of legalizing it?
- Why do politicians use obfuscating language – "medical aid to die" – for euthanasia? An Ipsos Marketing survey found that two-thirds of Quebecers did not understand that this meant a lethal injection, and 40 percent did not understand that euthanasia also meant that.
- Can we imagine physicians teaching medical students how to carry out euthanasia and clinically role-modelling it for them?
- Will many physicians decline work in institutions in which colleagues administer euthanasia? Imagine sitting down to lunch with a colleague who ten minutes before killed a patient.
- Will patients refuse to be admitted to institutions that provide euthanasia? Will they refuse palliative care and pain management for fear of being euthanized? The Netherlands and Belgium both show these are valid concerns.
- Why did Quebec politicians cite Belgium's law as a felicitous example when there is ample evidence of its abuse (the "practical slippery slope") and rapid and broad expansion of its application (the "logical slippery slope")?
- Would serious mental illness or anorexia nervosa be an "end-of-life condition" allowing euthanasia in Quebec, as in Belgium and the Netherlands? Likewise, as in those countries, once we become accustomed to euthanasia, will children become eligible for it? What about people with dementia?
- Will euthanasia be used as a cost-saving mechanism? Was it just a coincidence that Bill 52's passage into law immediately followed the Quebec budget bill?
- As Quebec politicians claim, will euthanasia be rarely used? In Belgium, five people die each day by euthanasia. In the Netherlands, 4 percent of all deaths are now by euthanasia, which is an underestimate and does not include deaths

through "continuous terminal sedation (CTS)" (Bill 52's term for "slow euthanasia"), which is being increasingly used, as its legal requirements are less onerous.

- Is euthanasia just an incremental expansion of current ethically and legally accepted end-of-life decisions such as refusals of life-support treatment, as pro-euthanasia advocates argue, or is acting with an intention to kill different in kind from allowing a natural death?
- Is euthanasia medical treatment?[25] What are the dangers of defining it as such to patients, the trust-based physician-patient relationship, and to medicine? Should we take the "medical cloak" off euthanasia and have some specially trained persons other than physicians mandated to administer it?[26]
- If euthanasia remains permitted, how do we think our great-grandchildren will die? What kind of society will we have left to them? Will it be one in which no reasonable person would want to live?
- Why don't most politicians and many Canadians recognize the momentousness of a decision to legalize euthanasia?

As I hope the answers to these questions will make people aware, legalizing euthanasia is not, as pro-euthanasia advocates argue, an incremental change. It is a radical and massive shift in our society's and civilization's foundational values. Indeed, as I wrote in chapter 1, I predict that history will see each society's decision about euthanasia, whether for or against it, as a major turning-point values decision of the twenty-first century.

Yet another question I was asked to answer about euthanasia, this a very direct one from an editor at the *Huffington Post*, was: "Why shouldn't euthanasia and assisted suicide be legalized?" In responding, I further clarified some of the differences between the pro-euthanasia and anti-euthanasia positions. Here's my answer, which summarizes many of the observations and arguments I have made about euthanasia in many parts of this book.

First, many people believe it is inherently wrong for one human being intentionally to kill another. The only legally recognized exceptions have traditionally been when that is the only way to save human life, as in self-defence or "just war." But utilitarians and moral relativists disagree. For them, nothing is inherently wrong, including euthanasia; rather its rightness or wrongness depends on all the circumstances and the values and preferences of the individual who wants it. They argue that euthanasia should be legal when its benefits for individual persons outweigh its risks and harms to them.

To get as many people as possible to agree with them, euthenasia advocates sanitize the language they use. For instance, they don't speak of killing, or even suicide, but, as in the Quebec government reports recommending that euthanasia be allowed, of "medically assisted death." We all want medical assistance – good palliative care, especially pain management – when we are dying. This euphemistic language conceals and creates confusion about what euthanasia involves, namely, killing another human, and a direct confrontation with that reality.

Another confusion used to promote euthanasia is the "no difference" argument, discussed in chapter 4. Pro-euthanasia advocates argue that currently accepted end-of-life treatment decisions, such as refusals of life-support treatment, result in shortening the patient's life but are ethical and legal, and that euthanasia is no different from them and that it is just another form of medical treatment. Therefore, to act consistently, they argue, euthanasia should be seen as ethical and legal. Anti-euthanasia proponents strongly disagree.

Pro-euthanasia advocates also argue that the right to refuse treatment establishes a right to die. But that is wrong; rights to refuse treatment are founded in respect for the right to inviolability, persons' right not to be touched, including by medical treatment, without their informed consent. Rights to refuse treatment do not recognize a right to die, let alone a right to be killed. At most, they establish a right to be allowed to die naturally.

Moreover, in respecting refusals of treatment, the physician does not have a primary intention to kill the patient as is true in euthanasia. Pro-euthanasia advocates respond that we cannot be sure what a physician's intention is. But courts across Canada determine an accused person's intentions every day in deciding on criminal culpability, where intention is a central element. We can assess a physician's intention according to whether the drugs given were medically indicated as reasonable treatment, for instance, to relieve pain, and were administered in appropriate doses.

Causation also differs between refusals of treatment and euthanasia. Refusals of life-support treatment result in natural death from underlying illness. In euthanasia, death results from a lethal injection or ingested drugs.

The "no difference" argument is also promoted by focusing on the ultimate outcome, namely death, and emphasizing that this occurs whether or not euthanasia is involved – "these people die anyway." But the issue is not *if* we die; we all die. It's *how* we die, and anti-euthanasia proponents believe there are valid ethical and legal distinctions between euthanasia and well-accepted medical practices at the end of life. A further difference is that anti-euthanasia advocates give priority to the value of respect for life, and pro-euthanasia ones privilege respect for individual autonomy, when, as in euthanasia, these values conflict. Unbridled "radical autonomy" is the cornerstone for many "progressive values" stances, including euthanasia. But can dying people really make free and informed (autonomous) decisions that they want "assistance to die"? Moreover, wanting assistance to die is not the same as "wanting to die," which many terminally ill people do want. New concepts such as "relational autonomy" – the idea that people are not isolated beings but exist in a context that influences their decisions, and that this must be taken into account when judging the validity of the voluntariness of those decisions[27] – can restrain individual autonomy gone wild.

Pro-euthanasia advocates often justify overriding the value of respect for life by labelling it as religious – they refer to it as "sanctity of life" – and as passé in a secular society such as Canada. But all societies in which reasonable people would want to live need to uphold respect for both individual human lives and human life in general, as the Canadian Charter of Rights and Freedoms affirms.

Focusing solely on individuals who want euthanasia, as pro-euthanasia advocates do, is not sufficient in deciding whether to legalize euthanasia. Euthanasia is not, as they argue, just a matter of personal decision-making. What we decide about it will affect others, our institutions, and society.

Implementing euthanasia requires changing the law to allow physicians to carry it out. How will this affect the value-carrying capacity of law and medicine, the two main institutions in a secular society carrying the value of respect for life? Legalizing euthanasia also means that society becomes complicit in inflicting death on some of its members. What long-term effects might result from that?

The final point I made in responding to the *Huffington Post* editor was that pro-euthanasia advocates adamantly deny there is any evidence in jurisdictions where euthanasia has been legalized of a "logical slippery slope" – that the situations in which euthanasia will be available will expand over time – or a "practical slippery slope" – that euthanasia will be used abusively. The latter is an especially relevant concern in relation to vulnerable people, including those who are old, disabled, or dying. But convincing evidence from the Netherlands and Belgium proves them wrong, as the High Court of Ireland affirmed after an extensive review of the evidence of the practical slippery slope.[28]

Advocates of legalizing euthanasia also reject slippery-slope arguments as constituting unfounded fear-mongering and claim that its use will always be restricted to rare cases of dying people with unrelievable, unbearable suffering. But, as the Netherlands and Belgium demonstrate, that's not what results in practice.

The logical and practical slippery slopes are unavoidable and inevitable, because those consequences are built into the act of legalization through its justification of inflicting death. Once we cross the clear line that we must not intentionally kill another person, there is no logical stopping point. Let me explain.

When euthanasia is first legalized, the usual necessary and sufficient justification for breaching that line is a conjunctive justification comprised of respect for individual autonomy and the relief of suffering. But as people and physicians become accustomed to euthanasia, they ask, "Why not just relief of suffering or respect for autonomy alone?" These become alternative justifications.

As a lone justification, relief of suffering allows euthanasia of those unable to consent for themselves. Pro-euthanasia advocates argue that allowing euthanasia is to do good to suffering, mentally competent people; consequently, denying it to mentally incompetent suffering people unable to consent is wrong, discrimination on the basis of mental handicap. So suffering people with dementia or disabled newborn babies or children should have access to euthanasia.

And if, as pro-euthanasia advocates also claim, one owns one's life and no one else has the right to interfere with one's decisions in that regard, then respect for the person's autonomy is a sufficient justification for euthanasia. That is, the person need not be suffering to have access; hence the proposal in the Netherlands that euthanasia should be available to those "over seventy and tired of life."

Once the initial justification for euthanasia is expanded, why not allow some other justifications, for instance, savings on health-care costs, especially with an aging population? Until very recently this was an unaskable question. Now, it is being raised in relation to euthanasia. In my own experience, a final-year medical student in a class I was teaching at McGill University became angry with me because I rejected his insistent claim that legalizing euthanasia was essential to save the health-care costs of an aging population.

The practical slippery slope is unavoidable because familiarity with inflicting death causes us to lose a sense of the awesomeness of what euthanasia involves – killing another human being. The same is true in making euthanasia a medical act. Both result in its logical extension and its abuse in practice becoming much more likely, indeed, inevitable. We need to stay firmly behind the clear line that establishes that we do not intentionally kill each other.

The strongest case for euthanasia is made by a seriously suffering person, such as the highly respected Canadian public health physician Dr Donald Low, who, when dying from a brain tumour, made a video pleading for "medically assisted death." He asked us to put ourselves "in his body" and imagine what we would want. Our hearts, understanding, and compassion rightly went out to him. His plea resonated with something Sue Rodriguez said: "How can you be so cruel as to deny this [physician-assisted suicide] to me? Even a man condemned to death is given his last wish." Such people make riveting television, and their impact is augmented because the media, which is largely pro-euthanasia, tends to feature them. For example, media coverage of Quebec's Bill 52, after it initially failed to be put to a vote, featured suffering people who wanted access to euthanasia lamenting that it had not yet become law – not those with disabilities opposing the bill's enactment, who felt that they had been given a breathing space.

As noted before, the case against legalizing euthanasia is more difficult to present, especially visually. This is because the relevant risks and harms are intangible, inchoate at present or in the future. They include risks of abuse of vulnerable people, harm to the ethos and ethics of medicine, and harm to the law's capacity to enshrine and carry the message of respect for life. They include the risk of harm to the important, shared, fundamental values through which we bond to form society – that we care for each other, especially vulnerable people, and do not intentionally kill each other – and consequently a risk of leaving a seriously damaged society to future generations.

Yet if I were asked right now the question I have dealt with in this last section, "What will history see as the defining development of the first decades of the twenty-first century?" and forced to make only one choice, I am not sure that I would still choose legalizing euthanasia, important as I think the decision around it is. Perhaps an even more crucial development is new technology that will allow us to alter the human germline. Whether we choose to do so or to prohibit it is probably the most momentous decision humans will ever make.

The human germline is the genetic essence of human life. It is the genes passed on from generation to generation that have evolved over billions of years since the advent of life on earth, an evolution that has resulted in each one of us. We can now alter that evolution by changing an embryo's germline genes, and all descendants of that embryo will inherit those alterations.

Is that ethical?

The human germline has been described as "the common heritage of humankind that must be held in trust for future generations." Until very recently there was widespread agreement that intentional interference with that heritage was unethical and should not be allowed. The UNESCO Universal Declaration on the Human Genome and Human Rights (1997) characterizes germline interventions as "practices that could be contrary to human dignity."[29] The Council of Europe's European Convention on Human Rights and Biomedicine

(Oviedo Convention, 1997) bans interventions on the human genome that could be inherited, that is, on the human germline.[30] The Canadian Assisted Human Reproduction Act 2004 prohibits "alter[ing] the genome of a cell of a human being or in-vitro embryo such that the alteration is capable of being transmitted to descendants;"[31] and the vast majority of bioethicists have agreed with this stance.

Until very recently, however, these were theoretical prohibitions, because the biotechnology needed to alter germline genes did not exist. But that changed with human gene-editing technologies such as CRISPR-Cas9, which Chinese scientists in April 2015 reported using on non-viable human embryos.

In response to such developments, the US National Academy of Sciences (NAS) and the National Academy of Medicine (NAM) announced that they were "launching a major initiative to guide decision-making about controversial new research involving human gene editing." They explain: "Human gene-editing technologies, such as CRISPR-Cas9, may lead to promising new treatments for disease. However, recent experiments to attempt to edit human genes also have raised important questions about the potential risks and ethical concerns of altering the human germline. Future advances are likely to raise new questions." The NAS-NAM initiative will include an international summit in the fall of 2015 "to explore the scientific, ethical and policy issues associated with human gene-editing research."[32]

The White House Office of Science and Technology Policy (OSTP) responded immediately with a "Note on Genome Editing." The OSTP "applauds NAS and NAM for convening this dialogue and fully supports a robust review of the ethical issues associated with using gene-editing technology to alter the human germline. The administration believes that altering the human germline for clinical purposes is a line that should not be crossed at this time," pointing out that "this year [2015] scientists called for a moratorium on germline-editing research *until the safety and ethical issues could be explored by the community*."[33] As my emphasis shows, the belief that it is inherently wrong to alter the human germline, that is, to create intentionally "genetically altered humans," does not seem to be an informing principle. Rather, it's a matter of taking a precautionary approach and weighing risks and benefits.

And this is where the rubber will hit the road. In May 2015, Harvard experimental psychologist Steven Pinker and I strongly disagreed at the BEINGS 2015 (Biotechnology and the Ethical Imagination: A Global Summit) meeting held in Atlanta, Georgia. I argued that holding the human germline in trust means it must not be intentionally altered. Pinker's view was that bioethicists should get out of the way if they were inhibiting advances in health technology such as germline alteration that could extend life expectancy and alleviate suffering. He used the example of deleting the gene for Huntington's disease and asked if I would reject that. This question is not theoretical: it has since been announced that two "Bama minipigs were engineered with CRISPR technology to lack two genes linked to Parkinson's disease."[34]

So, will our powerful desire to relieve suffering, no matter the cost, override all other concerns, so that we will be practising eugenics, designing our children, "enhancing" them (or even "dis-enhancing" some, because the superintelligent enhanced will be unsuited to doing menial but necessary jobs)? Will we create a new class-based society of the "gene rich" and "gene poor"? Is there a human right not to be designed, even if that is done with benevolent intentions?

The White House "Note" concludes with a warning: "The full implications of … [human germline editing] could not be known until a number of generations had inherited the genetic changes made – and choices made in one country could affect all of us."

What may we do? What must we not do? What values will prevail in the battle between doing great good by eliminating dreadful diseases and the suffering they entail, and doing great harm in designing human beings? Our decisions will determine the future nature of human nature.

These questions, which involve the beginning of life, are echoed by those we are facing at the end of life in deciding about euthanasia: What may we do? What must we not do? What values will prevail in the battle between what is perceived as doing good by eliminating suffering through legalizing euthanasia, and doing great harm in the resulting abuse of vulnerable people and great harm to the value of respect for life? What we decide will determine the future nature of human society.

◆◆◆

In concluding this chapter on the communication of values, particularly in relation to unprecedented scientific breakthroughs, the research by Nottingham University professors Brigitte Nerlich and David Clarke is informative. The two psychologists studied the distinctive role that staged media events play in the public understanding of genetics, analyzing as a case study such an event staged by two fertility experts in 2001. Their research showed, as they summarize it in the abstract of their article, that such events "can focus the attention of the media, scientists and the public on the risks and benefits of genetic advances in cloning [the case under study]; they can accelerate policy changes by exposing scientific, legal and ethical uncertainties; the use of images, metaphors, clichés and cultural narratives by scientists and the media engaged in this event can reinforce stereotypical representations of cloning, but can also expose fundamental clashes in arguments about cloning."[35]

The communication of values through all forms of media, including social media, has never been more powerful, ubiquitous, or important in determining what our shared values will be. We need to take great care with the substance of the messages we deliver and to be questioning and wisely critical recipients of those we receive. We must also keep in mind that persuasion, not imposition, is the approach most likely to convince others that they too should adopt the values we see as important to maintain if we are to balance ethically a respect for individual autonomy and the protection of the common good.

And so I come to the end of this book with yet one more question that can only be answered by others: What will humans, their physical world, their societies, and their individual and shared values look like one hundred years from now?

APPENDICES

APPENDIX A

The Best Teacher I Ever Had Was My Father, George Patrick Ganley

Finally, on a personal note …

I am quite often asked how I "ended up" doing the work I do, and where my values, ideas, opinions, beliefs, attitudes and so on come from. In view of the title and content of this book, I thought I should try to pre-empt that question by attempting to answer it, in part.

I came to realize what a powerful influence my father had been with respect to my values and philosophy of life when, in the mid-1990s, Professor Alex Michalos asked me to contribute to a book he was editing, which consisted of essays by members of the Royal Society of Canada, each starting with the phrase, "The best teacher I ever had was …" My essay was called, "Margaret A. Somerville on George Patrick Ganley."[1] The dedication read: "This text is dedicated to my mother, the late Gertrude Honora Ganley, with deep gratitude for her wisdom in choosing my father for me."

Here is that essay, written in 1996.

◆◆◆

The best teacher I ever had was my father, George Patrick Ganley. He loved learning and powerfully communicated this love to me. He quietly transmitted a sense of awe, wonder, joy, and intense curiosity about the tangible and intangible worlds that surround us. He was as interested in talking to me about the stars in the night sky and how to approach an animal in a way that would not frighten it as about how he felt about world affairs and music. Perhaps unusually for someone I've described as the best teacher I ever had, my father never seemed to be seeking to teach me, and I am almost certain he never thought of himself as trying to do this. Rather, I felt that he wanted to share with me that which he cared about deeply and which moved him profoundly.

On summer nights, my father, brother, and I used to sleep on the lawn in the back garden, and my father would identify the stars and their constellations and tell us the stories that surrounded them. As a boy, he had lived in the Outback of Australia and, at a young age, had worked with his father on vast station properties where the usual roof over their heads at night was the starry universe. My father also used the coming of the day to teach me. My mother told me that when I was a baby, he would take me for a walk each morning as the dawn broke to "show me the birds getting up."

As a four-year-old, I can remember rising very early and returning home while it was still dark; we had been out distributing pamphlets in letter boxes. Much later in my life, I learned that these were flyers for the Australian Communist Party which, at the time of our campaigning, the Commonwealth Government was trying to outlaw as an illegal organization in Australia. (In the *Communist Party* cases in the High Court of Australia, the legislation was struck down and political freedom and freedom of speech upheld.) My mother was a member of a conservative ladies' morning-tea group. Some days I was co-opted into two distributions: pamphlets before dawn and later, dressed in flower-sprigged voile with a blue sash tied in a large bow at the back, offering plates of sliced cake to "the ladies" at tea. I sometimes muse that being exposed at a young age to this radical duality was probably good training, not only for trying "to see the other side" when faced with persons who disagree with me (I was once told that I am referred to by some CBC journalists as Margo "on-the-other-hand" Somerville), but also for learning to live as comfortably as possible with unavoidable uncertainty. I often tell my students that the latter is one of the most important lessons they can learn, because it is essential to exercising good judgment in the stressful situations that they will face as physicians or lawyers in professional practice.

Throughout his life, my father rose before the sun and usually sat on the front verandah of our house waiting for the morning newspaper to arrive. He would devour it from front to back before setting off for work. News about the world, in particular international politics, was his passion. I used to think that he read every word of every article in the newspaper – and probably all the classified advertisements as well. A major pleasure in my everyday life is to read the newspaper each morning, no matter where I am in the world.

When I was eleven years old, the first part of my daily journey to school was on the same bus that my father took to work in the city of Adelaide. The passengers included a group of men with similar interests to my father's in "life, God, art, and world." I was accepted as an equal participant in these discussions, somebody who was respected, listened to, and disagreed with. I was not discriminated against on the basis of age or sex, the latter rare behaviour indeed among men in the Australia of the late 1950s. But my father did not generalize this tolerance. He would sometimes make remarks that I found expressed discriminatory attitudes to women. I would remind him that he did not see me in that way and he would say, "Oh, but you're different, Margo."

Likewise, probably because my father never saw himself as old, he was intolerant of old people. When he was in the last stages of his life and in a hospice, I asked him if he would like to attend a concert that was being performed for the patients. He said, "Those people are all too old for me." He was probably right in terms of their intellectual and psychological approaches to life as compared to his – he remained intensely intellectually curious and active to the end of his life. One of my most treasured compliments was from a man to whom I was complaining that I was growing old. He responded, "You're so crazy, Margo, you will be young when you're eighty-five." I hope so and, if it proves true, the approach to life that results in this is yet another gift from my father.

My father also taught me to love the experience of making music. He had a beautiful tenor voice – he would sometimes sing at weddings, and my mother would accompany him on the organ. Saturday nights were often music nights at our house; family and friends would gather to play instruments and sing. My brother and I were expected to be active contributors to the music-making. When I was reluctant to practise the piano, my father would ask me play for him. His appreciation of the music was so rewarding that I could not refuse his requests for the pieces I was struggling to perfect for my music examinations or to compete in an eisteddfod. I often think that surviving the latter as a five-year-old has given me the confidence I need to address audiences today.

One morning when my father was much older, and many years after I had become resident at McGill University in Canada and was back in Australia on vacation, I found him very upset and asked him what had happened. He told me that he had found his "friend" – a wild blackbird that would hover near his shoulder as he turned over the soil in the garden and dive down to take the worms that were exposed – dead in the garden. I asked him what he had done with the bird, and he said that he had buried him under the orange tree, the place where, with manifest grief and rituals of passing and parting, he and I had buried the beloved cats of my youth. (Perhaps it is only in death that the cats and the birds – the lions and the lambs – lie down together.) I tried to console my father, but he was obviously deeply affected by this loss. When I saw him again the next day, however, he was joyful. His eyes sparkled and he told me that it had been another bird that he had buried; his bird friend had returned that morning. My father's bond with this wild creature captures for me the complex interaction of *earned trust* and *blind trust* that is essential in our intimate human relationships, in particular, friendships. The bird manifested both kinds of trust in my father. Today some people would call that an interspecies friendship.

When my father arrived home each night from his office, he would stop at the front gate post, where my Siamese cat would be perched waiting for him to arrive, and scratch the cat behind his ears (what my father called "doing his ears") and tell the cat of the tensions and troubles of the day. He said that by the time he came into the house – to first kiss my mother, as he did each evening upon arrival home, and then me, if I were there – his worries and tensions had disappeared. They had been given to the cat, and the cat had accepted them. Through such examples, my father introduced me to the mystery of our interaction with other species and manifested his profound belief in the deeply embedded place of humans in nature as a whole.

We were a Catholic family, although at various times in his life my father had been a card-carrying atheist and, later, an agnostic and, later still, perhaps neither of these. One Sunday morning, when I was seven years old, I protested about going to Mass and said to my mother, "I don't see why I have to go when my father doesn't." She replied, "Your father will go to hell." The next day Sister Rosemary, the nun who was our class teacher, asked everyone in the class who wanted to go to heaven to raise their hand. Everyone did, except me. She said, "Where do you want to go?" and I said, "Hell." She was speechless. To the extent that I have courage, I believe I learnt it from my father. No matter how much it might have benefited him to do so, he would never agree with something that contravened his own personally determined central beliefs as to what was morally right and wrong.

When my father was dying, he told me that there was only one thing that he regretted in his life; it was that he had killed a kangaroo. His hero in life, of whom he spoke often, was Mahatma Ghandi, the man of peace. My father was a pacifist and abhorred war and cruelty. He expressed this in simple but profound ways. Again as a young child, I can remember screaming because I had found a large spider in my bed. My father came and said, "Don't be frightened. We just need to find him a new home." We encouraged the spider to crawl onto the bristles of a soft broom, carefully took him into the garden, and placed him in a large pine tree. That time, and many other times in my life, my father told me, "You should never destroy anything that you can't create, unless it is necessary to do so to protect people from danger." I continue to find new homes for insects, including, in the summer, transferring tiny spiders, ladybugs, and so on from the basil, picked from pots on the terrace and brought into the kitchen to make pesto, to the leaves of my inside house plants.

In the same vein, my father, although he was not a vegetarian, refused to eat what he called "factory" chicken, because of the cruel ways in which these animals are raised as "market produce." His example was in my mind on two recent occasions. I was asked to review the report of an expert committee of the Royal Society of Canada to advise Health Canada on the future treatment of a large colony of macaque monkeys, established by Health Canada for medical research purposes. I could hear in my mind my father's humane and concerned voice as I pondered the options. Health Canada is also considering the issues raised by xenotransplantation – the transplantation of animal organs to humans. One of the major issues is whether the treatment of the animals that is necessary to make them medically acceptable as a source of organs is ethically acceptable. Because these animals must be kept as pathogen free as possible, they will live in completely artificial, sterile conditions – even more so than the chickens my father refused to eat, and they will have no vestige of normal animal life. At Health Canada's consultative conference, one spokesperson for the xenotransplantation industry referred to the organ donor pigs (most often referred to by the stigmatizing, negative-emotion-eliciting term "swine") as his "manufacturing plant." I cannot think of any greater contrast with the way in which my father would have described these animals.

In the early days of my academic career at McGill, because of my work in the then-emerging field of medicine, ethics, and law, I started to receive some publicity in the media. One of the early articles was headLined, "I'm a Perpetual Student Says Margo Somerville." Several of my colleagues came to me concerned that I would be upset about being described in this way. They thought that it was demeaning and that I would feel that it was not sufficiently respectful of my newly acquired status as an assistant professor. In fact, I had not been perturbed by the title; indeed, I had not even noticed that it said anything unexpected or unusual. But the way in which my colleagues had perceived it made me wonder whether I had been insufficiently sensitive to its proper nuance. Shortly after this article appeared, I went to Australia and took a copy of it with me. I showed it to my father. His face immediately lit up and he said, "What a superb compliment that they would think that you are a perpetual student." I was as surprised by his perception as I had been by that of my colleagues, and asked him to explain why he thought this. He said that it is the most wonderful thing in life to be always learning, to be open-minded, intellectually curious, exploring and discovering, and that it was a great honour to be regarded as a person who seeks to live life doing this.

When my father was dying, I asked him if he would like to see a priest. He asked why I thought that he would want to do this, and I replied that he was one of the most religious people – although "spiritual" would have been a better word – I had ever met. He laughed and said that was not correct. I explained to him that I found his profound connection with nature, his way of seeing the world, his love of ideas and the "things of the human spirit" an expression of intense spirituality. He smiled and said, "Margo, that is not religion; that is living with the universe." A priest friend to whom I told this story remarked that this was perhaps one of the best definitions of religion that he had ever encountered. The word "religion," after all, comes from *re ligere*, to bind together, and the universe is the grandest scale on which we can do this.

My father was engaged in life and the universe in the ways I have described until the last seconds of his life. The palliative care nurse who happened to be with him when he died said that he and she were participating in a lively conversation about the Falklands War taking place at that time. She turned around to adjust some equipment in his room and, when she turned back, he was dead, literally leaving this world in mid-sentence. It is sometimes said that we die in the way we have lived. This certainly was true of my father, and it was his final important lesson for me.

Several years after my father died, I gave a speech I called "Gazing at Stars and Patting Cats." Its basic theme was that in order to live with equanimity and hope, to experience awe, wonder, and joy, and to deal with our tragedies, despairs, and sorrows, we humans need to have one hand patting an animal or in the earth at the same time as we reach out with the other to the stars – to the universe. In a way, we humans are the medium through which the Earth and the Universe meet, the window through which they can see each other. This speech was one of a series that included a previous one entitled "Spacing Out and Spacing In: Searching for the Purple-Pink Middle." In that speech, I had looked at how the range of our knowledge had been exponentially increased at the end of the twentieth century by our new science – our exploration of vast outer space, on the one hand, and vast inner space, through genetics and molecular biology, on the other hand – and mused about how we humans could cope with the enormity, the mind-altering nature, of what we had learnt. I proposed that we needed to search for ethics and, in order to do so, to change the colour of each of the poles of the spectrum, on which we place each other's views on ethics, from black and white, respectively, to red and blue. This strategy would help us to avoid fighting about whether we or our opponents were white or black (good or evil) and allow us to focus instead on the issues on which we disagreed. It would also give rise to a purple-pink middle – the colour of the imagination – rather than grey – the colour of depression – in which to search for ethics.

It is only now, looking back, that I can see the great extent to which concepts and ideas such as those I've mentioned above came from lessons that my father taught me. In fact, it was only in responding to the invitation to write about "the best teacher I ever had" that I fully realized this. The incidents and conversations described in this short paper are just examples of the richness of the teaching my father gave me throughout his life. I am coming to see how much I am indebted to him and that, in a sense, I am heir to his philosophy of life.

Patri gratias.

APPENDIX B

Three Statements on Academic Freedom

Association of Universities and Colleges of Canada (AUCC) Statement on Academic Freedom

Academic freedom is the freedom to teach and conduct research in an academic environment. Academic freedom is fundamental to the mandate of universities to pursue truth, educate students and disseminate knowledge and understanding.

In teaching, academic freedom is fundamental to the protection of the rights of the teacher to teach and of the student to learn. In research and scholarship, it is critical to advancing knowledge. Academic freedom includes the right to freely communicate knowledge and the results of research and scholarship.

Unlike the broader concept of freedom of speech, academic freedom must be based on institutional integrity, rigorous standards for enquiry and institutional autonomy, which allows universities to set their research and educational priorities.

https://www.aucc.ca/media-room/news-and-commentary/canadas-universities-adopt-new-statement-on-academic-freedom/

Canadian Association of University Teachers (CAUT) Policy Policy Statement on Academic Freedom

1 Post-secondary educational institutions serve the common good of society through searching for, and disseminating, knowledge

and understanding and through fostering independent thinking and expression in academic staff and students. Robust democracies require no less. These ends cannot be achieved without academic freedom.

2 Academic freedom includes the right, without restriction by prescribed doctrine, to freedom to teach and discuss; freedom to carry out research and disseminate and publish the results thereof; freedom to produce and perform creative works; freedom to engage in service to the institution and the community; freedom to express one's opinion about the institution, its administration, and the system in which one works; freedom to acquire, preserve, and provide access to documentary material in all formats; and freedom to participate in professional and representative academic bodies. Academic freedom always entails freedom from institutional censorship.

3 Academic freedom does not require neutrality on the part of the individual. Academic freedom makes intellectual discourse, critique, and commitment possible. All academic staff must have the right to fulfil their functions without reprisal or repression by the institution, the state, or any other source. Contracts which are silent on the matter of academic freedom do not entitle the employer to breach or threaten in any way the academic freedom of academic staff employed under such collective agreements or other employment contracts.

4 All academic staff have the right to freedom of thought, conscience, religion, expression, assembly, and association and the right to liberty and security of the person and freedom of movement. Academic staff must not be hindered or impeded in exercising their civil rights as individuals including the right to contribute to social change through free expression of opinion on matters of public interest. Academic staff must not suffer any institutional penalties because of the exercise of such rights.

5 Academic freedom requires that academic staff play a major role in the governance of the institution. Academic staff members shall constitute at least a majority on committees or collegial governing bodies responsible for academic matters including but not limited to curriculum, assessment procedures and standards, appointment, tenure and promotion.

6 Academic freedom must not be confused with institutional autonomy. Post-secondary institutions are autonomous to the extent that they can set policies independent of outside influence. That very autonomy can protect academic freedom from a hostile external environment, but it can also facilitate an internal assault on academic freedom. Academic freedom is a right of members of the academic staff, not of the institution. The employer shall not abridge academic freedom on any grounds, including claims of institutional autonomy.

Approved by the CAUT Council, November 2011.
http://archive.caut.ca/pages.asp?page=247&lang=1

The UNESCO Recommendation Concerning the Status of Higher-Education Teaching Personnel, 11 November 1997

VI Rights and freedoms of higher-education teaching personne

A Individual rights and freedoms: civil rights, academic freedom, publication rights, and the international exchange of information

25 Access to the higher education academic profession should be based solely on appropriate academic qualifications, competence and experience and be equal for all members of society without any discrimination.

26 Higher-education teaching personnel, like all other groups and individuals, should enjoy those internationally recognized civil, political, social and cultural rights applicable to all citizens. Therefore, all higher-education teaching personnel should enjoy freedom of thought, conscience, religion, expression, assembly and association as well as the right to liberty and security of the person and liberty of movement. They should not be hindered or impeded in exercising their civil rights as citizens, including the right to contribute to social change through freely expressing their opinion of state policies and of policies affecting higher education. They should not suffer any penalties simply because of the exercise of such rights. Higher-education teaching personnel

should not be subject to arbitrary arrest or detention, nor to torture, nor to cruel, inhuman or degrading treatment. In cases of gross violation of their rights, higher-education teaching personnel should have the right to appeal to the relevant national, regional or international bodies such as the agencies of the United Nations, and organizations representing higher-education teaching personnel should extend full support in such cases.

27 The maintaining of the above international standards should be upheld in the interest of higher education internationally and within the country. To do so, the principle of academic freedom should be scrupulously observed. Higher-education teaching personnel are entitled to the maintaining of academic freedom, that is to say, the right, without constriction by prescribed doctrine, to freedom of teaching and discussion, freedom in carrying out research and disseminating and publishing the results thereof, freedom to express freely their opinion about the institution or system in which they work, freedom from institutional censorship and freedom to participate in professional or representative academic bodies. All higher-education teaching personnel should have the right to fulfil their functions without discrimination of any kind and without fear of repression by the state or any other source. Higher-education teaching personnel can effectively do justice to this principle if the environment in which they operate is conducive, which requires a democratic atmosphere; hence the challenge for all of developing a democratic society.

28 Higher-education teaching personnel have the right to teach without any interference, subject to accepted professional principles including professional responsibility and intellectual rigour with regard to standards and methods of teaching. Higher-education teaching personnel should not be forced to instruct against their own best knowledge and conscience or be forced to use curricula and methods contrary to national and international human rights standards. Higher education teaching personnel should play a significant role in determining the curriculum.

29 Higher-education teaching personnel have a right to carry out research work without any interference, or any suppression, in accordance with their professional responsibility and subject to

nationally and internationally recognized professional principles of intellectual rigour, scientific inquiry and research ethics. They should also have the right to publish and communicate the conclusions of the research of which they are authors or co-authors, as stated in paragraph 12 of this Recommendation.

30 Higher-education teaching personnel have a right to undertake professional activities outside of their employment, particularly those that enhance their professional skills or allow for the application of knowledge to the problems of the community, provided such activities do not interfere with their primary commitments to their home institutions in accordance with institutional policies and regulations or national laws and practice where they exist.

APPENDIX C

Use of the Concept of Human Dignity in Four International Instruments

The Universal Declaration of Human Rights

Preamble

Whereas recognition of the inherent dignity and of the equal and inalienable rights of all members of the human family is the foundation of freedom, justice and peace in the world ...

Whereas the peoples of the United Nations have in the Charter reaffirmed their faith in fundamental human rights, in the dignity and worth of the human person and in the equal rights of men and women and have determined to promote social progress and better standards of life in larger freedom...

Article 1 All human beings are born free and equal in dignity and rights ...

Article 22 Everyone, as a member of society, has the right to social security and is entitled to realization, through national effort and international co-operation and in accordance with the organization and resources of each State, of the economic, social and cultural rights indispensable for his dignity and the free development of his personality.

Article 23 ... (3) Everyone who works has the right to just and favourable remuneration ensuring for himself and his family an existence worthy of human dignity, and supplemented, if necessary, by other means of social protection.

The UNESCO Universal Declaration on Bioethics and Human Rights (2005)

Preamble

... Recognizing that ethical issues raised by the rapid advances in science and their technological applications should be examined with due respect to the dignity of the human person and universal respect for, and observance of, human rights and fundamental freedoms ...

Also noting international and regional instruments in the field of bioethics, including the Convention for the Protection of Human Rights and Dignity of the Human Being with regard to the Application of Biology and Medicine ...

Recognizing that, based on the freedom of science and research, scientific and technological developments have been, and can be, of great benefit to humankind in increasing, inter alia, life expectancy and improving the quality of life, and emphasizing that such developments should always seek to promote the welfare of individuals, families, groups or communities and humankind as a whole in the recognition of the dignity of the human person and universal respect for, and observance of, human rights and fundamental freedoms;

... Proclaims the principles that follow and *adopts* the present Declaration.

General provisions

Article 1 *Scope*

1 This Declaration addresses ethical issues related to medicine, life sciences and associated technologies as applied to human beings, taking into account their social, legal and environmental dimensions.
2 This Declaration is addressed to States. As appropriate and relevant, it also provides guidance to decisions or practices of individuals, groups, communities, institutions and corporations, public and private.

Article 2 *Aims*

... (c) to promote respect for human dignity and protect human rights, by ensuring respect for the life of human beings, and fundamental freedoms, consistent with international human rights law;

... Article 3 *Human dignity and human rights*
1 Human dignity, human rights and fundamental freedoms are to be fully respected.
2 The interests and welfare of the individual should have priority over the sole interest of science or society ...

Article 10 *Equality, justice and equity*
The fundamental equality of all human beings in dignity and rights is to be respected so that they are treated justly and equitably.

Article 11 *Non-discrimination and non-stigmatization*
No individual or group should be discriminated against or stigmatized on any grounds, in violation of human dignity, human rights and fundamental freedoms.

Article 12 *Respect for cultural diversity and pluralism*
The importance of cultural diversity and pluralism should be given due regard. However, such considerations are not to be invoked to infringe upon human dignity, human rights and fundamental freedoms, nor upon the principles set out in this Declaration, nor to limit their scope ...

Article 28 *Denial of acts contrary to human rights, fundamental freedoms and human dignity*
Nothing in this Declaration may be interpreted as implying for any State, group or person any claim to engage in any activity or to perform any act contrary to human rights, fundamental freedoms and human dignity.

Universal Declaration on the Human Genome and Human Rights (1997)

... *Recalling* that the Preamble of UNESCO's Constitution refers to "the democratic principles of the dignity, equality and mutual respect of men," rejects any "doctrine of the inequality of men and races"...

Recognizing that research on the human genome and the resulting applications open up vast prospects for progress in improving the health of individuals and of humankind as a whole, but *emphasizing* that such research should fully respect human dignity, freedom and human rights, as well as the prohibition of all forms of discrimination based on genetic characteristics …
Proclaims the principles that follow and *adopts* the present Declaration.

A. Human dignity and the human genome
Article 1 The human genome underlies the fundamental unity of all members of the human family, as well as the recognition of their inherent dignity and diversity. In a symbolic sense, it is the heritage of humanity.
Article 2 (a) Everyone has a right to respect for their dignity and for their rights regardless of their genetic characteristics.
(b) That dignity makes it imperative not to reduce individuals to their genetic characteristics and to respect their uniqueness and diversity …
Article 6 No one shall be subjected to discrimination based on genetic characteristics that is intended to infringe or has the effect of infringing human rights, fundamental freedoms and human dignity …

C. Research on the human genome
Article 10 No research or research applications concerning the human genome, in particular in the fields of biology, genetics and medicine, should prevail over respect for the human rights, fundamental freedoms and human dignity of individuals or, where applicable, of groups of people …
Article 11 Practices which are contrary to human dignity, such as reproductive cloning of human beings, shall not be permitted. States and competent international organizations are invited to co-operate in identifying such practices and in taking, at national or international level, the measures necessary to ensure that the principles set out in this Declaration are respected.
Article 12 (a) Benefits from advances in biology, genetics and medicine, concerning the human genome, shall be made available to all, with due regard for the dignity and human rights of each individual …

Article 15 States should take appropriate steps to provide the framework for the free exercise of Research on the human genome with due regard for the principles set out in this Declaration, in order to safeguard respect for human rights, fundamental freedoms and human dignity and to protect public health. They should seek to ensure that research results are not used for non-peaceful purposes …

Article 21 States should take appropriate measures to encourage other forms of research, training and information dissemination conducive to raising the awareness of society and all of its members of their responsibilities regarding the fundamental issues relating to the defence of human dignity which may be raised by research in biology, in genetics and in medicine, and its applications …

Article 24 The International Bioethics Committee of UNESCO should contribute to the dissemination of the principles set out in this Declaration and to the further examination of issues raised by their applications … in particular regarding the identification of practices that could be contrary to human dignity, such as germ-line interventions.

Convention on the Rights of Persons with Disabilities (2006)

Preamble

The States Parties to the present Convention,

Recalling the principles proclaimed in the Charter of the United Nations which recognize the inherent dignity and worth and the equal and inalienable rights of all members of the human family as the foundation of freedom, justice and peace in the world,

Recognizing that the United Nations, in the Universal Declaration of Human Rights and in the International Covenants on Human Rights, has proclaimed and agreed that everyone is entitled to all the rights and freedoms set forth therein, without distinction of any kind,

Reaffirming the universality, indivisibility, interdependence and interrelatedness of all human rights and fundamental freedoms and the need for persons with disabilities to be guaranteed their full enjoyment without discrimination …

Recognizing that disability is an evolving concept and that disability results from the interaction between persons with impairments and attitudinal and environmental barriers that hinders their full and effective participation in society on an equal basis with others …

Recognizing also that discrimination against any person on the basis of disability is a violation of the inherent dignity and worth of the human person …

Convinced that a comprehensive and integral international convention to promote and protect the rights and dignity of persons with disabilities will make a significant contribution to redressing the profound social disadvantage of persons with disabilities and promote their participation in the civil, political, economic, social and cultural spheres with equal opportunities, in both developing and developed countries,

Have agreed as follows:

Article 1 Purpose

The purpose of the present Convention is to promote, protect and ensure the full and equal enjoyment of all human rights and fundamental freedoms by all persons with disabilities, and to promote respect for their inherent dignity.

Persons with disabilities include those who have long-term physical, mental, intellectual or sensory impairments which in interaction with various barriers may hinder their full and effective participation in society on an equal basis with others …

Article 3 General principles

The principles of the present Convention shall be:

Respect for inherent dignity, individual autonomy including the freedom to make one's own choices, and independence of persons …

Article 8 Awareness-raising

1. States Parties undertake to adopt immediate, effective and appropriate measures:

To raise awareness throughout society, including at the family level, regarding persons with disabilities, and to foster respect for the rights and dignity of persons with disabilities …

Article 16 *Freedom from exploitation, violence and abuse ...*
4. States Parties shall take all appropriate measures to promote the physical, cognitive and psychological recovery, rehabilitation and social reintegration of persons with disabilities who become victims of any form of exploitation, violence or abuse, including through the provision of protection services. Such recovery and reintegration shall take place in an environment that fosters the health, welfare, self-respect, dignity and autonomy of the person and takes into account gender- and age-specific needs ...

Article 24 *Education*
1. States Parties recognize the right of persons with disabilities to education. With a view to realizing this right without discrimination and on the basis of equal opportunity, States Parties shall ensure an inclusive education system at all levels and life long learning directed to:
The full development of human potential and sense of dignity and self-worth, and the strengthening of respect for human rights, fundamental freedoms and human diversity ...

Article 25 *Health*
States Parties recognize that persons with disabilities have the right to the enjoyment of the highest attainable standard of health without discrimination on the basis of disability. States Parties shall take all appropriate measures to ensure access for persons with disabilities to health services that are gender-sensitive, including health-related rehabilitation. In particular, States Parties shall ...

Require health professionals to provide care of the same quality to persons with disabilities as to others, including on the basis of free and informed consent by, inter alia, raising awareness of the human rights, dignity, autonomy and needs of persons with disabilities through training and the promulgation of ethical standards for public and private health care ...

APPENDIX D

The Declaration of Montreal

Declaration That Access to Pain Management Is a Fundamental Human Right

We, as delegates to the International Pain Summit (IPS) of the International Association for the Study of Pain (IASP) (comprising IASP representatives from Chapters in 64 countries plus members in 129 countries, as well as members of the community), have given in-depth attention to the unrelieved pain in the world,

Finding that pain management is inadequate in most of the world because:

There is inadequate access to treatment for acute pain caused by trauma, disease, and terminal illness and failure to recognize that chronic pain is a serious chronic health problem requiring access to management akin to other chronic diseases such as diabetes or chronic heart disease.

There are major deficits in knowledge of health care professionals regarding the mechanisms and management of pain.

Chronic pain with or without diagnosis is highly stigmatized.

Most countries have no national policy at all or very inadequate policies regarding the management of pain as a health problem, including an inadequate level of research and education.

Pain Medicine is not recognized as a distinct specialty with a unique body of knowledge and defined scope of practice founded on research and comprehensive training programs.

The World Health Organization (WHO) estimates that 5 billion people live in countries with low or no access to controlled medicines and have no or insufficient access to treatment for moderate to severe pain.

There are severe restrictions on the availability of opioids and other essential medications, critical to the management of pain.

And, recognizing the intrinsic dignity of all persons and that withholding of pain treatment is profoundly wrong, leading to unnecessary suffering which is harmful; we declare that the following human rights must be recognized throughout the world:

Article 1 The right of all people to have access to pain management without discrimination.[1]

Article 2 The right of people in pain to acknowledgment of their pain and to be informed about how it can be assessed and managed.[2]

Article 3 The right of all people with pain to have access to appropriate assessment and treatment of the pain by adequately trained health care professionals.[3]

In order to assure these rights, we recognize the following obligations:
1 The obligation of governments and all health care institutions, within the scope of the legal limits of their authority and taking into account the health care resources reasonably available, to establish laws, policies, and systems that will help to promote, and will certainly not inhibit, the access of people in pain to fully adequate pain management. Failure to establish such laws, policies, and systems is unethical and a breach of the human rights of people harmed as a result.
2 The obligation of all health care professionals in a treatment relationship with a patient, within the scope of the legal limits of their professional practice and taking into account the treatment resources reasonably available, to offer to a patient in pain the management that would be offered by a reasonably careful and competent health care professional in that field of practice. Failure to offer such management is a breach of the patient's human rights.

Note: This Declaration has been prepared having due regard to current general circumstances and modes of health care delivery in the developed and developing world. Nevertheless, it is the responsibility of: governments, of those involved at every level of health care administration, and of health professionals to update the modes of implementation of the Articles of this Declaration as new frameworks for pain management are developed.

NOTES

1 This right includes, but is not limited to, discrimination on the basis of age, sex, gender, medical diagnosis, race or ethnicity, religion, culture, marital, civil or socioeconomic status, sexual orientation, and political or other opinion. See International Covenant on Economic, Social and Cultural Rights (ICESCR) (1966). The state parties of the ICESCR recognize "the right of everyone to the highest attainable standard of physical and mental health" (Art. 12), creating the "conditions which would assure to all medical service and medical attention in the event of sickness." See also Universal Declaration of Human Rights (1948): Rights to Health (Article 25); Convention on the Rights of a Child (Article 24); Convention on the Elimination of All Forms of Discrimination against Women (Article 12); Convention on the Elimination of All Forms of Racial Discrimination (Article 5(e) (iv)). See also the Committee on Economic, Social and Cultural Rights. General Comment No. 14, 22nd Session, April-May 2000 E/C12/2000/4. "Core obligations" of all signatory nations included an obligation to ensure access to health facilities, goods, and services without discrimination, to provide essential drugs as defined by WHO, and to adopt and implement a national health strategy.

2 Committee on Economic, Social and Cultural Rights. General Comment No. 14, 22nd Session, April-May 2000, E/C 12/2000/4, para. 12. General Comment No. 14 stated that health accessibility "includes the right to seek, receive and impart information and ideas concerning health issues."

3 Appropriate assessment includes recording the results of assessment (e.g., pain as the "5th vital sign," can focus attention on unrelieved pain, triggering appropriate treatment interventions and adjustments). Appropriate treatment includes access to pain medications,

including opioids and other essential medications for pain, and best-practice interdisciplinary and integrative non-pharmacological therapies, with access to professionals skilled in the safe and effective use of these medicines and treatments and supported by health policies, legal frameworks, and procedures to assure such access and prevent inappropriate use. Given the lack of adequately trained health professionals, this will require providing educational programs regarding pain assessment and treatment in all of the health care professions and programs within the community for community care workers delivering pain care. It also includes establishment of programs in pain medicine for the education of specialist physicians in pain medicine and palliative medicine. Accreditation policies to assure appropriate standards of training and care should also be established.

Failure to provide access to pain management violates the United Nations 1961 Single Convention on Narcotic Drugs declaring the medical use of narcotic drugs indispensable for the relief of pain and mandating adequate provision of narcotic drugs for medical use.

The UN Universal Declaration of Human Rights (1948) (Article 5) states: "No one shall be subjected to torture or to cruel, inhuman or degrading treatment ..." Comment: Deliberately ignoring a patient's need for pain management or failing to call for specialized help if unable to achieve pain relief may represent a violation of Article 5.

The UN Special Rapporteur on the Right to Health and the UN Special Rapporteur on the question of torture and other cruel, inhuman, and degrading treatment has stated: "The failure to ensure access to controlled medicines for the relief of pain and suffering threatens fundamental rights to health and to protection against cruel, inhuman and degrading treatment."

REFERENCES

ANZCA. "Statement on Patients' Rights to Pain Management." ANZCA PS 45 45 (2001). www.anzca.edu.au.

Brennan, F., D.B Carr, and M.J. Cousins. "Pain Management: A Fundamental Human Right." *Anesthesia & Analgesia* 105 (2007): 205–21.

Cousins, M.J., F. Brennan, and D.B. Carr. "Pain Relief: A Universal Human Right." *Pain* 112 (2004): 1–4.

FEDELAT (Latin American Federation of Associations for the Study of Pain). Proclamation of Pain Treatment and the Application of Palliative Care as Human Rights, 22 May 2008.

IAHPC (International Association for Hospice and Palliative Care). "Joint Declaration and Statement of Commitment on Palliative Care and Pain Treatment as Human Rights." www.hospice care.com.

Scholten, W., H. Nygren-Krug, and H.A. Zucker. "The World Health Organization Paves the Way for Action to Free People from the Shackles of Pain." *Anesthesia & Analgesia* 105 (2007): 1–4.

Somerville, M. "Death of Pain: Pain, Suffering, and Ethics." In *Proceedings of the 7th World Congress on Pain: Progress in Pain Research and Management*. Vol. 2, edited by G.F. Gebhart, D.L. Hammond, and T.S. Jensen, 41–58. Seattle: IASP Press 1994.

Notes

PREFACE

1 Samuel Huntingdon, *The Clash of Civilizations and the Remaking of World Order* (New York: Simon & Schuster 1996).
2 http://link.springer.com/article/10.1007/s13238-015-0153-5/fulltext.html.

INTRODUCTION

1 John Ralston Saul's term for history. See John Ralston Saul, *The Unconscious Civilization* (Toronto: House of Anansi Press 1995).
2 See, for example, Peter H. Ditto, David A. Pizzaro, and David Tannenbaum, "Motivated Moral Reasoning," in *The Psychology of Learning and Motivation*, vol. 50, ed. Daniel L. Bartels, Christopher W. Bauman, Linda J. Sitka, and Douglas L. Medin (Burlington: Academic Press 2009), 307–38.
3 Jonathan Haidt, *The Righteous Mind: Why Good People Are Divided by Politics and Religion* (New York: Pantheon 2012).
4 Marc Farinella, "The 'Real' Issues Lying beneath the Surface of Political Debate," 1 December 2012, http://politicsofthemind.com/2012/12/01/the-six-moral-foundations-the-real-issues-lying-beneath-the-surface-of-political-debate/.
5 *Suffering and Bioethics*, ed. Ronald M. Green and Nathan J. Palpant (New York: Oxford University Press 2014), chapter 10, "Exploring Interactions between Pain, Suffering, and the Law," 201–27.
6 First published as Margaret Somerville, "'Law Marching with Medicine but in the Rear and Limping a Little': Ethics as 'First Aid' for Law," in *Ethik und Recht- Die Ethisierung des Rechts* (Ethics and

law – the ethicalization of law), ed. Silja Voneky, Britta Beylage-Haarmann, Anja Holfelmeier, and Anna-Katharina Hubler (Heidelberg, New York, Dordrecht, London: Springer 2013), 67–102.

CHAPTER ONE

1 I was asked by an editor at a Canadian newspaper for which I write as a freelancer to draft a commentary article responding to the question "What do I believe is currently the world's most dangerous idea?" (This article is included as part of chapter 5.) I was curious to know what my colleagues and friends would say. All of those I asked said "religion." I don't agree, but that is a discussion for another occasion.
2 I explain what I mean by the "human spirit" later in this chapter. See also, in general, Margaret Somerville, *The Ethical Imagination: Journeys of the Human Spirit* (Toronto: House of Anansi Press; Fitzroy: Melbourne University Press 2006).
3 George Weigel, "Freedom, Sanctity, and the Future," *EPPC Online*, posted 10 August 2009, http://www.eppc.org/programs/catholic studies/publications/pubID.3904,programID.16/pub_detail.asp.
4 http://www.consciencelaws.org/updates/2011-05-01.html#01, accessed 11 May 2011.
5 http://www.cofec.org/sermons/7816.
6 Somerville, *Ethical Imagination*.
7 Somerville, "Searching for a Shared Ethics – Challenging Richard Dawkins' 'The God Delusion,'" *The Sydney Papers*, ed. Anne Henderson (Sydney: Sydney Institute) 19, no. 3 (Winter 2007): 20–35.
8 See pp. 68–9.
9 Jürgen Habermas, *The Future of Human Nature* (Cambridge, UK: Polity Press 2003).
10 See p. 21, and Somerville, *Ethical Imagination*, 96–7, 104.
11 Colleen Carroll Campbell, "A Legacy of Connection and Common Ground in a Fragmented World," *St Louis Post-Dispatch*, 15 January 2009.
12 Somerville, *Ethical Imagination*, 40, 70–1, 166, 205.
13 Michael Valpy, "Is This the End of the Age of Our Social Cohesion?," *Toronto Globe and Mail*, 29 August 2009, A17.
14 Somerville, "Why Are Atheists So Passionate about Disbelief?," *Toronto Globe and Mail*, 16 November 1996, D2.
15 Somerville, *Ethical Imagination*, 96–7, 104. See also Somerville, "Children's Human Rights to Natural Biological Origins and Family Structure," HeinOnline IJJF library 2011, http://heinonline.org/

HOL/Page?handle=hein.journals/ijjf1&id=1&collection=journals, *International Journal of the Jurisprudence of the Family* 1 (2011): 35.

16 I hasten to note that I am not a genetic reductionist and am not suggesting that spirituality or being religious is nothing more than a hard-wired expression of certain genetic characteristics. Rather, it might be that we have genes that cause us to seek to experience spirituality – just as we have genes that allow us to know of our other essential human needs: for instance, that we are hungry or thirsty.

17 Paul Nathanson and Katherine K. Young, *Spreading Misandry: The Teaching of Contempt for Men in Popular Culture* (Montreal: McGill-Queen's University Press 2001), 209–10.

18 See Somerville, "Searching for a Shared Ethics," 20–35.

19 "'Yellow Ants,' Fundamentalists, and Cowboys: An interview with Rémi Brague," *Clarion Review* (29 October 2009), http://www.clarionreview.org/main/article.php?article_id=38#.

20 I wish to make it very clear here, although I do not address the issue in this chapter, that I consider a nation state based just on religion equally unacceptable and as dangerous as one based just on secular principles and beliefs.

21 *Chamberlain v. Surrey School District* (2000) 191 D.L.R. (4th) 128; [2000] 10 W.W.R. 393; 26 Admin. L.R. (3d) 297; 80 B.C.L.R. (3d) 181.

22 *School Act*, R.S.B.C. 1996, c. 412.

23 See note 21.

24 *Chamberlain v. Surrey District School Board No. 36*, [2002] 4 S.C.R. 710, 2002 SCC 86.

25 *Loyola High School v. Quebec (Attorney General)*, 2015 SCC 12. Numbers in square brackets refer to paragraphs in the judgment.

26 Jennifer Marshall, "Culture Wars and the Political Future of the US," http://www.mercatornet.com/articles/view/culture_wars_and_the_political_future_of_the_u.s/.

27 Michael Cook, "Ted Kennedy's Ambiguous Legacy," 29 August 2009, http://www.mercatornet.com/articles/view/ted_kennedys_ambiguous_legacy/.

28 Colleen Carroll Campbell, "A Legacy of Connection and Common Ground in a Fragmented World," *St Louis Post-Dispatch*, 15 January 2009.

29 Somerville, "A Simple Answer to Quebec's Simple Adoption Question," 13 October 2009, http://www.theglobeandmail.com/news/opinions/a-simple-answer-to-quebecs-simple-adoption-question/article1322352/.

30 Ibid., Tendercomrade, Comments, 15 October 2009.

31 Somerville, "Why We're Debating Euthanasia Now," *Ottawa Citizen*, 23 October 2009, http://www.ottawacitizen.com/debating+euthanasia/2134980/story.html#.

32 http://www.ottawacitizen.com/opinion/op-ed/debating+euthanasia/2134980/story.html#Comments, accessed 27 October 2009.

33 Somerville, "Is Jack Layton Obliged to Disclose His Health Details? No," 29 July 2011, http://www.theglobeandmail.com/news/opinions/opinion/is-jack-layton-obliged-to-disclose-his-health-details-no/article2114979/.

34 http://www.theglobeandmail.com/news/opinions/opinion/is-jack-layton-obliged-to-disclose-his-health-details-no/article2114979/comments/jmac123.

35 David Armstrong, "New Conflict Rules at Medical Journals," *Wall Street Journal*, 14 October 2009, http://online.wsj.com/article/SB125547553843083589.html?mod=dist_smartbrief.

36 Somerville, "Facing Up to the Dangers of the Intolerant University: Bird on an Ethics Wire," in "Ethics in the Academy," special issue, *Academic Matters*, May 2009, 58–61.

37 Ian McCullough, "Did Mozilla CEO Brendan Eich Deserve to Be Removed from His Position?" http://www.forbes.com/sites/quora/2014/04/11/did-mozilla-ceo-brendan-eich-deserve-to-be-removed-from-his-position-due-to-his-support-for-proposition-8/.

38 I am indebted to Professor Torrance Kirby, Faculty of Religious Studies, McGill University, for this insight.

39 Somerville, "The Case against Same-Sex Marriage," brief submitted to the Standing Committee on Justice and Human Rights, Parliament of Canada, 2003, http://www.marriageinstitute.ca/images/somerville.pdf; Somerville, "Focus on Same Sex Marriage. The Case against. Whose Rights Do We Value Most: Those of Children or of homosexual Adults?," *MercatorNet.com*, 28 July 2011, http://www.mercatornet.com/articles/view/the_case_against_same-sex_marriage/.

40 John Ralston Saul, *The Unconscious Civilization* (Toronto: House of Anansi Press 1995).

41 Jamie Doward and Denis Campbell, "British Women Treat Abortion as the Easy Option, Claims Angry Archbishop," *Observer*, 21 October 2007, http://www.guardian.co.uk/uk/2007/oct/21/religion.health.

42 Jennifer Roback Morse, "My Sister's Keeper," 27 August 2009, http://www.mercatornet.com/articles/view/my_sisters_keeper/.

43 This section is based on my book *Death Talk: The Case against Euthanasia and Physician-Assisted Suicide* (Montreal: McGill-Queen's

University Press 2001), chapter 6, "Legalizing Euthanasia: Why Now?," 105–18, where relevant references can be found.

44 Jay Katz, "The Silent World of Doctor and Patient" (New York, London: Free Press 1986).

45 Michael Higgins, "Why the English Don't Like to Mix the Spiritual and the Temporal," *Globe and Mail*, Commentary, 31 July 2009.

46 *Rodriguez v. British Columbia (Attorney General)* [1993] 3 S.C.R. 519.

47 In *Carter v. Canada (Attorney General)* 2013 BCCA 435, a majority of the British Columbia Court of Appeal overturned the first instance judgment, *Carter v. Canada (Attorney General),* 2012 BCSC 886, in which the trial judge ruled that the prohibition of assisted suicide was constitutionally invalid in certain circumstances that were present in the case. The Supreme Court of Canada allowed the plaintiffs' appeal, affirming the trial judge's decision. *Carter v. Canada (Attorney General)*, 2015 SCC 5. See chapter 4.

48 This is not my original idea. See R.M. Sade and M.F. Marshall, "Legistrothanatory: A New Specialty for Assisting in Death," *Perspectives in Biology and Medicine* 39, no. 4 (1996): 547–9.

49 See Somerville, *The Ethical Canary: Science, Society and the Human Spirit* (Toronto: Viking/Penguin 2000).

50 This issue is discussed in more detail in chapter 5.

51 Peter Singer, *Animal Liberation* (New York: Avon 1991).

52 Rodney Brooks, *Flesh and Machines: How Robots Will Change Us* (New York: Pantheon 2002).

53 Somerville, *Ethical Imagination.*

54 See chapter 5, under the heading "What Is Currently the World's Most Dangerous Idea?" for further discussion of this point.

CHAPTER TWO

1 Thomas Homer-Dixon, "How Free Is Academic Freedom?," *Globe and Mail*, 14 May 2012, A11. See also Appendix B for some descriptions of what academic freedom encompasses.

2 Ibid.

3 CSWA National Office, "Prime Minister, Please Unmuzzle the Scientists," 16 February 2012 http://sciencewriters.ca/2012/02/16/prime-minister-please-unmuzzle-the-scientists/.

4 Canadian Charter of Rights and Freedoms, Being Part I of the Constitution Act, 1982.

5 For the origins of these concepts see Jay Katz, *The Silent World of Doctor and Patient* (New York and London: Free Press 1986).

6 Tristan Claridge, *Definitions of Social Capital,* posted 7 January 2004, http://www.socialcapitalresearch.com/literature/definition.html. References omitted.

7 Milton Friesen, "Remembering How to Innovate," http://www.cardus.ca/blog/2013/07/remembering-how-to-innovate?utm_source=newsletter&utm_medium=email&utm_campaign=daily.

8 Francis Fukuyama, *Trust: The Social Virtues and the Creation of Prosperity* (London: Hamish Hamilton 1995), 10.

9 Fukuyama 1997, as cited in Claridge, *Definitions of Social Capital.*

10 Ronald Inglehart, *Modernization and Post-Modernization: Cultural, Economic and Political Change in Forty-Three Societies* (Princeton: Princeton University Press 1997), 188, as cited in Claridge, *Definitions of Social Capital.*

11 Robert D. Putnam, "Bowling Alone: America's Declining Social Capital," *Journal of Democracy* 6: 65–78; Putnam, *Bowling Alone: The Collapse and Revival of American Community* (New York, London: Simon & Schuster 1995), 67, as cited in Claridge, *Definitions of Social Capital.*

12 Joseph Brean, "Marginalized and on the Defensive, University Conservatives Forced to Grow Tougher," *National Post*, 13 March 2009, http://newsle.com/article/0/66271794/.

13 Somerville, "Three Genetic Parents," *Ottawa Citizen*, 17 July 2013, A-11, http://www.ottawacitizen.com/opinion/op-ed/ethics+three+genetic+parent+embryos/8672523/story.html. Republished as "The Dubious Ethics of Three-Genetic-Parent Embryos," *MercatorNet*, 23 July 2013, http://www.mercatornet.com/articles/view/the_dubious_ethics_of_creating_children_with_three_genetic_parents.

14 Jürgen Habermas, *The Future of Human Nature* (Oxford: Blackwell 2003). For further discussion, see chapter 3.

15 Hans Jonas, *Philosophical Essays: From Ancient Creed to Technological Man*) Chicago and London: University of Chicago Press 1974), chapter 7, "Biological Engineering – A Preview," 141–67.

16 *Starson v. Swayze*. Collection, Supreme Court Judgments, 6 June 2003. Neutral citation, 2003 SCC 32. Report citation, [2003] 1 S.C.R. 722.

17 Mark Bourrie, "RIGHTS: Canada, U.S. Courts Limit Forced Treatment of Mentally Ill," IPS Correspondents Reprint, http://ipsnews2.wpengine.com/2003/06/rights-canada-us-courts-limit-forced-treatment-of-mentally-ill/.

18 J.J. Furedy, "Free Speech and the Issue of Academic Freedom: Is the Canadian Velvet Totalitarian Disease Coming to Australian Cam-

puses?" *University of Queensland Law Journal* 30, no. 2: 279–86, http://www.psych.utoronto.ca/users/furedy/Papers/af/Free_Speech_AU11.docGillard's Asian 'cargo cult' .

19 John Furedy, "Academic Freedom vs Culture of Comfort at U of T: Notes from a Forty-Year Perspective," *Senior College Encyclopedia* (2011), www.psych.utoronto.ca/users/furedy/Papers/af/Academ_40yr.doc.

20 John Courtney Murray, "Creeds at War Intelligibly: Pluralism and the University," 30 September 2014, http://woodstock.georgetown.edu/library/Murray/whtt_c5_1958e.htm.

21 Peter Rosenthal, "Our Case against the Queen's Oath," *Globe and Mail*, 4 July 2013, A11.

22 Press release, University of Ottawa Students for Life and University of Ottawa Medical Students for Life, "Abortion Debate Heats Up at the University of Ottawa," 10 November 2011.

23 The Justice Centre for Constitutional Freedoms, news release, 24 September 2013, "New Report: 51% of Canadian Universities Fail to Uphold Free Expression Rights on Campus," http://www.jccf.ca/wp-content/uploads/2013/01/0924_JCCFNewsRelease1.pdf.The "2013 Campus Freedom Index" is a report that measures the state of free speech at forty-five Canadian public universities.

24 Sarah Boesveld, "Campus Free Speech 'Abysmal', Report," *National Post*, 1 November 2012, A4.

25 Ibid.

26 John J. Furedy and Christine Furedy, "From the Socratic to the Sophistic," *Quadrant* 56, no. 11 (November 2012).

27 Ibid., Australian Broadcasting Commission, 3 September 2012.

28 Parts of this sections are also published in Somerville," Brave New Ethicists": A Cautionary Tale," in *The Public Intellectual in Canada*, ed. Nelson Wiseman (Toronto: University of Toronto Press 2013), chapter 15, 212–32.

29 James Bradshaw, "Profs Sign Letter Criticizing University," *Globe and Mail*, 20 November 2012, A7.

30 "Report Vindicates Queen's Prof, Calls for Apology," CAUT *Bulletin*, October 2012, A8.

31 Somerville, "Facing Up to the Dangers of the Intolerant University: Bird on an Ethics Wire," in "Ethics in the Academy," special issue, *Academic Matters*, May 2009, 58–61.

32 Herbert Pimlott, Review of *The Assault on Universities: A Manifesto for Resistance*, edited by Michael Bailey and Des Freedman, CAUT *Bulletin*, May 2012, A9.

33 Rex Murphy, "A Creature of His Environment," *National Post*, 26 January 2013, A18.
34 Brean, "Marginalized and on the Defensive."
35 For a wider discussion of religion in the public square, see chapter 1, Somerville, "Should Religion Be Evicted from the Public Square?," monograph, Warrane Lecture 2011 (Sydney: Warrane College 2011), 44.
36 Murray, "Creeds at War Intelligibly."
37 This information on abortion statistics was first published as Somerville, "Democracy Hurt by Abortion Stats Secrecy," *Calgary Herald*, Tuesday, 22 May 2012, http://www2.canada.com/calgaryherald/news/theeditorialpage/story.html?id=6336e2d5-6263-4d5b-872d-4aa1e1a5ca3a.
38 CSWA National Office, "Prime Minister, Please Unmuzzle the Scientists," 16 February 2012, http://sciencewriters.ca/2012/02/16/prime-minister-please-unmuzzle-the-scientists/.
39 CBC News, "Trinity Western Law School Loses B.C. Law Society Vote," 10 June 2014, http://www.cbc.ca/news/canada/british-columbia/trinity-western-law-school-loses-b-c-law-society-vote-1.2670688. The Law Society of Upper Canada in Ontario voted against approving the TWU law school in April 2014; See CBC News, "Trinity Western Law School Rejected by Ontario Law Society," http://www.cbc.ca/news/canada/british-columbia/trinity-western-law-school-rejected-by-ontario-law-society-1.2621211.
40 See discussion above page 59 and Appendix B for CAUT's "Policy Statement on Academic Freedom."
41 Nick Martin, "Profs' Union Red-Flags Faith-Based Providence," *Winnipeg Free Press*, 15 March 2012, http://www.winnipegfreepress.com/local/profs-union-red-flags-faith-based-providence-142745885.html.
42 Furedy and Furedy, "From the Socratic to the Sophistic."
43 John Furedy, "Academic Freedom vs Culture of Comfort."
44 Ibid., references omitted.
45 *An Act Respecting End-of-Life Care*, C 2014, section 31.
46 Michael Cook, "Forcing Compliance: The Australian State of Victoria Has a World First: A Law Which Forces Doctors to Refer Women for Abortion or to Do It Themselves – Even If They Have a Conscientious Objection," http://www.mercatornet.com/articles/view/forcing_compliance/#sthash.fd3IxHgS.dpuf.
47 This discussion is excerpted from Somerville, "Respect for Con-

science Must Be a Social Value," *Mercatornet*, 17 October 2008, http://www.mercatornet.com/articles/view/respect_for_conscience_must_be_a_social_value.

48 http://www.ohrc.on.ca/en/submission-ontario-human-rights-commission-college-physicians-and-surgeons-ontario-regarding-draft-0.

49 Somerville, "Denying Doctors Free Conscience Unconscionable," *Calgary Herald*, 18 September 2008, A10. The college subsequently softened its position but is once again, as I write this, seeking public input on revising it.

50 http://www.msfc.org/.

51 See, for example, the 2013 Environics poll "Canadians' Attitudes towards Abortion," http://www.lifecanada.org/images/National%20Polls/Environics%20-%20LifeCanada%20Abortion%20Report%202013%20FINAL.pdf.

52 Sean Murphy and Stephen J. Genuis, "Freedom of Conscience in Health Care: Distinctions and Limits," *Journal of Bioethical Inquiry* 10, no. 3 (2013): 347–54, http://link.springer.com/article/10.1007/s11673-013-9451-x/fulltext.html.

53 Ibid.

54 http://www.cpso.on.ca/Policies-Publications/Policy/Professional-Obligations-and-Human-Rights.

55 "Ethical Cleansing in Ontario," Protection of Conscience Project, 12 January 2015, http://consciencelaws.org/blog/?p=5535.

56 Somerville, "Should Religion Be Evicted from the Public Square?," and chapter 1.

57 *Chamberlain* v. *Surrey School District*, (2000) 191 D.L.R. (4th) 128; [2000] 10 W.W.R. 393; 26 Admin. L.R. (3d) 297; 80 B.C.L.R. (3d) 181; Chamberlain v. Surrey District School Board No. 36, [2002] 4 S.C.R. 710, 2002 SCC 86, Chamberlain case.

58 For further discussion, see chapter 1.

59 "Report of the Select Committee of the Assemblée Nationale of Québec on 'Dying with Dignity, Mourir dans la Dignité'" (chair, Maryse Gaudreault), March 2012.

60 Habermas, *Future of Human Nature*.

61 Somerville, *The Ethical Imagination: Journeys of the Human Spirit* (Toronto: House of Anansi 2006).

62 See chapter 5, under the heading "What is Currently the World's Most Dangerous Idea?"

63 See above, pp. 64–6.

64 Personal communication, 23 August 2013.

65 Murray, "Creeds at War Intelligibly."
66 *Loyola High School v. Quebec (Attorney General)*, 2015 SCC 12. Numbers in square brackets refer to paragraphs in the judgment.
67 Homer-Dixon, "How Free Is Academic Freedom?"
68 For links to a series of articles and letters on this event, see the Society for Academic Freedom and Scholarship, "University of Calgary: Academic Freedom and Professor Flanagan," February 2013, http://www.safs.ca/universitycalgarymain.html.
69 Somerville, "Medical Interventions and the Criminal Law: Lawful or Excusable Wounding?," *McGill Law Journal* 26, no. 1 (1980) 82–96.
70 CAUT *Bulletin* 58, no. 10 (December 2011): A3. See also Appendix B.
71 CAUT *Bulletin*, ibid., A1.
72 Ibid., A3
73 Homer-Dixon, "How Free Is Academic Freedom?"
74 Jane Jacobs, *Systems of Survival: A Dialogue on the Moral Foundations of Commerce and Politics* (New York: Vintage 2003).
75 Graham Lloyd, "Climate Chair Left High and Dry by Uni," *The Australian*, 12 July 2013.
76 Union of Concerned Scientists, "An Open Letter on Science to Canadian Prime Minister Stephen Harper," https://secure3.convio.net/ucs/site/Advocacy?cmd=display&page=UserAction&id=4025, accessed 27 June 2014.
77 Alberto Giubilini and Francesca Minerva, "After-Birth Abortion: Why Should the Baby Live?," *Journal of Medical Ethics* 39 (2013) 261-3, doi:10.1136/medethics-2011-100411, http://jme.bmj.com/content/early/2012/03/01/medethics-2011-100411.full.
78 Nic van Beek, "Education Lost: A Conversation with Professor Douglas Farrow," *McGill Daily*, 5 January 2011, http://www.mcgill daily.com/2011/01/education-lost/; see also Douglas Farrow, "The (Lost) Idea of the University," Newman Lecture Series, 25 November 2010.
79 Personal email to the author from Mark Mercer, 28 May 2015.

CHAPTER THREE

1 Universal Declaration of Human Rights (UDHR), Preamble.
2 Ibid.
3 Ibid., article 1.
4 Ibid., article 22.

5 Ibid., article 23.
6 Universal Declaration on Bioethics and Human Rights (UDBHR), Preamble.
7 Ibid., article 2(c).
8 Ibid., article 12.
9 Ibid., article 28.
10 Universal Declaration on the Human Genome and Human Rights (UDHGHR), Preamble.
11 Ibid., article 1.
12 Ibid., article 2(a).
13 Ibid., article 2(b).
14 Ibid., article 6.
15 Ibid., article 10.
16 Ibid., article 11.
17 Ibid., article 15.
18 Ibid., article 21.
19 Ibid., article 24.
20 Convention on the Rights of Persons with Disabilities (CRPD), Preamble.
21 Ibid.
22 Ibid., article 1.
23 Ibid., article 16.
24 Adam Schulman, "Bioethics and the Question of Human Dignity," in *Human Dignity and Bioethics, Essays Commissioned by the President's Council on Bioethics* (hereafter *President's Council Report*) (Washington, DC, 2008), chapter 1, 13.
25 Sergio Vieira de Mello, "A World of Dignity" (2002 lecture on the universal character of human dignity). Vieira de Mello was a prominent human rights advocate and the United Nations special representative in Iraq. This speech was republished on 24 August 2009 to mark his passing as a result of violence. See more at http://www.mercatornet.com/articles/view/a_world_of_dignity#sthash.c9FSAsvf.dpuf.
26 Ibid.
27 Daniel Sulmasy, "Dignity and Bioethics: History, Theory, and Selected Applications," *in President's Council Report*, chapter 18, 485.
28 *President's Council Report* (2008).
29 Ruth Macklin, "Dignity as a Useless Concept," *British Medical Journal* 327 (2003): 1419–20.
30 Leon Kass, "Defending Human Dignity," in *President's Council Report*, chapter 12, 298.

31 Daniel Brudney, "Losing Dignity," *Perspectives in Biology and Medicine* 52 (2009): 454–7.
32 Diana Schaub, "Commentary on Meilaender and Lawler," in *President's Council Report*, chapter 11, 292.
33 Holmes Rolston III, "Human Uniqueness and Human Dignity: Persons in Nature and the Nature of Persons," in *President's Council Report*, chapter 6, 144, 150.
34 Charles Rubin, "Human Dignity and the Future of Man," in *President's Council Report*, chapter 7, 167.
35 Gilbert Meilaender "Commentary on Churchland," in *President's Council Report*, chapter 5, 124.
36 Robert P. Kraynak, "Human Dignity and the Mystery of the Human Soul," in *President's Council Report*, chapter 4, 80.
37 Somerville, *The Ethical Imagination: Journeys of the Human Spirit* (Toronto: House of Anansi Press 2006), 270.
38 Ibid., 7–8.
39 Richard John Neuhaus, "Human Dignity and Public Discourse," in *President's Council Report*, chapter 9, 226.
40 David Gelernter "The Irreducibly Religious Character of Human Dignity," in *President's Council Report*, chapter 15, 394.
41 Roger Scruton, "A Carnivore's Credo," from "Eating Your Friends," *Harper's*, April/May 2006, 21–6.
42 Somerville, *The Ethical Canary: Science, Society and the Human Spirit* (Toronto: Viking/Penguin 2000).
43 Somerville, *Ethical Imagination.*
44 Paul Nathanson and Katherine K. Young, *Spreading Misandry: The Teaching of Contempt for Men in Popular Culture* (Montreal: McGill-Queen's University Press 2001), 209–10.
45 Nick Bostrom, "Dignity and Enhancement," in *President's Council Report*, chapter 8, 199.
46 Gilbert Meilaender, "Human Dignity: Exploring and Explicating the Council's Vision," *President's Council Report*, chapter 11, 255.
47 Sulmasy, "Dignity and Bioethics," 474–5.
48 Samuel J. Kerstein, "Kantian Condemnation of Commerce in Organs," *Kennedy Institute of Ethics Journal* 19 (2009): 151.
49 Ibid., 157.
50 Ibid., 156.
51 Michael Sandel, *What Money Can't Buy: The Moral Limits of Markets* (New York: Farrar, Strauss & Giroux 2012).
52 Associated Press, 8 October 1933, http://query.nytimes.com/gst/abstract.html?res=9504E3DF1731E333A25751C2A9669.

53 As cited in Klaus Hoeyer, *Exchanging Human Bodily Material: Rethinking Bodies and Markets* (New York: Springer 2012), 17.
54 Schulman, "Bioethics and the Question of Human Dignity," 4.
55 Kass, Defending Human Dignity," 297–8.
56 Meilaender, "Human Dignity," 273–4.
57 Kerstein, "Kantian Condemnation," 151
58 Ibid., 151.
59 Sandel, *What Money Can't Buy.*
60 Harvey Max Chochinov, "Dignity-Conserving Care – A New Model for Palliative Care: Helping the Patient Feel Valued," *Journal of the American Medical Association* 287, no. 7 (2002): 2253–60.
61 Harvey Max Chochinov, Thomas Hack, Thomas Hassard, Linda J. Kristjanson, Susan McClement, and Mike Harlos, "Dignity Therapy: A Novel Psychotherapeutic Intervention for Patients near the End of Life," *Journal* of *Clinical Oncology* 23 (2005) 5520–5. See also Chochinov, *Dignity Therapy: Final Words for Final Days* (New York: Oxford University Press 2012), 224.
62 From "Dignity Therapy," by Harvey Max Chochinov et al. Published with the kind permission of Dr Chochinov.
63 Chochinov et al., "Dignity-Conserving Care," 2253–60.
64 Meilaender, "Human Dignity," 264.
65 Jürgen Habermas, *The Future of Human Nature* (Oxford: Blackwell 2003).
66 Bostrom, "Dignity and Enhancement," 175
67 Habermas, *Future of Human Nature*, vii, 32.
68 I have explored this issue in "Life's Essence Bought and Sold: What Are Children's Rights When It Comes to Their Origins?," *Globe and Mail*, 10 July 2010, A17. http://www.theglobeandmail.com/news/opinions/lifes-essence-bought-and-sold/article1635165/.
69 I discuss these issues in chapter 7.
70 Charles Morris, review of Richard John Neuhaus's *American Babylon*: *Notes of a Christian Exile*, *Sunday New York Times Magazine*, 12 April 2009.
71 The following discussion of the search for human perfections was first published as Somerville, "The Flawed Quest for Perfection," *Ottawa Citizen*, 7 August 2009, A9.
72 Somerville, *Ethical Imagination*, 270.
73 Edmund Pellegrino, "The Lived Experience of Human Dignity," *President's Council Report*, chapter 20, 535.

CHAPTER FOUR

1 Eric Cassel, "The Nature of Suffering and the Goals of Medicine," *New England Journal of Medicine* 326 (21 May 1992): 1440–1, doi:10.1056/NEJM199205213262119.

2 Somerville, "Human Rights and Medicine: The Relief of Suffering," in *International Human Rights Law: Theory and Practice,* ed. Irwin Cotler and F. Pearl Eliadis (Montreal: Canadian Human Rights Foundation 1992), 505–22. Also published in Somerville, *Death Talk: The Case against Euthanasia and Physician-Assisted Suicide* (Montreal: McGill-Queen's University Press 2001), chapter 13, 205–17.

3 See Daniel Callahan, "When Self-Determination Runs Amok," *Hastings Center Report* 22, no. 2. (March–April 1992): 52–5.

4 *Death Talk,* 205–17.

5 This story about my students first appeared as part of an opinion article published as Somerville, "The Case against Euthanasia," *Ottawa Citizen,* 27 June 2008.

6 The analysis of the trial level judgment of the *Carter* case was first published in *Suffering and Bioethics*, ed. Ronald M. Green and Nathan J. Palpant (New York: Oxford University Press 2014), chapter 10, "Exploring Interactions between Pain, Suffering, and the Law," 201–27. I am grateful for the kind permission of the editors and publisher to use that material as a basis for this chapter.

7 *Carter v. Canada (Attorney General),* 2012 BCSC 886.

8 *Rodriguez v. British Columbia (Attorney General)*, [1993] 3 S.C.R. 519.

9 *Carter v. Canada (Attorney General)* 2013 BCCA 435.

10 *Carter v. Canada (Attorney General)*, 2015 SCC 5.

11 *Carter v. Canada* (BCSC).

12 Criminal Code, R.S.C., 1985, c. C-46 (as amended).

13 Canadian Charter of Rights and Freedoms, The Constitution Act, 1982, being Schedule B to the Canada Act 1982 (UK), 1982, c. 11.

14 Numbers in square brackets referencing a court's holding refer to paragraphs in the Supreme Court of Canada's judgment, those in round brackets to paragraphs in the trial court's judgment in the *Carter* case.

15 Canadian Charter, note 13.

16 *Rodriguez v. British Columbia.*

17 Canadian Charter, note 13, sec. 7.

18 Expert Panel of the Royal Society of Canada (chair, Udo Schuklenk), *End-of-Life Decision Making* (Ottawa: Royal Society of Canada 2011).
19 Tom Koch, "End of Life, Year after Year after Year," *Canadian Medical Association Journal* 181, no. 11 (2009): 868.
20 Susan Sontag, *Illness as Metaphor and AIDS and Its Metaphors* (New York Anchor books/Doubleday, 1978), 3.
21 P.D. James, *The Children of Men* (Toronto: Knopf Canada 1992), 68–79.
22 As cited in T. Koch, *Thieves of Virtue: When Bioethics Stole Medicine* (Cambridge, MA: MIT Press 1990), chapter 3.
23 Daniel Callahan, *Setting Limits: Medical Goals in an Aging* Society (New York: Simon & Schuster 1987).
24 *Reibl v. Hughes,* [1980] 2 S.C.R. 880; *Hopp v. Lepp,* [1980] 2 S.C.R. 192.
25 Keith G. Wilson, Harvey Max Chochinov, Christine J. McPherson et al., "Desire for Euthanasia or Physician-Assisted Suicide in Palliative Cancer Care," *Health Psychology* 26, no. 3 (2007): 314–23, and the work of Dr Harvey Max Chochinov, a Manitoba psychiatrist who specializes in psychiatric care of terminally ill people, referred to in chapter 3.
26 *Rodriguez v. British Columbia.*
27 I am indebted to Canadian bioethicist Dr Tom Koch for this formulation of the issue.
28 *Rodriguez v. British Columbia.*
29 Expert Panel of the Royal Society of Canada.
30 "Report of the Select Committee of the Assemblée Nationale of Québec on 'Dying with Dignity, Mourir dans la Dignité'" (chair, Maryse Gaudreault), March 2012.
31 Alberto Giubilini and Francesca Minerva, "After-Birth Abortion: Why Should the Baby Live?," *Journal of Medical Ethics*, doi:10.1136/medethics-2011-100411.
32 Eduard Verhagen and Pieter J.J. Sauer, "The Groningen Protocol – Euthanasia in Severely Ill Newborns," *New England Journal of Medicine* 352 (10 March 2005): 959–96, doi:10.1056/NEJMp058026.
33 Expert Panel of the Royal Society of Canada.
34 Report of the Select Committee of the Assemblée Nationale.
35 In this section in using the word *euthanasia*, I intend it to include physician-assisted suicide.

36 Somerville, "Euthanasia by Confusion," *University of New South Wales Law Journal* 20, no. 3 (1997): 550–75. Also published in *Death Talk*, 119–43.
37 Jocelyn Downie, *Dying Justice: A Case for Decriminalizing Euthanasia and Assisted Suicide in Canada* (Toronto: University of Toronto Press 2004).
38 Lauren Vogel, "Line between Acts and Omissions Blurred, Euthanasia Critics Argue," *Canadian Medical Association Journal* 184, no. 1 (2012): E19–20, doi:10.1503/cmaj.109-4061 PMCID: PMC325 5188.
39 See pp. 131–2, 135, 136.
40 *Fleming* v. *Ireland & Ors*, [2013] IEHC 2.
41 http://www.ibtimes.com/deaf-twins-euthanized-belgian-brothers-marc-eddy-verbessem-wanted-die-because-they-were-going-blind, accessed 20 February 2013.
42 Johan Bilsen et al., "Medical End-of-Life Practices under the Euthanasia Law in Belgium," *New England Journal of Medicine* 361, no. 11 (2009): 1119–21, http://www.nejm.org/doi/pdf/10.1056/NEJMc0904292.
43 J. Donald Boudreau and Margaret A. Somerville, "Euthanasia Is Not Medical Treatment," *British Medical Bulletin* 106 (2013): 45–66, doi:10.1093/bmb/ldt010, http://bmb.oxfordjournals.org/content/early/2013/03/26/bmb.ldt010.full?keytype=ref&ijkey=IKP7zm8pfcR3lNH.
44 Report of the Select Committee of the Assemblée Nationale.
45 This proposal is not my original idea. See R.M. Sade and M.F. Marshall, "Legistrothanatory: A New Specialty for Assisting in Death," *Perspectives in Biology and Medicine* 39, no. 4 (1996): 547–9.
46 As noted, the High Court of Ireland came to the opposite conclusion after reviewing the evidence on which Justice Smith relied.
47 Somerville, "'Law Marching with Medicine but in the Rear and Limping a Little': Ethics as 'First Aid' for Law," in *Ethik und Recht – Die Ethisierung des Rechts* (Ethics and law – the ethicalization of law), ed. Silja Voneky, Britta Beylage-Haarmann, Anja Holfelmeier, and Anna-Katharina Hubler (Heidelberg, New York, Dordrecht, London: Springer 2013), 67–102.
48 Charter, note 13, sec. 33.
49 Criminal Code, R.S.C., 1985, c. C-46 (as amended), sec. 14.
50 Farzaneh Zahedi, Bagher Larijani, and Javad Tavakoly Bazzaz, "End of Life Ethical Issues and Islamic Views," *Iran Journal of Allergy Asthma and Immunology* 6, suppl. 5 (2007): 9.

51 Expert Panel of the Royal Society.
52 Report of the Select Committee of the Assemblée Nationale.
53 My translation; "La valeur du caractère sacré de la vie a subi une transformation notable."
54 Report of the Select Committee of the Assemblée Nationale (English version), 62.
55 Jurgen Habermas, *The Future of Human Nature* (Cambridge, UK: Polity Press 2003).
56 Somerville, *The Ethical Imagination: Journeys of the Human Spirit* (Toronto: House of Anansi Press 2006).
57 Somerville, *Death Talk*, 205–17.
58 Julia Addington-Hall, "Who Should Measure Quality of Life?," *British Medical Journal* 322 (2001): 1417–20. PMCID: PMC1120 479.
59 Somerville, *Ethical Imagination*, 28–31, 62–72.
60 Leonie Welberg, "The Moral Brain," *Nature Reviews Neuroscience* 8 (May 2007): 326, http://www.nature.com/nrn/journal/v8/n5/full/nrn2141.html.
61 Somerville, *Ethical Imagination*, 28–31, 53–93.
62 Somerville, "Legalizing Euthanasia: Why Now?," in *Death Talk*, 105–18.
63 *Death Talk*, 218–32.

CHAPTER FIVE

1 Hans Urs von Balthasa, *Seeing the Form*, vol. 1 of *The Glory of the Lord: A Theological Aesthetics*, 7 vols. (Edinburgh: T&T Clark 1982–91; first published 1961–69).
2 Wesley J. Smith, *A Rat Is a Pig Is a Dog Is a Boy: The Human Cost of the Animal Rights Movement* (New York: Encounter Books 2009).
3 See pp. 43–4, 114. Peter Singer, *Animal Liberation* (New York: Avon 1981).
4 Singer, *Practical Ethics*, 2nd ed. (New York: Cambridge University Press 2006), 57–61, 83.
5 Thomas I. White, *In Defence of Dolphins: The New Moral Frontier* (Oxford: Blackwell 2007); Lori Marino, "Dolphins Are People Too: Dolphins Are Sophisticated, Self-Aware, Highly Intelligent Beings with Personalities, Autonomy and an Inner Life – Sound Familiar?," *Ottawa Citizen*, 16 January 2010, http://www.ottawacitizen.com/technology/Dolphins+people/2449863/story.html.

6 Alberto Giubilini and Francesca Minerva, "After-Birth Abortion: Why Should the Baby Live?," *Journal of Medical Ethics*, doi:10.1136/medethics-2011-100411.

7 Francis Fukuyama, Special Report, "Transhumanism," *Foreign Policy*, 2 September 2004, http://www.foreignpolicy.com/articles/2004/09/01/transhumanism.

8 Somerville, "Legalizing Euthanasia: Why Now?" *Australian Quarterly* 68 (1996): 1–14. Republished as Somerville, *Death Talk: The Case against Euthanasia and Physician-Assisted Suicide* (Montreal and Kingston: McGill-Queen's University Press 2002), chapter 6, 105–18.

9 Carol Gilligan, *In a Different Voice: Psychological Theory and Women's Development* (Cambridge, MA: Harvard University Press 1982).

10 Jay Katz, *The Silent World of Doctor and Patient* (New York and London: Free Press 1986).

11 Somerville, "Why We Should Talk about Sex-Selective Abortions," *Calgary Herald*, 27 March 2013, http://www.calgaryherald.com/news/Somerville+should+talk+about+selective+abortions/8154813/story.html#ixzz2Ozzi5sKS. Republished as "Why Is Canada's Parliament Tip-Toeing around Sex-Selective Abortion?," *MercatorNet*, 9 April 2013, http://www.mercatornet.com/articles/view/why_is_canadas_parliament_tip_toeing_around_sex_selective_abortion.

12 Scancomark.se Team, 17 July 2011, http://www.scancomark.se/Competitiveness/Plans-on-the-way-to-make-Denmark-a-Down-syndrome-free-perfect-society.html; http://www.cphpost.dk/news/scitech/92-technology/51921-downs-syndrome-dwindling.html.

13 *Globe and Mail*, 11 August 2011, L6.

14 Audrey Cole, personal communication, 2011.

15 Prabhat Jha, Maya A. Kesler, Rajesh Kumar, Faujdar Ram, Usha Ram, Lukasz Aleksandrowicz, Diego G. Bassani, Shailaja Chandra, and Jayant K. Banthia, "Trends in Selective Abortions of Girls in India: Analysis of Nationally Representative Birth Histories from 1990 to 2005 and Census Data from 1991 to 2011," *The Lancet* 377 (4 June 2011), http://ac.els-cdn.com/S0140673611606491/1-s2.0-S0140673611606491-main.pdf?_tid=fa1fd7d4-0df0-11e4-8f42-00000aab0f26&acdnat=1405629116_b4f8dc29b1cc7034e503535ba79297bd.

16 Mara Hvistendahl, *Unnatural Selection: Choosing Boys over Girls, and the Consequences of a World Full of Men* (New York: Public Affairs 2011).

17 Rajendra Kale, "It's a Girl!" — Could Be a Death Sentence, *Canadian Medical Association Journal* 184 (6 March 2012): 387–8, http://www.*cmaj*.ca/content/early/*2012*/01/*16*/*cmaj*.120021.full.pdf.
18 See pp. 52–3, 109.
19 Somerville, "The Flawed Quest for Perfection," *Ottawa Citizen*, 7 August 2009, A9.
20 Alexandra Molotrow, "DIY Sensation Is a Cause for Optimism," *Globe and Mail*, 16 August 2014, R4.
21 Giubilini and Minerva, "After-Birth Abortion."
22 Opening and closing remarks and chair, "*Human Evolution, Space Migration, and a Need for Global Space Governance*," opening session, 2nd Manfred Lachs International Conference on Global Space Governance, Montreal, 29–31 May 2015.
23 BEINGS 2015, Biotech and the Ethical Imagination: A Global Summit (a gathering of global thought leaders to reach consensus on the direction of biotechnology for the 21st century), Atlanta, GA, 17–19 May 2015.
24 Jean Vanier, *Our Life Together: A Memoir in Letters* (Toronto: Harper Collins 2007).
25 Ibid., 1.
26 Ibid., 498.

CHAPTER SIX

1 http://www.weneedalaw.ca/blog/229-margaretsomerville, 26 November 2012.
2 Lola French, personal communication to author.
3 http://lifecharity.org.uk/findinghope/, accessed 3 September 2014.
4 Margaret Somerville, *The Ethical Imagination: Journeys of the Human Spirit* (Toronto: House of Anansi Press 2006).
5 *Reibl v. Hughes* [1980] 2 S.C.R. 880.
6 Richard Stith, "Stith: Arguing with Pro-Choicers," *First Things*, 4 November 2006, http://www.firstthings.com/web-exclusives/2006/11/stith-arguing-with-pro-choicer.
7 *National Post*, 31 August 2011.
8 "9/11 Memorial Lists 'Unborn,'" *NBC New York*, 11 September 2011.
9 *R. v. Morgentaler*, [1988] 1 S.C.R. 30.
10 *Globe and Mail*, 7 January 2012.
11 http://www.newswire.ca/en/story/861395/ontario-taxpayers-demand-that-abortion-be-defunded.

12 See pp. 56–7.
13 Cristina Odone, “A Modest Proposal,” 3 September 2011, http://www.telegraph.co.uk/women/sex/sexual-health-and-advice/8739589/Abortion-reform-a-modest-proposal-gone-awry.html.
14 Ibid.
15 Priscilla K. Coleman, “Abortion and Mental Health: Quantitative Synthesis and Analysis of Research Published 1995–2009,” *British Journal of Psychiatry* 199, no. 3 (2011): 180–6, doi:10.1192/bjp.bp.110.077230.
16 David van Gend, “Cool Heads Are Needed on the Abortion-Breast Cancer Link: Ostracism, Scorn and Denial Are Not Good Strategies for Dealing with an Important Public Health Issue,” *Mercatornet*, 27 August 2014. http://www.mercatornet.com/articles/view/cool_heads_are_needed_on_the_abortion_breast_cancer_link .
17 See pp. 207–9; also Stith, “Stith: Arguing with Pro-Choicers.”
18 Somerville, *Ethical Imagination*.
19 *New York Times Magazine*, 10 August 2011.
20 Patrick B. Craine, “Shock: No Jail Time for Woman Who Strangled Newborn Because Canada Accepts Abortion, Says Judge,” *lifesite-news.com,* 12 September 2011.
21 Somerville, “Reflections on Canadian Abortion Law: Evacuation and Destruction, Two Separate Issues,” *University of Toronto Law Journal* 31, no. 1 (1981): 1–26.
22 See, for example, “Nebraska Challenges Roe v. Wade with Bogus ‘Fetal Pain’ Law,” http://jezebel.com/5516862/nebraska-challenges-roe-v-wade-with-bogus-fetal-pain-law, accessed 9 July 2014.
23 http://www.lifenews.com/2015/05/29/federal-court-strikes-down-pro-life-idaho-law-banning-abortions-after-20-weeks/.
24 See Somerville,”Selective Birth in Twin Pregnancy,” Correspondence, *New England Journal of Medicine* 305, no. 20 (1981): 1218–19.
25 *R. v. Morgentaler*, [1988] 1 S.C.R. 30.

CHAPTER SEVEN

1 This chapter originated in a speech I was invited to deliver at the Ethicalization of Law Symposium, held at the Max Planck Institute at the University of Freiburg, Germany. The informing theme of the symposium was the contemporary relation of law and ethics, and whether ethics was benefiting or harming the law. My speech, “What is the Relation of Ethics and Law and Why Does It Matter?

Ethics as 'First Aid' for Law," was subsequently published as "'Law Marching with Medicine but in the Rear and Limping a Little': Ethics as 'First Aid' for Law," in *Ethik und Recht- Die Ethisierung des Rechts* (Ethics and law – the ethicalization of law), edited by Silja Voneky, Britta Beylage-Haarmann, Anja Holfelmeier, and Anna-Katharina Hubler (Heidelberg, New York, Dordrecht, London: Springer 2013, 67–102).

2 *Mount Isa Mines v Pusey*, (1970) 125 CLR 383, per Windeyer J., at 395.

3 *Bourhill v. Young*, [1943] AC 92 (House of Lords), at 110.

4 *Mount Isa Miners v. Pusey*, at 402.

5 Somerville, *The Ethical Imagination: Journeys of the Human Spirit* (Toronto: House of Anansi Press 2006), 29–31, 70–1, 166, 205 (McGill-Queen's University Press edition, 2008).

6 Ibid.

7 I note that determining when a person is dead is again a current issue as a result of some hospitals instituting DCD ("donation after cardiac death") policies, the requirements of which, some people believe, do not mean that the organ donor is dead. See Seema K. Shah, Robert D. Truog, and Franklin D. Miller, "Death and Legal Fictions," *Journal of Medical Ethics*, doi:10.1136/jme.2011.045385, http://jme.bmj.com/content/early/2011/08/02/jme.2011.045385.ful. Even more controversially, there are recent proposals to take organs from dying people who are "beyond suffering" and have given their informed consent but are not yet dead. See Rodríguez-Arias, Smith, Lazar, "Donation after Circulatory Death: Burying the Dead Donor Rule," *American Journal of Bioethics* " 11, no. 8 (2011): 36–43.

8 For a description of a coroner's enquiry that relied heavily on ethicists as expert witnesses, see Somerville, *The Ethical Canary: Science, Society and the Human Spirit* (Toronto: Viking/Penguin 2000), 152–74.

9 Robert S. French, "Ethics at the Beginning and Ending of Life," *University of Notre Dame Australia Law Review* 5 (2003): 1–13.

10 Ibid., 2.

11 Ibid., 6.

12 Ibid., 12.

13 Ibid.

14 See Somerville, *Ethical Canary*, 266–7.

15 The text of the Declaration of Montreal is attached as Appendix D.

16 Subsequently, I decided to use human rights language, again in a very similar way to my use of it in relation to trying to ensure

people's access to pain management. This next time I am using it in the context of the need for ethics to inform the law governing reproductive technologies. I argue that for every person the most fundamental human right of all is to be born from natural human biological origins, and this right should be legally recognized. I discuss this proposal shortly.

17 Hélène Boussard, "An Ambiguous Relationship between Ethics and Law: Study of the Future Declaration on Universal Norms on Bioethics," in M.H. Sanati, ed., *Proceedings of the International Congress of Bioethics 2005, Tehran, Iran, 26–28 March* (Tehran: Baraye-Farda), 3.
18 For a discussion of the concept of human dignity, see chapter 3.
19 Boussard, "Ambiguous Relationship," 3–4.
20 Ibid., 5.
21 Ibid., 8.
22 Boussard, "Ambiguous Relationship," 15.
23 Human Rights Watch, "Needless Pain: Government Failure to Provide Palliative Care for Children in Kenya," http://www.hrw.org/en/news/2010/09/02/kenya-provide-treatment-children-pain.
24 Canadian Charter of Rights and Freedoms, Being Part I of the Constitution Act, 1982.
25 Ronald Dworkin, "Freedom's Law: The Moral Reading of the American Constitution" (Cambridge, MA: Harvard University Press 1997).
26 *Pratten v. British Columbia (Attorney General)*, 2011 BCSC 656.
27 *Canada (Attorney General) v. PHS Community Services Society*, [2011] SCC 44 (30 September 2011, Supreme Court of Canada).
28 Neal Hall, "B.C. Government Appeals Landmark Sperm Donor Ruling," *Vancouver Sun,* 17 June 2011, http://www.vancouversun.com/health/government+appeals+landmark+sperm+donor+ruling/4966861/story.html#ixzz1VImvMa5D.
29 Canadian Charter of Rights and Freedoms, Being Part I of the Constitution Act, 1982, section 1.
30 Ibid., section 7.
31 *Pratten v British Columbia (Attorney General)* 2012 BCCA 480.
32 See Somerville, "Children's Human Rights to Natural Biological Origins and Family Structure," *International Journal of the Jurisprudence of the Family* 1 (2011): 35.
33 See *Canada (Attorney General) v. PHS Community Services Society.*
34 Controlled Drugs and Substances Act S.C 1996 c.19.

35 See also Somerville, "Is the Charter 'Applied Ethics' in Law's Clothing?," *Globe and Mail*, 14 November 2011, A11.
36 Somerville, "Children's Human Rights," 35.
37 *Pratten v. British Columbia (Attorney General)*; see pp. 242–6; Somerville, "Children's Human Rights," 35.
38 Somerville, Children's Human Rights," 35.
39 Somerville, "'Brave New Ethicists': A Cautionary Tale," in Nelson Wiseman, ed., *The Public Intellectual in Canada* (Toronto: University of Toronto Press 2013), 212–32.
40 Somerville, "Children's Human Rights," 35.
41 See pp. 176–82.
42 As noted in chapter 1, these topics include euthanasia and physician-assisted suicide; withdrawal of life-support treatment; treatment of seriously disabled newborn babies; access to health care, especially expensive new treatments; abortion; prenatal genetic screening; assisted human reproduction technologies; "designer babies"; cloning; human embryo stem cell research; artificial sperm and ova (making embryos from two same-sex adults); same-sex marriage; polygamy; sex education of children; the use of animals in research; "manimals" (embryos with both human and animal genes); synthetic biology; xenotransplantation (the use of animal organs in humans); transplant tourism; being soft/hard on crime and drugs; needle exchange clinics; safe injecting sites; capital punishment (should physicians give lethal injections?); law and ethics governing armed conflict, including health-care professionals' involvement in "extreme questioning" (query torture), treatment of wounded enemy combatants; the ethics of robotic warfare; business ethics – the pharmaceutical industry; corruption – fraud in medical science; environmental ethics – the impact of environmental damage on health; population health; aid to developing countries (does everyone have a right to some minimal level of health care?); bioterrorism and scientific research – the "dual use" dilemma; and so on. See, in general, Somerville, *Ethical Imagination*.
43 Andrew Purvis, "IVF: The Business of Making Babies," *Management Today*, 1 February 2011, http://www.managementtoday.co.uk/news/1050516/IVF-business-making-babies/?DCMP=ILC-SEARCH. Purvis writes, "The fertility game is truly global. In India, this lucrative surrogacy industry is expected to be worth $2.3bn (£1.9bn) a year by 2012." Note that this amount is just for surrogacy services in only one country.

44 For a more extensive discussion of the issues raised here, see chapter 1; also Somerville, *Death Talk: The Case against Euthanasia and Physician-Assisted Suicide* (Montreal: McGill-Queen's University Press 2002), chapter 6, "Legalizing Euthanasia: Why Now?," 105–18, from which some material in this section has been taken.

45 See Somerville, *Ethical Imagination.*

46 Paul Nathanson and Katherine Young, *Spreading Misandry: The Teaching of Contempt for Men in Popular Culture* (Montreal: McGill-Queen's University Press 2001), 209–10. See also chapter 1.

47 Jurgen Habermas, *The Future of Human Nature* (Oxford: Blackwell 2003), chapter 3, "The Embedding of Morality in an Ethics of the Species."

CHAPTER EIGHT

1 http://www.nybooks.com/blogs/nyrblog/2013/jan/07/haneke-film-not-to-see/.

2 Span, "The Brutal Truth of 'Amour,'" http://newoldage.blogs.nytimes.com/2013/01/22/the-brutal-truth-of-amour/?src=rechp.

3 Wency Leung, "How to Defend against Dementia," *Globe and Mail*, 21 January 2013, http://www.theglobeandmail.com/life/health-and-fitness/health/conditions/how-to-defend-against-dementia/article 7577041/.

4 Marie de Hennezel, *Intimate Death: How the Dying Teach Us How to Live*, Carol Janeway, trans. (New York: Alfred A. Knopf 1997).

5 Transcript of the film provided to Margaret Somerville.

6 Harvey Max Chochinov, Thomas Hack, Thomas Hassard, Linda J. Kristjanson, Susan McClement, and Mike Harlos, "Dignity Therapy: A Novel Psychotherapeutic Intervention for Patients near the End of Life," *Journal of Clinical Oncology* 23 (2005): 5520–5.

7 See pp. 67, 280–4, 288–9.

8 Personal communication, 20 August 2014.

9 Kazuo Ishiguro, *Never Let Me Go* (Toronto: Knopf Canada 2005).

10 D. Ysebaert, G. Van Beeumen, K. De Greef, J.P. Squifflet, O. Detry, A. De Roover, M.-H. Delbouille, W. Van Donink, G. Roeyen, T. Chapelle, J.-L. Bosmans, D. Van Raemdonck, M.E. Faymonville, S. Laureys, M. Lamy, and P. Cras, "Organ Procurement after Euthanasia: Belgian Experience," *Transplantation Proceedings* 41 (2009): 585–6.

11 Participants in the International Summit on Transplant Tourism and Organ Trafficking, convened by the Transplantation Society and International Society of Nephrology in Istanbul, Turkey, 30 April to 2

May 2008. See "The Declaration of Istanbul on Organ Trafficking and Transplant Tourism," *Kidney International* 74, no. 7 (2008): 854–9.

12 Assisted Human Reproduction Act S.C. 2004, c2, section 5(1)(a).

13 Nick Bostrom,"A History of Transhumanist Thought," http://www.nickbostrom.com/papers/history.pdf.

14 Somerville, *The Ethical Imagination: Journeys of the Human Spirit* (Toronto: House of Anansi 2006), 157–98.

15 Although the pigs have been created, there have been no transplants into humans for ethical reasons. There has been a major controversy about whether clinical trials should be allowed. See the closing section of this chapter.

16 F.H. Bach, Christiane Ferran, Miguel Soares, Christopher J. Wrighton, Josef Anrather, Hans Winkler, Simon C. Robson, and Wayne W. Hancock "Modification of Vascular Responses in Xeno-transplantation: Inflammation and Apoptosis," *Nature Medicine* 3 (1997): 944–8.

17 Criminal Code, R.S.C., 1985, c. C-46 (as amended).

18 Bill C-384, An Act to Amend the Criminal Code (Right to Die with Dignity), introduced 13 May 2009, http://www.parl.gc.ca/Content/LOP/ResearchPublications/2010-68-e.htm.

19 "Report of the Select Committee of the Assemblée Nationale of Québec on 'Dying with Dignity, Mourir dans la Dignité'" (chair, Maryse Gaudreault), March 2012.

20 Jean-Pierre Ménard, Jean-Claude Hébert, and Michelle Girou, *Rapport du comité de jurists experts sur la mise en oeuvre des re-commendations de la commission speciale de l'Assemblée Nationale sur la question de mourir dans la dignité*, January 2013, www.msss.gouv.qc.ca/presse.

21 An Act Respecting End-of-Life Care, RSQ c S-32.0001.

22 Ibid., section 3(6).

23 Criminal Code, R.S.C., 1985, c. C-46 (as amended), sec. 229.

24 For a contrary view, see J. Donald Boudreau and Margaret A. Somerville, "Euthanasia Is Not Medical Treatment," *British Medical Bulletin* 106 (2013): 45–66, doi:10.1093/bmb/ldt010, http://bmb.oxfordjournals.org/content/early/2013/03/26/bmb.ldt010.full?keytype=ref&ijkey=IKP7zm8pfcR3lNH.

25 Ibid.

26 Ibid. See also Boudreau and Somerville, "Euthanasia and Assisted Suicide: A Physician's and Ethicist's Perspectives," *Medicolegal and Bioethics* 4 (2014): 1–12 (Dove Press Open Access, 17 July 2014).

27 Jennifer Nedelsky, *Law's Relations: A Relational Theory of Self, Autonomy, and Law* (New York: Oxford University Press 2011).
28 *Fleming v. Ireland & Ors*, [2013] IEHC 2.
29 http://unesdoc.unesco.org/images/0012/001229/122990eo.pdf, 5.
30 http://www.coe.int/t/dg3/healthbioethic/Activities/07_Human_genetics_en/default_en.asp.
31 "Prohibited Activities," http://laws-lois.justice.gc.ca/eng/acts/a-13.4/page-2.html.
32 "News from the National Academies," 18 May 2015, http://academies246.rssing.com/browser.php?indx=30073578&item=121.
33 "A Note on Genome Editing," 26 May 2015, https://www.whitehouse.gov/blog/2015/05/26/note-genome-editing.
34 "Image of the Day: CRISPR Pigs," *The Scientist*, 29 May 2015, http://www.the-scientist.com/?articles.view/articleNo/43098/title/Image-of-the-Day—CRISPR-Pigs/.
35 B. Nerlich and D.D. Clarke, "Anatomy of a media event: how arrangements clashed in the 2001 human cloning debate," *New Genetics and Society* 22, no. 1 (2003): 43–59.

APPENDIX A

1 Margaret Somerville, "Margaret A. Somerville on George Patrick Ganley," in *The Best Teacher I Ever Had*, ed. Alex Michalos (London, ON: Althouse Press 2003), 247–52.

Index

Abella, Rosalie, 78
abortion: of babies with Down syndrome, 113, 136, 177–9, 220; in Canada, lack of legal restrictions on, 206–7, 208, 211; in Canada, statistics of, 32, 63, 179, 209; in China, 182; comparison with infanticide, 216–17; consequences of, 203, 206, 225; coverage by Ontario Health Insurance Plan, 211; on demand, 222; ethical issues, 222; as feticide, 181; freedom of conscience and, 67–8; funding of, 211; on the ground of sex selection, 180; impact on societal values, 181, 224–6; in India, 182; informed consent to, 205, 213; justification of, 214, 215, 218, 219–20; Justin Trudeau on, 223–4; legal aspects of, 182; medical restrictions on, 179–80; mental health and, 213; as moral choice, 32–3; need for legislation on, 223; need for prevention programs, 201; non-restricting access to, 218; in Ontario, privacy and, 63; parental testing and, 176; politics and, 69, 223–4; as private matter, 180; public perception of, 202–3, 210, 221–2; risks associated with, 213; study of, 10; in United Kingdom, 212; in the United States, 219; women's human rights and, 62
abortion debate: attempts to suppress, 31, 211–12; on Canadian university campuses, 56–7; democracy and, 63–4; importance of language in, 218; points of agreement in, 228; polar views in, 221; public opinion of Canadians in, 221–2; scientific advances and, 212; silent Canadians in, 226; use of labels in, 220–1
Abraham, Carolyn, 209
academia: culture of comfort in, 55; role of trust in, 82
academic freedom: Association of Universities and Colleges of Canada on, 80–1; Canadian Charter of Rights and Freedoms and, 51; characteristics of, 79, 86; concept of, 9; context of, 47–8; examples of violations of, 48, 59, 84; institutional autonomy and, 79; political correctness and, 46; as privilege, 85; proper understanding of, 47; reaction to abuse of, 85; in relation to freedom of thought, 48, 53; religious pluralism and, 55–6; threats to, 81
Act Respecting End-of-Life Care (Bill 52), 67, 280
Act to Prevent Coercion of Pregnant Women to Abort (Roxanne's Law), 210
Adair, Elaine, 242, 243

Adelin (protagonist in *End Credits*), 268–9, 270
adolescent progressivism, 6
Adoption Act. *See* British Columbia Adoption Act
Affordable Health Care Act (Obamacare), 257
Agnost, Joe, 30
Allan, James, 58
all life is beautiful: idea of, 169. *See also* beauty
Alton, Roger, 35
amazement, wonder, and awe: experience of, 191–3, 194, 196, 227
American Medical Association's opinion on relation of law and ethics, 235
Amour (film): absence of hope in, 265; depiction of love, 264–5; funeral theme, 266; as illustration of failure of society to provide palliative care, 265; music in, 264–5, 266; plot, 262–4; reviews of, 262; study of, 11, 261; viewers' perception of, 262, 267
Anderson, Benedict, 20
animals: as non-human persons, 171–2, 216
Anne (protagonist), 262–4
antiques, 190
applied ethics, 10–11, 229, 231–2, 233, 234. *See also* ethics
appraisal respect, 97
Assange, Julian, 71
assisted reproductive technologies. *See* reproductive technologies
assisted suicide. *See* euthanasia
atheism, 21
autonomy: versus common good, 152–3; euthanasia and right to, 119; as moral principle, 101; priority of individual's, 135

Bach, Fritz, 278
Balthasar, Hans Urs von, 168
Bamiyan Buddhas: destruction of, 169
Barnard, Christiaan, 232
Battin, Margaret, 151–2
beauty: Confucius on, 168; human life and, 10; link to value and respect, 169; as part of the essence of God, 168; perceptions of, 169; predominance of physical, 168, 174; suffering and, 167; truth and, 168
Beijing Summer Olympic Games opening ceremony: controversy over representation of, 187–9, 190
Belgium: euthanasia of Verbessem twins in, 145; law on assisted suicide in, 143–4; practice of euthanasia and organ donation in, 273, 283; pro-euthanasia movement in, 270; results of legalizing euthanasia in, 133, 287
Bennett, Carolyn, 226
Beyleveld, Deryck, 102
Bill 52 (Act Respecting End-of-Life Care), 67, 280
Binder, Amy, 61
bioethics, 102, 229–30, 236
Biotechnology and the Ethical Imagination: A Global Summit (BEINGS 2015), 291
birds: as metaphor of freedom, 3
birth: in postmodern context, 5
Bondo, Lillian, 177
Bostrom, Nick, 96, 109
Boudreau, Donald, 149, 268
Bourhill v. Young, 231
Boussard, Hélène, 236
Brague, Rémi, 23
Brendstrup, Ulla, 177
British Columbia: controversy over Western Trinity University law school, 66; policy on assisted suicide, 158–9
British Columbia Adoption Act, 242
British Columbia Law Society, 66
Brooks, Rodney, 43
Brown, Louise, 233
Brownsword, Roger, 102
Buckingham, Janet, 76

Callahan, Daniel, 128
Campaign Life Coalition Youth, 211

Campbell, Colleen Carroll, 19, 28
Campus Freedom Index, 57
Canadian Assisted Human Reproduction Act, 290
Canadian Association of Pregnancy Support Services (CAPSS), 10, 200
Canadian Association of University Teachers, 66
Canadian Charter of Rights and Freedoms, 36, 48, 72; and adopted children's right to access to information, 242–44; on founding principles of Canada, 26; giving preference to individual claims in law, 252; as justification of absence of law on abortion, 226; as legal instrument for embedding ethics in law, 241, 244; physician-assisted suicide and, 120–1, 125; protection of academic freedom and, 51, 86; respect for life and, 76, 160, 286; and secularism, 79
Canadian Institute for Health Information (CIHI), 208
Canadian Medical Association Journal, 182
Canadian Radio-Television Telecommunications Commission (CRTC), 60
Carter v. Canada: analysis of, 153; brief, 9, 119–22; central issue of, 152, 163–4; evidence in, 131–2; impact on societal values, 155; Supreme Court's decision on, 165
Cassel, Eric, 117
Chamberlain v. Surrey School District, 25
Charter of Rights and Freedoms. *See* Canadian Charter of Rights and Freedoms
charters of rights: ethical impact of, 241–2
children: rights of, 249, 250
Children of Men, The (P.D. James), 127
China: collective culture of, 188; disproportion of population in, 182; sex-selection abortions in, 182
Chochinov, Harvey Max, 9, 106, 108, 266
Chow, Tiffany, 263
Church, George, 112
Clarke, David, 292
Cole, Audrey, 179
Coleman, Priscilla, 213
collective human imagination, 20
collective values, 15, 32
College of Physicians and Surgeons of Ontario, 68, 71–2
common good, 152–3, 195
Confucius, 167–8
consumerism, 39–40
Convention on the Rights of Persons with Disabilities (CRPD), 87, 88
Cook, Michael, 28
Cosyns, Marc, 268, 270
Creutzfeldt-Jakob disease, 279
Criminal Code of Canada, 120, 121, 157, 280, 281
crisis pregnancy, 10, 202–4
culture wars, 15, 86, 212, 252
cynicism, 194

Darwall, Stephen, 96
Dawkins, Richard, 17, 18, 22
death: characteristics of, 135–6; control over human, 42; in entertaining programs, exposure of, 36; ethics of, 137; fear of, 38, 175–6; in modern society, perception of, 35; mystery of, 163, 192; as norm, 271; in postmodern context, 5; presence of hope and, 266; responsibilities of physicians and danger of inflicting, 163; as result of refusal of treatment, 139
death talk, 37–8
Declaration of Istanbul on Organ Trafficking and Transplant Tourism, 103, 274
Declaration of Montreal on access to pain management, 235, 236, 237
Declaration on Science and the Use of Scientific Knowledge, 82
Decommere, Alexander, 268
"Defund Abortion" rally, 211

democracy: debates on abortion and, 63; freedom of conscience as pillar of, 72; moral reasoning as foundation of, 28; principles of, 22; religion and, 29
Dennett, Daniel, 17
designer babies, 52, 53
dignity: as aristocratic concept, 91; intrinsic and extrinsic, 97, 98–9; limitation of concept of, 111. *See also* human dignity
dignity of choice, 146, 147
dignity therapy, 106–7, 108, 266–7
disability: opportunities provided by, 196–7, 198
Dorries, Nadine, 212
Downie, Jocelyn, 138
Down syndrome: abortion of babies with, 113, 136, 177–9, 220; Denmark as society free of, 177
Dworkin, Ronald, 241
dying: as act of life, 176; fear of, 175–6
dying people: feelings of, 106; importance of legacy for, 198–9
"Dying with Dignity" report, 75, 150, 159–60, 280

ecosystem, xiv, 114, 166, 196. *See also* metaphysical ecosystem
Effert, Katrina, 216
Eich, Brendan, 30
embryo: characteristics of, 208; cloning of, 275; human dignity of, 109–10; legal controversy over, 233; recognition as person, 217; treatment of, 110. *See also* fetus; unborn child
End Credits (documentary): depiction of euthanasia in, 268–9; experience of dying patients in, 270; main theme, 268; première at Marda Loop Justice Film Festival, 268; study of, 11, 261
end in itself, 98
end-of-life population, 126–7, 155
environmentalism, 22
epigenetics, 21
Escamilla, Arthur, 13
ethical obligations, 235
ethical universals, 19
ethics: changing nature of, 231; in court decisions, 242; danger of commercialization of, 234; of death, 137; integrity as core of, 189; neuroscience of, 52; questions of, 261; in relation to law, 5, 229, 234–5, 245, 246, 260; religion and, 5; technoscience and, 113–14, 260. *See also* applied ethics
ethics of complexity, 256
ethics of neuroscience, 51
ethics of potentiality, 256
ethics of uncertainty, 256
European Convention on Human Rights and Biomedicine, 289
euthanasia: abuses of, 132–3, 151; as act of killing, 37; arguments against legalizing, 284–5; in Australia, 215; calls for legalizing, 34; in Canada, attempts to legalize, 120–1; Catholic church on, 100; consequences of legalizing, 165, 166, 281–3, 287; damage of human spirit by, 176; versus death from natural causes, 140; as example of death talk, 37–8; freedom of conscience and, 67; in Germany, 100; Groningen protocol on, 136; harm from, 35, 271; health-care costs saving and, 288; hopelessness and desire for, 40; impact on future generations, 162–3; individuals' rights to autonomy and, 119; justifications of, 124, 135, 147–9, 287–8; "medical cloak" of, 37; as medical treatment, 149, 150, 151; nonrelevance to medicine, 166; organ donation and, 273; pain management and, 138; pain relief treatment versus, 138; palliative care and, 128, 149; primary intention of, 139; problem of authorized practitioners to carry, 150–1; Protestant church on, 100; purpose of prohibition of, 122, 123; in

Quebec, introduction of legislation on, 280; questions concerning awareness of, 282–4; versus refusal of treatment, 142–3, 286; risks of legalizing, 282; sanctity of life and, 158; secular sacred and, 95–6; sedation as slow, 145; versus suicide, 129–30; Supreme Court of Canada on, 133–4; use of euphemizing language to describe, 175; of Verbessem twins, 145; vote in Canadian Parliament on legalizing, 156
euthanasia debate: current state of, 34; essence of, 43, 137; human dignity and, 101, 105–6, 117–18; impact on societal values, 255; importance of outcome of, 164; legal positivism in, 39; nature of, 146, 163; Nazis and contemporary, 99–100; "no difference" argument in, 137, 285, 286; political aspect of, 282; respect for human life and, 255; slippery-slope arguments in, 287, 288; societal values and, 289; use of obscure language in, 283, 285
euthanasia in Canada: media coverage of, 288–9; prohibition under Criminal Code, 281; public support of, 280–1; Supreme Court on, 281
Eva (protagonist in *End Credits*), 268–9
experience: of amazement, wonder, and awe, 191–3, 194, 196, 227; importance of personal, 193; of transcendence, 194

failures: dealing with, 193–4
false certainty, 256
fear: of death, 38; law as response to, 38; of mystery, 40–1
Federation for the Humanities and Social Sciences (Congress 2008), 59–60
Federation of Law Societies of Canada, 65
female genital mutilation, 80
Fernando, Roxanne, 210
fertility industry, 254, 274
fetus: constructionist approach to, 209; developmental approach to, 207, 213–14; as potential human life, 209; in selective reduction, killing of, 215. *See also* embryo; unborn child
Finding Hope organization, 204
Finlay, Ilora, 132
Finnis, John, 229
Flanagan, Tom, 80
Francis, Pope, 6
Fraser, Andrew, 66
freedom: idea of, 48; in relation to religion, 24; respect to others', 70; restrictions on, 3, 7; suppression of, 8
freedom in fetters, 3, 48, 164
freedom of belief, 65
freedom of conscience: definition of, 67; "perfective" and "preservative," 70–1; of physicians, 68; as pillar of democracy, 72; risk of harm and, 71
freedom of expression, 56
freedom of information, 63, 64
Freedom of Information and Protection of Privacy Act (FIPPA), 63
freedom of religion, 27, 74–5, 79
freedom of speech: in academia, 54–5; importance of, 58; political correctness and, 58; privacy as tool to restrict, 62; self-censorship and, 62; suppression of, 31, 61–2; threats to, 55
freedom of thought, 51–4
freedom to learn, 77
Freiburg Symposium on the Ethicalization of Law, 259
French, Lola, 200–2
French, Robert, 233
Fukuyama, Francis, 50, 173
Furedy, Christine, 58, 66
Furedy, John, 54, 58, 66

Gabel, Marc, 72, 73

gamete donation, 245–6
Garland, Alex, 272
gay community, 251: debates on transmission of life and, 249
Gelernter, David, 94
genetic control, 52–3
George, Robert P., 229
Georges (protagonist), 262–3, 262–4
germline interventions, xiii, 9, 52, 89, 195, 289–91
Gibbon, Edward, 4
Globe and Mail, 20, 29, 60, 209, 263
Golfman, Noreen, 59, 60
Golob, Alissa, 211
Gonthier, Charles, 26
Gough, Hugh, 67
Gray, Kathleen, 206
Green, Ronald, 9
Groningen protocol on euthanasia of ill newborn, 136, 172

Habermas, Jürgen: on altering human genes, 52; on designed persons, 109; on ethics of human species, 19, 76, 160, 259; *The Future of Human Nature*, 109; on human embryos, 110
Haidt, Jonathan, 7
Haneke, Michael, 262, 264
Hanifan, L.J., 49, 50
Harper, Stephen, 182
Harris, Sam, 17
health: definition of, 258; as secular religion, 257
health-care system in Canada, 257, 282, 288
health-care professionals: freedom of conscience, 67–9, 72, 258–9; and pain management, 234, 237
healthism, 256
heart transplant: first appearance of, 232
Hebbert, Rebekah, 191
Hendin, Herbert, 132
Hennezel, Marie de, 265
history: as human memory, 4, 32
Hitchens, Christopher, 17
Homer-Dixon, Thomas, 47, 79, 81
hope, 194, 228
hopelessness, 40
human beings: versus animals, 111, 171; categories of, 216; commodification of, 104, 105; criticism of idea of, 43; definition of, 44; expansion of technological opportunities for, 183; language and dehumanization of, 174–5; meaning of being human, 43–6; as persons, 171, 172; respect for, 170, 172–3; unethical interventions on, 173
human dignity: absence of definition of, 89; bioethics and, 102; characteristic of, 89; in comparison with justice, 103; concepts of, 9, 87, 91–2, 114–15; connection with religion, 93; connection with sacredness, 93–4; as constraint, 102–3; debates on euthanasia and, 105–6, 117–18; as empowerment, 102; end in itself and, 98; genetic research and, 88; of human embryos, 109–10; human rights and, 90; in international instruments, 87–8; Kant on respect of, 101, 103–4; meaning of, 87, 93; as part of human nature, 98; Pellegrino's report on, 115–16; people with disabilities and, 99; perception of dependence as loss of, 265; respect for, 98, 101, 114, 115; secular sacred and, 96; technoscience and, 111–12; themes, definitions, and implications, 106–7. *See also* dignity
human embryo. *See* embryo
human ethics, 19, 76, 160, 236–7, 238
human exceptionalism, 170
human genome: legislation and international conventions on, 289–90; moratorium on editing, 290; societal values and research on, 290, 291
human immunodeficiency virus (HIV), 279
human life: as beautiful, 10, 167,

168, 199; characteristics of, 172; competing worldviews of, 42–3; euthanasia debate and respect for, 255; idea of, 9–10; inviolability of, 156–7; "just war" and, 161; mystery of, 163; narratives of, 270–1; perceptions of, 75–6, 227; possibility to prolong, 184; preservation of, 126, 135, 156; protection of, 157–8; quality of, 161–2; respect for, 154–6; sanctity of, 158–61; suffering and, 174; transmission of, 248; values related to, 153
human perfection, 112–13, 114, 186–7
human race: scenarios of end of, 276, 278
human responsibility, 236–7, 238
human rights: concept of, 235–6, 238; horror of breaches of, 239–40; human dignity and, 90; nature of, 236; for people in pain, 235; relations to human responsibility and human ethics, 236–7, 238; threats to, 7, 164; of unborn child, 248
human spirit, 93
human ways of knowing, 19, 32, 195
Huppert, Isabelle, 262

illness: as sin, 257–8
imagination: importance of, 195
immortality, 42
Incipientposthuman.com website, 183
India: disproportion of population in, 182; sex-selection abortion in, 182
indifference: as opposite of hate and love, 21
individual autonomy, 195
individualism, 34–5
infanticide, 172, 182, 192, 216
infant male circumcision (IMC), 80
informed consent: to abortion, 205, 213; doctrine of, 54, 157
Inglehart, Ronald, 50
Insite case, 242, 246–8
institutional autonomy, 81
integrity: definition of, 189
intelligence: definition of, 173
International Association for the Study of Pain (IASP), 235
Intimate Death (de Hennezel), 265
Ishiguro, Kazuo, 271

Jacobs, Jane, 81
James, P.D., 127
Jefferson, Thomas, 193
Judaism, 23
Justice Centre for Constitutional Freedom (JCCF), 57

Kant, Immanuel, 97–8, 101, 103–4, 239
Kass, Leon, 91, 102, 184
Keats, John, 167
Kennett, Jeff, 95–6
Kerstein, Samuel, 97, 98, 103, 104
Kevorkian, Jack, 36
Kraynak, Robert, 93

Lalonde, Francine, 280
Lamer, Antonio, 130
Lammin, Richard, 128
law: applied ethics and, 10–11; bioethics and, 236; ethical norms in, 241; Justice Windeyer's description of, 231; in relation to ethics, 5, 229, 234–5, 246, 260; values institutionalized in, 4
LAWER (life-ending acts without explicit request), 143, 144
legalism, 39
liberty rights, 11
life. *See* human life
life-support treatment: versus euthanasia, refusal of, 142–3; primary intention of withdrawal of, 138–9
Low, Donald, 288
Loyola High School v. Quebec, 27, 78

Mackenzie, Kenneth C., 25
Macklin, Ruth, 90

Macquarie University (Australia), 84
mad cow disease, 279
Marshall, Jennifer, 28
Mason, Crystal, 167
materialism, 39–40
McLachlin, Beverley, 27
media: and abortion debate, 200; communication of values through, 292; as component of public square, 35–6, 202; individualism and, 35, 188, 283, 288–9; secularism and, 18
media ethics, 202
medical profession: ethical and moral issues in, 69–70, 72, 254–5
Medical Students for Choice group, 69
medical treatment, 54, 140, 150; euthanasia as, 37, 119, 121, 134, 137, 149–51, 166, 281
medicare: as symbol of Canadian identity, 257
medicine: progress in, 253–4; as secular religion, 256, 257, 258; societal values and ethics of, 253
Meilaender, Gilbert, 92, 97, 102, 109
Mello, Sérgio Vieira de, 90
mental injury, 230–1
Mercer, Mark, 86
metaphysical ecosystem, xiv, 196, 250. *See also* ecosystem
Moldaver, Michael J., 27
Moon, Richard, 79
moral intuition, 40, 181, 188, 222, 231, 274
morality: politics and, 28; versus religion, 25–6
moral reasoning: as foundation of democracy, 28; in public square, role of, 28–9
moral relativism, 161
moral syndromes, 81–2
Morgentaler case, 208, 223
Morris, Charles, 111
Morse, Jennifer Roback, 32
Mount Isa Mines v. Pusey, 230–1
Murphy, Rex, 60
Murphy, Sean, 72
Murray, John Courtney, 55, 62, 77
mystery, xi, 40–1, 42, 93, 163, 176, 185, 192, 200, 227

Nathanson, Paul, 21, 95
National Health Services (NHS), 212
National Post, 214
natural law, 259
Nazir-Ali, Michael, 17
neo-atheists, 17–18
Nerlich, Brigitte, 292
Netherlands: Groningen protocol on euthanasia of disabled babies, 136, 172; law on assisted suicide in, 144; practice of euthanasia in, 283; results of legalizing euthanasia in, 139, 287; use of palliative sedation in, 145–6
Neuhaus, John, 28, 29, 94
neuroethics, 173
Never Let Me Go (film), 11, 261; depiction of dehumanized children, 272–3; lessons learned from, 272, 274, 275–6; plot, 271–2; use of language in, 274–5
New England Journal of Medicine, 220
"new natural law" theory, 229
New York Times, 99, 188, 214
Nicholson, Rob, 210
Nitschke, Philip, 215
Note on Genome Editing, 290, 291

Olympic Games, 189. *See also* Beijing Summer Olympic Games opening ceremony
Onfray, Michel, 17
Ontario Human Rights Commission (OHRC), 68
organizational ethics, 83
organ trafficking, 103, 104–5
organ transplantation, 232, 278
original: versus replica, 187
Ottawa Citizen, 30, 76, 80
Our Life Together (Jean Vanier), 197
Ovid, 4

PACE (Parliamentary Assembly of the Council of Europe), 180
Padawar, Ruth, 214
Pain-Capable Unborn Child Protection Act, 219
pain management, 138, 239, 240
palliative care, 128
Palpant, Nathan, 9
parental love, 178–9, 183
parental screening, 178–9
Parkinson's disease, 291
Pellegrino, Edmund, 115
Penner, Barry, 242
Pereira, Jose, 132
physical ecosystem, 196
physician-assisted suicide. *See* euthanasia
physicians: freedom of conscientious and, 68, 72; popular view of, 69; problem of facilitation of abortion by, 72; responsibilities of, 163; right of conscientious, 73–4; as secular priests, 258; as technicians, 258–9
Pinker, Steven, 291
Plourde, Nathanael, 210
pluralism, 27
political correctness: academic freedom and, 46, 61; elimination of values with, 8, 46; freedom of speech and, 58; suppression of freedoms by, 8; as threat to universities, 58–9
Pratten, Olivia, 242, 243–4, 274
Pratten v. British Columbia (Attorney General), 242–3; breach of constitutional rights in, 243–4; British Columbia Court of Appeal on, 244; ethical aspect of, 245; Justice Adair's ruling on, 243–4; legal and ethical view of, 245; public perception of decision on, 244–5
pregnancy, 204, 207, 213–14, 215
preservation of life, 152–3, 154, 156
privileging secularism, 22–3
progressive values, 6, 259
Prose, Francine, 262
protection of life, 157–8
public square: exclusion of religious voices from, 8, 13, 29–31, 33–4, 45; issues debated in, 14–15; media as component of, 35–6; moral values based on religious beliefs and, 24–5; "naked," 29; role of moral reasoning in, 28–9; secular voices in, 45
Putnam, Robert, 50

quality of life: concept of, 124–5, 162–3; death and argument of, 136; problem of assessment of, 162; versus sanctity of life, 161. *See also* human life
Quebec: Act Respecting End-of-Life Care (Bill 52), 149, 269–70, 280; lack of support of pregnant women in, 204; Legislative Assembly Committee's report "Dying with Dignity," 136–7, 150; public perception of abortion in, 203, 204
Quebec College of Physicians and Surgeons, 150

refusal to provide service, 70
regenerative medicine, 272
relational autonomy: concept of, 286
religion: call for elimination of, 18; collective human imagination and, 20; decline of, 232; democracy and, 29; ethics and, 5; etymology of word, 21, 158; expulsion from public square, 8, 13, 29–31, 33–4, 45; hostility toward, 16; link to medicine, 257; versus morality, 25–6; "none" as America's new religion, 22; public perceptions of, 16; in Quebec, 75; in relation to freedom, 24; secularism and, 27; as store of traditional knowledge and wisdom, 33; in university curriculum, 77; values and, 15, 253; as world's most dangerous idea, 76
religious belief, 25
religious pluralism, 55–6
replica: versus original, 187
reproductive technologies, 4, 5, 182–3, 240, 251–2

respect for human beings, 173
respect for life, 154–6, 166, 286
right not to be born, 249
right to die, 139
right to life, 154
right to refuse treatment, 139, 285
Riva, Emmanuelle, 262
Roberts, Stephen, 67
Rodriguez, Sue, 36, 288
Rodriguez v. British Columbia (Attorney General), 119, 121–2, 129, 131, 140, 143
Roe v. Wade, 218
Rolston, Holmes, III, 91
Romanek, Mark, 272
Royal Society panel report on euthanasia, 137
Rubin, Charles, 92

sacred: concept of, 94, 95
Salby, Murry, 84
same-sex marriage, 250–1
sanctity of life, 75, 158–61
Sandel, Michael, 98, 105
Saul, John Ralston, 32
Schaub, Diana, 91
Schulman, Adam, 89, 102
Schweitzer, Albert, 138
science: ability to change human body, 96; ethics and, 195–6, 260; human nature and, 184; law and rapid development of, 232–3; in search for human perfection, 112, 185–6; as secular religion, 22
scientism, 22, 195
scientists in Canada, 64
Scruton, Roger, 94
secularism, 17, 22, 27, 29
secularist society, 74
secular religions, 21–2, 256
secular sacred: concept of, 95, 96
secular society: changes in, 34; consumerism in, 39–40; definition of, 19–20; freedom of religion in, 79; intense individualism in, 34–5; legalism in, 39; scientific progress in, 41; versus secularist society, 74; separation of church and state in, 24
sedation, 145
selective reduction of fetuses, 219–20
self-censorship, 62
Selley, Chris, 207, 214
separation of church and state: doctrine of, 24
sex-selection abortion, 179–82
sexual reproduction: versus asexual replication, 248; ethics of, 248–9
Shapiro, Bernard, 80
shared ethics, 15–16, 241–2
shared values: in law, implementation of, 241
Singer, Peter, 171, 216
Smith, Lyn: assumptions about euthanasia, 134–5; on attempted suicide, 129; on Charter of Rights and physician-assisted suicide, 125; consideration of personal stories of patients, 141; on end-of-life population, 126–7; on inequality, 131; on inequality and decisions regarding lives, 130; interpretation of right to life by, 125–6; on inviolability of life, 156–7; on justification of physician-assisted suicide, 141; on legalizing euthanasia, 137, 149; on physician-assisted suicide as medical treatment, 151; on positive and negative effects of legalizing physician-assisted suicide, 142; on preservation of life, 156; on protection of life, 157–8; reference to sanctity of life, 158–9; reliance on empirical evidence, 131–2; on respect for life, 154–5; on respect of autonomous choice, 146; on right to life, 154; on risks and benefits of physician-assisted suicide, 133; ruling on physician-assisted suicide, 119, 120, 122, 123, 128; on sanctity of life, 160; slippery slope arguments in rulings of, 143–4; on suffering, 121, 147; on suicide, 129; use of "no difference" approach by, 145; on values related to human life, 153

Smith, Wesley J., 92
Snowden, Edward, 71
social capital, 49–51
social trust: culture of, 189
societal values, 253
Socrates, 66
Somerville, Margaret: *Death Talk: The Case against Euthanasia and Physician-Assisted Suicide,* 118; *The Ethical Canary,* 94; *The Ethical Imagination,* 94, 114; media on, 30; presentation of euthanasia debate by, 118–19; speech on searching for purple pink, 195
Sontag, Susan, 127
South African Bill of Rights, 241
Span, Paula, 262
Starson, Scott, 53
Stith, Richard, 207
suffering: assisted death as response to, 148–9; beauty of life and, 167, 174; cost of relieve, 291; danger of romanticizing, 197; definition of, 117; ethical and legal limits to freedom to alleviate, 164; as justification for euthanasia, 124, 151–2; as loss of dignity, 117; meanings in, 149; perceptions of, 118–19; stories of individuals', 124; suicide and, 148–9
suicide: decriminalization of, 129; versus physician-assisted suicide, 129–30; right to choose to commit, 130–1; suffering and, 148–9
Sulmasy, Daniel, 90, 97
Sumner, Wayne, 135, 156
Supreme Court of Canada: assumptions about euthanasia, 134–5; on choice of suffering individuals, 132; on ethics of end-of-life practices, 140–1; on freedom of belief, 65; on informed consent to euthanasia, 128; judgement on prohibition of euthanasia, 122–3, 124; on Judge Smith's arguments on assisted suicide, 144–5; on lack of access to physician-assisted death, 147; "no difference" approach in decisions of, 140, 141; on physician-assisted suicide, 131, 133–4, 140, 141, 148, 150; on protection of autonomy and common good, 152; on rights to liberty and security of person, 142; on right to life, 126; ruling on Rodriguez case, 120; ruling on Stratton case, 53–4; on sanctity of life, 161
Switzerland: law on assisted suicide in, 144
Systems of Survival (Jane Jacobs), 81

Taylor, Gloria, 120, 123, 124, 125–6, 147, 154
Techno sapiens, 277
technoscience: ethics and, 113–14
Telegraph, 212
Tennyson, Alfred, Lord, 267
test-tube baby, 233
Tharaud, Alexandre, 263
tolerance, 31
transhumanism, 5, 173, 183–5, 276–7
transmission of life, 249
transplant tourism, 103
Tremonti, Anna Maria, 226
Trigg, Roger, 16
Trinity Western University, 64–6
Trintignant, Jean-Louis, 262
Trudeau, Justin, 223–4, 226
trust: in academia, role of, 82; blind and earned, 49; virtual reality and loss of, 189–90
truth: beauty and, 168
two kingdoms: metaphor of, 127

Uldbjerg, Niels, 177
"Ulysses" (Tennyson), 267
unborn child: commemoration of, 208; dehumanization of, 207; human rights of, 248; as non-person, 216; perceptions of, 6, 227–8; as potential human being, 207–8; rights of, 249–50; right to kill, 218, 219. *See also* embryo; fetus
Unborn Victims of Crime Act (Bill C-484), 209–10

UNESCO Universal Declaration on the Human Genome and Human Rights, 289
United States President's Council on Bioethics, 90
Universal Declaration of Human Rights (UDHR), 87, 90
Universal Declaration on Bioethics and Human Rights (UDBHR), 87
Universal Declaration on the Human Genome and Human Rights (UDHGHR), 87
universal human personhood, 217
universities: condemnation of Christian, 66; controversy over teaching about religion in, 77; evaluation of freedoms in Canadian, 57; freedom of conscience in, 71; freedom to learn in, 77; importance of protection of freedom of speech in, 60–1; obligations to students, 83; organizational ethics in, 83–4; political correctness in, 8; protection of reputation of, 80; religious pluralism in, 62
utilitarianism, 135, 161
utopian totalitarianism, 6

Valpy, Michael, 20
value of choice, 146
values: decision-making based on, 7; importance of public discussion about, 12; institutionalized in law, 4; intrinsic versus instrumental, 97; in law, implementation of shared, 241; political correctness and elimination of, 46; progressive, 6, 259; progressives/permissives advocates of, 6; promotion of progressive, 17; public perception of, 5; religious voices and, 44–5; role of media in communication of, 292; of sanctity of life, 75
values conflict, 15–17
Vanier, Jean, 196, 197, 198, 199
Veit, Joanne, 216
Verbessem twins, 145

ways of knowing. *See* human ways of knowing
Weigel, George, 16
western culture: individualistic nature of, 188
White House Office of Science and Technology Policy (OSTP), 290
Williams, Rowan, 32
Windeyer, William, 230, 231
wisdom, 208
women with crisis pregnancy, 202–4, 205, 206
world's most dangerous idea, 170, 276
World Transhumanist Association, 185

xenotransplantation, 278, 279

Yachnin, Paul, 270
Yang, Peiyi, 188
Young, Katherine, 21, 95